Fodor's 20

ROME

Welcome to Rome

Italy's vibrant capital lives in the present, but no other city on Earth evokes its past so powerfully. For over 2,500 years, emperors, popes, artists, and common citizens have left their mark here. Ancient ruins, art-filled churches, and the Vatican's treasures vie for your attention, but Rome is also a wonderful place to practice the Italian-perfected *il dolce far niente*, the sweet art of idleness. Your most memorable experiences may include sitting at a café or strolling a beguiling piazza. As you plan your upcoming travels to Rome, please confirm that places are still open and let us know when we need to make updates by writing to us at corrections@fodors.com.

TOP REASONS TO GO

★ **History:** The Colosseum and the Forum are just two amazing archaeological musts.

★ **Food:** From pasta and pizza to innovative fare, great meals at trattorias or *enoteche*.

★ **Art:** Works by Michelangelo, Raphael, Bernini, and Caravaggio.

★ **Churches:** From the Byzantine to the Baroque.

★ **Landmarks:** The Pantheon, St. Peter's, the Spanish Steps—to name but a few.

★ **Shopping:** Chic boutiques in Piazza di Spagna, flea markets in Trastevere.

Contents

Fodor's Features

Ancient Rome:
Rome Wasn't Built in a Day 80

Heavens Above:
The Sistine Ceiling 116

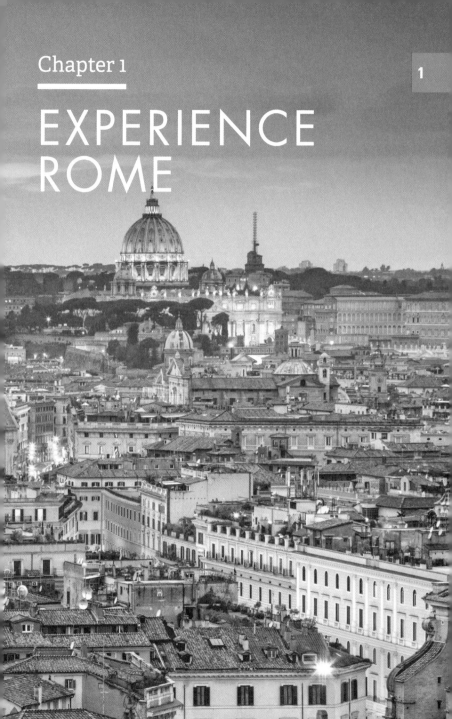

Chapter 1

EXPERIENCE ROME

24 ULTIMATE EXPERIENCES

Rome offers terrific experiences that should be on every traveler's list. Here are Fodor's top picks for a memorable trip.

1 Piazza Navona

One of the most popular public spaces in Rome, the magnificent, oval-shaped Piazza Navona is lined with restaurants, gelaterias, souvenir shops, and Baroque art by both Bernini and Borromini. *(Ch. 5)*

2 MAXXI Museum

One of Rome's best modern art museums is the Zaha Hadid–designed MAXXI (Museo Nazionale delle Arti del XXI Secolo or Museum of 21st Century Art). *(Ch. 8)*

3 Gelato

Gelato is generally denser and less fatty than normal ice cream. Rome has no shortage of excellent gelaterias, but it's smart to stick to the artisanal shops. *(Ch. 3–11)*

4 Palazzo Barberini/ Galleria Nazionale

The impressive palace that was once home to the powerful Barberini family today contains a splendid collection of art, including works by Raphael and Caravaggio. *(Ch. 7)*

5 Via Appia Antica

Known as the Queen of Roads, this ancient road is lined with ruins and the underground graves of Rome's earliest Christians; the spooky yet mesmerizing catacombs can still be visited today. *(Ch. 11)*

6 The Jewish Ghetto

Rome's Jewish population lived in this closed community from the 16th century until 1870. It still is the cultural home of Jewish Rome, with historic synagogues and excellent Jewish restaurants. *(Ch. 5)*

7 Churches

Roman churches, from Santa Maria della Vittoria to San Luigi dei Francesi, are full of impressive art and architecture from Renaissance and Baroque masters. *(Ch. 3–11)*

8 Shopping in Piazza di Spagna

Piazza di Spagna and nearby Via dei Condotti and Via del Corso are where you can find major intentional chains and the flagship stores of Italian designer brands. *(Ch. 6)*

9 The Roman Forum

The Forum was a political playground, a center of commerce, and a place where justice was dispensed during the days of the Roman Republic and Empire. *(Ch. 3)*

10 The Vatican Museums

As the home base for the Catholic Church and the papacy, the Vatican sees millions of annual visitors, who come to explore its museums and Michelangelo's Sistine Chapel. *(Ch. 4)*

11 Espresso and Caffè

When in Rome, you must drink espresso (drip coffee doesn't even exist here). Stop by a classic caffè and sit down to enjoy one of the city's most beloved traditions. *(Ch. 3–11)*

12 Campo de' Fiori

Shopping for fresh fruit and vegetables at the *mercato* (market) is a way of life for many Romans; one of the city's most popular is held every day but Sunday in Campo de' Fiori. *(Ch. 5)*

13 Gran Priorato di Roma dell'Ordine di Malta

At the Priory of the Knights of Malta in Piazza dei Cavalieri di Malta, the keyhole of a nondescript door offers a perfectly framed view of Saint Peter's Basilica across the city. *(Ch. 10)*

14 Ostia Antica

Located about 40 minutes outside Rome, this ancient port city is one of the best-preserved archaeological sites in Italy. *(Ch. 12)*

15 The Pantheon

This best-preserved pagan temple of ancient Rome was rebuilt in the 2nd century AD and has survived intact because it was consecrated as a Christian church. *(Ch. 5)*

16 Trastevere

This charming, village-like neighborhood is a maze of cobblestone streets, traditional Roman trattorias, and medieval houses. *(Ch. 9)*

17 The Colosseum

The most internationally recognized symbol of Rome, this mammoth amphitheater was the site of gladiatorial combats and animal fights. *(Ch. 3)*

18 St. Peter's Basilica

Within the world's most important Catholic church, visit the site of the martyrdom and burial of St. Peter and marvel at Michelangelo's cupola. *(Ch. 4)*

19 Aperitivo

After work, Romans love to meet for aperitivo, the Italian happy hour. Any bar worth its salt offers snacks and a selection of cocktails, including the classic Aperol Spritz. *(Ch. 3–11)*

20 Piazza del Popolo

This huge circular piazza was once the northern entrance to the city, and, with its obelisk and twin churches, it's still a favorite spot for people-watching. *(Ch. 8)*

21 Capitoline Museums

On the smallest and most sacred of Rome's seven hills, you'll find the world's first public museums, with a greatest-hits collection of Roman art through the ages. *(Ch. 3)*

22 La Cucina Romana

Roman specialties tend to be simple, prepared using few ingredients and tried-and-true methods. Classics include fried artichokes, carbonara, and cacio e pepe. *(Ch. 3–11)*

23 Trevi Fountain

One of the few fountains in Rome actually more absorbing than the people crowding around it, the Fontana di Trevi is nothing short of magical. *(Ch. 6)*

24 Galleria Borghese

Only the best could satisfy the aesthetic taste of Cardinal Scipione Borghese, whose artistic holdings within this museum epitomize Baroque Rome. *(Ch. 8)*

WHAT'S WHERE

1 Ancient Rome. No other archaeological park in the world has so compact a nucleus of fabled sights; nearby Monti has artisan shops, restaurants, bars, and high-end boutiques.

2 The Vatican. An independent sovereign state, the pope's residence draws millions to St. Peter's Basilica and the Vatican Museums. Borgo and Prati are the neighborhoods right outside the Vatican.

3 Piazza Navona, Campo de' Fiori, and the Jewish Ghetto. The Piazza Navona and Campo de' Fiori are busy meeting points, surrounded by restaurants and cafés, with the Pantheon nearby. The Jewish Ghetto, the historical center of Jewish life in the city, is home to Rome's main synagogue.

4 Trevi and Piazza di Spagna. The Spanish Steps are iconic, and the surrounding area is the place to window-shop, thanks to upscale fashion boutiques. The Trevi Fountain is a short walk away.

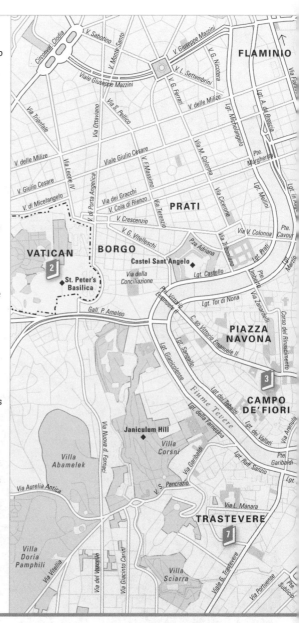

5 **Repubblica and Quirinale.** These areas bustle with government offices during the day, but are also home to several churches and sights, including Bernini's Baroque Sant'Andrea al Quirinale.

6 **Villa Borghese and Environs.** The Villa Borghese, Rome's vast city park, is home to dazzling museums while nearby Piazza del Popolo is prime people-watching territory.

7 **Trastevere and Monteverde.** These picturesque neighborhoods attract locals and visitors to its restaurants and wine bars. The Janiculum Hill has incomparable views.

8 **Aventino and Testaccio.** These off-the-usual-track neighborhoods have the vibrancy of true Rome. Aventino is an elegant residential area; traditionally working-class Testaccio is rapidly gentrifying and has a hip nightlife scene.

9 **Esquilino and Environs.** Some of Rome's least touristy and most beloved neighborhoods have plenty of ancient sights and spectacular churches. The verdant Via Appia Antica leads past the landmark church of Domine Quo Vadis to the catacombs and beyond.

What to Eat and Drink in Rome

SALUMI AND PROSCIUTTO

Romans often start a meal with a meat-and-cheese board featuring prosciutto, salami, mortadella, and other charcuterie. You can order such meats in restaurants and buy them at stores and delis like the famed Roscioli Salumeria con Cucina, which also has a restaurant in the back.

PIZZA

Rome has two main pizza styles: *pizza tonda* (round pizza) and *pizza al taglio* (by the slice). The typical Roman pizza tonda has a very thin crust and is cooked in a wood-burning oven that reaches extremely hot temperatures; the pizzerias that serve this style tend to open for dinner only. Al taglio pizza has a thicker, focaccia-like crust and is cut into squares; it's sold by weight in places that are generally open all day.

CACIO E PEPE

Meaning "cheese and pepper," this is a simple pasta dish from the *cucina povera*, or rustic cooking, tradition. It's a favorite Roman primo, usually made with *tonnarelli* (fresh egg pasta a bit thicker than spaghetti) and coated with pecorino-cheese sauce and lots of freshly ground black pepper. You can find it at most classic Roman trattorias.

GELATO

For many visitors, their first taste of Italian gelato is revelatory. Its consistency is a cross between regular American ice cream and soft-serve, and the best versions are extremely flavorful and made fresh daily. When choosing a gelateria, avoid the places hawking industrially made gelato in unnatural colors and flavors and opt for the places serving the artisanal stuff.

FRITTI

The classic Roman starter (especially at a pizzeria) is *fritti,* an assortment of fried treats, usually crumbed or in batter. Popular options include *filetti di baccala* (salt cod in batter), *fiori di zucca* (zucchini flowers, usually stuffed with anchovies and mozzarella), and *supplì* (rice balls stuffed with mozzarella and other ingredients).

AMARO COCKTAILS

You can find creations that include *amaro,* the popular bittersweet Italian liqueur, in most cocktail bars in Rome (it's a main ingredient in drinks like the Aperol Spritz and Negroni). But the best place to sample this Italian staple is Il Marchese, Europe's first amaro bar, where you can choose from around 550 different bottles.

ESPRESSO

Few Romans can live without *il caffè,* so there's no shortage of coffee bars. Real Italian espresso consists of a thimbleful of aromatic black liquid, prepared by a barista in a variety of ways and enjoyed quickly while standing at the bar or leisurely while sitting down (to-go cups are not a thing here).

ARTICHOKES

Winter through spring is artichoke season, and restaurants all over Rome put them on menus as appetizers or side dishes. There are two styles to know: *carciofi alla romana*, i.e., Roman-style artichokes, which are stuffed with garlic and wild Roman mint and cooked in olive oil and water, and *carciofi alla giudia*, Jewish-style artichokes, which are smashed so the leaves open up and then fried to crispy perfection. The former can be found in trattorias all over the city; the place to get the latter is the Jewish Ghetto.

PASTA ALL'AMATRICIANA

The origins of *amatriciana* are in the Lazio town of Amatrice, hence the name. Although it might be made with *bucatini* (spaghetti-like but hollow), *mezze maniche* (short grooved pasta tubes), or rigatoni, this pasta dish always has a tomato-based sauce with *guanciale* (cured pork cheek) and pecorino cheese. You'll find it just about everywhere Roman classics are served.

CODA ALLA VACCINARA

Rome's largest slaughterhouse in the 1800s was in the Testaccio neighborhood, and that's where you'll still find dishes like "oxtail in the style of the cattle butcher." This dish is made from ox or veal tails stewed with tomatoes, carrots, celery, and wine, and usually seasoned with cinnamon. It's simmered for hours and then finished with raisins and pine nuts or bittersweet chocolate.

LA CARBONARA

One of the city's most iconic pasta dishes, carbonara is made with eggs, guanciale, pecorino, and freshly cracked black pepper—never cream. It's sometimes served with spaghetti or rigatoni and is a staple of Roman trattorias.

MARITOZZO

Cornetti (the Italian version of a croissant) are a ubiquitous breakfast staple all over Italy, but if you want to try a true Roman pastry, opt for a *maritozzo*. A soft bun split in half and filled with cream, it's often available at bars and bakeries around the city.

What to Buy in Rome

GOURMET FOOD PRODUCTS

Thanks to the impressive selection of Italian produce, Rome has no shortage of specialty food stores, gourmet outlets, and artisan shops. From Roman wine biscuits to locally produced olive oil, vinegar, condiments, and coffee, the city is a great place to stock up on some basics for your kitchen.

LEATHER ITEMS

Italian leather is renowned the world over for its high quality, supple feel, and sturdy craftsmanship. Roman stores that carry leather products abound and range from high fashion designers to boutique shops. Handbags, wallets, belts, and jackets can make unique (but be warned, pricey) souvenirs.

HANDMADE CHOCOLATE

Roman desserts have a unique charm thanks to tasty concoctions like amaretti or *brutti ma buoni* cookies (which literally translates to "ugly but good"). But the best tasty treat to bring home is handmade chocolate from an old-school confection shop.

SHOES

From sexy stilettos to strappy sandals to stylish *stivali* (boots), Rome has a *scarpa* (shoe) for every foot. The best place to get your feet wet is in the swanky Piazza di Spagna area, but other (less expensive) boutiques can be found around Piazza Navona and Campo de' Fiori.

DESIGNER CLOTHING

Italians know fashion; that much is indisputable. There are plenty of upscale flagship stores of world-famous brands in Rome, including the likes of Prada, Fendi, and Valentino. But try to browse the city's smaller boutiques, too; you'll be sure to find a piece or two from a lesser-known designer to liven up your wardrobe.

CERAMICS AND DECORATIVE ARTS

Unique pottery, beautiful ceramics, and other decorative arts are at the top of most souvenir shoppers' lists, and Rome is a great place to search for Italian-made items. The best finds are at artisan shops tucked away on winding cobblestone streets. Whether you fancy a ceramic serving bowl or a marble plaque carved by hand with a funny saying, you won't go home empty-handed.

JEWELRY

Over the years, several delightful boutiques featuring unique handmade jewelry have made their debut in the Eternal City. Don't leave Rome without stepping foot in a specialized *oreficeria*.

LAZIO WINE

Lazio might not have the reputation of Piedmont or Tuscany when it comes to wine, but some local wineries are finally putting the region on the map. Bottles of local wine can be purchased at *enoteche* (wine shops) across the city and even in wine bars and supermarkets.

ANTIQUES AND PRINTS

Rome is one of Italy's happiest hunting grounds for antiques and bric-a-brac. You'll find streets lined with shops groaning under the weight of gilded Rococo tables, charming Grand Tour memorabilia, fetching 17th-century engravings of realistic scenes, and many intriguing curios.

VINTAGE CLOTHING

For many, looking good means not looking like anyone else. Luckily Rome has a wide range of vintage shops (mainly in the Monti and Piazza Navona areas), where you can find some great couture from the *Dolce Vita* days and other classic time periods. Spend some time going through the racks, and you never know what treasures you might find.

FLEA MARKETS

Treasure seekers and bargain hunters alike will appreciate Rome's *mercati all'aperto* (open-air markets), which are great spots to unearth some really good finds both old and new. Every Sunday, all of Rome tends to gravitate to Trastevere for the Porta Portese flea market, where tents overflow with cheap luggage, new and vintage clothes, and nearly anything else you can think of.

PECORINO ROMANO

Rome's famed sheep's milk cheese, known as pecorino romano, is the star of many classic Roman dishes, from cacio e pepe to carbonara. You can purchase some to take home from multiple delicatessens and cheese shops around town.

Best Museums in Rome

MACRO
The former Peroni brewery in the Repubblica district houses this museum with a focus on Italian art from the 1960s through the present. The building, with its striking red structure and glass walkways, was designed by French architect Odile Decq and is worth a visit in and of itself.

MUSEI CAPITOLINI
Second in size only to the Vatican Museums, the Capitoline Museums were the world's first public art museums. Two buildings on Michelangelo's Piazza del Campidoglio house a collection spanning from ancient Rome to the Baroque era, with masterpieces that include Caravaggio's *St. John the Baptist*.

GALLERIA NAZIONALE D'ARTE MODERNA E CONTEMPORANEA
A huge, white, Beaux-Arts building in Villa Borghese has one of Italy's most important collections of 19th- and 20th-century art. You'll find works by Degas, Monet, Courbet, Cézanne, and Van Gogh, but there's also an emphasis on Italian Modernism.

GALLERIA BORGHESE
It would be hard to find a more beautiful villa filled with a must-see collection of masterpieces by Bernini, Caravaggio, Raphael, Rubens, and Titian. Cardinal Scipione Borghese had the gorgeous Renaissance villa built in 1612 to display his collection, though it has undergone many changes since.

MUSEO NAZIONALE ETRUSCO DI VILLA GIULIA
The pre-Roman Etruscans appeared in Italy around 2,000 BC, though no one knows exactly where they originated. To learn more about them, plan a visit to this museum in Villa Giulia, which was built for Pope Julius III in the mid-1500s.

PALAZZO DORIA PAMPHILJ
For a look at aristocratic Rome, visit this museum in the 15th-century palazzo of the Doria Pamphilj family just south of the Piazza di Spagna. Wander through the Hall of Mirrors—fashioned after the one at Versailles—but don't miss the Old Master paintings.

MUSEI VATICANI

One of the largest museum complexes in the world, the Vatican palaces and museums comprise some 1,400 rooms, galleries, and chapels. By far the most famous attraction is the Sistine Chapel painted by Michelangelo and a team of others, but the Raphael Rooms come in a close second when it comes to must-see works.

MAXXI

Tucked away in the quiet Flaminio neighborhood, the Museo Nazionale delle Arti del XXI Secolo (National Museum of 21st Century Arts)—or MAXXI, for short—proves that there's more to Rome than ancient and Baroque art.

CENTRALE MONTEMARTINI

Nowhere else is the theme of gods and machines more apparent than at this museum. Situated in the Testaccio district, Rome's first power plant now houses the overflow from collections at the Capitoline Museums; the sculptures of men in togas and women in dresses form a poignant contrast to the machinery.

Best Ancient Sites in Rome

COLOSSEUM
Perhaps the monument most symbolic of ancient Rome, the Colosseum is one of the city's most fascinating—and popular—tourist attractions. It officially opened in AD 80 with 100 days of games, including wild-animal fights and gladiatorial combat.

FORO DI TRAIANO
Trajan's Forum was the last of imperial Rome's forums—and the grandest. Comprising a basilica, two libraries, and a colonnade surrounding a piazza, it's connected to a market that once bustled with commercial activity.

PANTHEON
Built as a pagan temple, the Pantheon is Rome's best-preserved ancient site, perhaps because it was later consecrated as a church. Step inside, and you'll be amazed at its perfect proportions and the sunlight streaming in from the 30-foot-wide oculus. It's truly a wonder of ancient engineering.

ROMAN FORUM
One of the Eternal City's most emblematic sites, the Roman Forum stretches out between the Capitoline and Palatine hills. This vast area filled with crumbling columns and the ruins of temples, palaces, and shops was once the hub of the ancient world and the center of political, commercial, and religious life in the city.

CIRCUS MAXIMUS
It might be hard to imagine now, but the grassy area between the Palatine and Aventine hills was once the site of the largest hippodrome in the Roman Empire. The huge oval course was rebuilt under Julius Caesar and later enlarged by subsequent emperors. During its heyday, it hosted epic chariot races and competitions that sometimes lasted for up to 15 days.

BOCCA DELLA VERITÀ
Legend has it the mouth in this ancient stone face will bite off the hand of a liar, and tourists line up to stick their hand inside the mouth and put it to the test. (Gregory Peck's character tricks Audrey Hepburn's Princess Ann into thinking he lost a hand inside it in a scene from *Roman Holiday*.) You'll find the enigmatic face in the portico of the Church of Santa Maria in Cosmedin, near the Circus Maximus.

TEATRO MARCELLO

What looks a bit like a smaller version of the Colosseum was once ancient Rome's largest and most important theater. Julius Caesar ordered the land for the theater to be cleared, but he was murdered before it was built. It was inaugurated in AD 12 by Augustus and hosted performances of drama and song. It's kept that purpose even today, at least during the summer, when it hosts concerts.

APPIA ANTICA

Head to the southeastern edge of the city to Appia Antica Park and you can walk on the stones—which are incredibly well-preserved—that ancient Roman soldiers and citizens once trod. This thoroughfare once stretched all the way to Brindisi on the Adriatic Coast. Today, the first 16 km (10 miles) are part of a regional park, and it's a perfect spot for bike rides and picnics in the grass under the shadow of Rome's emblematic umbrella pines.

ARA PACIS AUGUSTAE

Now housed in a modern glass-and-travertine building designed by renowned American architect Richard Meier, the Ara Pacis Augustae has some of the most incredible reliefs you'll see on any ancient monument. It was commissioned to celebrate the Emperor Augustus's victories in battle and the Pax Romana, a peaceful period that followed. It's definitely worth a visit and is centrally located on the Tiber River in the Piazza di Spagna district.

TERMI DI CARACALLA

A testament to ancient Rome's bathing culture, this site on the Aventine Hill was essentially a massive spa, with saunas, baths, what would be an Olympic-size pool, and two gymnasiums for boxing, weight lifting, and wrestling.

Best Churches in Rome

SANTA MARIA DEL POPOLO

It would be easy to bypass this church on the corner of Piazza del Popolo, but do go inside to see its artistic treasures. Raphael designed an entire chapel within the church, and there are two altar paintings by Caravaggio: *Crucifixion of Saint Peter* and the *Conversion of Saint Paul*.

BASILICA DI SAN PIETRO

The world's largest church and one of the world's holiest places, St. Peter's Basilica was built on the site of Saint Peter's tomb. The greatest architectural achievement of the Renaissance, it's a testament to the Catholic Church's wealth and power.

SAN LUIGI DEI FRANCESI

Among art lovers, the secret's out about this small church near Piazza Navona dedicated to Saint Louis, the patron saint of France. Inside, the Contarelli Chapel is adorned by three Caravaggios, each one more splendid than the last. Gaze up at his three depictions of Saint Matthew (the *Calling of Saint Matthew*, *Saint Matthew and the Angel*, and the *Martyrdom of Saint Matthew*) and you'll understand why Caravaggio was the master of chiaroscuro.

SAN GIOVANNI IN LATERANO

Built by the Emperor Constantine 10 years prior to the Basilica di San Pietro, the monumental Arcibasilica di San Giovanni in Laterano is actually the ecclesiastical seat of the Pope. Before you enter, look up to admire the 15 monumental statues depicting the 12 apostles, plus Jesus Christ, the Virgin Mary, and John the Baptist. The intricate mosaic floors are the work of the Cosmati family. To learn more about them, join Personalized Italy's Cosmatesque Tour of Rome led by a charming art historian who illuminates the incredible craftsmanship that went into this and other churches.

PANTHEON

Originally a pagan temple and later consecrated as a church, the Pantheon counts itself among Rome's most famous monuments for good reason. It's considered the world's only architecturally perfect building by some, because of its proportions (the diameter is equal to its height). Of Rome's many ancient sites, it's the best preserved. It's also the final resting place of Raphael and other important figures from Italy's history.

SCALA SANTA

Devout Catholic pilgrims travel to Rome's San Giovanni district from far and wide to climb the Scala Santa—the marble staircase from Pontius Pilate's palace in Jerusalem—on their knees. At the top is the Sancta Sanctorum (Holy of Holies), a small chapel ornately decorated with marble, frescoes, and Cosmatesque mosaic floors. Note that you can also climb non-sanctified side stairs to reach the top and admire the Sancta Sanctorum, which was the Pope's chapel before the Sistine Chapel.

BASILICA DI SAN CLEMENTE

The 12th-century Basilica di San Clemente in the Celio district is known as the "lasagna church" because the deeper you descend, the farther back in time you go. It was built on top of a 4th-century church, which was built atop not only a 2nd-century pagan temple dedicated to the cult of Mithras, but also a collection of 1st-century Roman houses. Pay the nominal entry fee to access the lower levels, where the mysterious cult once worshipped, and you'll feel like you're peeling back the layers of ancient history.

SANTA MARIA DELLA VITTORIA

Bernini's genius is on full display in this church near Piazza della Repubblica. Though the structure's architect was Carlo Maderno, Bernini was responsible for the Cornaro Chapel, where you can admire his somewhat controversial sculpture, the *Ecstasy of Saint Teresa*. It's meant to depict the saint abandoning herself to the divine love of god, but her expression seems to imply she's experiencing a more earthly pleasure. Pay this church a visit and decide for yourself.

SAN PIETRO IN VINCOLI

The reason to visit this otherwise unremarkable church in Monti is to lay eyes on Michelangelo's *Moses*. Pope Julius II had commissioned the statue for his tomb, but after he died, his successor—a rival from the Medici family—abandoned the tomb and left the statue here instead. Scholars debate whether the two things on Moses's head are meant to be horns or rays of light. Either way, the statue is one of Michelangelo's best.

SANT'AGOSTINO

This church tucked behind Piazza Navona contains a triple-whammy of incredible art. Not only is it home to Caravaggio's *Madonna of the Pilgrims*, but also Raphael's *Isaiah*, which may have been inspired by Michelangelo's prophets on the ceiling of the Sistine Chapel (the artist snuck a peek despite orders of secrecy) and Sansovino's sculpture *St. Anne and the Madonna with Child*. It's definitely worth a detour.

Under-the-Radar Things to Do in Rome

Gardens on Aventine Hill

STREET ART IN OSTIENSE, SAN LORENZO, AND PIGNETO

Beyond the *centro storico* (historic center), the gritty neighborhoods of Ostiense, San Lorenzo, and Pigneto may not be on your Rome bucket list, but they're a must-see for fans of street art. Entire buildings are covered top-to-bottom in murals, and well-known street artists have left their mark.

PALAZZO ALTEMPS

This small museum near Piazza Navona was once the aristocratic home of Cardinal Altemps. It now houses ancient Roman statues that are part of the collection of the Museo Nazionale Romano, but the real reason to come is to admire the gorgeous loggia with its colorful frescoes and busts of the Caesars.

CULTURAL PROGRAMMING AT THE VILLA MEDICI

You wouldn't know it from the outside, but this gorgeous Renaissance palace on the Pincio Hill houses the Academy of France in Rome, which hosts visiting artists and scholars and puts on cultural events.

THE CAPUCHIN CRYPT

As if preserving saintly relics wasn't creepy enough, the Capuchin order of friars used the bones of some 4,000 brothers to decorate the crypt under the Church of Santa Maria della Concezione. This site isn't for the faint of heart. A sign that reads "What you are, we once were. What we are, you will someday be" serves as a poignant reminder of our mortality.

CONCERTS AT THE ORATORIO DEL GONFALONE

Hidden behind a nondescript door in the centro storico lies a room decorated wall-to-wall with incredibly well-preserved frescoes depicting scenes of the passion of the Christ. Painted in the 16th century by a team of mannerist painters, the site has been called "the Sistine Chapel of Mannerism."

SHOPPING ON VIA DI MONSERRATO

Via del Corso and Via dei Condotti may be Rome's most famous shopping streets, but for truly unique finds, you need to get off the beaten path and head to Via di Monserrato near the Campo de' Fiori. This charming cobblestone street is home to a collection of high-end boutiques.

PARCO DEGLI ACQUEDOTTI

On the city's southeastern outskirts, this massive green park is a peaceful oasis where locals come to jog, walk their dogs, and just hang out. The aqueducts are relics of the Roman Empire and you can walk along the remains of an ancient cobblestone road that once formed part of the Appia Antica.

GARDENS ON AVENTINE HILL

If you happen to be in Rome in the spring, when the Roseto Comunale on the Aventine Hill is in bloom, it's worth a stop. Once a Jewish cemetery, the garden's paths are fittingly shaped like a menorah. With more than 1,000 different varieties of roses, it's one of the most romantic spots in Rome.

QUARTIERE COPPEDÈ

This charming microneighborhood near Villa Torlonia may be a bit off the beaten path, but it's a fascinating spot for architecture fans. A collection of 27 buildings were designed in a whimsical Art Nouveau style by architect Gino Coppedè in the 1910s. Don't miss the Fontana delle Rane (Fountain of the Frogs).

Best Free Things to Do in Rome

VITTORIANO MONUMENT

Near the Piazza di Spagna, this monument to Italy's first king, Victor Emmanuel II, has polarized locals since its construction, but it still has some of the best views in the city. It also holds the Tomb of the Unknown Soldier and its eternal flame.

SPANISH STEPS

Located within the elegant Piazza di Spagna, the largest staircase in Europe definitely deserves a visit, and luckily it doesn't cost a thing. You can walk up the stairs for great views from the famed church, Trinità dei Monti. Bernini's fountain, La Barcaccia, stands at the bottom of the stairs and is a great example of Baroque art and design.

PIAZZA NAVONA

For the finest example of Baroque Roman architecture, head to Piazza Navona. Here you'll find one of Bernini's most important masterpieces, the Fountain of the Four Rivers, topped by the obelisk of Domitian. The square is filled daily with street performers and artists. You can also enter the church Sant'Agnese in Agone by Borromini from the piazza.

CAMPO DE' FIORI

Campo de' Fiori hosts the oldest and most famous market in Rome. Watch the stand owners boisterously interact as they show off their wares, and admire the central monument to the philosopher Giordano Bruno. Around the corner, you'll find some of Rome's best *pizza bianca* (focaccia-style bread) at Forno Roscioli or Forno Campo de' Fiori.

KEYHOLE OF THE KNIGHTS OF MALTA

High up on Aventine Hill, the Gran Priorato di Roma dell'Ordine di Malta (Grand Priory of the Knights of Malta), which is set in the Piazza dei Cavalieri di Malta, has an unusual and enchanting attraction. Through the tiny keyhole of a nondescript door, you can see the gorgeous dome of St. Peter's Basilica. This perfectly framed view gives you a unique taste of three separate nations: Malta, Italy, and the Vatican.

ORANGE GARDEN

Located on elegant Aventine Hill, the Orange Garden (as it's known by locals) is officially named Savello Park, named for the family who lived there throughout the 13th century. The setting is filled with orange trees planted in honor of San Domenico, who founded the neighboring convent, hence the reason for its colloquial name. Today, it's an enchanting garden space perfect for a stroll or picnic. But most of all, visitors love coming here for the spectacular panoramic views of the city.

ISOLA TIBERINA

The only island in Rome, Tiber Island sits in the middle of the Tiber River between the Jewish Ghetto and Trastevere. The small boat-shaped island is home to a hospital (here since the 16th century), a church, a pharmacy, and two restaurants. It's connected to the mainland by bridges on either side, one of which is pedestrian-only. From

here, city views stretch out across the river, and in the summer months, there is an outdoor cinema and seasonal restaurants and bars.

GIANICOLO

While not officially one of the famed Seven Hills of Rome, the Janiculum (Gianicolo in Italian) is certainly the one Romans are fondest of. From it, sprawling panoramic views of the city stretch out like a postcard; it's often the location for a wedding photo shoot, first kiss, or proposal. Walk the paths that feature significant historical statues and busts, and take in the beauty of the Fontana di Acqua Paola; referred to by locals as the *fontanone* (the big fountain), it's said to be where you go to weep and mourn a broken heart.

ROME'S BASILICAS

It's completely free to walk right into Rome's four major papal basilicas, the four highest-ranking Roman Catholic church buildings in the world. These include Arcibasilica di San Giovanni in Laterano (the official seat and parish of the Pope), as well as San Pietro, San Paolo Fuori le Mura, and Santa Maria Maggiore. Each has unique architecture and style.

VIA MARGUTTA

Walk in Audrey Hepburn and Gregory Peck's footsteps à la *Roman Holiday* on a stroll down one of the city's prettiest streets. Via Margutta (at number 51, to be precise) was the location of Peck's character's apartment in the film, and where many scenes were shot. This short street with a long history is now filled with antiques stores and galleries.

VILLA BORGHESE

As the most famous park in Rome, Villa Borghese is a lush oasis in the northern part of the city center. It has a man-made lake where you can rent canoes, and there are plenty of spaces for a picnic. You could easily spend the entire day here, and there's a café for light meals and snacks, too.

Rome Today

Rome, the Eternal City, is 28 centuries old and yet is still constantly reinventing itself. Here, the glories of ancient times, the pomp of the Renaissance Papacy, and the futuristic architecture of the 20th and 21st centuries all blend miraculously into a harmonious whole. The fact that you can get Wi-Fi in the shadow of 2,000-year-old ruins sort of sums things up, and it's this fusion of old and new and the casual way that Romans live with their weighty history that make this city so unique.

NEW ARCHITECTURE

Rome may be firmly anchored in the distant past, but that's never been an obstacle to its journey into the new millennium. Just look at some of the architectural marvels that have emerged in the last 25 years: the Auditorium Parco della Musica (Renzo Piano, 2002); the Jubilee Church (formerly Chiesa di Dio Padre Misericordioso, Richard Meier, 2003); the Museo dell'Ara Pacis (Richard Meier, 2006); MACRO (Odile Decq, 2010); and the MAXXI (Zaha Hadid, 2010).

In 2011, Rome also built a new bridge— the grandiose Ponte della Musica—over the Tiber River. Looking like two giant white harps rising from the ground, it can be used only by pedestrians and cyclists. In addition, the Massimiliano Fuksas–designed Roma Convention Center, nicknamed "La Nuvola" for its futuristic suspended cloud shape, opened in 2016.

NEW MODES OF TRANSPORTATION

Romans are anxiously awaiting the completion of the new Metro Linea C, which will cut through the city center at Piazza Venezia and link with both the A and B lines at Ottaviano for St. Peter's and the Colosseum, respectively. Although it is expected to ease surface-traffic congestion considerably, progress on the new line has gone slowly, because every time a shaft is sunk in Roman ground, it reveals some new important archaeological site, and all work halts for the ensuing excavation. Currently, only the peripheral section of Line C is running, connecting with Line A at San Giovanni and continuing eastward to Pigneto and beyond.

More eco-friendly modes of transportation are appearing, too. E-bikes by Uber Jump and electric scooters can be found around the city. You can rent one from Helbiz, Lime by Uber, and Bird via each company's app. Just be careful—riding on the sidewalks is prohibited, and drivers can be rather aggressive.

NEW FOOD TRENDS

Although it's still true that Romans love Roman food, the city's dining scene is becoming (slightly) more international. Rome might never have the diversity of New York or London, but some of its trendiest restaurants and bars serve Mexican tacos and margaritas, sushi, Danish bread and pastries, and even ramen.

You'll also find traditional Roman or Italian restaurants where menus include a few surprising items, like burgers. As puzzling as this tendency might be, it can be nice to have alternatives to the usual trattoria fare.

MORE HOTEL OPTIONS

The pandemic caused a lot of hotel clo-sures, but there's since been a flurry of openings, with lots more to come—and hotels are seriously upping the ante for travelers looking for a fabulous place to stay.

International hospitality companies are investing big in the Eternal City. Some of the new trendy hotels offer unprecedent-ed levels of luxury whereas others offer great style at relatively low price points. Yes, there are classic Marriott and Hilton outposts here, but British brands Hoxton and Soho House, French brand Mama Shelter, and American brands W and EDI-TION have also arrived on the scene.

In addition, Thai brand Anantara has taken over Palazzo Naiadi on Piazza della Repubblica, and Six Senses has revamped a historic palazzo just off Via del Corso. The Rome-born jewelry brand Bulgari made a splash when it opened a namesake hotel on Piazza Augusto Imperatore. Also watch out for ultra-lux-urious openings by Four Seasons and Rosewood.

The influx of new places to stay coupled with pandemic-induced woes means that some older hotels have gone out of busi-ness, but others, like the illustrious Hotel de Russie, are gussying up their spaces and revamping their offerings. Overall, it's good news for travelers.

What to Read and Watch

LA DOLCE VITA
Just as the names Raphael, Botticelli, Michelangelo, and Da Vinci reign over the Italian art world, filmmakers like Fellini, Rossellini, De Sica, and Antonioni are essential for appreciating Italian (and Roman) cinema. Federico Fellini's classic *La Dolce Vita* follows the busy days and nights of journalist Marcello, taking viewers throughout Rome and its most notable landmarks. Among the film's more artistic and nuanced aspects are gorgeous scenes of nightlife, dining, and general folly in the ancient city's ruin and splendor.

HISTORY OF THE DECLINE AND FALL OF THE ROMAN EMPIRE BY EDWARD GIBBON
Okay, so maybe you do get through all six volumes of this classic text, or maybe they just sit on your bookshelf looking pretty (we're not here to judge). But while there have since been many historical and archaeological discoveries that add to and challenge the conclusions Gibbon made in the late 1700s, this text remains famous and respected for its comprehensive attempt to understand ancient Rome and the causes of its decline. For a more contemporary and abridged source of Roman history, try *SPQR: A History of Ancient Rome* by Mary Beard.

BICYCLE THIEVES
Many Roman films highlight a spirit of unsettling resistance, confusion, and pain during the aftermath of Mussolini's fascist regime—a time that came to define much of contemporary Italy and its art. Vittorio de Sica's neorealist masterpiece captures this atmosphere through the story of a father, son, and one stolen bicycle, taking us through the desperate, dusty streets of Rome after World War II.

THE YOUNG POPE
Although it's unclear how realistic the Vatican politics depicted in this HBO series actually are, this tale about the rise of an unlikely, power-hungry young pope and his ensuing deviance, manipulations, and power-grabs makes for great television. The clever writing and skilled performances (especially by a creepy Jude Law as Pius XIII, the world's first American pope) elevate the show, as does the gorgeous cinematography.

AENEID BY VIRGIL
Because so much of Roman literature (and history) has been built upon the early greats, it's helpful to get some classical poetry under your belt before a trip to Rome. Virgil, Ovid, Horace, or Catullus (and even Dante or Keats) will do just fine, but the *Aeneid* is arguably the most Roman poem in existence. The long harrowing journey of Aeneas and his soldiers, as they head out of Troy and toward the Italian peninsula, is outlined in this long epic poem, which ends with the early finding (and founding) of Rome, making it a unique literary origin story.

ROMAN HOLIDAY
When all the fascism and papal politics start to get too heavy, turn instead to a light Roman film, the classic *Roman Holiday*. In it, the charms of Gregory Peck and Audrey Hepburn and their whirlwind romance make great vacation fodder, as they ride Vespas through Roman streets, and gallivant through the Piazza del Popolo, around the Colosseum, and other landmarks.

A CLASH OF CIVILIZATIONS OVER AN ELEVATOR IN PIAZZA VITTORIO BY AMARA LAKHOUS
While the plot centers around a murder that takes place in a small apartment building on the Piazza Vittorio, this novel is really about the tenants of said building, a culturally diverse group, whose

differences shape the complexity of what it means to be Roman. An author of Algerian descent, Lakhous has a knack for delving into shifting points of view, particularly shining a much needed light on the Muslim immigrant experience in Italy.

THE BORGIAS
This historical television drama series gives a fictionalized tale of the very real, very corrupt Borgia family that came from Spain and rose to power and the papacy in Renaissance Italy. Although the show takes historical liberties to build drama, most of the juiciest scandals—torture, bribery, and even incest—are based on real events or longtime rumors about the infamous family.

LA GRANDE BELLEZZA (THE GREAT BEAUTY)
Paolo Sorrentino's Academy Award–winning film follows an aging writer in contemporary Rome as he examines both his past and present life choices. Moving through the protagonist's partying lifestyle, the film is a modern-day version of *La Dolce Vita* that highlights some of the more lavish, indulgent aspects of Roman life.

THE AGONY AND THE ECSTASY BY IRVING STONE
Reading this 1961 novel provides great context for those who plan to visit the Vatican's most popular artistic sight, the Sistine Chapel. This fictionalized biography of Michelangelo's arduous process details the genius and struggle (along with the politics) that went into his masterful creation. As material for the novel, Stone sourced Michelangelo's original correspondence during the time (almost 500 letters), spent long periods in Rome and Florence, and even worked in a marble quarry and as a sculptor's apprentice.

EAT, PRAY, LOVE
Elizabeth Gilbert's memoir on what she ate, learned, and loved after leaving a failed marriage to travel the world is divided into three sections and her time spent in Italy, India, and Bali, respectively. The "Eat" portion of Gilbert's journey (the four months she spent in Rome) is perhaps the most enjoyable to read, and provides important travel advice: when in Rome, indulge with abandon. In the movie version, Rome and its feasts are less detailed but more cinematic (and on the plus side, you have Julia Roberts playing Gilbert).

LOVE AND ANARCHY
Much like her mentor Federico Fellini, Lina Wertmüller—one of Italy's most impressive female directors and the first woman to be nominated for the Best Director Oscar—has a knack for combining humor and folly with political critique and human heartbreak. The film's lovable, blundering star is a countryman determined to murder Mussolini, finding love and friendship in a Roman brothel along the way. This beautiful work is full of Roman sentiment, style, and history, making it a must-see in Italian cinema, as is Wertmüller's slightly darker work, *Seven Beauties*.

GLADIATOR
Russell Crowe takes on ancient Rome as a powerful general who, after a fall from political grace, is taken as a slave and forced to fight as a gladiator in the (digitally re-imagined) Colosseum. The epic film, full of high stakes and high emotions, was a huge box-office hit when it opened in 2000. Although it contains some historical inaccuracies, it's an enjoyable watch for those fascinated by the ins and outs of the political and social structures, power plays, and daily violence of ancient Rome.

Rome with Kids

There are plenty of ways to keep the younger set occupied in Rome—plus, getting them to eat isn't usually a problem, with options like pizza, pasta, and gelato on the menu.

ARCHAEOLOGY

If your kids are into archaeology or gladiators, traipsing the ruins of ancient Rome can provide hours of entertainment. Who can resist climbing the giant steps of the **Colosseum**? For the true enthusiast, the Roman Gladiator School offers group and private lessons in which your little one (or big one) can dress up like Spartacus and learn sword-fighting techniques and a bit about the lives of these warriors.

Roman Gladiator School. Two-hour lessons in how to be a gladiator include clothing to dress up in as well as "weapons" and shields—it's great fun and a great way to get some history lessons. The instructors are top-quality, and experienced at dealing with participants of varying levels. There's a viewing platform for those who prefer to observe their friends and family. ⊕ *www.romegladiatorschool.com* ✉ *From €120.*

PARKS

Take little ones to see the Teatrino Pulcinella's open-air puppet show weekends on the Janiculum Hill, where you can also enjoy a great view of the city, or to the San Carlino puppet theater weekends on Viale dei Bambini in **Villa Borghese Park.** (Tips for the puppeteers are greatly appreciated.) Villa Borghese is also home to other kid-oriented attractions such as the **Bioparco** (zoo), with more than 1,000 animals in peaceful landscaped surroundings.

Rent a bike (at Bici Pincio at Via di Campo Marzo or on Viale Goethe) and explore the vast Borghese estate. You can also take a rowboat out on the Laghetto di Villa Borghese. At only €5 per person for 20 minutes, it's one of the best ways to explore the park's incredible sculptures, temples, and natural beauty.

CREEPY STUFF

Rome's catacombs (underground cemeteries) are intriguing enough to wipe the boredom off most teenagers' faces, and the best are the **Catacombe di San Callisto** on the Via Appia Antica. It's hard not to be impressed by the labyrinth of dark corridors and grisly tales of Christian martyrs.

The **Capuchin Crypt** under Santa Maria della Concezione is also gruesomely mesmerizing, with the skulls and bones of 3,700 friars arranged on the walls and ceiling in fanciful patterns. Or take the kids to the Bocca della Verità (Mouth of Truth) at **Santa Maria in Cosmedin,** and warn them that it bites off liars' hands.

WATER FOUNTAINS

The public water fountains in Rome are free (and perfectly safe) to drink from; the only problem is figuring out how to do it without getting wet. A good trick is to block a hole under the spout with your finger to create a fountain, or bring bottles to fill up.

Chapter 2

TRAVEL SMART

Updated by
Laura Itzkowitz

★ **CAPITAL:**
Rome

⚥ **POPULATION:**
4,471,094

💬 **LANGUAGE:**
Italian

$ **CURRENCY:**
Euro

☎ **COUNTRY CODE:**
39

⚠ **EMERGENCIES:**
112

🚗 **DRIVING:**
On the right

⚡ **ELECTRICITY:**
220V/50Hz; Continental-style
plugs, with two or three
round prongs

🕑 **TIME:**
Six hours ahead of New York

🌐 **WEB RESOURCES:**
www.turismoroma.it
www.wantedinrome.com
www.italymagazine.com
www.060608.it

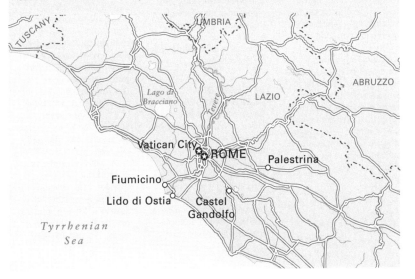

Know Before You Go

TAKE ADVANTAGE OF THE ROMA PASS.
In addition to single- and multiday transit passes, a three-day Roma Pass (€52) covers unlimited use of buses, trams, and the Metro, plus free admission to two museums or archaeological sites of your choice and discounted entrance to others. A two-day pass is €32 and includes one museum.

NAVIGATING THE CITY IS ACTUALLY PRETTY EASY.
Many of Rome's main attractions are concentrated in the *centro storico* (historic center), which encompasses what stood inside the city's 3rd-century walls. The district's borders are roughly the Vatican to the west, Villa Borghese to the north, Termini station to east, and the Colosseum to the south. Although this large area is easier to fully navigate when divided into smaller modern neighborhoods, some main sights are close to one another, making them relatively easy to visit on foot. In addition, Rome has a good network of public transport, both above and below ground. The Metro Linea A will take you to Termini station, the Trevi Fountain (Barberini stop), the Spanish Steps (Spagna stop), St. Peter's (Ottaviano stop), and the Vatican Museums (Cipro), to name a few.

IT'S HELPFUL TO KNOW HOW TO READ ADDRESSES.
In the centro storico, most street names are posted on ceramic-like plaques on the side of buildings, which can make them hard to see. Addresses are fairly straightforward: the street name is followed by the street number, but it's worth noting that Roman street numbering, even in the newer outskirts of town, can be erratic. Usually numbers are even on one side of the street and odd on the other, but sometimes numbers are in ascending consecutive order on one side of the street and descending order on the other side.

BE AWARE OF EXTRA CHARGES.
As is common in many big cities, tourists can be taken advantage of in establishments near major sights, and Rome is no different, so always check your final bill carefully. It's common to see table service charges or cover charges on menus, but they should be specified, and the cover charge should include a bread basket. These charges mean tipping is not mandatory, although locals generally round up to the nearest euro of the total amount; at a casual trattoria or pizzeria, some coins on the table is good enough. If any surprise fees are on your final bill, don't be afraid to bring this up to the waitstaff. If you're at a bar having coffee, it's customary to leave a coin for your barista. Other charges to be aware of include paying to use the bathroom in some public places and the Tourist City Tax, imposed by the City of Rome—this is a compulsory per night, per person charge for all hotels, B&Bs, and even Airbnb bookings.

DRESS (AND ACT) APPROPRIATELY WHEN VISITING CHURCHES.
If you're planning to visit the Vatican, in particular St. Peter's Basilica, appropriate clothing and attire must be worn and, at a minimum, shoulders have to be covered. Low-cut or sleeveless tops, miniskirts, and hats are not allowed. Scarves and shawls are available for purchase in and around the Vatican if you turn up unprepared. Modest dress and behavior should also be observed when visiting other religious sites and churches in the city. Do not enter a church while eating or drinking—keep all food items in a bag. Avoid entering altogether when a service is being held. All mobile phones must be on silent. If there are signs

reading "No photography" or "No flash photography," abide by these rules.

PRACTICE SOME BASIC ITALIAN ETIQUETTE.

Although you may find Rome much more informal than many other European cities, Romans will nevertheless appreciate attempts to abide by local etiquette. When entering an establishment, the key phrases to know are: *buongiorno* (good morning), *buona sera* (good evening), and *salve* (a neutral greeting). When exiting, it's polite to say *grazie* (thank you) or *arrivederci* (goodbye). Italians greet friends with a kiss, usually first on the right cheek, and then on the left. When you meet a new person, shake hands and say *piacere* (*pee-ah-chair-ay*).

IT HELPS TO LEARN SOME ITALIAN, TOO.

You can always find someone who speaks at least a little English in Rome, albeit with an accent. Remember that the Italian language is pronounced exactly as it's written, so many Italians try to speak English as it's written—sometimes with bewildering results. You may run into a language barrier outside big cities, but a phrase book and close attention to the Italian use of expressive gestures will go a long way. Try to master a few phrases for daily use, and familiarize yourself with the terms you'll need to decipher signs and museum labels. Many museum exhibitions only have descriptions in Italian.

BE PREPARED FOR ROMAN TIME.

In Italy, almost nothing starts on time except for (sometimes) a theater, opera, or movie showing. Italians even joke about a "15-minute window" before actually being late somewhere. In addition, the day starts a little later than normal here with many shops not opening until 10 am, lunch never happening before 1 pm, and dinner rarely before 8 pm. On Sunday, many independent shops close, and on Monday, most state museums and exhibition halls, plus many restaurants are closed. Daily food shop hours generally run 10 am–1 pm and 4 pm–7:30 pm or 8 pm, but other stores in the center usually observe continuous opening hours. Pharmacies tend to close for a lunch break and keep night hours (*ora rio notturno*) in rotation. As for churches, most open at 8 or 9 in the morning, close noon to 3 or 4, then reopen until 6:30 or 7. St. Peter's, however, has continuous hours 7 am–7 pm (until 6 pm in the fall and winter), and the Vatican Museums are open Monday but closed Sunday (except for the last Sunday of the month).

IT'S USUALLY BEST TO AVOID AUGUST.

If you can avoid it, don't travel at all in Italy in mid-August, when much of the population is on the move, especially around Ferragosto, the August 15 national holiday, when cities such as Rome are deserted and many restaurants and shops are closed.

If you've done the tourist circuit several times, though, you may enjoy a quieter, emptier version of the city during this time. Other national holidays are New Year's Day (January 1); Epiphany (January 6); Easter Sunday and Monday; Liberation Day (April 25); Labor Day (May 1); Republic Day (June 2); All Saint's Day (November 1); Immaculate Conception (December 8); Christmas Day and the feast of Saint Stephen (December 25 and 26). Rome-specific holidays are Rome's birthday (April 21) and St. Peter and Paul Day (June 29).

THERE ARE WAYS TO AVOID THE CROWDS.

Millions of tourists visit Rome each year, and you should plan your sightseeing ahead of time, especially for the most popular sights like the Colosseum and the Vatican. While travelers seem to be catching on to what used to be low season in Rome, January, February, and November are still when the city is a little quieter than usual. Advance tickets and private tours that let you skip the ticket lines are highly recommended to ensure hours aren't lost queuing for the major attractions. While the city center is the most aesthetically spectacular part of the city, spend some time in the less busy neighborhoods like Testaccio, Monti, or San Giovanni if tourist crowds aren't your thing.

Getting Here and Around

Air

Flying time to Rome is 7½–8½ hours from New York, 9–10 hours from Chicago, 11–12 hours from Los Angeles, and 2½ hours from London.

AIRPORTS

The principal airport for flights to Rome is Leonardo da Vinci Airport, more commonly known as Fiumicino (FCO). It's 30 km (19 miles) southwest of the city. There is a direct train link with Rome's Termini station on the Leonardo Express train, and there's a local train to Trastevere and Ostiense stations. Rome's other airport is Ciampino (CIA), on Via Appia Nuova, 15 km (9 miles) south of downtown. Ciampino is a national and international hub for many low-cost airlines. There is a train linking Ciampino to Termini station, but you have to take a bus to Ciampino station. There are also a number of shuttle buses running daily.

TRANSFERS BETWEEN AIRPORTS

It's not easy to move from one airport to another in Rome—the airports aren't connected by a railway system or by the Metro. The only way to make the transfer is by car, taxi, or a combination of bus, Metro, and train. The latter option is not advisable because it would take you at least two to three hours to get from one airport to the other. A taxi ride from Fiumicino Leonardo Da Vinci Airport to Ciampino Airport will take approximately 45 minutes and could cost roughly €50.

TRANSFERS BETWEEN CIAMPINO AND DOWNTOWN

By car, go north on the Via Appia Nuova into downtown Rome. The taxi fare law implemented by the Comune di Roma that affects Fiumicino applies to this airport, too. All taxi drivers are supposed to charge a fixed fare of €31 (including luggage handling) if your destination is within the Aurelian walls. If your hotel is outside the walls, the cab ride can run you about €60, plus *supplementi* (extra charges) for luggage. The ride takes about 30 minutes. Take only official white cabs with the "taxi" sign on top; unofficial cabs often overcharge disoriented travelers.

Airport Connection Services (⊕ *www.airportconnection.it*) has shuttles that cost €22 for the first passenger and €28 for two. **Airport Shuttle** (⊕ *www.airportshuttle.it*) charges €71.69 for up to three people. The **ATRAL bus** connects Ciampino airport with Termini station via a bus to Ciampino station and then a train. Buses depart from in front of the airport terminal frequently 6:15 am–10:40 pm. The fare is €2.70, and tickets can be bought on the bus. Travel time is approximately 40 minutes.

TRANSFERS BETWEEN FIUMICINO AND DOWNTOWN

If you're driving into the city, follow the signs for Rome and the GRA (the ring road that circles Rome). The direction you take on the GRA depends on where your lodging is located. If you're staying in the centro storico, follow indications for Roma Centro. Get a map and directions from the car-rental service, and if you aren't using one on your phone, considering renting a GPS as well.

A law implemented by the Comune di Roma requires all Rome taxi drivers to charge a fixed fare of €50 (including four passengers and luggage handling) if your destination is within the Aurelian walls (this covers the centro storico, most of Trastevere, most of the Vatican area, and parts of San Giovanni). If you aren't sure if your hotel falls within the Aurelian walls, ask when you book your room. If your hotel is outside the walls, the cab ride can run you upwards of €60 plus supplementi for luggage. (Of course, this also depends on traffic.) The ride from the airport to the city center takes about 30–45 minutes.

Private limousines can be booked at booths in the Arrivals hall; they charge more than taxis but can carry more passengers. The Comune di Roma now has a representative in place outside the International Arrivals hall (Terminal 3), where the taxi stand is located, to help tourists get into a taxi cab. Use only licensed white taxis. When in doubt, always ask for a receipt and write the cab company and taxi's license number down (it's written on a metal plate on the inside of the passenger door). Avoid unauthorized drivers who may approach you in the Arrivals hall; they charge exorbitant, unmetered rates.

Airport Connection charges €22 for one passenger, €28 for two, and minimal fees for each additional passenger. Booking ahead is required. **Airport Shuttle Express** (⊕ www.airportshuttleexpress.it) offers a daily service from/to FCO with stops at all major hotels in the center of Rome. It costs €20 one-way for one passenger, €30 for two, and €10 for each additional passenger. (The rate includes two bags per person.) **Airport Shuttle** provides door-to-door shuttle service, at a cost of €44 for up to three people. Advance booking is recommended.

Two trains link downtown Rome with Fiumicino—a nonstop express and a local. Inquire at the APT tourist information counter in the International Arrivals hall or the train information counter near the tracks to determine which takes you closest to your destination in Rome. The 32-minute nonstop Airport–Termini express (called the **Leonardo Express**)

goes directly to Tracks 23 or 24 at Termini station, which is well served by taxis and is a hub of Metro and bus lines. Departures to Termini station run approximately every 15 minutes beginning at 5:38 am from the airport, with a final departure at 11:53 pm. Trains depart Termini station from Tracks 23 and 24 to the airport starting at 4:50 am and the last train leaves at 11:05 pm. Tickets cost €14.

Trenitalia's **FL1,** the commuter rail, leaves from the same tracks and runs to Rome and beyond. The main stops in Rome are at Trastevere (26 minutes), Ostiense (31 minutes), and Tiburtina (48 minutes); at each you can find taxis and public transport connections to other areas of the city. FL1 regional trains run from Fiumicino between 5:57 am and 11:27 pm, with departures every 15 minutes; the schedule is similar going to the airport. Tickets cost €8. For either train, you can buy your ticket at a vending machine, at ticket counters at the airport and at some stations (Termini, Trastevere, Tiburtina), or online at ⊕ www.trenitalia.com.

At the airport, stamp the ticket at the gate. At other stations, remember to stamp the ticket in the little yellow or red machine near the track *before* you board. If you fail to stamp your ticket before you board, you could receive a hefty fine, as much as €100 on top of the ticket price. If you book your ticket online, you don't need to print it, but you do need to validate it via a link you'll receive when you book it. You can show the PDF to the ticket controller using your smartphone.

At night, take **COTRAL buses** from the airport to Tiburtina station or Termini station in Rome (50 minutes) and vice versa. Timetables are subject to last-minute changes, so be sure to check before traveling. Tickets either way cost €5 (€7 if purchased on board).

Getting Here and Around

Bus

An extensive network of bus lines that covers all of Lazio (the surrounding geographical region of which Rome is the capital) is operated by **COTRAL** (⊕ *www.cotralspa.it*), which stands for Consorzio Trasporti Lazio. There are several main bus stations. Long-distance and suburban COTRAL bus routes terminate either near Tiburtina station or at outlying Metro stops, such as Rebibbia and Ponte Mammolo (Linea B) and Anagnina (Linea A).

ATAC (⊕ *www.atac.roma.it*), Rome's city transport service, offers reasonable fares for travel in and around Rome, especially with the BIRG (Biglietto Integrale Regionale Giornaliero), which allows you to travel on all the lines (and some railroad lines) up to midnight on the day of the ticket's first validation. The cost of a BIRG depends upon the distance to your destination and how many "zones" you travel through. Because of the extent and complexity of the system, it's a good idea to consult with your hotel concierge, review ATAC's website, or to telephone COTRAL's central office when planning a trip.

COTRAL has several buses that leave daily from Rome's Ponte Mammolo (Linea B) Metro station for the town of Tivoli, where Hadrian's Villa and Villa D'Este are located. Flixbuses (⊕ *www.flixbus.it*) leave from Rome's Tiburtina Metro and train station (Linea B) and will take you to Siena and other towns in Tuscany.

While the bus may be an affordable way of moving around, keep in mind that buses can be crowded due to commuter traffic. Just because you've managed to purchase a ticket doesn't mean you're guaranteed a seat. Make sure to arrive early and stand your ground in line. If you are not able to procure a seat, you may be standing for the entire ride.

Car

Driving in Rome isn't recommended, but if you must do so, the main access routes from the north are the A1-E35 (Autostrada del Sole) from Milan and Florence and the A12–E80 highway from Genoa, and the principal route to or from points south, including Naples, is the A1-E45. All highways connect with the Grande Raccordo Anulare Ring Road (GRA), which channels traffic into the city center. Markings on the GRA are confusing: take time to study the route you need. For driving directions, check out ⊕ *www.tuttocitta.it*.

Be extremely mindful of pedestrians and mopeds. Romans are casual jaywalkers who pop out frequently from between parked cars, and scooter drivers weave in and out of traffic.

PARKING

Parking in Rome can be a nightmare. The situation is greatly compounded by the fact that private cars without permits are not allowed access to the centro storico on weekdays 6:30 am–6 pm, Saturday 2 pm–6 pm, or Friday and Saturday nights (11 pm–3 am). Other areas, including Trastevere, Testaccio, and San Lorenzo, are closed to cars at various times. Check the **Roma Mobilità** website for the most up-to-date information. These areas, known as Zona Traffico Limitato (ZTL), are marked by electric signs, and bordering streets have video cameras for photographing license plates. Fines are sent directly to car-rental companies and added to your bill. Check with your hotel regarding appropriate places to park nearby.

Most parking is metered and costs €1–€1.50 per hour (depending on the area) with a limit on total parking time allowed in many places. Spaces with white lines are free; spaces with blue lines are paid; and spaces with yellow lines are for the handicapped only. All other color-coded spaces are reserved for residents or carpooling and require special permits. If you park in one without a permit, your car could be ticketed or towed. Note that there are parking facilities near the Villa Borghese and the Vatican.

RENTAL CARS

When you reserve a car, ask about cancellation penalties, taxes, drop-off charges (if you're planning to pick the car up in one city and leave it in another), and surcharges (for additional drivers, say, or for driving across regional or country borders or beyond a specific distance from your point of rental). All these things can add substantially to your costs, as can car seats, GPS, and other extras—all of which are best arranged when booking.

Rates in Rome begin at around €40 per day for an economy car with air-conditioning, a manual transmission (note that automatic transmissions are rarer), and unlimited mileage. This includes the 20% Value-Added Tax (VAT, or "IVA" in Italian) on car rentals.

It's usually cheaper to rent a car in advance rather than on arrival. Indeed, booking ahead on a rental company's website can save you as much as €10 per day. There are other reasons to book ahead, though: to ensure availability during busy times of the year or to ensure that you get certain types of cars (automatic transmission, vans, SUVs, exotic sports cars).

In Italy, you must be 21 years of age to rent an economy or subcompact car, and most companies require customers under the age of 23 to pay by credit card. There are no special restrictions on senior-citizen drivers. Upon rental, all companies require credit cards as a warranty; to rent bigger cars (2,000 cc or more), you must often show two credit cards. Debit or check cards are not accepted.

Your own driver's license is acceptable if accompanied by an official translation in Italian. But to be extra safe, an International Driving Permit is a good idea; some rental agencies even require it (ask when booking). It's available from the American or Canadian Automobile Association and, in the United Kingdom, from the Automobile Association or Royal Automobile Club. These international permits are universally recognized, and having one in your wallet may save you a problem with the local authorities.

RULES OF THE ROAD

Driving is on the right, and speed limits are 50 kph (31 mph) in Rome, 110 kph (70 mph) on state and provincial roads, and 130 kph (80 mph) on autostrade, unless otherwise marked. Fines for speeding are uniformly stiff: 10 kph (6 mph) over the speed limit can warrant a fine in the hundreds and even thousands of euros; over 10 kph, and your license could be taken away.

Talking on a mobile phone while driving is strictly prohibited, and if caught, the driver will be issued a fine. Not wearing a seat belt is also against the law. The blood-alcohol content limit for driving is 0.5 gr/l with fines up to €6,000 and the possibility of 12 months imprisonment for surpassing the limit. ■TIP→ **Note that Italian police have the power to levy on-the-spot fines.**

Whenever the city implements an "Ecological Day" to reduce smog levels, commuters are prohibited from driving their cars during certain hours of the day and in certain areas of the city. These days are usually organized and announced ahead of time, so ask the rental company and/or your hotel if there are any planned.

Getting Here and Around

Ⓜ Public Transport

Although most of Rome's sights are in a relatively circumscribed area, and you can expect to do a lot of walking, the city as a whole is too large to be seen entirely on foot. Rome's integrated transportation system includes buses and trams (ATAC), the Metropolitana (the subway, or Metro), suburban trains and buses (COTRAL), and the commuter rail run by the state railway (Trenitalia). You can get free city and transit maps at municipal information booths.

Tickets are sold at tobacco shops, newsstands, some coffee bars, automatic ticket machines in Metro stations, some bus stops, and at ATAC ticket booths. You can purchase individual or multiple tickets or a rechargeable contactless card. It's always a good idea to have a few tickets handy so you don't have to hunt for a vendor when you need one.

A ticket (BIT), valid for 100 minutes on any combination of buses and trams and one entrance to the Metro, costs €1.50. A Roma24H ticket, or *biglietto integrato giornaliero* (integrated daily ticket), is valid for 24 hours (from the moment you stamp it) on all public transit and costs €7. You can also purchase a Roma48H (€12.50), a Roma72H (€18), and a CIS (Carta Integrata Settimanale), which is valid for one week (€24). Each option gives unlimited travel on ATAC buses, COTRAL urban bus services, trains for the Lido and Viterbo, and Metro.

If you're going farther afield, or planning to spend more than a week in Rome, think about getting a BIRG (daily regional ticket) or a CIRS (weekly regional ticket) from the railway station. These give you unlimited travel on all state transport throughout the region of Lazio. This can take you as far as the Etruscan city of Tarquinia or medieval Viterbo.

All tickets must be validated by tapping contactless cards or time-stamping tickets in the red or yellow meter boxes aboard buses or in Metro stations immediately prior to boarding. Failure to validate your ticket will result in a fine of €54.90, which you can pay on the ATAC website, in post offices and authorized shops, or by wire transfer. Pay immediately as the fine increases to €104.90 after five days. Some ticket inspectors may be equipped for payment by mobile POS; do not pay the inspectors in cash.

CITY BUS AND TRAM

Although not as fast as the Metro, bus and tram travel within Rome is very scenic and fairly efficient. Note, though, that at peak times, buses can be quite crowded, making walking or taking a taxi a better alternative.

ATAC city buses are red or gray; trams are green. Remember to board at the rear and exit at the middle; some drivers won't let you out the front door, leaving you to scramble through the crowd to exit. Also, don't forget to buy your ticket before boarding and to stamp (validate) it in a machine as soon as you enter. The ticket is good for a transfer and one Metro trip within the next 100 minutes.

Buses and trams run 5:30 am–midnight, after which time there's an extensive network of *notturno* buses (late-night buses) with less-frequent service throughout the city. Be sure the bus you're waiting for is actually running. At bus stops, regular buses are either cited as *feriali,* which means "daily," or don't have any special distinction. Notturno buses have an "N" sign just above the bus number; their schedules are listed beside those for the regular day buses. *Deviata* buses have been rerouted due to road construction or public demonstrations, and *festivi* buses only run on Sunday and holidays; like notturno buses, they have less-frequent service.

The ATAC has a website (⊕ *www.atac.roma.it*) that helps you determine the bus route you need; it even calculates the number of stops and gives you a map directing you to them. To navigate the site, look for the British flag in the upper right-hand corner to change the website into English. Or do as the locals do, and use the Moovit app.

METRO

The Metro (subway), which has three lines, is the easiest and fastest way to get around Rome. There are stops near most main attractions, and street entrances are marked with red "M" signs.

Linea A (red, though indicated in orange on some transit maps) runs from the southeastern part of the city, with stops at San Giovanni in Laterano, Piazza Barberini, Piazza di Spagna, Piazzale Flaminio (Piazza del Popolo), and Ottaviano/San Pietro near the Basilica di San Pietro and Musei Vaticani. **Linea B** (blue), which intersects with Linea A at Termini station, stops near the Colosseum, Circus Maximus, Pyramid (Ostiense station, with trains for Ostia Antica), and Basilica di San Paolo Fuori le Mura. **Linea C** (green) runs from the city's eastern outskirts through Pigneto and meets Linea A at San Giovanni.

The Metro opens at 5:30 am, and the last trains leave the terminus station at either end at 11:30 pm (1:30 am on Friday and Saturday nights). As with buses and trams, it's best to avoid taking the Metro during rush hours, when cars can be extremely crowded. Midmorning and midday through early afternoon tend to be less busy.

Scooter

Mopeds/scooters are everywhere in Rome. Riders are required to wear helmets, and traffic police are tough in enforcing this law. Producing your country's driver's license should be enough to convince most rental firms that they're not dealing with a complete beginner, but if you're unsure of exactly how to ride a scooter, think twice, as driving one in Rome is not like you see it in the movies. It can be very dangerous, and Roman drivers tend to be ruthless; at least ask the attendant for a detailed demonstration. If you don't feel up to braving the Roman traffic on a moped, you can hire a Segway or electric bicycle to explore the seven hills of Rome.

Taxi

Taxis may stop if you flag them down, but they don't cruise the city looking for fares. In general, to hire a taxi in Rome you go to a taxi stand or arrange service by phone or via an app, in which case you'll be charged a supplement (the meter will already be running when you're picked up). The various taxi services are considered interchangeable and are referred to by their phone numbers rather than names. Taxicabs can be reserved the night before only if you're traveling to or from the airport or the train station. All taxis are required to accept credit cards, but sometimes the driver will tell you the machine isn't working, so it's good to have cash on hand.

The base meter fare is €3 during the day, €6.50 10 pm–6 am, and €4.50 on Sunday and holidays. Supplemental charges, such as for luggage or even for pick up at Termini station, are added to the meter fare. When in doubt, ask for a receipt (*ricevuta*). This will encourage the driver

Getting Here and Around

to be honest and charge you the correct amount. Women traveling alone via taxi 10 pm–6 am are entitled to a 10% discount; the same discount applies if your destination is a public hospital (make sure to ask for it).

Use only licensed, metered white cabs, identified by a numbered shield on the side, an illuminated taxi sign on the roof, and a plaque next to the license plate reading "*servizio pubblico.*" Avoid unmarked, unauthorized, unmetered cabs (numerous at Rome airports and train stations), whose drivers actively solicit your trade and may demand astronomical fares.

Although ride-sharing apps like Uber and Lyft are not yet big in Rome, apps like ItTaxi (⊕ *www.ittaxi.it*) and FreeNow (⊕ *www.free-now.it*) provide a quick and easy way to book an official taxi with a smartphone. You can choose to pay by app or with cash, and can rate your driver after the ride.

🚊 Train

State-owned Trenitalia trains are part of the Metrebus system and also serve some destinations that are side trips from Rome. The main Trenitalia stations in Rome are Termini, Tiburtina, Ostiense, and Trastevere. Suburban trains use all of these stations. The Ferrovie COTRAL line departs from a terminal in Piazzale Flaminio, connecting Rome with Viterbo.

Only Trenitalia trains such as Frecciarossa, Frecciargento, and Intercity Plus have first- and second-class compartments. Local trains can be crowded early in the morning and in the evening as many people commute to and from the city, so try to avoid traveling at these times. Plan on arriving early to secure a seat or be ready to stand.

On long-distance routes (to Florence and Venice, for instance), you can either travel by the cheap (but slow) *regionale* trains or the fast, but more expensive, Intercity, Frecciarossa, or Frecciargento, which require seat reservations, available at the station when you buy your ticket, online, or through a travel agent. The state railways' excellent and user-friendly site will help you plan any rail trips in the country. It's best to book ahead to make sure you get the lowest price.

Italy's rails have a private competitor, Italo, whose gorgeous and very fast trains travel between large cities including Naples, Rome, Florence, Bologna, Milan, Venice, and Torino. In Rome, Italo trains stop at Termini and Tiburtina stations.

Essentials

Dining

Rome has been known since antiquity for its grand feasts and banquets, and dining out has always been a favorite Roman pastime. Until recently, however, the *buongustaii* (gourmands) often pointed out that the city was distinguished more by its enthusiasm for eating out than for having a multitude of world-class restaurants—but this is changing.

There is a growing slow-food movement—featuring sustainably and locally sourced produce—as well as an increasing focus on catering to diners who want to spend less. The result has been the rise of "street food" restaurants, selling everything from inexpensive, creative takes on the classic *supplì* (Roman fried-rice balls) to sandwiches made using organic ingredients.

Generally speaking, Romans like Roman food, and that's what you'll find in many of the city's trattorias and wine bars. Most chefs prefer freshness over fuss and simplicity of flavor and preparation over complex cooking techniques. Most also stick with the traditional, excelling at dishes that have taken hundreds, sometimes thousands, of years to perfect. Hence, the basic trattoria menu is more or less the same wherever you go, and even the top chefs feature their takes on simple classics like carbonara.

Still, people move to the nation's capital from every corner of the Italian peninsula, so Sicilian, Tuscan, Pugliese, Bolognese, Marchegiano, Sardinian, and northern Italian dishes are all represented. There's also a growing number of restaurants offering good-quality international cuisines—particularly Japanese, Indian, and Ethiopian.

Oddly enough, though, for a nation that prides itself on *la bella figura* ("looking good"), most Romans don't fuss about music, personal space, lighting, or decor. After all, who needs flashy interior design when so much of Roman life takes place outdoors, when dining alfresco in Rome can take place in the middle of a glorious ancient site or a centuries-old piazza?

RESTAURANT TYPES

There used to be a distinct hierarchy of restaurant types in Rome. A *ristorante* was typically elegant and expensive; a *trattoria* served more traditional, home-style fare in a relaxed atmosphere; and an *osteria* was even more casual, essentially a wine bar and gathering spot that also served food. All these places still exist, but their distinction has blurred considerably. Now, for instance, an osteria in the center of town may be pricier than a ristorante across the street. In addition, *enoteca* is the more contemporary term for a casual wine bar that also serves food.

Although Rome may not boast the grand **cafés** (here known as *caffè*) of Paris or Vienna, it does have hundreds of small places on pleasant side streets and piazze. The coffee is routinely of high quality. Locals usually stop in for a quickie at the bar, where prices are much lower than for the same drink taken at the table. If you place your order at the counter, ask if you can sit down: some places charge more for table service. Usually you'll pay a cashier first, then give your *scontrino* (receipt) to the person at the counter who fills your order.

HOW TO ORDER: FROM PRIMO TO DOLCE

In a Roman sit-down restaurant, whether a ristorante, trattoria, or osteria, you're expected to order at least two courses. It could be a *primo* (first course, usually pasta, risotto, or soup) followed by a *secondo* (second course, really a "main course" in English parlance, usually meat

Essentials

or fish); an *antipasto* (starter) followed by a primo or secondo; or a primo or secondo and a *dolce* (dessert). Many people consider a full meal to consist of an antipasto, a primo or secondo, and a dolce.

If you're not too hungry, try a pizzeria (*pizzerie*), where it's common to order just one dish. The handiest places for an afternoon snack are bars, cafés, and pizzerie. For a quick lunch or dinner, head to a *tavola calda*, kind of like a cafeteria where you can order from what's available at the counter and sit and eat at a table.

MEAL TIMES AND RESERVATIONS

Breakfast (*la colazione*) is usually served 7 am–10:30 am, lunch (*il pranzo*) 12:30 pm–2:30 pm, dinner (*la cena*) 7:30 pm–11 pm. Peak times are around 1:30 pm for lunch and 9 pm for dinner. Enoteche are sometimes open in the morning and late afternoon for snacks. Most pizzerie open at 7 or 8 pm and close around midnight or 1 am. Most bars and cafés are open 7 am–8 or 9 pm. Almost all restaurants close one day a week (in most cases Sunday or Monday) and for at least two weeks in August. The city is zoned, however, so that there are always some restaurants in each zone that remain open.

The pace of a sit-down meal may be slower than what you're used to and you won't receive *il conto* (the bill) until you ask for it. Because most Roman restaurants are small and aren't in the business of turning tables, it's best to reserve in advance. Popular restaurants tend to book up days or weeks ahead of time. Even if you walk into a restaurant at 7 pm and see empty tables, the host might not seat you because you likely won't finish your meal before the diners who booked those tables arrive.

⇨ *Restaurant reviews throughout this guide have been shortened. For full information, visit Fodors.com. Restaurant prices are the average cost of a main course at dinner or, if dinner is not served, at lunch.*

What It Costs in Euros			
$	$$	$$$	$$$$
AT DINNER			
under €15	€15–€24	€25–€35	over €35

 ## Health

Throughout Italy, smoking is banned in all public places. This includes trains, buses, and offices, as well as restaurants, pubs, and dance clubs (unless the latter have separate smoking rooms). Fines for breaking the law are exorbitant. Most people skirt it by sitting on open-air terraces. If you're bothered by smoke, sit inside at restaurants, many of which now have air-conditioning.

It's best to travel with your own trusted medications. Should you need medicine while in Italy, though, speak with a physician so you can ensure it is the proper kind and get a prescription for it if necessary. Pharmacies sell aspirin (*l'aspirina*), ibuprofen, acetaminophen, cough syrup, antiseptic creams, and other over-the-counter remedies. Pharmacists are happy to dispense advice and, in the city center especially, almost always speak some English.

Immunizations

 Proof of COVID-19 vaccination, recovery, or a negative test result is no longer required for visits to Italy.

🛏 Lodging

Whether you want a simple place to rest your head or a complete cache of exclusive amenities, you have plenty of choices. Indeed, Rome has a wide selection of high-end hotels, bed-and-breakfasts, and designer boutique hotels—options that run the gamut from whimsical to luxurious.

Luxury hotels are justly renowned for sybaritic comforts: fluffy towels, postcard views over Roman rooftops, and silver flatware on white linen atop a groaning breakfast-buffet table. In the more modest categories, however, Rome's hotels don't always meet the standards of space, comfort, quiet, and service found in comparable U.S. properties. Hence, you may find places that have tiny rooms, lumpy beds, and anemic air-conditioning. The good news: if you're flexible, there are happy mediums aplenty.

Location is a good place to start when picking a lodging, and proximity to the main sights is only one consideration. For instance, if a picturesque location is important, stay in one of the small hotels around Piazza Navona or Campo de' Fiori. If luxury is a priority, opt for Piazza di Spagna or beyond the city center, where quality/price ratios are better, and some hotels have swimming pools.

⇨ *Hotel reviews throughout this guide have been shortened. For full information, visit Fodors.com. Hotel prices are for a standard double room in high season.*

What It Costs in Euros			
$	$$	$$$	$$$$
LODGING FOR TWO			
under €125	€125–€200	€201–€300	over €300

🍸 Nightlife

For a great night out, you need only wander as there's entertainment on every corner. Most visitors head to the centro storico; Piazza Navona, Pantheon, Campo de' Fiori, and even Trastevere may be filled with tourists, but they're also beginning to attract niche and boutique bars. (In contrast, the Spanish Steps area is a ghost town by 9 pm.) Monti has lots of bars with al fresco seating and a more local crowd.

Alternatively, you could leave the comfort zone by heading to the Testaccio, San Lorenzo, and Pigneto areas. Indeed, when it comes to clubs and discos, Testaccio is a mecca. Its Via Galvani is Rome's Sunset Strip, where hybrid restaurant-clubs, largely identical in music and crowd, jockey for top ranking. On average, drinks range between €10 and €15, and one is often included with the entrance (€10–€20). In summer, though, many clubs relocate to the beach or the Tiber, so check ahead.

Wherever you go, be sure to follow Rome's rule of thumb: if you see an enoteca, stop in. Though most are tiny and offer a limited antipasti menu, their wine lists are expansive, and they often have a charming gang of regulars. For the linguistically timid, the city also has English and Irish pubs, complete with a steady stream of Guinness; dartboards; and oversize, flat-screen TVs showing rugby and soccer, as well as American football, baseball, and basketball—ideal for those who don't want to miss a playoff game.

Rome offers a cornucopia of evening bacchanalia, from ultra-chic to super-cheap, but most people agree that finding "the scene" requires patience and pursuit. Although word-of-mouth is the best source, entertainment guides like **Romeing** (⊕ *www.romeing.it*) and **2night**

Where Should I Stay?

	NEIGHBORHOOD VIBE	PROS	CONS
Around the Vatican: Borgo and Prati	Touristy and not especially atmospheric but has good restaurants and cafés.	Close to the Vatican; pretty quiet at night.	Far from other major attractions and nightlife.
Piazza Navona, Campo de' Fiori, and Jewish Ghetto	Surrounded by most of Rome's major attractions.	Walking distance to good restaurants and shops, as well as museums and monuments.	Convenient but pricey. Lots of hustle and bustle, so street noise can be an issue (the Jewish Ghetto is quieter, though).
Piazza di Spagna	Frequented by high rollers and A-listers.	Has the crème de la crème of Rome's hotels and shops.	Everything is expensive; not very close to central hot spots.
Repubblica	Has a beautiful piazza and is near Termini station without the grungy feel.	Hotels are much cheaper than elsewhere in Rome; convenient to Termini station.	Basic accommodations; the area surrounding Termini station can be iffy.
Villa Borghese and Piazza del Popolo, Monte Mario, and Parioli	Somewhat outside the hubbub and a bit more refined, with fancy boutiques and hotels.	Close to the Piazza di Spagna and shopping; lots of dining options nearby.	Pricey and a bit removed from Piazza Navona and Campo de' Fiori.
Trastevere	Villagelike, with cobblestone alleys, beautiful churches, and mom-and-pop trattorias.	Fun area with great restaurants, bars, and cafés.	Full of students; can be rowdy at night and rambunctious on weekends.
Aventino and Testaccio	Aventino is a relaxing hilltop retreat. Working-class Testaccio is the heart of Rome's nightlife.	Tranquility, amazing views, and spacious rooms await in Aventino. Party in Rome's famous nightlife district, Testaccio.	Transportation difficult on the Aventine Hill; Testaccio is crowded on weekends.
Esquilino	Has some of the more hip and funky neighborhoods in Rome.	Hotels are cheaper than elsewhere in the city; close to Termini station.	Far from main tourist attractions.

(⊕ *2night.it/roma*) have great general information and up-to-date listings of bars and clubs.

■**TIP**➜ **Romans love an after-party, so plenty of nightlife doesn't start until midnight.**

⊕ Passports and Visas

All U.S., Canadian, Australian, and New Zealand citizens, even infants, need a valid passport to enter Italy for stays of up to 90 days.

In 2024, Italy and other European Union countries implemented an electronic visa waiver program designed for foreign visitors to the EU from countries that don't require a visa to visit. If you are a citizen of one of the 60 or so non-EU countries that don't require a visa to visit the EU (this includes the United States and the United Kingdom), this means you will now have to "pre-register" your trip through a simple online process that costs €7; this pre-registration covers multiple trips and lasts three years or until your passport expires—whichever comes first. The vast majority of applications should be approved within minutes, but it's still smart to not book flights or hotels until your application is approved. Visit the official ETIAS website at ⊕ *travel-europe.europa.eu/etias_en* to apply. For more helpful information, check out ⊕ *www.etias.com*.

⊕ Performing Arts

Rome has stunning venues both ancient and modern. Here you can see a classical opera in the 3rd-century-AD Terme di Caracalla, enjoy an experimental dance show in the postindustrial Teatro India, or catch a contemporary performance at the Renzo Piano–designed Auditorium Parco della Musica.

To find arts and cultural event listings, scan the "Cronaca and Cultura" section of Italian newspapers, including *Metro,* the free publication found at Metro stops and on trams. The monthly, English-language periodical **Wanted in Rome** (⊕ *www.wantedinrome.com*) also has good coverage of arts events and is available at many newsstands.

Romeing (⊕ *www.romeing.it*), a website written exclusively for the English-speaking community, and **2night** (⊕ *2night.it/roma*) are great online sources. For directory information, like addresses, **060608** (⊕ *www.060608.it/en*) has listings of every cultural site (monument, church, museum, art space, etc.) in the city.

⊕ Safety

Rome is like any other major Western city: generally quite safe but with occasional instances of pickpocketing or bag snatching, especially in the busy summer months. Wear your purse, bag, or camera slung across your body bandolier-style, and don't put your belongings on a table or beneath or hanging from a chair at a sidewalk café or restaurant.

Pickpockets—who often work in teams—tend to be active wherever tourists gather, including the Roman Forum, Spanish Steps, Piazza Navona, and Piazza di San Pietro. They're also an issue on public transportation, especially buses such as No. 64 (Termini–Stazione di San Pietro); No. 40 Express; and No. 46, which takes you close to St. Peter's Basilica. You should also be wary of pickpockets in transit stations, as well as on subways and trains, especially when making your way through crowded cars.

Women traveling alone will feel safe but should take the same precautions as in any other major Western city. Although

Essentials

Rome doesn't have as big of a gay scene as other European cities, and Italy is still a rather conservative country (gay marriage isn't legal, for instance), LGBTQ+ travelers should, nevertheless, feel welcome and safe here.

🛍 Shopping

Perhaps it's the sight of a fashionably bespectacled, Giorgio Armani–attired commuter deftly zipping through traffic on his Vespa or maybe it's the memories of films starring Anita Ekberg, Audrey Hepburn, or Julia Roberts that make us long to be Roman—or at least shop like one—if only for a day. With limited time, however, knowing where to put your best fashion foot forward is crucial in this city where shopping is an art form. Luckily, you can fit your retail sprees in amid visits to sights.

A stop at the Trevi Fountain, for instance, lets you relive the movie classic *Three Coins in a Fountain,* and puts you close to the 18th-century Piazza di Spagna, where you can snap a selfie while keeping an eye on that sweet little bag in the window at Dolce & Gabbana. Nearby, designer powerhouses like Fendi and Armani are among the stores strung tightly together along three main fashion arteries: Via dei Condotti, Via Borgogno-na, and Via Frattina.

To the south and within striking distance of the Colosseum is the Monti neighborhood, a colorful hive where a plethora of artisans and independent shops sell everything from bespoke jewelry to vintage clothing. Across the Tiber River in Trastevere, you'll not only find one of Rome's oldest and grandest churches (Santa Maria in Trastevere) but also one of Italy's largest flea markets (Porta Portese), as well as an array of funky boutiques.

DUTY-FREE SHOPPING
Value-Added Tax (VAT, or IVA in Italian) is 22% on clothing and luxury goods, but is already included in the amount on the price tag for consumer goods. All non–EU citizens visiting Italy are entitled to a reimbursement of this tax when purchasing nonperishable goods that total more than €154.95 in a single transaction. If you buy goods in a store that does not participate in the "Tax-Free Italy" program, ask the cashier to issue you a special invoice known as a *fattura,* which must be made out to you and includes the phrase "*Esente IVA ai sensi della legge 38 quarter.*" The bill should indicate the amount of IVA included in the purchase price. Present this invoice and the goods purchased to the Customs Office on your departure from Italy to obtain your tax reimbursement.

ITALIAN SIZES
Unfortunately, Italian sizes are not standard—it is therefore always best to try things on. If you wear a "small," you may be surprised to learn that in Italy, you are a medium. Children's sizes are just as complicated; they are typically based on Italian children's ages. Check labels on all garments, as many are dry clean–only or non–tumble dry. When in doubt about the proper size, ask the shop attendant—most will have an international size chart handy. At open-air markets, where there often isn't any place to try on garments, you'll have to take your best guess: if you're wrong, you may or may not be able to find the vendor the next day to exchange.

Tipping

In Italy, service is almost always included in the menu prices. It's customary to leave an additional 5%–10% tip, or a couple of euros, for the waiter, depending on the quality of service. Tip checkroom attendants €1 per person, restroom attendants €0.50. In both cases tip more in expensive hotels and restaurants. Tip €0.05–€0.10 for whatever you drink standing up at a coffee bar, €0.20–€0.50 or more for table service in a café. At a hotel bar, tip €1 and up for a round or two of cocktails, more in the grander hotels.

For tipping taxi drivers, it is acceptable if you round up to the nearest euro, minimum €0.50. Give a barber €1–€1.50 and a hairdresser's assistant €1.50–€4 for a shampoo or cut, depending on the type of establishment and the final bill; 5%–10% is a fair guideline.

On private sightseeing tours, tipping your guides 10% is customary. In museums and other places of interest where admission is free, a contribution is expected; give anything from €0.50 to €1 for one or two people, more if the guardian has been especially helpful. Service station attendants are tipped only for special services. On off-hours there may be station attendants not in uniform working just for tips. Give €0.50 to €1 if they fill up your tank.

In hotels, give the *portiere* (concierge) about 15% of his bill for services, or €2.50–€5 if he has been generally helpful. For two people in a double room, leave the chambermaid about €1 per day, or about €4–€6 a week, in a moderately priced hotel; tip a minimum of €1 for valet or room service. Increase these amounts by one half in an expensive hotel, and double them in a very expensive hotel.

Tours and Guides

With engaging commentary, friendly guides, and fellow sightseers from every country under the sun, bus tours can be fun. They can also help you get your bearings and decide which sights you'd like to visit at leisure later on.

The least expensive organized sightseeing tour of Rome is the one run by **CitySightseeing Roma** (⊕ *www.city-sight-seeing.it/rome*). Double-decker buses leave every 8–16 minutes (depending on the season) between 9 am and 7:30 pm from Via Marsala, beside Termini station, but you can also hop on at any of the nine stops. A full-day ticket (€26), which you can buy on board, lets you get off and on as often as you like and includes an audioguide system in six languages. The total tour takes about two hours and covers the Colosseum, Piazza Navona, St. Peter's, the Trevi Fountain, and Via Veneto. Two- and three-day tickets are also available.

You can also book other types of tours, including small group tours, Vespa tours, jogging tours, and exclusive private tours. Tour operators can provide a luxury car for up to three people, a limousine for up to seven, or a minibus for up to nine—all with an English-speaking driver (guide service is extra, however).

★ **Scooteroma**
PRIVATE GUIDES | For the quintessential Roman experience of cruising around on a Vespa, this is the company to choose. Just hop on the back and one of the experienced driver-guides will show you the sights. Themed tours include a classic tour, a street art tour, a cinema tour, and a foodie tour. The three- to four-hour private tours always include a stop for coffee or gelato. ⊠ *Rome* ⊕ *www. scooteroma.com* ✉ *From €180.*

Helpful Italian Phrases

BASICS

Yes/no	Sí/No	see/no
Please	Per favore	pear fa-**vo**-ray
Thank you	Grazie	**grah**-tsee-ay
You're welcome	Prego	**pray**-go
I'm sorry (apology)	Mi dispiace	mee dis-pee-**atch**-ay
Excuse me, sorry	Scusi	**skoo**-zee
Good morning/ afternoon	Buongiorno	bwohn-**jor**-no
Good evening	Buona sera	**bwoh**-na **say**-ra
Good-bye	Arrivederci	a-ree-vah-**dare**-chee
Mr. (Sir)	Signore	see-**nyo**-ray
Mrs. (Ma'am)	Signora	see-**nyo**-ra
Miss	Signorina	see-nyo-**ree**-na
Pleased to meet you	Piacere	pee-ah-**chair**-ray
How are you?	Come sta?	**ko**-may-**stah**
Hello (phone)	Pronto?	**proan**-to

NUMBERS

one-half	mezzo	**mets**-zoh
one	uno	**oo**-no
two	due	**doo**-ay
three	tre	Tray
four	quattro	**kwah**-tro
five	cinque	**cheen**-kway
six	sei	Say
seven	sette	**set**-ay
eight	otto	**oh**-to
nine	nove	**no**-vay
ten	dieci	dee-**eh**-chee
eleven	undici	**oon**-dee-chee
twelve	dodici	**doh**-dee-chee
thirteen	tredici	**trey**-dee-chee
fourteen	quattordici	kwah-**tor**-dee-chee
fifteen	quindici	**kwin**-dee-chee
sixteen	sedici	**say**-dee-chee
seventeen	dicissette	dee-chah-**set**-ay
eighteen	diciotto	dee-chee-**oh**-to
nineteen	diciannove	dee-chee-ahn-**no**-vay
twenty	venti	**vain**-tee
twenty-one	ventuno	**vent**-oo-no
thirty	trenta	**train**-ta
forty	quaranta	kwa-**rahn**-ta
fifty	cinquanta	cheen-**kwahn**-ta
sixty	sessanta	seh-**sahn**-ta
seventy	settanta	seh-**tahn**-ta
eighty	ottanta	o-**tahn**-ta
ninety	novanta	no-**vahn**-ta
one hundred	cento	**chen**-to
one thousand	mille	**mee**-lay
one million	un milione	oon **mill**-oo-nay

COLORS

black	Nero	**nair**-ro
blue	Blu	bloo
brown	Marrone	ma-**rohn**-nay
green	Verde	**ver**-day
orange	Arancione	ah-rahn-**cho**-nay
red	Rosso	**rose**-so
white	Bianco	bee-**ahn**-koh
yellow	Giallo	**jaw**-low

DAYS OF THE WEEK

Sunday	Domenica	do-**meh**-nee-ka
Monday	Lunedi	loo-ne-**dee**
Tuesday	Martedi	mar-te-**dee**
Wednesday	Mercoledi	**mer**-ko-le-**dee**
Thursday	Giovedi	jo-ve-**dee**
Friday	Venerdì	ve-ner-**dee**
Saturday	Sabato	**sa**-ba-toh

MONTHS

January	Gennaio	jen-**ay**-o
February	Febbraio	feb-**rah**-yo
March	Marzo	**mart**-so
April	Aprile	a-**pril**-ay
May	Maggio	**mahd**-joe
June	Giugno	**joon**-yo
July	Luglio	**lool**-yo
August	Agosto	a-**gus**-to
September	Settembre	se-**tem**-bre
October	Ottobre	o-**toh**-bre
November	Novembre	no-**vem**-bre
December	Dicembre	di-**chem**-bre

USEFUL WORDS AND PHRASES

Do you speak English?	Parla Inglese?	**par**-la een-**glay**-zay
I don't speak Italian	Non parlo italiano	non **par**-lo ee-tal-**yah**-no
I don't understand	Non capisco	non ka-**peess**-ko
I don't know	Non lo so	non lo **so**
I understand	Capisco	ka-**peess**-ko
I'm American	Sono Americano(a)	**so**-no a-may-ree-**kah**-no(a)
I'm British	Sono inglese	so-no een-**glay**-zay
What's your name?	Come si chiama?	**ko**-may see kee-**ah**-ma
My name is ...	Mi chiamo...	mee kee-**ah**-mo
What time is it?	Che ore sono?	kay **o**-ray **so**-no
How?	Come?	**ko**-may
When?	Quando?	**kwan**-doe
Yesterday/today/ tomorrow	Ieri/oggi/domani	**yer**-ee/ **o**-jee/ do-**mah**-nee

This morning	Stamattina/Oggi	sta-ma-**tee**-na/ o-jee
Afternoon	Pomeriggio	po-mer-**ee**-jo
Tonight	Stasera	sta-**ser**-a
What?	Che cosa?	kay **ko**-za
What is it?	Che cos'è?	kay ko-**zey**
Why?	Perchè?	pear-**kay**
Who?	Chi?	**Kee**
Where is ...	Dov'è...	doe-**veh**
the train station?	la stazione?	la sta-tsee-**oh**-nay
the subway?	la metropolitana?	la may-tro-po-lee-**tah**-na
the bus stop?	la fermata dell'autobus?	la fer-**mah**-ta del-ow-tor-**booss**
the airport	l'aeroporto	la-er-roh-**por**-toh
the post office?	l'ufficio postale	loo-**fee**-cho po-**stah**-lay
the bank?	la banca?	la **bahn**-ka
the hotel?	l'hotel...?	lo-**tel**
the museum?	Il museo	eel moo-**zay**-o
the hospital?	l'ospedale?	lo-spay-**dah**-lay
the elevator?	l'ascensore	la-shen-**so**-ray
the restrooms?	...il bagno	eel **bahn**-yo
Here/there	Qui/là	kwee/la
Left/right	A sinistra/a destra	a see-**neess**-tra/a **des**-tra
Is it near/far?	È vicino/lontano?	ay vee-**chee**-no/ lon-**tah**-no
I'd like ...	Vorrei...	vo-**ray**
a room	una camera	**oo**-na **kah**-may-ra
the key	la chiave	la kee-**ah**-vay
a newspaper	un giornale	oon jore-**nah**-vay
a stamp	un francobollo	oon frahn-ko-**bo**-lo
I'd like to buy ...	Vorrei comprare...	vo-**ray** kom-**prah**-ray
a city map	una mappa della città	**oo**-na **mah**-pa **day**-la chee-**tah**
a road map	una carta stradale	**oo**-na **car**-tah stra-**dahl**-lay
a magazine	una revista	**oo**-na ray-**vees**-tah
envelopes	buste	**boos**-tay
writing paper	carta de lettera	**car**-tah dah **leyt**-ter-rah
a postcard	una cartolina	**oo**-na car-tog-**leen**-ah
a ticket	un biglietto	oon bee-**yet**-toh
How much is it?	Quanto costa?	**kwahn**-toe **coast**-a
It's expensive/ cheap	È caro/ economico	ay **car**-o/ ay-ko-**no**-mee-ko
A little/a lot	Poco/tanto	**po**-ko/**tahn**-to
More/less	Più/meno	pee-**oo/may**-no

Enough/too (much)	Abbastanza/ troppo	a-bas-**tahn**-sa/tro-po
I am sick	Sto male	sto **mah**-lay
Call a doctor	Chiama un dottore	kee-**ah**-mah-oondoe-**toe**-ray
Help!	Aiuto!	a-**yoo**-to
Stop!	Alt!	ahlt

DINING OUT

A bottle of ...	Una bottiglia di...	**oo**-na bo-**tee**-lee-ah dee
A cup of ...	Una tazza di...	**oo**-na **tah**-tsa dee
A glass of ...	Un bicchiere di...	oon bee-key-**air**-ay dee
Beer	La birra	la **beer**-rah
Bill/check	Il conto	eel **cone**-toe
Bread	Il pane	eel **pah**-nay
Breakfast	La prima colazione	la **pree**-ma ko-la-**tsee**-oh-nay
Butter	Il burro	eel **boor**-roh
Cocktail/aperitif	L'aperitivo	la-pay-ree-**tee**-vo
Dinner	La cena	la **chen**-a
Fixed-price menu	Menù a prezzo fisso	may-**noo** a **pret**-so **fee**-so
Fork	La forchetta	la for-**ket**-a
I am vegetarian	Sono vegetariano(a)	**so**-no vay-jay-ta-ree-**ah**-no/a
I cannot eat ...	Non posso mangiare	non **pose**-so mahn-gee-**are**-ay
I'd like to order	Vorrei ordinare	vo-**ray** or-dee-**nah**-ray
Is service included?	Il servizio è incluso?	eel ser-**vee**-tzee-o ay een-**kloo**-zo
I'm hungry/ thirsty	Ho fame/sede	oh **fah**-meh/**sehd**-ed
It's good/bad	È buono/cattivo	ay **bwo**-bo/ka-**tee**-vo
It's hot/cold	È caldo/freddo	ay **kahl**-doe/**fred**-o
Knife	Il coltello	eel kol-**tel**-o
Lunch	Il pranzo	eel **prahnt**-so
Menu	Il menu	eel may-**noo**
Napkin	Il tovagliolo	eel toe-va-lee-**oh**-lo
Pepper	Il pepe	eel **pep**-peh
Plate	Il piatto	eel pee-**aht**-toe
Please give me ...	Mi dia...	mee **dee**-a
Salt	Il sale	eel **sah**-lay
Spoon	Il cucchiaio	eel koo-kee-ah-yo
Tea	tè	tay
Water	acqua	**awk**-wah
Wine	vino	**vee**-noh

Great Itineraries

Rome is jam-packed with things to do and see. These are some of our suggested itineraries. Make sure to leave yourself time to just wander and get the feel of the city as well.

ROME IN 1 DAY

Rome wasn't built in a day, but if that's all you have to see it, take a deep breath, strap on some stylish-but-comfy sneakers, and grab a cappuccino to help you get an early start. Get ready for a spectacular sunrise-to-sunset tour of the Ancient City.

Begin near Piazza Navona by getting a coffee at the bar of Sant'Eustachio il Caffè right when it opens at 7:30 am. Close by are two opulently over-the-top monuments that show off Rome at its Baroque best: the church of Sant'Ignazio, with its stunning painted ceiling, and the princely Palazzo Doria Pamphilj, packed with great Old Master paintings. Midmorning, head west a few blocks to find the fabled Pantheon, still looking like Emperor Hadrian might arrive shortly. A few blocks north is San Luigi dei Francesi, home to Caravaggio's earliest major commissions.

Just before lunch, saunter a block or so westward into the gorgeous Piazza Navona, studded with Bernini fountains. Then take Via della Cuccagna (at the piazza's south end) and continue several blocks toward Campo de' Fiori's open-air food market. This is a great place to stop for lunch.

Two more blocks toward the Tiber brings you to one of the most romantic streets of Rome—Via Giulia—laid out by Pope Julius II in the early 16th century. Walk past 10 blocks of Renaissance palazzi and ivy-draped antiques shops to take a bus (from the stop near the Tiber) over to the Vatican.

Gape at St. Peter's Basilica, then hit the treasure-filled Musei Vaticani (for the Sistine Chapel) in the early afternoon. During lunch, the crowds thin out some, but you can avoid lines if you book online at ⊕ *tickets.museivaticani.va* (the €5 service fee is well worth the time saved). Wander for about two hours and then head for the Ottaviano stop near the museum and Metro your way to the Colosseo stop.

Climb up into the Colosseum and picture it full of screaming toga-clad citizens enjoying the spectacle of gladiators in mortal combat. Follow Via dei Fori Imperiali to the entrance of the Roman Forum. Photograph yourself giving a "Friends, Romans, Countrymen" oration (complete with upraised hand) by a crumbling column. At sunset, the Forum closes and the floodlights come on.

March down the Forum's ancient Via Sacra and back out into Via dei Fori Imperiali where you will head around "the wedding cake," the looming Vittorio Emanuele II Monument (Il Vittoriano), to the Campidoglio. Here, on the Capitoline Hill, tour the great ancient Roman art treasures of the Musei Capitolini, and admire the view over the Forum from the Tabularium and toward St. Peter's from the terrace by the museum's café. If you're not entering the museum, there is a spectacular view over the Forum from the Capitoline Hill (at the top of Via Monte Tarpeo).

After dinner, hail a cab—or take a long stroll (*passeggiata*) down *La Dolce Vita* memory lane—to the Trevi Fountain, a gorgeous sight at night. Don't forget to toss a coin in over your shoulder to ensure a trip back to Rome.

ROME IN 3 DAYS

More time in Rome will allow you to explore more of the Roman Forum and the Vatican Museums, check out some less touristy sights, and drink your way through hip neighborhoods like Trastevere.

DAY 1: ANCIENT ROME

Spend your first day exploring the likes of the Roman Forum, the Musei Capitolini, and the Colosseum. This area is pretty compact, but you can easily spend a full morning and afternoon exploring its treasures. Try to beat the crowds at the Colosseum by arriving right when it opens at 8:30 am (advance tickets help, too). A guided tour of the Forum is also a good way to make the most out of your afternoon. After your day of sightseeing, stop for a classic Roman dinner in nearby Monti.

DAY 2: THE VATICAN AND PIAZZA NAVONA

Another full day of sightseeing awaits when you make your way to the city-state known as the Vatican. To make the most of your time, book online reservations (for an extra €5) ahead of time, especially if you want a glimpse of the Sistine Chapel. Also, consider booking a tour of the Vatican Museums; most tours last two hours. Be sure to allow time to marvel at St. Peter's Basilica, too. Stop for lunch in nearby Prati, and, when you're done with the Vatican, cross the river and take in the glorious Piazza Navona and its sculptures. Stop by the Pantheon before heading to the area around Campo de' Fiori for dinner at an outdoor restaurant. Afterward, there are plenty of nearby bars to keep you occupied.

DAY 3: PIAZZA DI SPAGNA, VILLA BORGHESE, AND TRASTEVERE

Start your morning with breakfast near the Trevi Fountain. Do some window-shopping along Via Condotti or its surrounding streets as you make your way to the Spanish Steps. Pose for some postcard-worthy photos there before heading to nearby Villa Borghese. If you're sick of museums, feel free to explore Rome's main park and enjoy the great views; if you're up for some more art, the Galleria Borghese is one of the city's best art museums. Afterward, head to trendy Trastevere for dinner, and soak in the cobblestone streets and charming medieval houses as you bar-hop during your last night in town.

IF YOU HAVE MORE TIME

If you have an extra day, head out to Ostica Antica, an ancient port city that is now one of the best preserved archaeological ruins in all of Italy. A train to the site leaves every 15 minutes from the Porta San Paolo station; the trip takes a mere 35 minutes. Take your time exploring these impressive ruins, and be sure to stop for lunch in town, too. Other great day trips include the gorgeous villas in the town of Tivoli, the charming small villages of the Castelli Romani, and the whimsical gardens of Bomarzo.

If you'd rather stay in the city itself, you can take your time exploring churches and cathedrals like Sant'Ignazio or San Clemente. You can also visit gorgeous palaces like the Palazzo Doria Pamphilj, or check out lesser known but impressive museums like the MAXXI or the MACRO. Visiting the ancient Roman road known as the Via Appia Antica and its spooky yet mesmerizing catacombs is another great way to spend an afternoon immersed in Roman history.

Rome of the Emperors: A Roman Forum Walk

Looking down at the Roman Forum from the terraces of the Campidoglio (Capitoline Hill) allows you to take in two millennia of history in a single glance. Here, in one fabled panorama, are the world's most striking and significant concentrations of historic remains.

THE COLOSSEUM

Start just south of the Forum at ancient Rome's hallmark monument, the **Colosseum** (with its handy Colosseo Metro stop). Convincingly austere, the Colosseum is the Eternal City's yardstick of eternity. Take one of the elevators up to level one to glimpse the extensive subterranean passageways that once funneled all the unlucky animals and gladiators into the arena. Alternatively, see the passageways up close on a guided tour, which must be booked in advance.

THE ROMAN FORUM

Leaving the Colosseum behind, admire the **Arch of Constantine,** standing just to the north of the arena. The largest and best preserved of Rome's triumphal arches, it was erected in AD 315 to celebrate the victory of the emperor Constantine (280–337) over Maxentius—it was shortly after this battle that Constantine converted Rome to Christianity. You have to walk down Via dei Fori Imperiali to the entrance, located about halfway down the street from the Colosseum and across from Via Cavour, to enter the Forum. From there, you can take a left up the ancient Via Sacra to start at the Forum's southwestern point with the **Temple of Venus and Roma.** Off to your left, on the spur of hillside jutting from the Palatine Hill, stands the famed **Arch of Titus.** Through the arch, photograph the great vista of the entire Forum as it stretches toward the distant Capitoline Hill.

Rome of the Emperors: A Roman Forum Walk

HIGHLIGHTS:
Arches of Septimius Severus, Titus, and Constantine; the Colosseum; the Via Sacra; the Roman Forum

WHERE TO START:
Piazza del Colosseo, with its handy Colosseo Metro stop

WHERE TO STOP:
Inside the archaeological ruins, there are drinking fountains and a couple of vending machines (on the Palatine and the via Nova in the Forum) for hot days. Just a five-minute walk from the Colosseum on Via di San Giovanni, fresh and creamy gelato and homemade Sicilian specialties await you at several genuine shops and restaurants.

LENGTH:
Two to five hours, depending on your pace and how detailed you wish the visit to be

BEST TIME TO GO:
To avoid the harsh midday sun start your tour of the Forum early or in the late afternoon.

WORST TIME TO GO:
Midday, when the sun is high and merciless in the Forum, particularly in the summertime—remember, there are no roofs and few trees to shelter under at these archaeological sites. The Palatine has more shade (and a small air-conditioned museum). Crowds are at their thickest after 10 am.

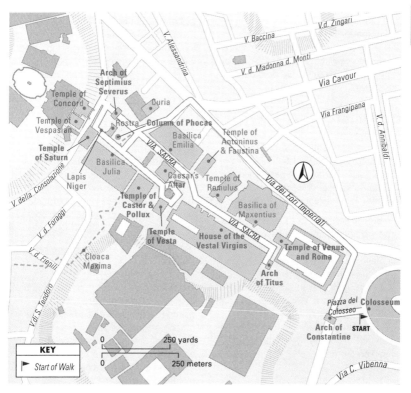

HAUNT OF THE VESTAL VIRGINS

Continue your walk toward the Capitoline Hill by strolling over to the **Temple of Castor and Pollux** and beyond to the circular **Temple of Vesta.** In a tradition going back to an age when fire was a precious commodity, the famous vestal virgins kept the fire of Rome burning here. Of the original 20 columns only three remain, behind which stretch the vast remains of the **House of the Vestal Virgins.** Crossing the central square and walking back toward the towering Capitoline Hill, you are now entering the midsection of the open area of the Forum proper; you can see to your left the **Column of Phocas.**

SEVERUS AND SATURN

Continue back down the Via Sacra, where towers one of the Forum's extant spectaculars, the **Arch of Septimius Severus.** Continuing left and up the Via Sacra, you reach the base of the celebrated **Temple of Saturn.** For a better sense of the whole area—a sort of archaeological gestalt—climb onto the Palatine (the stairs are very steep; easier access is up the path by the Arch of Titus) to the terrace at the Horti Farnesiani Gardens for a breathtaking view to put your walking into panoramic context.

On the Calendar

The City of Eternal Festivals has a bevy of internationally recognized events. In the fall and spring especially, you can see local and international talent in some of Rome's most beautiful venues, outside and in.

February

Equilibrio. This contemporary dance festival takes place at the Auditorium Parco della Musica, with performances by international choreographers and dancers. ⊕ www.auditorium.com.

Street Food Festival. For three days, Eataly's third floor becomes a haven for street food fans. Buy tokens and redeem them for Sicilian *panelle* (chickpea fritters), Tuscan *lampredotto* (tripe sandwiches), *arrosticini* (grilled lamb skewers) from Abruzzo, and more delicacies. Note that although this festival has traditionally been held in February, its scheduling has been in flux in recent years, so check ahead on the timing of it. ⊕ www.eataly.net.

March

Green Market Festival. Dedicated to artisan goods and wellness, this relatively new festival features not only craftspeople selling sustainable creations but also a roster of yoga, Tai Chi, Pilates, and mindfulness classes. ⊕ www.greenmarketfestival.it.

Spring FAI Days. The Fondo Ambiente Italiano (FAI) produces two series of open days yearly throughout Italy—one in spring and one in fall—during which incredible off-limits treasures of architecture and art are made accessible to the public. Past locations in Rome have included the Casino dell'Aurora Ludovisi, a 16th-century villa with the only ceiling painting attributed to Caravaggio, the prestigious Accademia Nazionale dei Lincei inside Palazzo Corsini (Galileo Galilei was a member), and the 16th-century Palazzo del Collegio Romano, which now houses the Ministry of Culture. ⊕ fondoambiente.it.

April

Il Tempietto. This series of unforgettable concerts takes place throughout the year in otherwise inaccessible sites, like the 1st-century Teatro di Marcello. Music runs the gamut from classical to contemporary. ⊕ www.tempietto.it.

June

Estate Romana. Many of the things offered in this summer-long, city-sponsored cultural series are free and take place outdoors along the Tiber River and in piazzas all around the city. Look for cinema events, art programs, theater, book fairs, and guided tours of monuments by night. ⊕ www.culture.roma.it.

I Concerti nel Parco. This June-through-August concert series is held in a small park near the Via Appia Antica. Performances start at sunset, last late into the evening, and showcase a variety of musical genres from classical to contemporary. There are some winter events, including Christmas concerts, as well. ⊕ www.iconcertinelparco.it.

Pride Week. Much like Pride celebrations across Europe and the U.S., Pride Week in Rome consists of concerts, book and film presentations, and other events—all culminating in a parade. Revelers decked out in drag or swaddled in rainbow flags march from Piazza della Repubblica down Via Merulana toward the Colosseum in an epic celebration of the city's LGBTQ+ community. The parade usually takes place the second Saturday of June. ⊕ *www.romapride.it.*

Rock in Roma. From June through August, various locations throughout Rome, including the massive Ippodromo, host rock's top acts from all over the world. ⊕ *www.rockinroma.com.*

Roma Summer Fest. Past editions of this music festival, which takes place at the Auditorium Parco della Musica from June through August, have included concerts by Elton John, Sting, Leonard Cohen, Bob Dylan, Patti Smith, and Arctic Monkeys. ⊕ *www.auditorium.com.*

Villa Ada Festival. World-class headliners and a beautiful location (in a former monarch's villa) make this one of Europe's most impressive music festivals. ⊕ *www.villaadafestival.it.*

September

RomaEuropa. For six weeks in early fall, this multivenue, avant-garde performing and visual arts program showcases international artists. ⊕ *www.romaeuropa.net.*

October

Festa del Cinema di Roma. Cinephiles head to Rome for two packed weeks of cinema celebration and celebrity spotting. The festival showcases Hollywood hits, Italian indie and experimental films, retrospectives and shorts, and conversations with global cinema icons. ⊕ *www.romacinemafest.it.*

November

Roma Jazz Festival. Throughout the month of November, the Auditorium Parco della Musica is the site of performances by local and international jazz musicians. ⊕ *www.romajazzfestival.it.*

December

Natale Festival. From early December through early January, the Auditorium Parco della Musica hosts a Christmas festival replete with pop, rock, jazz, and gospel concerts as well as ice-skating. ⊕ *www.auditorium.com.*

Vitala Festival. This philanthropic festival, which runs from December through June, presents concerts of soul, rock, and blues at Teatro San Genesio in Prati. ⊕ *www.teatrosangenesio.it.*

Chapter 3

ANCIENT ROME

3

Updated by
Laura Itzkowitz

👁 Sights	🍴 Restaurants	🛏 Hotels	🛍 Shopping	🍸 Nightlife
★★★★★	★★☆☆☆	★★☆☆☆	★★★☆☆	★★★☆☆

NEIGHBORHOOD SNAPSHOT

MAKING THE MOST OF YOUR TIME

This area is relatively compact, but extremely rich in history with plenty to see. Serious history buffs should allow a full day to do the area justice, including an hour in the Colosseum, a few hours in the Forum and on the Palatine Hill, and a couple more hours in the Musei Capitolini. Even for ancient Rome experts, taking a tour can be helpful, but be sure to book a guide in advance instead of picking up one of those trying to shill their expertise on-site.

The longest line in Rome, aside from the one at the Vatican Museums, is at the Colosseum, so book a timed slot online ahead of time (⊕ www.coopculture.it). Even with timed entrances, the security line can be long and the interior crowded. From April through October and on weekends year-round, try to book your visit for before 10 am or for an hour or so before closing, when many tour buses have started to depart. There is little to no shade in the Forum, so it gets very hot and dusty in summertime—another reason to either go early or start late.

Outside the main tourism area, give yourself some time to explore the neighborhood of Monti itself, which surrounds the Colosseum, with its artisans' shops, fine trattorias, and great bars—the best of old and new Rome, all in one tiny, proud *rione* (district).

TOP REASONS TO GO

The Colosseum: Clamber up the stands above the imperial box and imagine the gory games as Trajan saw them.

The Roman Forum: Walk through crumbling, romantic ruins—a trip back 2,000-plus years—to the heart of one of the greatest empires the world has ever seen.

The Campidoglio: Watch the sun go down over the Forum from the Campidoglio, the best view in town.

Capitoline Museums: See eye to eye with the ancients—the busts of emperors and philosophers are more real than ideal.

GETTING HERE

■ The Colosseo Metro station is right across from the Colosseum and a short walk from both the Roman and Imperial forums, as well as the Palatine Hill. Walking from the very heart of the historic center will take about 20 minutes, much of it along the wide Via dei Fori Imperiali. The little electric Bus No. 117 from the center or No. 85 from Termini will also deliver you to the Colosseum's doorstep. Any of the following buses will take you to or near the Roman Forum: Nos. 51, 60, 75, and 87.

VIEWFINDER

■ As you walk down Via dei Serpenti in Monti, you'll see a slice of the Colosseum framed cinematically between the buildings on either side of the street, which becomes Via del Fagutale as you cross Via Cavour. At the end of the street, you'll find this little hill with fantastic views. When you're done taking photos, head down the steps on the left and you'll be right across the street from the Colosseum.

If you ever wanted to feel like an emperor—with all of ancient Rome (literally) at your feet—head to Michelangelo's famed Piazza del Campidoglio, and make a beeline for the terrace flanking the side of the center building, the Palazzo Senatorio, Rome's ceremonial city hall. The panorama is breathtaking from this balcony atop the Capitoline Hill.

Spread out before you is the entire Roman Forum, the *caput mundi*—the capital of the known world—for centuries and where many of the world's most important events in the past 2,500 years happened. Here, all Rome shouted as one, "Caesar has been murdered," and crowded to hear Mark Antony's eulogy for the fallen leader. Here, legend has it that St. Paul traversed the Forum en route to his audience with Nero. Here, Roman law and powerful armies were created, keeping the rest of the world at bay for a millennium. And here the Roman emperors staged the biggest blow-out extravaganzas ever mounted for the entire population of a city, outdoing even Elizabeth Taylor's entrance in *Cleopatra*.

But after a more than 27-century-long parade of pageantry, you'll find that much has changed in this area. The marble fragments scattered over the Forum area makes all but students of archaeology ask: is this the grandeur that was Rome? It's not surprising that Shelley and Gibbon once reflected on the adage that *sic transit gloria mundi*—"thus passes the

glory of the world." Yet spectacular monuments—the Arch of Septimius Severus, the Palatine Hill, and the Colosseum (looming in the background), among them—remind us that this was, indeed, the birthplace of much of Western civilization.

Before the Christian era, before the emperors, before the powerful republic that ruled the Mediterranean, Rome was founded on seven hills. Two of them, the Capitoline and the Palatine, surround the Roman Forum, where the Romans of the later Republican and imperial ages worshipped deities, debated politics, and wheeled and dealed. It's all history now, but this remains one of the world's most striking and significant concentrations of ancient remains: an emphatic reminder of the genius and power that made Rome the fountainhead of the Western world.

Outside the actual ancient sites, you'll find neighborhoods like Monti and Celio, rioni which are just as much part of Rome's history as its ruins. These are the city's oldest neighborhoods, and today are a charming mix of the city's past and present. Once you're done exploring ancient Rome, these are the easiest places to head for a bite to eat or some shopping.

The Campidoglio

Your first taste of ancient Rome should start from a point that embodies some of the city's earliest and greatest moments: the Campidoglio. Here, on the Capitoline Hill (which towers over the traffic hub of Piazza Venezia), a meditative Edward Gibbon was inspired to write his 1764 tome, *The History of the Decline and Fall of the Roman Empire.*

Of Rome's famous seven hills, the Capitoline is the smallest and the most sacred. It has always been the seat of Rome's government, and its Latin name echoes in the designation of the national and state capitol buildings of every country in the world.

Although there are great views of the Roman Forum from the terrace balconies to either side of the Palazzo Senatorio, the best view is from the 1st century BC Tabularium, now part of the Musei Capitolini. The museum café is on the Terrazza Caffarelli, with a magical view toward Trastevere and St. Peter's, and is accessible without a museum ticket.

◉ Sights

Basilica di Santa Maria in Aracoeli
CHURCH | Perched atop 124 steps, on the north slope of the Capitoline Hill, Santa Maria in Aracoeli occupies the site of the temple of Juno Moneta (Admonishing Juno), which also housed the Roman mint. According to legend, it was here that the Sibyl, a prophetess, predicted to Augustus the coming of a Redeemer. Augustus responded by erecting an altar, the Ara Coeli (Altar of Heaven). This was eventually replaced by a Benedictine monastery and then by a church, which

was passed in 1250 to the Franciscans, who restored and enlarged it in Romanesque-Gothic style.

Today, the Aracoeli is best known for the Santo Bambino, a much-revered olivewood figure of the Christ Child (a copy of the 15th-century original, which was stolen in 1994). At Christmas, everyone pays homage to the "Bambinello" as children recite poems from a miniature pulpit. In true Roman style, the church interior is a historical hodgepodge, with classical columns and large marble fragments from pagan buildings, as well as a 13th-century cosmatesque pavement. The richly gilded Renaissance ceiling commemorates the naval victory at Lepanto in 1571 over the Turks. The first chapel on the right is noteworthy for Pinturicchio's frescoes of St. Bernardino of Siena (1486). ⊠ *Via del Teatro di Marcello, Piazza Venezia* ☎ *06/69763839* Ⓜ *Colosseo.*

Carcere Mamertino (*Mamertine Prison*)
RUINS | The state prison of the ancient city has two subterranean cells where Rome's enemies, most famously the Goth, Jugurtha, and the indomitable Gaul, Vercingetorix, were imprisoned and died of either starvation or strangulation. Legend has it that, under Nero, saints Peter and Paul were imprisoned in the lower cell, and they used the water from a miraculous spring that appeared to baptize their jailers. A church, San Giuseppe dei Falegnami, now stands over the prison. The multimedia tour has received mixed reviews: it focuses on the Christian history of the site, and the audio is more fluffy than historical. ⊠ *Clivo Argentario 1, Piazza Venezia* ☎ *06/69924652* ⊕ *www.omniavaticanrome.org/en* 🎟 *€10* Ⓜ *Colosseo.*

Le Domus Romane di Palazzo Valentini
RUINS | If you find your imagination stretching to picture Rome as it was two millennia ago, then check out this "new" ancient site just a stone's throw from Piazza Venezia. As was common practice in Renaissance-era Rome, 16th-century

builders simply filled in ancient structures with landfill, using them as part of the foundation for Palazzo Valentini. In doing so, the builders also unwittingly preserved the ruins beneath, which archaeologists rediscovered during excavations in 2007. It took another three years for the two opulent, imperial-era *domus* (upscale urban houses) to open to the public.

Descending below Palazzo Valentini is like walking into another world. Not only are the houses luxurious and well preserved—retaining their beautiful mosaics, inlaid marble floors, and staircases—but the ruins have been made to "come alive" through multimedia. Sophisticated light shows re-create what it all would have looked like, while a dramatic, automated voice-over accompanies you as you walk through the rooms, pointing out cool finds: the heating system for the private baths, the mysterious fragment of a statue, the marks left by wooden beams used to fill in the foundations of Palazzo Valentini during the Renaissance, and a WWII bunker and escape tunnel connected to the domus. If it sounds corny, hold your skepticism: it's an effective, excellent way to actually "experience" the houses as ancient Romans would have—and to learn a lot about ancient Rome in the process. A multimedia presentation halfway through also shows you the detailed battle scenes sculpted onto Trajan's Column above the site.

The multimedia tour takes about an hour. There are limited spots, so book in advance over the phone, online, or in person; make sure you book one of the English tours (at 11 am, 2 pm, and 5 pm). ✉ *Via Foro Traiano 84, Piazza Venezia* ☎ *06/87165343* ⊕ *www.palazzovalentini.it* 💶 *€13.50, including booking fee* ⊗ *Closed Tues.* Ⓜ *Colosseo.*

★ **Musei Capitolini**

ART MUSEUM | Surpassed in size and richness only by the Musei Vaticani, the world's first public museum—with the greatest hits of Roman art through the ages, from the ancients to the Baroque—is housed in the Palazzo dei Conservatori and the Palazzo Nuovo, which mirror one another across Michelangelo's famous piazza. The collection was begun by Pope Sixtus IV (the man who built the Sistine Chapel) in 1473, when he donated a room of ancient statuary to the people of the city. This core of the collection includes the She Wolf, which is the symbol of Rome, and the piercing gaze of the Capitoline Brutus.

Buy your ticket and enter the Palazzo dei Conservatori where, in the first courtyard, you'll see the giant head, foot, elbow, and imperially raised finger of the fabled seated statue of Constantine, which once dominated the Basilica of Maxentius in the Forum. Upstairs is the resplendent Sala degli Orazi e Curiazi (Hall of the Horatii and Curatii), decorated with a magnificent gilt ceiling, carved wooden doors, and 16th-century frescoes depicting the history of Rome's legendary origins. At each end of the hall are statues of two of the most important popes of the Baroque era, Urban VIII and Innocent X.

The heart of the museum is the modern Exedra of Marcus Aurelius (Esedra di Marco Aurelio), which displays the spectacular original bronze statue of the Roman emperor whose copy dominates the piazza outside. To the right, the room segues into the area of the Temple of Jupiter, with the ruins of part of its vast base rising organically into the museum space. A reconstruction of the temple and the Capitoline Hill from the Bronze Age to the present day makes for a fascinating glimpse through the ages. On the top floor, the museum's *pinacoteca,* or painting gallery, has some noted Baroque masterpieces, including Caravaggio's *The Fortune Teller* and *St. John the Baptist.*

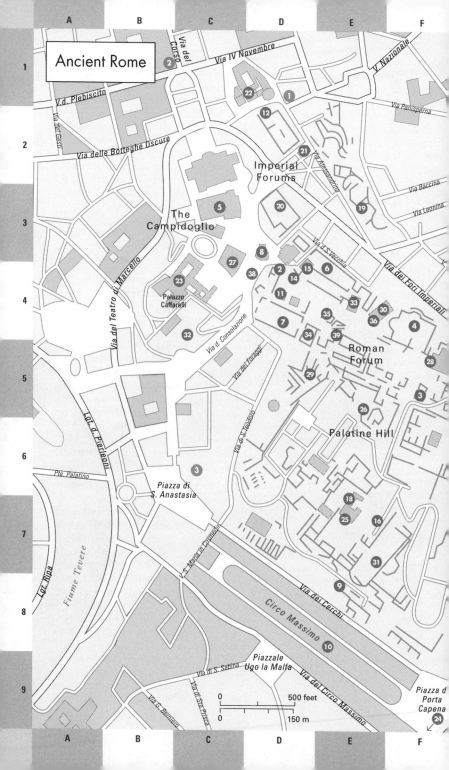

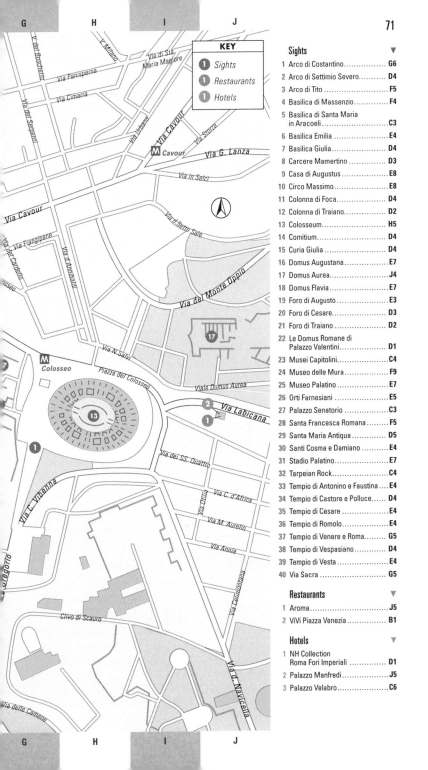

KEY

1 Sights

1 Restaurants

1 Hotels

Sights ▼

1 Arco di Costantino **G6**
2 Arco di Settimio Severo **D4**
3 Arco di Tito **F5**
4 Basilica di Massenzio **F4**
5 Basilica di Santa Maria
   in Aracoeli **C3**
6 Basilica Emilia **E4**
7 Basilica Giulia **D4**
8 Carcere Mamertino **D3**
9 Casa di Augustus **E8**
10 Circo Massimo **E8**
11 Colonna di Foca **D4**
12 Colonna di Traiano **D2**
13 Colosseum **H5**
14 Comitium **D4**
15 Curia Giulia **D4**
16 Domus Augustana **E7**
17 Domus Aurea **J4**
18 Domus Flavia **E7**
19 Foro di Augusto **E3**
20 Foro di Cesare **D3**
21 Foro di Traiano **D2**
22 Le Domus Romane di
   Palazzo Valentini **D1**
23 Musei Capitolini **C4**
24 Museo delle Mura **F9**
25 Museo Palatino **E7**
26 Orti Farnesiani **E5**
27 Palazzo Senatorio **C3**
28 Santa Francesca Romana **F5**
29 Santa Maria Antiqua **D5**
30 Santi Cosma e Damiano **E4**
31 Stadio Palatino **E7**
32 Tarpeian Rock **C4**
33 Tempio di Antonino e Faustina **E4**
34 Tempio di Castore e Polluce ... **D4**
35 Tempio di Cesare **E4**
36 Tempio di Romolo **E4**
37 Tempio di Venere e Roma **G5**
38 Tempio di Vespasiano **D4**
39 Tempio di Vesta **E4**
40 Via Sacra **G5**

Restaurants ▼

1 Aroma **J5**
2 ViVi Piazza Venezia **B1**

Hotels ▼

1 NH Collection
   Roma Fori Imperiali **D1**
2 Palazzo Manfredi **J5**
3 Palazzo Velabro **C6**

72

To get to the Palazzo Nuovo section of the museum, take the stairs or elevator to the basement of the Palazzo dei Conservatori, where the corridor uniting the two contains the Epigraphic Collection, a poignant assembly of ancient gravestones. Just over halfway along the corridor, and before going up into the Palazzo Nuovo, be sure to take the staircase to the right to the Tabularium gallery and its unparalleled view over the Forum.

On the stairs inside the Palazzo Nuovo, you'll be immediately dwarfed by Mars in full military rig and lion-topped sandals. Upstairs is the noted Sala degli Imperatori, lined with busts of Roman emperors, and the Sala dei Filosofi, where busts of philosophers sit in judgment—a fascinating who's who of the ancient world. Within these serried ranks are 48 Roman emperors, ranging from Augustus to Theodosius. Nearby are rooms filled with sculptural masterpieces, including the famed *Dying Gaul*, the *Red Faun* from Hadrian's Villa, and a *Cupid and Psyche*. ⊠ *Piazza del Campidoglio 1, Piazza Venezia* ☎ *06/0608* ⊕ *www.museicapitolini.org* ⊠ *€11.50 (€16 with exhibitions); €13.50 with access to Centrale Montemartini; €7 audio guide* Ⓜ *Colosseo.*

Palazzo Senatorio
GOVERNMENT BUILDING | During the Middle Ages, this city hall looked like those you might see in Tuscan hill towns: part fortress and part assembly hall. The building was entirely rebuilt in the 1500s as part of Michelangelo's revamping of the Campidoglio for Pope Paul III; the master's design was adapted by later architects, who wisely left the front staircase as the focus of the facade. The ancient statue of Minerva at the center was renamed the Goddess Rome, and the river gods (the River Tigris remodeled to symbolize the Tiber, to the right, and the Nile, to the left) were hauled over from the Terme di Costantino on the Quirinal Hill. Today, it is Rome's city hall and is not open to the public. ⊠ *Piazza del Campidoglio, Piazza Venezia* Ⓜ *Colosseo.*

Tarpeian Rock
RUINS | In ancient Rome, traitors were hurled to their deaths from here. In the 18th and 19th centuries, the Tarpeian Rock became a popular stop for people making the Grand Tour because of the view it gave of the Palatine Hill. Today, the Belvedere viewing point has been long shuttered for restoration, but you can proceed a short walk down to Via di Monte Tarpeo, where the view is spectacular enough. It was on this rock that, in the 7th century BC, Tarpeia betrayed the Roman citadel to the early Romans' sworn enemies, the Sabines, only asking in return to be given the heavy gold bracelets the Sabines wore on their left arm. The scornful Sabines did, indeed, shower her with their gold, and added the crushing weight of their heavy shields, also carried on their left arms. ⊠ *Via del Tempio di Giove, Piazza Venezia* Ⓜ *Colosseo.*

🍴 Restaurants

ViVi Piazza Venezia
$$ | BISTRO | For an alternative to the heavy pastas typically found in Roman restaurants, this cheerful bistro inside Palazzo Bonaparte is a great choice. There are plenty of healthy options like excellent salads and poké bowls, as well as heartier fare such as burgers and, yes, pasta. **Known for:** fresh, healthy food; vegan and gluten-free desserts; shabby-chic design. Ⓢ *Average main: €15* ⊠ *Piazza Venezia 5, Piazza Venezia* ☎ *06/69228769* ⊕ *www.vivi.it* Ⓜ *Colosseo.*

The Roman Forum

Whether it's from the main entrance on Via dei Fori Imperiali or by the entrance at the Arch of Titus, descend into the extraordinary archaeological complex that is the Foro Romano and the Palatine Hill, once the very heart of the Roman world.

Entry Tickets

Admission to many of the sights in Ancient Rome is via a combined ticket that you should purchase in advance online at ⊕ *coopculture.it*. (There's a ticket office at Largo della Salaria Vecchia, but tickets often sell out days or weeks in advance.) The basic combo ticket costs €16 and is good for one entrance to the Roman Forum and the Palatine Hill—which are part of a single continuous complex and include some Imperial Forums sights—and a single, timed-admission entry to the Colosseum. This ticket must be used within 24 hours.

The "Full Experience" ticket is good for two consecutive days, costs €22, and allows access to additional attractions.

In the Roman Forum and Imperial Forums, this ticket covers the Curia Giulia, Santa Maria Antiqua, Tempio di Romolo (temporarily closed to the public), and Foro di Augusto; on the Palatine Hill, it includes the Casa di Augusto, the Domus Tiberiana, and the Museo Palatino.

Both tickets carry an extra €2 booking fee, and audio guides cost another €7.50. To avoid the lines to pick up tickets, choose the print-at-home ticket option (a PDF on a smartphone works, too). Note, too, that although the Roman Forum–Palatine Hill complex is open daily, some sights within it are not.

The Forum began life as a marshy valley between the Capitoline and Palatine hills—a valley crossed by a mud track and used as a cemetery by Iron Age settlers. Over the years, a market center and some huts were established here, and, after the land was drained in the 6th century BC, the site became a political, religious, and commercial center: the Forum.

Hundreds of years of plunder reduced the Forum to its current desolate state. But this enormous area was once Rome's pulsating hub, filled with stately and extravagant temples, palaces, and shops and crowded with people from all corners of the empire. Adding to today's confusion is the fact that the Forum developed over many centuries; what you see today are not the ruins from just one period but from a span of almost 900 years, from about 500 BC to AD 400. Nonetheless, the enduring romance of the place, with its lonely columns and great broken fragments of sculpted marble and stone, makes for a quintessential Roman experience.

⊙ Sights

★ Arco di Settimio Severo
(Arch of Septimius Severus)
RUINS | One of the grandest triumphal arches erected by a Roman emperor, this richly decorated monument was built in AD 203 to celebrate Severus's victory over the Parthians. It was once topped by a bronze statuary group depicting a chariot drawn by four (or perhaps as many as six) life-size horses. Masterpieces of Roman statuary, the stone reliefs on the arch were probably based on huge painted panels depicting the event, a kind of visual report on his foreign campaigns that would have been displayed during the emperor's triumphal parade in Rome to impress his subjects (and, like much statuary then, were originally painted in florid, lifelike colors). ✉ *West end of Foro Romano, Monti* ⊕ *www.coopculture.it* 🎫 *€16 24-hour ticket required* Ⓜ *Colosseo.*

Arco di Tito (*Arch of Titus*)

RUINS | Standing at the northern approach to the Palatine Hill on the Via Sacra, this triumphal arch was erected in AD 81 to celebrate the sack of Jerusalem 10 years earlier, after the First Jewish–Roman War. The superb view of the Colosseum from the arch reminds us that it was the emperor Titus who helped finish the vast amphitheater, begun earlier by his father, Vespasian. Under the arch are two great sculpted reliefs, both showing scenes from Titus's triumphal parade along this very Via Sacra. You still can make out the spoils of war plundered from Herod's Temple, including a gigantic seven-branched candelabrum (menorah) and silver trumpets. During his sacking of Jerusalem, Titus killed or deported most of the Jewish population, thus initiating the Jewish diaspora—an event that would have far-reaching historical consequences. ✉ *East end of Via Sacra, Monti* ⊕ *www.coopculture.it* ✉ *€16 24-hour ticket required* Ⓜ *Colosseo.*

Basilica di Massenzio (*Basilica of Maxentius*)

RUINS | Although its great arched vaults still dominate the north side of the Via Sacra, only about one-third of the original of this gigantic basilica (in the sense of a Roman courthouse and meeting hall) remains, so you can imagine what a wonder this building was when first erected. Begun under the emperor Maxentius about AD 306, the edifice was a center of judicial and commercial activity, the last of its kind to be built in Rome. Over the centuries, like so many Roman monuments, it was exploited as a quarry for building materials and was stripped of its sumptuous marble and stucco decorations. Its coffered vaults, like that of the Pantheon's dome, were later copied by many Renaissance artists and architects. ✉ *Via Sacra, Monti* ⊕ *www.coopculture.it* ✉ *€16 24-hour ticket required* Ⓜ *Colosseo.*

Basilica Emilia

RUINS | Once a great colonnaded hall, this served as a meeting place for merchants and as a courthouse from the 2nd century BC; it was rebuilt by Augustus in the 1st century AD. To the right as you enter the Forum from Via dei Fori Imperiali, a spot on one of the basilica's preserved pieces of floor testifies to one of Rome's more harrowing moments—and to the hall's purpose. That's where bronze coins melted, leaving behind green stains, when Rome was sacked and the basilica was burned by the Visigoths in 410 AD. The term "basilica" refers here to the particular architectural form developed by the Romans: a rectangular hall flanked by colonnades, it could serve as a court of law or a center for business and commerce. The basilica would later become the building type adopted for the first official places of Christian worship in the city. ✉ *Monti* ✛ *On right as you descend into Roman Forum from Via dei Fori Imperiali entrance* ⊕ *www.coopculture.it* ✉ *€16 24-hour ticket required* Ⓜ *Colosseo.*

Basilica Giulia

RUINS | The Basilica Giulia owes its name to Julius Caesar, who ordered its construction; it was later completed by his adopted heir, Augustus. One of several such basilicas in the center of Rome, it was where the Centumviri, the hundred-or-so judges forming the civil court, met to hear cases. The open space between the Basilica Emilia and this basilica was the heart of the Forum proper—the prototype of Italy's Renaissance piazzas and the center of civic and social activity in ancient Rome. ✉ *Via Sacra, Monti* ⊕ *www.coopculture.it* ✉ *€16 24-hour ticket required* Ⓜ *Colosseo.*

Colonna di Foca (*Column of Phocas*)

RUINS | The last monument to be added to the Forum was erected in AD 608 in honor of the Byzantine emperor Phocas who had donated the Pantheon to Pope Boniface IV. It stands 44 feet high and remains in good condition. ✉ *West end of Foro Romano, Monti* ⊕ *www.coop-culture.it* 🎫 *€16 24-hour ticket required* Ⓜ *Colosseo.*

Comitium

RUINS | The open space in front of the Curia was the political hub of ancient Rome. Julius Caesar had rearranged the Comitium, moving the Curia to its current site and transferring the imperial Rostra, the podium from which orators spoke to the people (decorated originally with the prows of captured ships, or *rostra,* the source for the term "rostrum"), to a spot just south of where the Arch of Septimius Severus would be built. It was from this location that Mark Antony delivered his funeral oration in Caesar's honor. On the left of the Rostra stands what remains of the Tempio di Saturno, which served as ancient Rome's state treasury. The area of the Comitium has been under excavation for several years and is currently not open to visitors. ✉ *West end of Foro Romano, Monti* ⊕ *www.coopculture.it* 🎫 *€16 24-hour ticket required* Ⓜ *Colosseo.*

Curia Giulia

RUINS | This large brick structure next to the Arch of Septimius Severus, restored during Diocletian's reign in the late 3rd century AD, is the Forum's best-pre-served building—thanks largely to having been turned into a church in the 7th century. By the time the Curia was built, the Senate, which met here, had lost practically all of the power and prestige that it had possessed during the Republican era. Still, the Curia appears much as the original Senate house would have looked. Note, especially, the intricately inlaid 3rd-century floor of marble and porphyry, a method called *opus sectile.* ✉ *Via Sacra, northwest corner of Foro Romano, Monti* ⊕ *www.coopculture.it* 🎫 *€22 2-day Full Experience ticket required* ◷ *Closed Tues.–Fri.* Ⓜ *Colosseo.*

Santa Francesca Romana

CHURCH | This church, a 10th-century edifice with a Renaissance facade, is dedicated to the patron saint of motorists. On her feast day, March 9, cars and taxis crowd the Via dei Fori Imperiali below for a special blessing—a cardinal and *carabinieri* (Italian military) are on hand and a special siren starts off the ceremony. The incomparable setting continues to be a favorite for weddings. ✉ *Piazza di Santa Francesca Romana, next to Colosseum, Monti* ⊕ *www.coopculture.it* 🎫 *€16 24-hour ticket required* Ⓜ *Colosseo.*

Santa Maria Antiqua

RUINS | The earliest Christian site in the Forum was originally part of an imperial structure at the foot of the Palatine Hill before it was converted into a church sometime in the late 5th century. Within it are some exceptional frescoes dating from the 6th to the 9th century. Buried by a 9th-century earthquake, the church was abandoned and a replacement was eventually built on top in the 17th century. This newer church was knocked down in 1900 during excavation work on the Forum, which revealed the early medieval church beneath. ✉ *South of Tempio di Castore and Polluce, at foot of Palatine Hill, Monti* ⊕ *www.coopculture.it* 🎫 *€22 2-day Full Experience ticket required* Ⓜ *Colosseo.*

Tempio di Antonino e Faustina

RUINS | Erected by the Senate in honor of Faustina, deified wife of Emperor Antoninus Pius (AD 138–161), Hadrian's successor, this temple was rededicated to the emperor as well upon his death. Because it was transformed into a church (San Lorenzo in Miranda), it's one of the best-preserved ancient structures in the Forum. ✉ *North of Via Sacra, Monti* ⊕ *www.coopculture.it* 🎫 *€16 24-hour ticket required* Ⓜ *Colosseo.*

Tempio di Castore e Polluce

RUINS | The three remaining Corinthian columns of this temple beautifully evoke the former grandeur and elegance of the

Forum. This temple was dedicated in 484 BC to Castor and Pollux, the twin brothers of Helen of Troy, who carried to Rome the news of victory at Lake Regillus, southeast of Rome—the definitive defeat of the deposed Tarquin dynasty. The twins flew on their fabulous white steeds 20 km (12 miles) to the city to bring the news to the people before mortal messengers could arrive. Rebuilt over the centuries before Christ, the temple suffered a major fire and was reconstructed by the future Emperor Tiberius in 12 BC, the date of the three standing columns. ⊠ *West of Casa delle Vestali, Monti* ⊕ *www.coopculture.it* ✉ *€16 24-hour ticket required* Ⓜ *Colosseo.*

Tempio di Cesare

RUINS | What survives of the base of the temple—built by Augustus, Julius Caesar's successor—stands over the spot where Caesar's body was cremated. A pyre was improvised by grief-crazed citizens who kept the flames going with their own possessions. ⊠ *Via Sacra, opposite the Tempio di Antonino e Faustina, Monti* ⊕ *www.coopculture.it* ✉ *€16 24-hour ticket required* Ⓜ *Colosseo.*

Tempio di Romolo

RUINS | This round brick temple with bronze doors behind the Basilica dei Santi Cosma e Damiano is believed to have been dedicated by the Emperor Maxentius to his son, Valerius Romulus, who died in 309 AD and was deified. In the 6th century, the temple was converted into a vestibule for the church. There are various wall decorations in the rotunda, including Christ enthroned between St. Mary Magdalene and St. Mary Salome. To the left of the entrance is a 13th-century painting attributed to Jacopo Torriti depicting the Madonna enthroned and Child between the Medici saints. ⊠ *Behind the Basilica dei Santi Cosma e Damiano, Monti* ☎ *06/39967700* ⊕ *www.coopculture.it* ✉ *€22 2-day Full Experience ticket required* Ⓜ *Colosseo.*

Tempio di Venere e Roma

RUINS | Once Rome's largest temple, was, in fact, originally two temples back-to-back. The half dedicated to Venus, facing the Colosseum, is the section seen today; its twin, which once faced the Forum, was dedicated to the goddess Roma, and is now the foundation of the church of Santa Maria Nova. Begun by Hadrian in AD 121, the temple is accessible from the end of the Forum near the Arch of Titus, and offers a great view of the Colosseum. ⊠ *East of Arco di Tito, Monti* ⊕ *www.coopculture.it* ✉ *€16 24-hour ticket required* Ⓜ *Colosseo.*

Tempio di Vespasiano

RUINS | All that remains of Vespasian's temple are three graceful Corinthian columns. They marked the site of the Forum through the centuries while the rest was hidden beneath overgrown rubble. Nearby is the ruined platform that was the Tempio di Concordia. ⊠ *West end of Foro Romano, Monti* ⊕ *www.coopculture.it* ✉ *€16 24-hour ticket required* Ⓜ *Colosseo.*

Tempio di Vesta

RUINS | Although only a fragment of the original building remains, this temple nevertheless conveys the sophisticated architectural elegance that was achieved in the later Roman Empire. Set off by florid Corinthian columns, the *tholos* (circular building) was rebuilt by Emperor Septimius Severus when he restored the temple (around AD 205), which is dedicated to Vesta, the goddess of the hearth. It was here that the six, highly privileged vestal virgins—chosen when they were between six and 10 years old to serve for 30 years—kept Rome's sacred flame burning, a tradition that dated from the very earliest days of the city, when guarding the community's precious fire was essential to its well-being.

Next to the temple, the Casa delle Vestali gives you a glimpse of the splendor in which these women lived. Marble statues of the vestals and fragments of mosaic pavement line the garden courtyard, which once would have been surrounded by lofty colonnades and at least 50 rooms. Their standing in Rome was considerable: among women, they were second in rank only to the Empress. Their intercession could save a condemned man, and they did, in fact, rescue Julius Caesar from the lethal vengeance of his enemy Sulla.

The virgins were handsomely maintained by the state, but if they allowed the sacred fire to go out, they were scourged by the high priest, and if they broke their vows of celibacy, they were buried alive (a punishment doled out only a handful of times throughout the cult's 1,000-year history). The vestal virgins were one of the last of ancient Rome's institutions to die out, enduring until the end of the 4th century AD—even after Rome's emperors had become Christian. ✉ *South side of Via Sacra, Monti* 🌐 *www.coopculture.it* 🎟 *€16 24-hour ticket required* [M] *Colosseo.*

Via Sacra
RUINS | The celebrated "Sacred Way," paved with local volcanic rock, runs through the Roman Forum, lined with temples and shrines. It was also the traditional route of religious and triumphal processions. Pick your way across the paving stones, some rutted with the ironclad wheels of Roman wagons, to walk in the footsteps of Julius Caesar and Marc Antony. ✉ *Monti* 🌐 *www.coopculture.it* 🎟 *€16 24-hour ticket required* [M] *Colosseo.*

🛏 Hotels

NH Collection Roma Fori Imperiali
$$$$ | **HOTEL** | It would be hard to find a modern hotel closer to the Roman Forum—the ancient ruins are practically right outside the door. **Pros:** incredible views of ancient Rome; rooftop serves a great aperitivo and refined dinners; restaurant Oro Bistrot by renowned chef Natale Giunta. **Cons:** breakfast foods are pre-packaged; not much public space; no spa or gym. [$] *Rooms from: €400* ✉ *Via di Santa Eufemia 19, Monti* ☎ *06/697689911* 🌐 *www.nh-collection.com/en/hotel/nh-collection-roma-fori-imperiali* 🛏 *42 rooms* 🍴 *No Meals* [M] *Colosseo.*

The Palatine Hill

Just beyond the Arco di Tito, the Clivus Palatinus—the road connecting the Roman Forum and the Palatine Hill—gently rises to the heights of the Colle Palatino (Palatine Hill), the oldest inhabited site in Rome and where Romulus is said to have founded the city that bears his name.

Despite a location overlooking the Forum's traffic and attendant noise, the Palatine Hill is charmingly bucolic, with pines and olive trees providing shade. It was, however, ancient Rome's most coveted address. During the Roman Republic, it was home to wealthy patrician families—Cicero, Catiline, Crassus, and Agrippa all had homes here. When Augustus (who had himself been born on the hill) came to power, declaring himself to be the new Romulus, it would thereafter become the home of emperors.

The House of Augustus is one of the hill's best-preserved structures, replete with fabulous frescoes. Tiberius extended this palace, and other structures followed, notably the gigantic extravaganza constructed for Emperor Domitian, which makes up much of what's seen today.

👁 Sights

★ **Casa di Augustus** (*House of Augustus*)
RUINS | First discovered in the 1970s and only open to the public since 2006, this was the residence of Octavian Augustus (27 BC–AD 14) after his victory at Actium. (Archaeologists have recently found two

The "Bel Air" of ancient Rome, the Palatine Hill was the address of choice for Cicero and Agrippa, as well as the emperors Tiberius, Caligula, and Domitian.

courtyards rather than one, though, in the style of Rome's ancient Greek kings, suggesting Augustus maintained this house after his ascension to prominence.) Four rooms have exquisite examples of decorative frescoes on the walls; startlingly vivid and detailed are the depictions of a narrow stage with side doors, as well as some striking comic theater masks. An exquisitely painted upper room has been identified as the Emperor's study. ⊠ *Northwest crest of Palatine Hill, Monti* ⊕ *www.coopculture.it* ✉ *€22 2-day Full Experience ticket required* Ⓜ *Colosseo.*

Circo Massimo (*Circus Maximus*)
RUINS | From the belvedere of the Domus Flavia on the Palatine Hill, you can see the Circus Maximus; there's also a great free view from Piazzale Ugo La Malfa on the Aventine Hill side. The giant space where 300,000 spectators once watched chariot races while the emperor looked on is ancient Rome's oldest and largest racetrack; it lies in a natural hollow between the two hills. The oval course stretches about 650 yards from end to

end; on certain occasions, there were as many as 24 chariot races a day, and competitions could last for 15 days. The charioteers could amass fortunes rather like the sports stars of today. (The Portuguese Diocles is said to have totted up winnings of 35 million sestertii.)

The noise and the excitement of the crowd must have reached astonishing levels as the charioteers competed in teams, each with their own colors—the Reds, the Blues, etc. Betting also provided Rome's majority of unemployed with a potentially lucrative occupation. The central ridge was the site of two Egyptian obelisks (now in Piazza del Popolo and Piazza San Giovanni in Laterano). Picture the great chariot race scene from MGM's *Ben-Hur*, and you have an inkling of what this was like. ⊠ *Between Palatine and Aventine Hills, Aventino* ☎ *06/0608* ✉ *€5* Ⓜ *Circo Massimo.*

Domus Augustana
RUINS | In the imperial palace complex, this area, named in the 19th century for the "Augustuses" (a generic term used for emperors, in honor of Augustus

himself), consisted of private apartments built for Emperor Domitian and his family. Here Domitian—"Dominus et Deus," as he liked to be called—would retire to dismember flies (at least, according to Suetonius), before eventually being assassinated. ⊠ *Southern crest of Palatine Hill, Monti* ⊕ *www.coopculture. it* ☎ *€16 24-hour ticket required* Ⓜ *Circo Massimo.*

Domus Flavia

RUINS | Domitian used this area of the imperial palace complex for official functions and ceremonies. It included a basilica where the emperor could hold judiciary hearings. There was also a large audience hall, a *peristyle* (a columned courtyard), and the imperial *triclinium* (dining room)—some of its mosaic floors and stone banquettes are still in place. According to Suetonius, Domitian had the walls and courtyards of this and the adjoining Domus Augustana covered with the shiniest marble to act as mirrors to alert him to any knife pointed at his back. They failed in their purpose: he died in a palace plot, engineered, some say, by his wife Domitia. ⊠ *Southern crest of Palatine Hill, Monti* ⊕ *www.coopculture. it* ☎ *€16 24-hour ticket required* Ⓜ *Circo Massimo.*

Museo Palatino

ART MUSEUM | The Palatine Museum charts the history of the hill from Archaic times, with quaint models of early villages (on the ground floor), to Roman times (on the ground and upper floors). There is a good video reconstruction of the hill in Room V on the ground floor, as well as a collection of colored stones used in the decorations of the palace, with a map showing the distant imperial regions whence they came. Upstairs, the room dedicated to Augustus houses painted terra-cotta moldings and sculptural decorations from various temples—notably the Temple of Apollo Actiacus, whose name derives from the god to whom

Octavian attributed his victory at Actium (the severed heads of the Medusa in the terra-cotta panels symbolize the defeated Queen of Egypt). There is also a selection of imperial portraits on the upper floor, including a rare surviving image of Nero. The museum closes early, at 3:30 pm. ⊠ *Northwest crest of Palatine Hill, Monti* ⊕ *www.coopculture.it* ☎ *€22 2-day Full Experience ticket required* Ⓜ *Colosseo.*

Orti Farnesiani

GARDEN | Alessandro Farnese, a nephew of Pope Paul III, commissioned the 16th-century architect Vignola to lay out this archetypal Italian garden over the ruins of the Palace of Tiberius, on the northern side of the Palatine, with a spectacular view over the Forum. This was yet another example of the Renaissance renewing an ancient Roman tradition. To paraphrase the poet Martial, the statue-studded gardens of the Flavian Palace were such as to make even an Egyptian potentate turn green with envy. ⊠ *Palatine Hill, Monti* ⊕ *www.coopculture.it* ☎ *€16 24-hour ticket required* Ⓜ *Colosseo.*

Stadio Palatino

RUINS | Built by Domitian and erroneously referred to since the 19th century as the "stadium," this was, in fact, a sunken garden that created a terrace on the slopes of the hill. It may also have been used to stage games (but not chariot races) and other amusements for the emperor's benefit. ⊠ *Southeast crest of Palatine Hill, Monti* ⊕ *www.coopculture.it* ☎ *€16 24-hour ticket required* Ⓜ *Circo Massimo.*

 Hotels

Palazzo Velabro

$$$$ | **HOTEL** | A member of Design Hotels, this 32-room boutique bolt-hole has spacious rooms and suites, the majority of which come equipped with a kitchenette and sofa bed—some have balconies with views of the Palatine Hill. **Pros:** spacious

Continued on page 92

ANCIENT ROME:
ROME WASN'T BUILT IN A DAY

by Robert I. C. Fisher

RE-CREATING THE ANCIENT CITY

Time has reduced ancient Rome to fields of silent ruins, but the powerful impact of what happened here, of the genius and power that made Rome the center of the Western world, echoes across the millennia. In this one compact area of the city, you can step back into the Rome of Cicero, Julius Caesar, and Virgil. You can walk along the streets they knew, cool off in the shade of the Colosseum that loomed over their city, and see the sculptures poised over their piazzas.

Today, this part of Rome, more than any other, is a perfect example of the layering of historic eras, the overlapping of ages, of religions, of a past that is very much a part of the present.

Although it has been the capital of the Republic of Italy only since 1946, Rome has been the capital of something for more than 2,500 years, and it shows. The magnificent ruins of the Palatine Hill, the ancient complexity of the Forum, the Renaissance harmony of the Campidoglio—all are part of Rome's identity as one of the world's most enduring seats of government.

This is not to say that it's been an easy 2½ millennia. The Vandal hordes of the 3rd century, the Goth sacks of the Middle Ages, the excavations of a modern-day Mussolini, and today's modern citizens—all played a part in transforming Rome into a city of fragments. Semi-preserved ruins of ancient forums, basilicas, stadiums, baths, and temples are strewn across the city like remnants of some Cecil B. DeMille movie set. No wonder first-time visitors feel that the only thing more intimidating than crossing a Roman intersection at rush hour is trying to make sense of the layout of ancient Rome.

The following pages detail how the new Rome overlaps the old, showing how the modern city is crammed with details of ageless walls and ancient sites, even though some of them now lie hidden underneath the earth. Written in these rocks is the story of the emperors, the city's greatest builders. Thanks in large part to their dreams of glory—combined with their architectural megalomania—Imperial Rome became the fountainhead of Western civilization.

(Left) Colosseum; (top) Head of Emperor Constantine, Musei Capitolini

THE WAY ROME WAS

Circus Maximus (Circo Massimo): Atop the Palatine Hill, the emperor's royal box looked down on the races and games of this vast stadium—most

Early Christians met their untimely end here, not in the Colosseum.

Capitoline Hill (Campidoglio): Most important of Rome's original

seven hills, and home to the Temple of Jupiter, the "capital" hill was strategically located high above the Tiber and became the hub of the Roman Republic.

Palatine Hill (Colle Palatino): The birthplace of Rome, settled by Romulus and Remus, the Palatine ultimately became Rome's "Beverly Hills,"

Rome in the Year 300 AD

for it was home to Cicero, Julius Caesar, and a dozen emperors.

Roman Forum
(Foro Romano): Downtown ancient Rome, this was the political heart of the republic and empire—the place for processions, tribunals, law courts, and orations, and it was here that Mark Antony buried Caesar and Cleopatra made her triumphant entry.

Colosseum
(Colosseo):
Before 50,000 spectators, gladiators fought for the chance to live another day in this giant arena built in a mere eight years and inaugurated in AD 80.

Domus Aurea:
Nero's "Golden House," a sprawling example of the excesses of Imperial Rome, once comprised 150 rooms, some shimmering with gold.

Via Flaminia

Forum of Trajan

QUIRINALE

VIMINALE

Roman Forum

SUBURRA

Domus Aurea

Basilica of Maxentius

ESQUILINO

Aqueduct of Acqua Claudia

Colosseum

Temple of Claudius

Acquaduct of Acqua Appia

CELIO

THEY CAME, THEY SAW, THEY BUILT

Remember the triumphal scene in the 2000 film *Gladiator*? Awesome expanses of pristine marble, a cast of thousands in gold-lavished costumes, and close-ups of Joaquin Phoenix (playing Emperor Commodus) on his way to the Colosseum: Rome à la Hollywood. But behind all the marble splendor seen in the film lies an eight-century-long trail that extends back from Imperial Rome to a tiny village of mud huts along the Tiber River.

Museo della Civiltà Romana's model of Imperial Rome

ROMULUS GOES TO TOWN

Legend has it that Rome was founded by Romulus and Remus, twin sons of the god Mars. Upon being abandoned in infancy by a wicked uncle, they were taken up and suckled by a she-wolf living on a bank of the Tiber. (Ancient gossip says the wolf was actually a woman nicknamed Lupa for her multiple infidelities to her shepherd husband.)

As young men, Romulus and Remus returned in 753 BC to the hallowed spot to found a city but came to blows during its building, ending in the death of Remus—which is how the city became Roma, not Rema.

Where myth ends, archaeology takes over. In 2007, Roman excavators uncovered a cavernous sanctuary dedicated to the brothers situated in the valley between the Palatine (Palatino) and Capitoline (Campidoglio) hills in central Rome. Often transformed into "islands" when the Tiber river overflowed, these two hills soon famously expanded to include seven hills, including the Esquiline, Viminale, Celian, Quirinale, and Aventine.

SIMPLY MARBLE-OUS

Up to 510 BC, the style of the fledging city had been set by the fun-loving, sophisticated Etruscans—Rome was to adopt their vestal virgins, household gods, and gladiatorial games. Later, when the republic took over the city (509 BC–27 BC), the austere values promulgated by its democratic Senate eventually fell to the power-mad triumvirate of Crassus, Pompey, and Julius Caesar, who waved away any detractors—including Rome's main power-players, the patrician Senators, and the populist Tribunes—by invoking the godlike sovereignty of emperorship.

Republican Rome's city was badly planned, in fact not planned at all, and the great contribution of the Emperor Augustus—who took over when his stepfather Caesar was assassinated in 43 BC—was to commence serious town planning, with results far surpassing even his own claim that he "found Rome brick and left it marble." Which was only fitting, as floridly colored marble began to flow into Rome from all of the Mediterranean provinces he had conquered (including obelisks transported from Egypt to flaunt his victory over Cleopatra).

Via Sacra in the Roman Forum, with the Temple of Saturn in the foreground and the Basilica Julia on the right.

A FUNNY THING HAPPENED ON THE WAY TO THE ROMAN FORUM

It was during Augustus's peaceful 40-year reign that Rome began its transition from glorified provincial capital into great city. While excavations have shown that the area of the Roman Forum was in use as a burial ground as far back as the 10th century BC, the importance of the Forum area as the political, commercial, and social center of Rome and, by extension, of the whole ancient world, grew immeasurably during Imperial times. The majestic ruins still extant are remnants of the massive complex of markets, civic buildings, and temples that dominated the city center in its heyday.

After Rome gained "empire" status, however, the original Forum was inadequate to handle the burden of the many trials and meetings required to run Western civilization, so Julius Caesar built a new forum. This apparently started a trend, as over the next 200-plus years (43 BC–AD 180), four different emperors—Augustus, Domitian, Vespasian, and Trajan—did the same. Oddly enough, the Roman Forum became four different Forums. They grew, in part, thanks to the Great Fire of AD 64, which Nero did not set but for which he took credit for laying waste to shabbier districts to build new ones.

For half a millennium, the Roman Forum area became the heart and soul of a worldwide empire, which eventually extended from Britain to Constantinople. Unfortunately, another thousand years of looting, sacking, and decay means you have to use your vivid imagination to see the glory that once was.

WHERE ALL ROADS LEAD

Even if you don't dig ruins, a visit to the archaeological sites in and around the Roman Forum is a must. Rome's foundation as a world capital and crossroads of culture are to be found here, literally. Overlapped with Rome's current streets, this map shows the main monuments of the Roman Forum (in tan) as they originally stood.

Basilica Julia

Via IV Novembre

Via C. Battisti

Trajan's Column

V. Alessandrina

TRAJAN'S FORUM

Via del Teatro di Marcello

C A M P I D O G L I O

Palazzo Senatorio

Tabularium

Carcere Mamertino

V. L. petroselli

TEMPLE OF JUPITER

Arch of Septimus Severus

Curia

Umbilcus Urbis Romae

The Rostra

Temple of Vespasian

Roman Forum

Basilica Julia

Tarpeian Rock

Temple of Saturn

Temple of Castor and Pollux

V. C. Jugario

V. della Consolazione

V. d. Foraggi

V. d. Fienili

V. di S. Teodoro

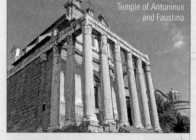
Temple of Antoninus and Faustina

Cloaca Maxima

TIBERIAN PALACE

M O N T E

House of Livia

V. del Velabro

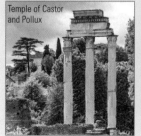
Temple of Castor and Pollux

Domitian's Palace

Circus Maximus

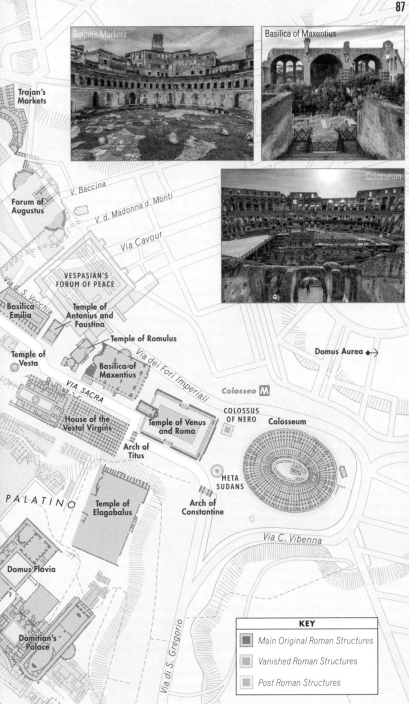

Trajan's Markets

Basilica of Maxentius

Colosseum

Trajan's Markets

Forum of Augustus

V. Baccina

V. d. Madonna d. Monti

Via Cavour

VESPASIAN'S FORUM OF PEACE

Via d. S. Vecchia

Basilica Emilia

Temple of Antonius and Faustina

Temple of Romulus

Temple of Vesta

Via dei Fori Imperiali

Basilica of Maxentius

Domus Aurea

VIA SACRA

Colosseo M

House of the Vestal Virgins

Temple of Venus and Roma

COLOSSUS OF NERO

Colosseum

Arch of Titus

META SUDANS

PALATINO

Temple of Elagabalus

Arch of Constantine

Domus Flavia

Via C. Vibenna

Domitian's Palace

Via di S. Gregorio

KEY		
■	*Main Original Roman Structures*	
■	*Vanished Roman Structures*	
■	*Post Roman Structures*	

URBIS ROMÆ: THE EXPANDING CITY

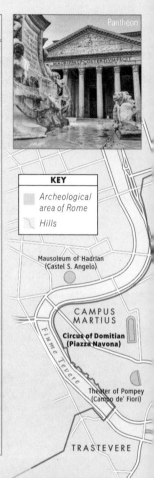

Pantheon

Today's Campitelli district—the historic area comprising the Forums and the Colosseum—was, in fact, a relatively small part of the ancient city. From the center around the Forum, the old city dramatically grew outwards and in AD 7, the emperor Augustus organized ancient Rome into 14 *regiones*, administrative divisions that were the forerunners of today's historic *rioni* (districts). Rome's first city walls went up in the 6th century BC when King Servius Tullius built an 8-mile ring. As the city's borders greatly expanded, however, the outlaying areas needed extra protection. This became a dire necessity in the 3rd century when Germanic tribes arrived to sack Rome while Emperor Aurelian was fighting wars on the southern border of the empire. Fueled by fear, the emperor commissioned an 11-mile bulwark to be built of brick between 271 and 275. Studding the Aurelian Walls were 380 towers and 18 main gates, the best preserved of which is the Porta di San Sebastiano, at the entrance to the Via Appia Antica. The Porta is now home to the Museo delle Mura, a small but fascinating museum that allows you to walk the ancient ramparts today; take Bus No. 118 to the Porta. From the walls' lofty perch you can see great vistas of the timeless Appian Way.

KEY

Archeological area of Rome

Hills

Mausoleum of Hadrian
(Castel S. Angelo)

CAMPUS MARTIUS

**Circus of Domitian
(Piazza Navona)**

Fiume Tevere

Theater of Pompey
(Campo de' Fiori)

TRASTEVERE

Pantheon: Built in 27 BC by Augustus's general Agrippa and totally rebuilt by Hadrian in the 2nd century AD, this temple, dedicated to all the pagan gods, was topped by the largest dome ever built (until the 20th century).

Baths of Caracalla: These gigantic thermal baths, a stunning example of ancient Roman architecture, were more than just a place to bathe—they functioned somewhat like today's swank athletic clubs.

Isola Tiberina: The Temple of Aesculapius once presided over this island—which was shaped by ancient Romans to resemble a ship, complete with obelisk mast and (still visible) marble ship prow—and was Rome's shrine to medicine.

Circus of Domitian: Rome's present Piazza Navona follows the shape of this ancient oval stadium built in 96 AD—houses now stand on top of the cavea, the original stone seating, which held 30,000 spectators.

Campus Borum: Today's Piazza della Bocca della Verità was ancient Rome's cattle market and the site of two beautifully preserved 2nd century BC temples, one dedicated to Fortuna Virilis, the other to Hercules.

Porta di San Sebastiano: The largest extant gate of the 3rd-century Aurelian Walls, located near the ancient aqueduct that once brought water to the nearby Baths of Caracalla, showcases the most beautiful stretch of Rome's ancient walls.

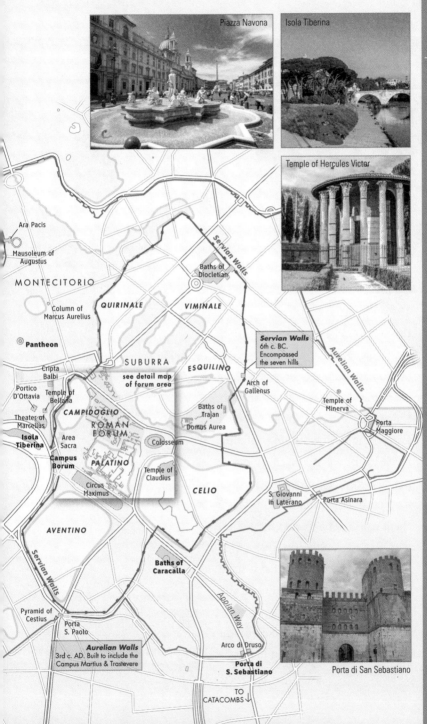

Piazza Navona

Isola Tiberina

Temple of Hercules Victor

Ara Pacis

Mausoleum of
Augustus

MONTECITORIO

Column of
Marcus Aurelius

Pantheon

Cripta
Balbi

Portico
D'Ottavia

Theater of
Marcellus

Isola
Tiberina

Campus
Borum

QUIRINALE

VIMINALE

Baths of
Diocletian

Servian Walls

Servian Walls
6th c. BC.
Encompassed
the seven hills

Aurelian Walls

SUBURRA

ESQUILINO

see detail map
of forum area

Temple of
Bellona

CAMPIDOGLIO

ROMAN
FORUM

Area
Sacra

PALATINO

Circus
Maximus

Arch of
Gallenus

Baths of
Trajan

Domus Aurea

Colosseum

Temple of
Claudius

CELIO

Temple of
Minerva

Porta
Maggiore

S. Giovanni
in Laterano

Porta Asinara

AVENTINO

Servian Walls

Baths of
Caracalla

Appian Way

Pyramid of
Cestius

Porta
S. Paolo

Aurelian Walls
3rd c. AD. Built to include the
Campus Martius & Trastevere

Arco di Druso

Porta di
S. Sebastiano

TO
CATACOMBS

Porta di San Sebastiano

BUILDING BLOCKS OF THE EMPERORS

Vespasian's Colosseum

The oft-quoted remark of Augustus, that he found Rome brick and left it marble, omits a vital ingredient of Roman building: concrete. The sheer size and spectacle of ancient Rome's most famous buildings owe everything to this humble building block. Its use was one of the Romans' greatest contributions to the history of architecture, for it enabled them not only to create vast arches, domes, and vaults—undreamed of before—but also to build at a scale and size never before attempted. The fall of the Roman Empire ultimately arrived, but great architectural monuments remain to remind us of its glory.

THE ARCH
VESPASIAN'S COLOSSEUM

Born in Riete, Titus Flavius Vespasian was the first of the new military emperors. A down-to-earth countryman with a realistic sense of humor, his dying words "I think I am in the process of becoming a god" have lived on. Along with generally restoring the city, which had burned down under Nero, he started the Colosseum, (his son, Titus, finished it in AD 80).Erected upon the swampy marsh that once held the stagnum, or lake, of Nero's Golden House, the Colosseum was vast; its dimensions underscored how much Romans had come to value audacious size. The main architectural motif were the arches—hundreds of them in four ascending birthday tiers, each tier adorned with a different style of column: Doric, Ionic, Corinthian, and Corinthian pilaster. Inside each arch was a statue (all of which have disappeared). Under these arches, called fornices, ancient Romans were fond of looking for bedfellows (so famously said the great poet Ovid), so much so that these arches gave a new word to the English language.

Nero's Domus Aurea

Hadrian's Pantheon

THE VAULT
NERO'S DOMUS AUREA

Most notorious of the emperors, but by no means the worst, Nero had domestic and foreign policies that were popular at first. However, his increasing megalomania was apparent in the size of his Domus Aurea, the "Golden House," so huge that the cry went up "All Rome has become a villa." Taking advantage of the Great Fire of AD 64, Nero wanted to re-create his seaside villa at Baia (outside Naples) right in the middle of Rome, building a vast palace of polychrome marble with a dining room with perforated ivory ceilings so that diners could be showered with flowers and perfume (designed by Fabullus, Nero's decorator). But the masterstrokes were the gigantic vaulted rooms—the Room of the Owls and the octagonal center room—designed by Nero's architects, Severus and Celer. Greek post-and-lintel architecture was banished for these highly dramatic spaces created by soaring vaults. You can still tour the ruins of Nero's "villa," but his 120-foot-high colossal bronze statue gave way to make room for the Colosseum.

THE DOME
HADRIAN'S PANTHEON

The concrete Roman dome at its most impressive can be seen in the Pantheon (around AD 125), a massive construction measuring 141 feet across. It is a fascinating feat of both design and engineering, for it is modeled on a sphere, the height of the supporting walls being equal to the radius of the dome. Larger than Saint Peter's, this dome of domes was constructed by the greatest Imperial builder of them all, the Emperor Hadrian. Poised on top of the dome's mighty concrete ring, the five levels of trapezoid-shaped coffers represent the course of the five then-known planets and their concentric spheres. Then, ruling over them, comes the sun, represented symbolically and literally by the so-called oculus—the giant "eye" open to the sky at the top. The heavenly symmetry is further paralleled by the coffers themselves: 28 to each row, the number of lunar cycles. In the center of each would have shone a small bronze star. In the 17th century, the Barberini popes had all of the dome's famous gilt trim stripped away and melted down so that it could be used to decorate the Vatican.

rooms and suites; nice restaurant and outdoor bar; screening room. **Cons:** rates increase based on occupancy; no spa; not many restaurants in the immediate vicinity. [$] *Rooms from: €500* ✉ *Via del Velabro 16, Aventino* ☎ *06/97619197* 🌐 *www.palazzovelabro.it* 🛏 *32 rooms* 🍴 *No Meals* [M] *Circo Massimo.*

The Imperial Forums

A compound of five grandly conceived complexes flanked with colonnades, the Fori Imperiali contain monuments of triumph, law courts, and temples. The complexes were tacked on to the Roman Forum, from the time of Julius Caesar in the 1st century BC until Trajan in the very early 2nd century AD, to accommodate the ever-growing need for administrative buildings as well as grand monuments.

From Piazza del Colosseo, head northwest on Via dei Fori Imperiali toward Piazza Venezia. Among the Fori Imperiali along the avenue, you can see the Foro di Cesare (Forum of Caesar) and the Foro di Augusto (Forum of Augustus). The grandest was the Foro di Traiano (Forum of Trajan), with its huge semicircular Mercati di Traiano and the Colonna Traiana (Trajan's Column).

You can walk through part of Trajan's Markets on the Via Alessandrina and visit the Museo dei Fori Imperiali, which presents the Imperial Forums and shows how they would have been used through ancient fragments, artifacts, and modern multimedia.

Sights

Colonna di Traiano (*Trajan's Column*)
RUINS | The remarkable series of reliefs spiraling up this column, which has stood in this spot since AD 113, celebrate the emperor's victories over the Dacians in today's Romania. The scenes on the column are an important primary source for information on the Roman army and its tactics. An inscription on the base declares that the column was erected in Trajan's honor and that its height corresponds to the height of the hill that was razed to create a level area for the grandiose Foro di Traiano. The emperor's ashes, no longer here, were kept in a golden urn in a chamber at the column's base; his statue stood atop the column until 1587, when the pope had it replaced with a statue of St. Peter. ✉ *Via del Foro di Traiano, Monti* [M] *Cavour.*

Foro di Augusto (*Forum of Augustus*)
RUINS | These ruins, along with those of the Foro di Nerva, on the northeast side of Via dei Fori Imperiali, give only a hint of what must have been impressive edifices. The three columns are all that remain of the Temple of Mars Ultor. ✉ *Via dei Fori Imperiali, Monti* 🌐 *www.coopculture.it* 🎫 *€22 2-day Full Experience ticket required* [M] *Colosseo.*

Foro di Cesare (*Forum of Caesar*)
RUINS | In an attempt to rival the Roman Forum, Julius Caesar had this extension built in the middle of the 1st century BC. Each year without fail, on the Ides of March, flowers are laid at the foot of Caesar's statue. ✉ *Via dei Fori Imperiali, Monti* ☎ *06/0608* 🌐 *www.coopculture.it* 🎫 *€16 24-hour ticket required* [M] *Colosseo.*

Foro di Traiano (*Forum of Trajan*)
RUINS | Of all the Fori Imperiali, Trajan's was the grandest and most imposing, a veritable city unto itself. Designed by architect Apollodorus of Damascus, it comprised a vast basilica, two libraries, and a colonnade laid out around the square—all at one time covered with rich marble ornamentation. Adjoining the forum were the Mercati di Traiano (Trajan's Markets), a huge, multilevel, brick complex of shops, taverns, walkways, and terraces, as well as administrative offices involved in the mammoth task of feeding the city.

The Museo dei Fori Imperiali (Imperial Forums Museum) takes advantage of the Forum's soaring vaulted spaces to showcase archaeological fragments and sculptures while presenting a video re-creation of the original complex. In addition, the series of terraced rooms offers an impressive overview of the entire forum. A pedestrian walkway, the Via Alessandrina, also allows for an excellent (and free) view of Trajan's Forum.

To build a complex of this magnitude, Apollodorus and his patrons clearly had great confidence, not to mention almost unlimited means and cheap labor at their disposal (readily provided by slaves captured in Trajan's Dacian Wars). The complex also contained two semicircular lecture halls, one at either end, which are thought to have been associated with the libraries in Trajan's Forum. The markets' architectural centerpiece is the enormous curved wall, or *exedra*, that shores up the side of the Quirinal Hill excavated by Apollodorus's gangs of laborers. Covered galleries and streets were constructed at various levels, following the exedra's curves and giving the complex a strikingly modern appearance.

As you enter the markets, a large, vaulted hall stands in front of you. Two stories of shops and offices rise up on either side. Head for the flight of steps at the far end that leads down to Via Biberatica. (*Bibere* is Latin for "to drink," and the shops that open onto the street are believed to have been taverns.) Then head back to the three retail and administrative tiers that line the upper levels of the great exedra and look out over the remains of the Forum. Empty and bare today, the cubicles were once ancient Rome's busiest market stalls. Though it seems to be part of the market, the Torre delle Milizie (Tower of the Militia), the tall brick tower that is a prominent feature of Rome's skyline, was actually built in the early 1200s. ⊠ *Via IV Novembre 94, Monti*

☎ *06/0608* ⊕ *www.mercatiditraiano.it* ⊠ *€11.50 (€13 with exhibits)* Ⓜ *Cavour.*

★ Santi Cosma e Damiano

CHURCH | Home to one of the most striking early Christian mosaics, this church was adapted in the 6th century from two ancient buildings: the library in Vespasian's Forum of Peace and a hall of the Temple of Romulus (dedicated to the son of Maxentius who had been named for Rome's founder). In the apse is the famous AD 530 mosaic of Christ in Glory. It reveals how popes at the time strove to re-create the splendor of imperial audience halls into Christian churches: Christ wears a gold, Roman-style toga, and his pose recalls that of an emperor addressing his subjects. He floats on a blue sky streaked with a flaming sunset—a miracle of tesserae mosaic work. To his side are the figures of Saint Peter and Saint Paul, who represent Cosmas and Damian (patron saints of doctors), two Syrian benefactors whose charity was such that they were branded Christians and condemned to death. Beneath this awe-inspiring work is an enchanting mosaic frieze of holy lambs. ⊠ *Via dei Fori Imperiali 1, Monti* ☎ *06/6920441* ⊕ *www.cosmadamiano.com* Ⓜ *Colosseo.*

The Colosseum and Environs

Legend has it that, as long as the Colosseum stands, Rome will stand—and when Rome falls, so will the world. No visit to Rome is complete without a trip to the obstinate oval that has been the iconic symbol of the city for centuries. Looming over a group of the Roman Empire's most magnificent monuments to imperial wealth and power, the Colosseum was the gigantic sports arena built by Vespasian and Titus. To its west stands the Arco di Costantino, a majestic, ornate triumphal arch, built solely as a tribute to the emperor Constantine; victorious armies purportedly marched under it on their return from war. To the east of the Colosseum, hidden under the Colle Oppio, is Nero's opulent Domus Aurea, a palace that stands as testimony to the lavish lifestyles of the emperors; it is accessible every day by joining a guided tour. Check ⊕ *www.coopculture.it* for details and reservations.

◉ Sights

Arco di Costantino (*Arch of Constantine*)
RUINS | This majestic arch was erected in AD 315 to commemorate Constantine's victory over Maxentius at the Milvian Bridge. It was just before this battle, in AD 312, that Constantine—the emperor who converted Rome to Christianity—legendarily had a vision of a cross and heard the words, "In this sign thou shalt conquer." Many of the costly marble decorations for the arch were scavenged from earlier monuments, both saving money and placing Constantine in line with the great emperors of the past. It is easy to picture ranks of Roman centurions marching under the great barrel vault. ⊠ *Piazza del Colosseo, Monti* Ⓜ *Colosseo.*

★ **Colosseum** (*Colosseo*)
RUINS | The most spectacular extant edifice of ancient Rome, the Colosseum has a history that is half gore, half glory. Once able to house 50,000 spectators, it was built to impress Romans with its spectacles involving wild animals and fearsome gladiators from the farthest reaches of the empire. Senators had marble seats up front, the vestal virgins took the ringside position, the plebs sat in wooden tiers at the back, and the masses watched from the top tier. Looming over all was the amazing velarium, an ingenious system of sail-like awnings rigged on ropes and maneuvered by sailors from the imperial fleet, who would unfurl them to protect the arena's occupants from sun or rain.

From the second floor, you can get a bird's-eye view of the hypogeum: the subterranean passageways that were the architectural engine rooms that made the slaughter above proceed like clockwork. In a scene prefiguring something from Dante's *Inferno*, hundreds of beasts would wait to be launched via a series of slave-powered hoists and lifts into the bloodthirsty sand of the arena above.

Designed by order of the emperor Vespasian in AD 72, and completed by his son Titus in AD 80, the arena has a circumference of 573 yards, and its external walls were built with travertine from nearby Tivoli. Its construction was a remarkable feat of engineering, for it stands on marshy terrain reclaimed by draining an artificial lake that formed part of the vast palace of Nero. Originally known as the Flavian amphitheater (Vespasian's and Titus's family name was Flavius), it came to be known as the Colosseum thanks to a colossal gilded bronze statue which once stood nearby.

The legend made famous by the Venerable Bede says that as long as the Colosseum stands, Rome will stand; and when Rome falls, so will the world … not that the prophecy deterred medieval and Renaissance princes and popes from using the Colosseum as a quarry. In the 19th century, poets came to view the arena by moonlight; today, mellow golden spotlights make the arena a spectacular sight at night, and evening visits are possible with guided tours from May through October.

■**TIP**→ **To enter, book a combination ticket (with the Roman Forum and Palatine Hill) in advance online, though if you have a Roma Pass, you can use it.**

Tickets cost €16 plus a €2 online booking surcharge. Aim for early or late slots to minimize lines, as even the preferential lanes get busy in the middle of the day. Alternatively, you can book a tour online with a company (do your research to

Hollywood got it wrong, historians got it right: plenty of gladiators died in the Colosseum, but early Christians only met their tragic fate in the nearby Circus Maximus arena.

make sure it's reputable) that lets you skip the line. Avoid the tours sold on the spot around the Colosseum; although you can skip the lines, the tour guides tend to be dry, the tour groups huge, and the tour itself rushed. To see the arena or the underground, you must purchase a special timed-entry ticket with those features, though the arena is included if you buy the Roman Forum–Palatine complex €22 two-day Full Experience ticket. ⊠ *Piazza del Colosseo, Colosseo* ☎ *06/39967700* ⊕ *www.coopculture. it* ⊠ *Requires either the €16 24-hour ticket or the €22 Full Experience ticket (can include the arena for no additional fee, but it must be specified during the purchase)* Ⓜ *Colosseo.*

Domus Aurea (*Golden House of Nero*)
RUINS | Legend has it that Nero fiddled while Rome burned. Fancying himself a great actor and poet, he played, as it turns out, his harp to accompany his recital of "The Destruction of Troy" while gazing at the flames of Rome's catastrophic fire of AD 64. Anti-Neronian

historians propagandized that Nero, in fact, had set the Great Fire to clear out a vast tract of the city center to build his new palace. Today's historians discount this as historical folderol (going so far as to point to the fact that there was a full moon on the evening of July 19, hardly the propitious occasion to commit arson).

Regardless, Nero did get to build his new palace, the extravagant Domus Aurea (Golden House)—a vast "suburban villa" that was inspired by the emperor's pleasure palace at Baia on the Bay of Naples. His new digs were huge and sumptuous, with a facade of pure gold; seawater piped into the baths; decorations of mother-of-pearl, fretted ivory, and other precious materials; and vast gardens. It was said that after completing this gigantic house, Nero exclaimed, "Now I can live like a human being!" Note that access to the site is exclusively via guided tours that use virtual reality headsets for part of the presentation. Booking ahead is essential. ⊠ *Viale della Domus Aurea 1, Monti* ☎ *06/39967700 booking information* ⊕ *www.coopcul-ture.it* 🎫 *€18 including booking fee and guided visit (Mon.–Thurs. only); €23 including booking fee, guided visit, and virtual reality experience (Fri.–Sun. only)* ⚠ *Reservations essential* Ⓜ *Colosseo.*

Museo delle Mura

RUINS | Rome's first walls were erected in the 6th century BC, but the ancient city greatly expanded over the next few centuries, and when Rome was at its peak, it didn't need walls. In the 3rd century AD, however, Emperor Aurelian commissioned a 12-mile wall to protect the city. Although many considered this a sign of weakness, it was more than a century before those walls were first breached in a siege that would herald the end of the empire. The ancient walls eventually became the fortifications of the papal city, and remained in use for 16 centuries until the unification of Italy in 1870. Studding the Aurelian Walls were 18 main gates, the best preserved of which is the Porta di San Sebastiano at the entrance to the Via Appia Antica. This gate is also home to a small museum that allows you to walk a section of the ancient ramparts and take in some truly wonderful views. Note that the museum closes relatively early, at 2 pm. ⊠ *Via di Porta San Sebastiano 18, Via Appia Antica* 🕿 *06/060608* ⊕ *www.museodellemuraro-ma.it* ☾ *Closed Mon.*

 Restaurants

Aroma

$$$$ | **MODERN ITALIAN** | The panoramas from this Michelin-starred restaurant atop the Palazzo Manfredi Hotel are undeniably stunning; it's the best unobstructed view of the Colosseum in Rome, so ask for a table on the terrace. With chef Giuseppe Di Iorio's tasting menus, each dish is an innovative twist on Italy's top cuisine. **Known for:** intimate 28-seat restaurant; sustainable fish and local produce; gluten-free tasting menu. 💲 *Average main: €150* ⊠ *Palazzo Manfredi, Via Labicana 125, Colosseo* 🕿 *06/77591380* ⊕ *www.aromarestaurant.it* ☾ *No lunch Mon.* ☞ *Tasting menus only* Ⓜ *Colosseo.*

Hotels

Palazzo Manfredi

$$$$ | **HOTEL** | If you dream of waking up to head-on views of the Colosseum, book into this boutique hotel, which is set in a 17th-century palazzo built over the ruins of the Ludus Magnus, the gymnasium used by Roman gladiators, and offers refined luxury. **Pros:** incredible views; unparalleled location; excellent restaurant and cocktail bar. **Cons:** not all rooms have Colosseum views; some guests complain about noise; no spa. 💲 *Rooms from: €600* ⊠ *Via Labicana 125, Colosseo* 🕿 *06/77591380* ⊕ *www.palazzoman-fredi.com* ⇲ *23 rooms* 🍴 *No Meals* Ⓜ *Colosseo.*

Nightlife

BARS

★ **The Court**

COCKTAIL BARS | For a winning combination of creative cocktails and incredible views of the Colosseum, this bar in Palazzo Manfredi can't be beat. Bar manager Matteo "Zed" Zamberlan cut his teeth in New York's top drinking establishments, and here his creativity is on full display. The cocktails are pricey, but they come with a bounty of snacks from the hotel's acclaimed restaurant. ⊠ *Via Labicana 125, Colosseo* 🕿 *06/77591380* ⊕ *www.manfredihotels.com/the-court-new* Ⓜ *Colosseo.*

Monti

As the hill starts to slope downward from Termini station, right around Santa Maria Maggiore, the streets become cobblestone, the palazzos prettier, and the boutiques higher-end. This is the area known as Monti, the oldest rione in

Rome. Gladiators, prostitutes, and even Caesar made their homes in this area that stretches from Santa Maria Maggiore down to the Forum. Today, Monti is one of the city's best-loved neighborhoods, known for its appealing mix of medieval streets, old-school trattorias, and hip boutiques.

 ## Sights

Palazzo delle Esposizioni

ART MUSEUM | The late-19th-century Palazzo delle Esposizioni holds temporary exhibitions showcasing everything from Etruscan art to Pixar movies. The complex also has a great bookshop (including some books in English), a coffee bar, and a restaurant. ⊠ Via Nazionale 194, Monti ☎ 06/696271 ⊕ www.palazzoesposizioni. it ⌨ €12.50; costs vary by exhibition ⊗ Closed Mon. Ⓜ Repubblica.

★ San Pietro in Vincoli

CHURCH | Michelangelo's *Moses,* carved in the early 16th century for the never-completed tomb of Pope Julius II, has put this church on the map. The tomb was to include dozens of statues and stand nearly 40 feet tall when installed in St. Peter's Basilica. But only three statues—*Moses* and the two that flank it here, *Leah* and *Rachel*—had been completed when Julius died. Julius's successor as pope, from the rival Medici family, had other plans for Michelangelo, and the tomb was abandoned unfinished.

The fierce power of this remarkable sculpture dominates its setting. People say that you can see the sculptor's profile in the lock of Moses's beard right under his lip and that the pope's profile can also be seen. As for the rest of the church, St. Peter takes second billing to Moses. The reputed sets of chains (*vincoli*) that bound St. Peter during his imprisonment by the Romans in both Jerusalem and Rome are in a bronze and crystal urn under the main altar. Other treasures include a 7th-century mosaic of St. Sebastian, in front of the second altar to the left of the main altar, and, by the door, the tomb of the Pollaiuolo brothers, two 15th-century Florentine artists. ⊠ Piazza di San Pietro in Vincoli, Monti ☎ 06/97844952 Ⓜ Cavour.

★ Santa Maria Maggiore

CHURCH | Despite its florid 18th-century facade, Santa Maria Maggiore is one of the city's oldest churches, built around 440 by Pope Sixtus III. One of Rome's four great pilgrimage churches, it's also the city center's best example of an early Christian basilica—one of the immense, hall-like structures derived from ancient Roman civic buildings and divided into thirds by two great rows of columns marching up the nave. The other three major basilicas in Rome (San Giovanni in Laterano, St. Peter's, and St. Paul Outside the Walls) have been largely rebuilt. Paradoxically, the major reason why this church is such a striking example of early Christian design is that the same man who built the undulating exteriors circa 1740, Ferdinando Fuga, also conscientiously restored the interior, throwing out later additions and, crucially, replacing a number of the great columns.

Precious 5th-century mosaics high on the nave walls and on the triumphal arch in front of the main altar bear splendid testimony to the basilica's venerable age. Those along the nave show 36 scenes from the Old Testament (unfortunately, tough to see clearly without binoculars), and those on the arch illustrate the Annunciation and the Youth of Christ. The resplendent carved-wood ceiling dates from the early 16th century; it's supposed to have been gilded with the first gold brought from the New World. The inlaid marble pavement (called cosmatesque, after the family of master artisans who developed the technique) in the central nave is even older, dating from the 12th century.

Did You Know?

"Sistine" refers to anything related to a pope with the name Sixtus, and Rome has several sistine chapels. The Monti district's Capella Sistina, in the basilica known as the Santa Maria Maggiore, was commissioned by Pope Sixtus V, whereas the Vatican's more famous one was commissioned by Pope Sixtus IV.

The Cappella Sistina (Sistine Chapel), in the right-hand transept, was created by architect Domenico Fontana for Pope Sixtus V in 1585. Elaborately decorated with precious marbles "liberated" from the monuments of ancient Rome, the chapel includes a lower-level museum in which some 13th-century sculptures by Arnolfo da Cambio are all that's left of what was the once richly endowed chapel of the *presepio* (Christmas crèche), looted during the Sack of Rome in 1527.

Directly opposite, on the church's other side, stands the Cappella Paolina (Pauline Chapel), a rich Baroque setting for the tombs of the Borghese popes Paul V—who commissioned the chapel in 1611 with the declared intention of outdoing Sixtus's chapel across the nave—and Clement VIII. The Cappella Sforza (Sforza Chapel) next door was designed by Michelangelo and completed by Della Porta. Just right of the altar, next to his father, lies Gian Lorenzo Bernini; his monument is an engraved slab, as humble as the tombs of his patrons are grand. Above the loggia, the outside mosaic of Christ raising his hand in blessing is one of Rome's most beautiful sights, especially when lighted at night. ⊠ *Piazza di Santa Maria Maggiore, Monti* ☎ *06/69886800* Ⓜ *Termini.*

★ **Santa Prassede**

CHURCH | This small, inconspicuous, 9th-century church is known above all for the exquisite Cappella di San Zenone, just to the left of the entrance. It gleams with vivid mosaics that reflect their Byzantine inspiration. Though much less classical and naturalistic than the earlier mosaics of Santa Pudenziana, they are no less splendid, and the composition of four angels hovering on the sky-blue vault is one of the masterstrokes of Byzantine art. Note the square halo over the head of Theodora, mother of St. Paschal I, the pope who built this church. It indicates that she was still alive when she was depicted by the artist.

The chapel also contains one curious relic: a miniature pillar, supposedly part of the column at which Christ was flogged during the Passion. It was brought to Rome in the 13th century. Over the main altar, the magnificent mosaics on the arch and apse are also in rigid Byzantine style. In them, Pope Paschal I wears the square halo of the living and holds a model of his church. ⊠ *Via di Santa Prassede 9/a, Monti* ☎ *06/4882456* Ⓜ *Cavour.*

★ **Santa Pudenziana**

CHURCH | Apart from Ravenna, Rome has some of Italy's most opulent mosaics, and this church has the earliest example. Commissioned during the papacy of Innocent I, its early 5th-century apse mosaic, depicting Christ teaching the apostles, sits above a Baroque altarpiece surrounded by a bevy of florid 18th-century paintings. The mosaic is remarkable for its iconography; at the center sits Christ Enthroned, shown as an emperor or as a philosopher holding court, surrounded by his apostles. Each apostle faces the spectator, literally rubbing shoulders with his companion (unlike later hieratic styles in which each figure is isolated) and bears an individualized expression. Above these figures and a landscape symbolizing Heavenly Jerusalem float the signs of the four evangelists in a blue sky flecked with the orange of sunset, made from thousands of *tesserae* (mosaic tiles).

To either side of Christ, saints Praxedes and Pudentiana hold wreaths over the heads of saints Peter and Paul. These two women were actually daughters of the Roman senator Pudens (probably the one mentioned in 2 Timothy 4:21), whose family befriended both apostles. During the persecutions of Nero, both sisters collected the blood of many martyrs before suffering their fate. Pudentiana transformed her house into a church, but her namesake church was constructed over a 2nd-century bathhouse. Beyond the sheer beauty of the mosaic work, the size, rich detail, and number of figures make this both the last gasp of ancient Roman art and one of the first major works of Early Christian art. ✉ *Via Urbana 160, Monti* ☎ *06/4817292* 🌐 *www.stpudenziana.org* 🕒 *Closed Sun.* [M] *Repubblica.*

🍴 Restaurants

La Taverna dei Fori Imperiali
$$ | **ROMAN** | Tucked on a cobblestone street at the edge of Monti, this cozy little family-run restaurant is one of the best places to eat near the Forum. An eclectic collection of sketches, photos, and paintings decorates the walls, and the menu offers traditional Roman trattoria fare as well as some creative twists on the classics, like cacio e pepe, usually a simple dish of pasta in a peppery cheese sauce but here featuring black truffle, and burrata-stuffed ravioli. **Known for:** la gricia pasta with seasonal fruit; cozy space with brick arches; friendly servers. [$] *Average main: €18* ✉ *Via della Madonna dei Monti 9, Monti* ☎ *06/6798643* 🌐 *www.lataverna-deiforiimperiali.com* 🕒 *Closed Tues.* [M] *Cavour.*

Rocco Ristorante
$$ | **ROMAN** | **FAMILY** | This slightly vintage, slightly trendy trattoria has a timeless quality, with terrazzo floors, vaulted brick ceilings, white tablecloths, vintage photos, sketches, and a Pink Floyd poster lending the place a hip yet easygoing vibe that attracts people of all ages. Or maybe it's the owner, a real Roman character who presides over the dining room, coming to your table and reciting the menu—written on a chalkboard—in case you can't read it. **Known for:** Italian comfort food; cool, welcoming atmosphere; local favorite spot. [$] *Average main: €18* ✉ *Via Giovanni Lanza 93, Monti* ☎ *06/4870942* 🌐 *www.instagram.com/roccoristorante* 🕒 *Closed Sun. No dinner Sat.* [M] *Vittorio Emanuele, Cavour.*

☕ Coffee and Quick Bites

★ **Fatamorgana Monti**
$ | **ICE CREAM** | **FAMILY** | The emphasis is on all-natural ingredients at this woman-owned gelateria, which has several locations in Rome, including one near Campo de' Fiori and another in Trastevere. Flavors change often but might include favorites like stracciatella (with chocolate shavings) and hazelnut as well as more unusual flavors like matcha or carrot cake. **Known for:** all natural ingredients; unusual flavors; gluten-free with many vegan options. [$] *Average main: €3* ✉ *Piazza degli Zingari 5, Monti* ☎ *06/48906955* 🌐 *www.gelateriafatamorgana.com* [M] *Cavour.*

★ **Zia Rosetta**
$ | **SANDWICHES** | Translating to "Aunt Rosetta," the name of this tiny sandwich shop is a play on words, since rosetta is not just a female name but also a type of roll commonly found in Rome. Here the rolls are used to make gourmet sandwiches with delicious combinations of meat, cheeses, veggies, or fish, such as the "Peggy Rockefeller" with prosciutto, crunchy parmigiano reggiano, and eggplant or the "Sora Lella" with anchovies, stracciatella, and puntarelle. **Known for:** gourmet sandwiches; vegan and gluten-free options; seasonal specials. [$] *Average main: €7* ✉ *Via Urbana 54, Monti* ☎ *06/31052516* 🌐 *www.ziarosetta.com* [M] *Cavour.*

🛏 Hotels

Nerva Boutique Hotel
$$$ | **HOTEL** | Step out of this charming, clean, well-run hotel, and you'll feel like you've landed in the middle of an ancient imperial stomping ground; a stone's throw from the Forum, it's surrounded by the breathtaking splendor of ancient ruins. **Pros:** close to the Forum; friendly staff; modern design. **Cons:** some showers are tiny; single rooms are only slightly bigger than a closet; breakfast

not included. $ *Rooms from: €300* ✉ *Via Tor de' Conti 3/4, Monti* ☎ *06/6781835* ⊕ *www.hotelnerva.com* ⤴ *18 rooms* ⍟ *No Meals* Ⓜ *Cavour, Colosseo.*

Nightlife

Lately, Monti has been wearing the crown as the "it" neighborhood, reigning supreme as an all-ages hipster hangout with trendy bars, top-notch restaurants, and artisan shops, as well as picturesque piazzas.

BARS

★ Ai Tre Scalini

WINE BAR | An ivy-covered wine bar in the center of Monti, Rome's trendiest 'hood, Ai Tre Scalini has a warm and cozy menu of delicious antipasti and light entrées to go along with its enticing wine list. After about 8 pm, be prepared to wait—this is one extremely popular spot with locals and they don't take reservations. ✉ *Via Panisperna 251, Monti* ☎ *06/48907495* ⊕ *www.aitrescalini.org* Ⓜ *Cavour.*

Blackmarket Hall

COCKTAIL BARS | This underground cocktail bar and lounge feels like a cross between a speakeasy and a gastropub. Mismatched vintage tables and chairs, rugs, exposed brick walls, and black-and-white photographs give it a shabby chic vibe. The creative cocktails are the main draw, but the burgers are also good. From 6 pm until 8 pm, you can get an aperitivo with a drink and a nice selection of small bites for €13–16. ✉ *Via de' Ciancaleoni 31, Monti* ☎ *349/1995295* ⊕ *www.blackmarkethall.com* Ⓜ *Cavour.*

★ Drink Kong

COCKTAIL BARS | Irish-Italian bartender Patrick Pistolesi worked his way up the ranks at establishments in Rome and New York City before opening this cocktail bar that's regarded as one of the world's best. His first solo venture is an expression of his bold aesthetic and philosophy of hospitality. Inspired by the Japanese cartoons he watched as a kid, the space is dark and dramatic with flashes of neon. The creative cocktails feature ingredients like lemongrass cordial and miso and arrive at your table impressively quickly. Pair them with Asian-inspired snacks like pork dumplings or codfish-filled bao. ✉ *Piazza di San Martino ai Monti 8, Monti* ☎ *06/23488666* ⊕ *www.drinkkong.com* Ⓜ *Cavour.*

JAZZ CLUBS

Charity Café

LIVE MUSIC | An intimate club with live music performances nightly, Charity hosts local and international jazz musicians in a relaxed atmosphere. ✉ *Via Panisperna 68, Monti* ☎ *06/47825881* ⊕ *www.charitycafe.it* ⊘ *Closed Mon.* Ⓜ *Cavour.*

Shopping

CLOTHING

Humana Vintage

VINTAGE | Run by the non-profit organization Humana People to People, which implements sustainable development projects in Africa, Asia, and Latin America, this shop is a popular destination for vintage and second-hand clothing for men and women. The racks are lined with all kinds of apparel from the 1960s through the '90s, from Levis jeans and Converse sneakers to made-in-Italy blazers and leather bags. There are also shops on Via Cavour and Corso Vittorio Emanuele II. ✉ *Via Leonina 38, Monti* ☎ *06/483831* ⊕ *www.humanavintage.it* Ⓜ *Cavour.*

Kokoro

CLOTHING | This pared-down little boutique on one of Monti's most charming streets sells women's clothes designed by owners Benedetta Piccirilli and David Anav. Their pieces tend to be familiar silhouettes made with colorful Italian fabrics and often feature botanical or Asian-inspired prints. Although each of their off-the-rack pieces is one-of-a-kind, they also make garments made to

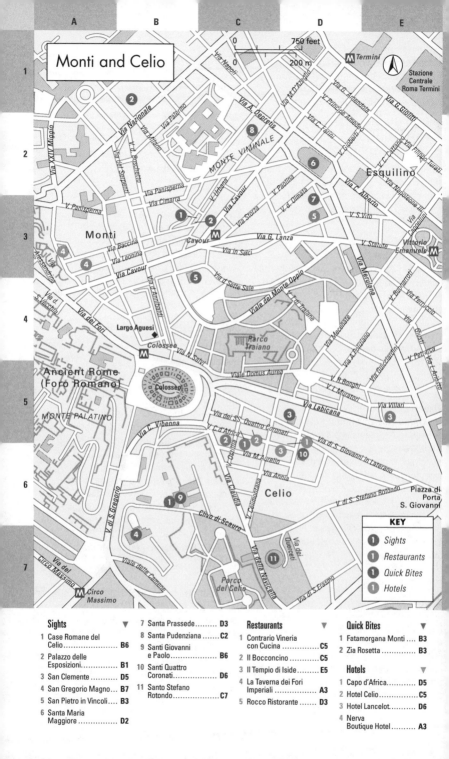

Monti and Celio

0 ————— 750 feet
0 ————— 200 m

Termini

Stazione
Centrale
Roma Termini

MONTE VIMINALE

Esquilino

Monti

Cavour

Vittorio
Emanuele

Ancient Rome
(Foro Romano)

MONTE PALATINO

Colosseo

Largo Aguesi

Colosseo

Parco
Traiano

Celio

Piazza di
Porta
S. Giovanni

Circo
Massimo

Parco
del Celio

KEY
- ① Sights
- ① Restaurants
- ① Quick Bites
- ① Hotels

measure. ✉ *Via del Boschetto 75, Monti* ☎ *349/7434694 WhatsApp* ⊕ *www.koko-roshop.it* Ⓜ *Cavour.*

★ **Sacripante**

CLOTHING | This tiny Monti art gallery/boutique/bar has some of the most sophisticated, retro-inspired garments in Rome. Its owner, Carlotta Cerulli, sells clothes by her mother, Wilma Silvestri, who cleverly combines vintage and contemporary fabrics for her label Le Gallinelle, creating stylish fashions with a modern edge made for everyday wear. ✉ *Via Panisperna 59, Monti* ☎ *06/48903495* ⊕ *www.facebook.com/sacripantegallery* Ⓜ *Cavour.*

FOOD

Grezzo Raw Chocolate

CHOCOLATE | This chocolate shop opened in 2014 and claims to be the first raw pastry shop in the world. Everything is 100% organic, vegan, gluten-free, dairy-free, and made without refined sugar—and nothing is cooked above 108 degrees Fahrenheit. If you're skeptical, seeing (or, in this case, tasting) is believing. The pralines and truffles are as delicious as traditional ones, and there are also cookies, organic nut and chocolate spreads, pastries, and gelato. There are also locations in the Jewish Ghetto and Parioli. ✉ *Via Urbana 130, Monti* ☎ *06/483443* ⊕ *www.grezzorawchocolate.com* Ⓜ *Cavour.*

JEWELRY

Art Privé Gioielli

JEWELRY & WATCHES | On one of Monti's steeply sloping streets is the small jewelry shop where Tiziana Salzano and Antonio Marino make elegant necklaces and earrings using the finest gold or silver and a combination of semiprecious gemstones. Most pieces are unique, so if you feel something tug at your heart be sure to grab it. They also take orders for bespoke pieces. ✉ *Via Panisperna 51, Monti* ☎ *06/47826347* ⊕ *www.facebook.com/ArtPriveGioielli* Ⓜ *Cavour.*

L'Artigianaio

JEWELRY & WATCHES | "The Artisan" is the place to go for handmade watches and rare vintage timepieces. The store's expert watchmakers specialize in nostalgic mechanical watches and chronographs from the early 1900s through the 1970s. Have an heirloom piece that has stopped working or that needs a little fine-tuning? Bring it to the shop, and the owners will get it ticking again in no time. ✉ *Via Urbana 103A, Monti* ☎ *06/4742284* Ⓜ *Cavour.*

Celio

Bordering Monti, from the Colosseum west toward Piazza San Giovanni, the Celio neighborhood is a tranquil, lovely residential area replete with medieval churches and ruins. Sights not to miss here include the Basilica of San Clemente, the church of Santi Quattro Coronati, and the church of Santo Stefano Rotondo.

 Sights

Case Romane del Celio

RUINS | Formerly accessible only through the church of Santi Giovanni e Paolo, this important ancient Roman excavation was opened in 2002 as a museum in its own right. An underground honeycomb of rooms, the site consists of the lower levels of a so-called *insula,* or apartment block, the heights of which were a wonder to ancient Roman contemporaries.

Through the door on the left of the Clivo di Scauro lane, a portico leads to the Room of the Genie, where painted figures grace the walls virtually untouched over two millennia. Farther on is the Confessio altar of Saint John and Saint Paul, officials at Constantine's court who were executed under Julian the Apostate. Still lower is the Antiquarium, where state-of-the-art lighting showcases amphorae, pots, and ancient Roman bricks, with stamps so fresh they might have been imprinted yesterday. ✉ *Via del Clivio di Scauro, Celio* ⊕ *www.caseromanedelcelio.it* 🖼 *€8* ⊘ *Closed Tues. and Thurs.* Ⓜ *Colosseo.*

★ San Clemente

CHURCH | One of the most impressive archaeological sites in Rome, San Clemente is a historical triple-decker. A 12th-century church was built on top of a 4th-century church, which had been built over a 2nd-century pagan temple to the god Mithras and 1st-century Roman apartments. The layers were uncovered in 1857, when a curious prior, Friar Joseph Mullooly, started excavations beneath the present basilica. Today, you can descend to explore all three.

The upper church (at street level) is a gem in its own right. In the apse, a glittering 12th-century mosaic shows Jesus on a cross that turns into a living tree. Green acanthus leaves swirl and teem with small scenes of everyday life. Early Christian symbols, including doves, vines, and fish, decorate the 4th-century marble choir screens. In the left nave, the Castiglioni chapel holds frescoes painted around 1400 by the Florentine artist Masolino da Panicale (1383–1440), a key figure in the introduction of realism and one-point perspective into Renaissance painting. Note the large Crucifixion and scenes from the lives of saints Catherine, Ambrose, and Christopher, plus the Annunciation (over the entrance).

To the right of the sacristy (and bookshop), descend the stairs to the 4th-century church, used until 1084, when it was damaged beyond repair during a siege of the area by the Norman prince Robert Guiscard. Still intact are some vibrant 11th-century frescoes depicting stories from the life of St. Clement. Don't miss the last fresco on the left, in what used to be the central nave. It includes a particularly colorful quote—including "Go on, you sons of harlots, pull!"—that's not only unusual for a religious painting,

but also one of the earliest examples of written vernacular Italian.

Descend an additional set of stairs to the Mithraeum, a shrine dedicated to the god Mithras. His cult spread from Persia and gained a foothold in Rome during the 2nd and 3rd centuries AD. Mithras was believed to have been born in a cave and was thus worshipped in cavernous, underground chambers, where initiates into the all-male cult would share a meal while reclining on stone couches, some visible here along with the altar block. Most such pagan shrines in Rome were destroyed by Christians, who often built churches over their remains, as happened here. ✉ *Via Labicana 95, Celio* ☎ *06/7740021* ⊕ *basilicasanclemente. com/eng* 🖼 *Archaeological area €10* ⚠ *Reservations required* Ⓜ *Colosseo.*

San Gregorio Magno

CHURCH | Set amid the greenery of the Celian Hill, this church wears its Baroque facade proudly. Dedicated to St. Gregory the Great (who served as pope 590–604), it was built about 750 by Pope Gregory II to commemorate his predecessor and namesake. The church of San Gregorio itself has the appearance of a typical Baroque structure, the result of remodeling in the 17th and 18th centuries. But you can still see what's said to be the stone slab on which the pious St. Gregory the Great slept; it's in the far right-hand chapel.

Outside are three chapels. The right chapel is dedicated to Gregory's mother, Saint Sylvia, and contains a Guido Reni fresco of the *Concert of Angels.* The chapel in the center, dedicated to Saint Andrew, contains two monumental frescoes showing scenes from the saint's life. They were painted at the beginning of the 17th century by Domenichino (*The Flagellation of St. Andrew*) and Guido Reni (*The Execution of St. Andrew*). It's a striking juxtaposition of the sturdy, if sometimes stiff, classicism of Domenichino with the more flamboyant and heroic Baroque manner of Guido Reni. ✉ *Piazza di San Gregorio al Celio 1, Celio* ☎ *06/7008227* ⊕ *www.monasterosangre-gorio.it* Ⓜ *Colosseo.*

★ Santi Giovanni e Paolo

CHURCH | Perched up the incline of the Clivio di Scauro—a magical time-machine of a street, where the dial seems to be stuck somewhere in the 13th century—Santi Giovanni e Paolo is an image that would tempt most landscape painters. Marked by one of Rome's finest Romanesque bell towers, it looms over a picturesque piazza. Underneath, however, are other treasures, whose excavations can be seen in the Case Romane del Celio museum.

A basilica erected on the spot was, like San Clemente, destroyed in 1084 by attacking Normans. Its half-buried columns, near the current church entrance, are visible through misty glass. The current church's origins date to the start of the 12th century, but most of the interior dates to the 17th century and later. The lovely, incongruous chandeliers are hand-me-downs from New York's Waldorf-Astoria hotel, a gift arranged by the late Cardinal Francis Spellman of New York, whose titular church this was. Spellman also initiated the excavations here in 1949. ✉ *Piazza di Santi Giovanni e Paolo 13, Celio* ☎ *06/772711* ⊕ *www.basilicassgiovanniepaolo.it* Ⓜ *Colosseo.*

Santi Quattro Coronati

CHURCH | Situated on one of those evocative cul-de-sacs in Rome where history seems to be holding its breath, this quiet citadel has resisted the tides of time and traffic. The church—which is both strongly imbued with the sanctity of the Romanesque era and marvelously redolent of the Middle Ages—dates from the 4th century and honors the Four Crowned Saints: the four brothers Severus, Severianus, Carpophorus, and Victorinus, all Roman officials who were whipped to death for their faith by Emperor Diocletian (284–305).

After its 9th-century reconstruction, the church was twice as large as it is now; the abbey was partially destroyed during the Normans' sack of Rome in 1084 but reconstructed about 30 years later. This explains the inordinate size of the apse in relation to the small nave. Don't miss the cloister, with its well-tended gardens and 12th-century fountain. The entrance is the door in the left nave; ring the bell if it's not open.

There's another medieval gem hidden away off the courtyard at the church entrance: the Chapel of San Silvestro. The chapel has remained, for the most part, as it was when consecrated in 1246. Some of the best-preserved medieval frescoes in Rome decorate the walls, telling the story of the Christian emperor Constantine's recovery from leprosy thanks to Pope Sylvester I. Note, too, the delightful *Last Judgment* fresco above the door, in which the angel on the left neatly rolls up sky and stars like a backdrop, signaling the end of the world. ✉ *Via dei Santi Quattro 20, Celio* ☎ *06/70475427* ⊕ *www.monacheagos-tinianesantiquattrocoronati.it* Ⓜ *Colosseo.*

Santo Stefano Rotondo

CHURCH | This 5th-century church is thought to have been inspired by the design of the Church of the Holy Sepulchre in Jerusalem. Its unusual round plan and timbered ceiling set it apart from most other Roman churches. So do the frescoes, which lovingly depict 34 of the goriest martyrdoms in Catholicism—a catalog, above the names of different emperors, of every type of violent death conceivable. (You've been warned: these are not for the fainthearted.) ✉ *Via Santo Stefano Rotondo 7, Celio* ☎ *06/421199* ⊕ *www.cgu.it/it/santo-stefano-rotondo* ⊗ *Closed Mon.* Ⓜ *Colosseo.*

🍴 Restaurants

★ Contrario Vineria con Cucina
$$ | MODERN ITALIAN | Wine bottles cover just about every inch of wall space in this intimate restaurant a few blocks from the Colosseum, which, perhaps unsurprisingly, also has an encyclopedic wine list. The friendly staff will happily help you navigate the options and suggest pairings for the dishes, which are rooted in tradition but often with a little twist, like the addition of artichokes in their version of *la gricia* (pasta with guanciale and pecorino romano). **Known for:** extensive wine list; slightly revisited versions of traditional dishes; welcoming, helpful staff. [$] *Average main: €24* ✉ *Via Ostilia 22, Celio* ☎ *06/7090606* 🌐 *www.ristorantecontrario.com* 🕒 *Closed Sun.* [M] *Colosseo.*

Il Bocconcino
$$ | ROMAN | This charming osteria with burgundy leather booths and vintage advertisements serves forgotten recipes from Rome and Lazio in addition to classic dishes like carbonara and an excellent cacio e pepe with homemade tonnarelli. Don't expect artichokes in July or eggplant in December—the cuisine is strictly seasonal and made using the finest local ingredients. **Known for:** forgotten Roman dishes; cozy interiors; good selection of local wines. [$] *Average main: €18* ✉ *Via Ostilia 23, Celio* ☎ *06/77079175* 🌐 *www.ilbocconcino.com* 🕒 *Closed Wed.* [M] *Colosseo.*

Il Tempio di Iside
$$$ | SEAFOOD | In an unassuming location between the Colosseum and Piazza San Giovanni, this elegant restaurant with exposed brick arches and white tablecloths serves some of the freshest seafood in the city—with tanks full of live lobsters and crabs to prove it. Owner Francesco Tripodi personally goes to the fish auctions in Fiumicino everyday and presides over the dining room, charismatically dispensing suggestions and taking orders. **Known for:** vast selection of raw appetizers; shrimp catalana; charismatic owner. [$] *Average main: €28* ✉ *Via Pietro Verri 1, Celio* ☎ *06/77204025* 🌐 *www.isideristorante.it* 🕒 *Closed Sun.* [M] *Manzoni.*

🛏 Hotels

Capo d'Africa
$$$ | HOTEL | A great location and amenities, plus outstanding customer service make a stay at this hotel worth every euro. **Pros:** quiet, comfortable rooms; fitness center and rooftop terrace; friendly, welcoming staff. **Cons:** hotel lacks a great view of Colosseum despite proximity; not a lot of restaurants in the immediate neighborhood; Wi-Fi can be spotty. [$] *Rooms from: €289* ✉ *Via Capo d'Africa 54, Celio* ☎ *06/772801* 🌐 *www.hotelcapodafrica.com* 🛏 *65 rooms* 🍴 *No Meals* [M] *Colosseo, Manzoni.*

Hotel Celio
$$ | HOTEL | At this hotel near the Colosseum, each of the small guest rooms is named after a famous Italian painter (Tiziano, Cellini, Michelangelo) and features decor that evokes the work of its namesake. **Pros:** beautiful rooftop garden; good location; comfortable beds. **Cons:** very small bathrooms; service can be iffy; breakfast not that substantial. [$] *Rooms from: €180* ✉ *Via dei Santissimi Quattro 35/c, Celio* ☎ *06/70495333* 🌐 *www.hotelcelio.com* 🛏 *20 rooms* 🍴 *Free Breakfast* [M] *Colosseo.*

Hotel Lancelot
$$$ | HOTEL | FAMILY | This friendly home-away-from-home in a quiet residential area close to the Colosseum has been run by the Khan family since 1971. **Pros:** hospitable staff; secluded and quiet; very family-friendly. **Cons:** some bathrooms are on the small side; no in-room refrigerators; some rooms are in need of redecorating. [$] *Rooms from: €210* ✉ *Via Capo d'Africa 47, Celio* ☎ *06/70450615* 🌐 *www.lancelothotel.com* 🛏 *61 rooms* 🍴 *Free Breakfast* [M] *Colosseo.*

Chapter 4

THE VATICAN

4

Updated by
Laura Itzkowitz

⊙ Sights	🍴 Restaurants	🛏 Hotels	🛍 Shopping	🍸 Nightlife
★★★★★	★★★☆☆	★★★☆☆	★★☆☆☆	★★☆☆☆

NEIGHBORHOOD SNAPSHOT

TOP REASONS TO GO

Michelangelo's Sistine Ceiling: The most sublime example of artistry in the world, this 10,000-square-foot fresco took the artist four long, neck-craning years to finish.

St. Peter's Dome: Climb the twisting Renaissance stairs to the top for a well-earned view (the elevator to the right of the main church portico goes up to the base of the dome, but there are still a lot of stairs afterwards).

Papal Blessing: Join the singing, flag-waving throngs from around the world at the Wednesday general audience on St. Peter's Square (usually only in spring, summer, and early fall).

Musei Vaticani: Savor one of the Western world's best art collections—from the *Apollo Belvedere* to Raphael's *Transfiguration.* It can be overwhelming though, so don't plan to see everything in one day.

St. Peter's Basilica: Stand in awe of the largest church in the world.

GETTING HERE

Metro stops Cipro or Ottaviano will get you within about a 10-minute walk of the entrance to the Musei Vaticani. Or, from Termini station, Bus No. 40 Express or the famously crowded No. 64 will take you to Piazza San Pietro. Both routes swing past Largo Argentina, where you can also get Bus No. 492 or 46.

A leisurely meander from the *centro storico* (historic center), across the exquisite Ponte Sant'Angelo, will take about a half hour.

HOW TO BEAT THOSE LONG LINES

■ Home to the Sistine Chapel and the Raphael rooms, the Musei Vaticani are among the most congested of all Rome's attractions, drawing up to 30,000 visitors per day in high season.

■ The best way to avoid long lines is to make reservations online for an extra €5 (⊕ *tickets.museivaticani. va/home*). Although reservations do minimize your wait time, it can still be extremely busy once you're inside, though afternoons are usually less crowded. The free Sunday is best avoided altogether unless you're feeling very brave and patient.

■ Another good idea is to schedule your visit during the Wednesday General Audience, held in the piazza of St. Peter's or at Aula Paolo VI, usually at 9:15 am when the pope is in town. To see the pope's calendar, visit ⊕ *www.papalaudience. org*.

■ Finally, you might book a tour, either with the Musei Vaticani directly or with a private agency that guarantees that you'll skip the line. The Vatican's own guided tour of the museums and Sistine Chapel, which can be booked online, costs €35 and lasts two hours.

For many, a visit to the Vatican is one of the top reasons to visit Rome, and it is a vast and majestic place, jam-packed with things to see. The Borgo and Prati are the neighborhoods immediately surrounding the Vatican, and it's worth noting that, while the Vatican may well be a priority, these neighborhoods are not the best places to choose a hotel, as they're quite far from other top sights in the city.

The Vatican

Climbing the steps to St. Peter's Basilica feels monumental, like a journey that has reached its climactic end. Suddenly, all is cool and dark … and you are dwarfed by the gargantuan nave and its magnificence.

Above is a ceiling so high it must lead to heaven itself. Great, shining marble figures of saints frozen mid-whirl loom from niches and corners. And at the end, a throne for an unseen king whose greatness, it is implied, must mirror the greatness of his palace. For this basilica is a palace, the dazzling center of power for a king and a place of supplication for his subjects. Whether his kingdom is earthly or otherwise may lie in the eye of the beholder.

The Vatican is an exercise in spirituality, requiring patience but delivering joy. Some come here for a transcendent glimpse of a heavenly Michelangelo fresco; others come in search of a direct connection with the divine. But what all visitors share, for a few hours, is an awe-inspiring landscape that offers a famous sight for every taste: rooms decorated by Raphael, antique sculptures like the *Apollo Belvedere*, famous paintings by Giotto and Bellini, and, perhaps most of all, the Sistine Chapel—for the lover of beauty, few places are as historically important as this epitome of faith and grandeur.

The story of this area's importance dates back to the 1st century, when St. Peter, the first Roman Catholic pope, was buried here. The first basilica in his honor rose on this spot some 250 years later under Emperor Constantine, who legitimized Christianity. It wasn't until the early 15th century, however, that the papacy decided to make this area not only a major spiritual center but the spot from which they would wield temporal power as well.

Today, it's difficult not to be reminded of that worldly power when you take in the massive Renaissance walls surrounding Vatican City—the international boundary of an independent sovereign state, established by the Lateran Treaty of 1929 between the Holy See and Mussolini's government.

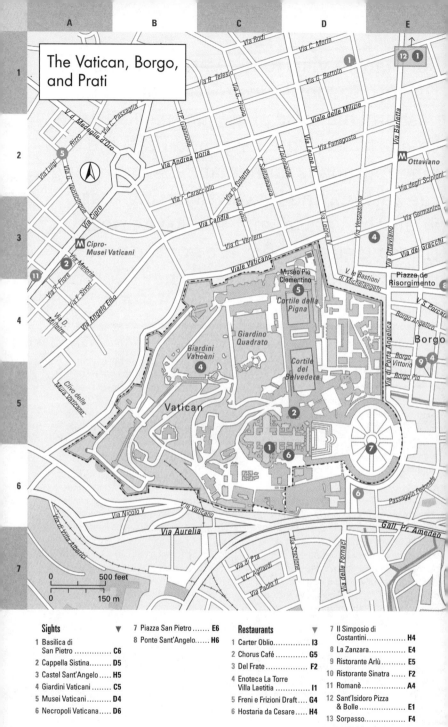

The Vatican, Borgo, and Prati

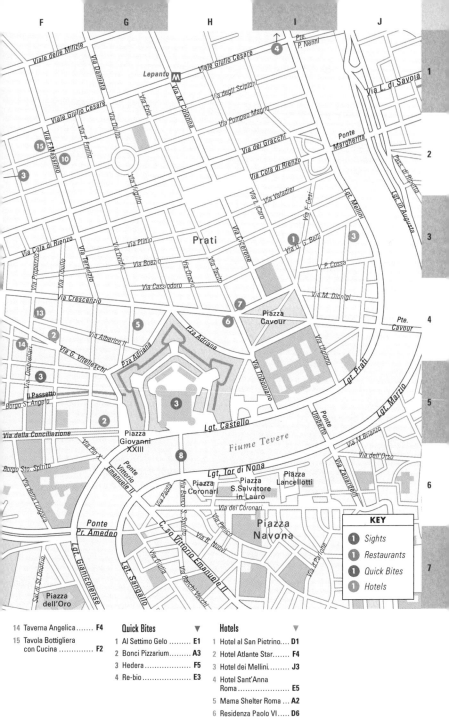

KEY
- 1 Sights
- 1 Restaurants
- 1 Quick Bites
- 1 Hotels

14 Taverna Angelica **F4**
15 Tavola Bottigliera
con Cucina **F2**

Quick Bites ▼
1 Al Settimo Gelo **E1**
2 Bonci Pizzarium **A3**
3 Hedera **F5**
4 Re-bio **E3**

Hotels ▼
1 Hotel al San Pietrino.... **D1**
2 Hotel Atlante Star....... **F4**
3 Hotel dei Mellini......... **J3**
4 Hotel Sant'Anna
Roma **E5**
5 Mama Shelter Roma ... **A2**
6 Residenza Paolo VI..... **D6**

Tips for Visiting the Vatican

To enter the Musei Vaticani, the Sistine Chapel, and the Basilica di San Pietro, you must comply with the Vatican's dress code or you may be turned away by the implacable custodians stationed at the doors. (Also: no penknives, which will show up in the metal detector.) For both men and women, shorts and tank tops are taboo, as are miniskirts and other revealing clothing. Wear a jacket or shawl over sleeveless tops, and avoid T-shirts with writing or pictures that could risk giving offense.

If you opt to start at the Musei Vaticani, note that the entrance on Viale Vaticano (there's a separate exit on the same street) can be reached by Bus No. 49 from Piazza Cavour, which stops right in front; on foot from Piazza del Risorgimento (Bus No. 81 or Tram No. 19); or a brief walk from the Via Cipro–Musei Vaticani stop on Metro Linea A.

The collections of the museums are immense, covering about 7 km (4½ miles) of displays. To economize on time and effort, once you've seen the frescoes in the Raphael rooms, you can skip much of the modern religious art in good conscience and get on with your tour.

You can rent a somewhat dry audio guide in English explaining the museums, including the Sistine Chapel and the Raphael rooms.

You cannot take any photographs in the Sistine Chapel. Elsewhere, you're free to photograph what you like—barring use of flash, tripod, or other special equipment, for which permission must be obtained.

With an average of 20,000 visitors per day, lines at the entrance to the Musei Vaticani can move slowly. It is always a good idea to reserve (⊕ www.museivaticani.va) tickets or tours in advance. The museum's Prime Experience tour lets you inside one hour before the official opening. The most exclusive (and most expensive) tour allows you to visit the empty museum with the key keeper at 6 am as he opens the doors and turns on the lights. It is sometimes possible to exit the museums from the Sistine Chapel into St. Peter's, saving further legwork.

Legally recognized as its own city-state, Vatican City covers 110 acres on a hill west of the Tiber and is separated from the city on all sides, except at Piazza di San Pietro, by high walls. Within the walls, about 840 people are permanent residents. The Vatican has its own daily newspaper (*L'Osservatore Romano*), issues its own stamps, mints its own coins, and has its own postal system (run by the Swiss). Within its territory are administrative and foreign offices, a pharmacy, banks, an astronomical observatory, a print shop, a mosaic school and art restoration institute, a tiny train station, a supermarket, a small department store, and several gas stations. The sovereign of the world's smallest state is the pope, Francis, elected in 2013 after his predecessor, Benedict XVI, stepped down (the first time a pope has "resigned" from office since 1415). His main role is as spiritual leader to the world's Catholic community.

Today, there are two principal reasons for sightseeing at the Vatican. One is to visit the Basilica di San Pietro, the most overwhelming architectural achievement of the Renaissance; the other is to visit the Musei Vaticani, which contain collections

For St. Peter's, Michelangelo originally designed a dome much higher than the one ultimately completed by his follower, Giacomo della Porta.

of staggering richness and diversity, from ancient Etruscan treasures and Egyptian mummies to an actual piece of the Moon.

Inside the basilica—breathtaking both for its sheer size and for its extravagant interior—are artistic masterpieces including Michelangelo's *Pietà* and Bernini's great bronze *baldacchino* (canopy) over the main altar. The Musei Vaticani, their entrance a 10-minute walk from the piazza, hold endless collections of many of the greatest works of Western art. The Laocoön, Leonardo's *St. Jerome in the Wilderness,* and Raphael's *Transfiguration* are all here. The Sistine Chapel, accessible only through these museums, is Michelangelo's magnificent artistic legacy, and his ceiling is the High Renaissance in excelsis in more ways than one.

◎ Sights

★ Basilica di San Pietro

CHURCH | The world's largest church, built over the tomb of St. Peter, is the most imposing and breathtaking architectural achievement of the Renaissance (although much of the lavish interior dates to the Baroque period). No fewer than five of Italy's greatest artists—Bramante, Raphael, Peruzzi, Antonio da Sangallo the Younger, and Michelangelo—died while striving to erect this new St. Peter's.

The history of the original St. Peter's goes back to AD 326, when the emperor Constantine completed a basilica over the site of the tomb of St. Peter, the Church's first pope. The original church stood for more than 1,000 years, undergoing a number of restorations and alterations, until, toward the middle of the 15th century, it was on the verge of collapse. In 1452, a reconstruction job began but was abandoned for lack of money.

In 1503, Pope Julius II instructed the architect Bramante to raze all the existing buildings and build a new basilica, one that would surpass even Constantine's for grandeur. It wasn't until 1626 that the new St. Peter's was completed and consecrated.

Basilica di San Pietro

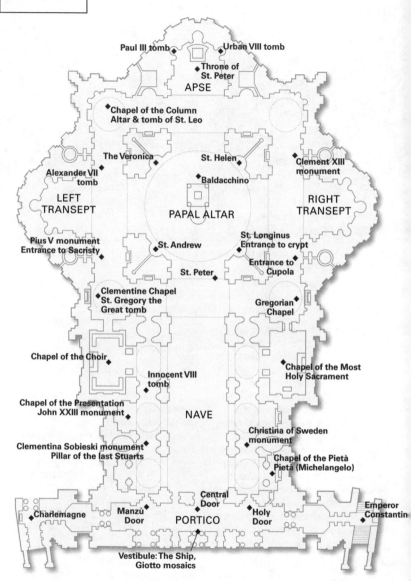

- Paul III tomb
- Urban VIII tomb
- Throne of St. Peter
- APSE
- Chapel of the Column Altar & tomb of St. Leo
- The Veronica
- St. Helen
- Clement XIII monument
- Alexander VII tomb
- Baldacchino
- LEFT TRANSEPT
- RIGHT TRANSEPT
- PAPAL ALTAR
- Pius V monument Entrance to Sacristy
- St. Andrew
- St. Longinus Entrance to crypt
- Entrance to Cupola
- St. Peter
- Clementine Chapel St. Gregory the Great tomb
- Gregorian Chapel
- Chapel of the Choir
- Chapel of the Most Holy Sacrament
- Innocent VIII tomb
- Chapel of the Presentation John XXIII monument
- NAVE
- Christina of Sweden monument
- Clementina Sobieski monument Pillar of the last Stuarts
- Chapel of the Pietà Pietà (Michelangelo)
- Central Door
- Emperor Constantin
- Charlemagne
- Manzù Door
- PORTICO
- Holy Door
- Vestibule: The Ship, Giotto mosaics

Highlights include the Loggia delle Benedizioni (Benediction Loggia), the balcony where newly elected popes are proclaimed; Michelangelo's *Pietà*; and Bernini's great bronze baldacchino, a huge, spiral-columned canopy—at 100,000 pounds, perhaps the largest bronze object in the world—as well as many other Bernini masterpieces. There are also collections of Vatican treasures in the Museo Storico-Artistico e Tesoro and the Grotte Vaticane crypt.

For views of both the dome above and the piazza below, take the elevator or stairs to the roof. Those with more stamina (and without claustrophobia) can then head up more stairs to the apex of the dome. ■TIP→ **The basilica is free to visit, but a security check at the entrance can create very long lines. Arrive before 8:30 or after 5:30 to minimize the wait and avoid the crowds.** ⊠ *Piazza San Pietro, Vatican* ⊕ *www.vatican.va* ✉ *Free* ☉ *Closed during Papal General Audience (Wed. until 1 pm) and during other ceremonies in piazza* Ⓜ *Ottaviano.*

★ **Cappella Sistina** (*Sistine Chapel*)
ART MUSEUM | In 1508, the redoubtable Pope Julius II commissioned Michelangelo to fresco the more than 10,000 square feet of the Sistine Chapel's ceiling. (*Sistine*, by the way, is simply the adjective form of *Sixtus*, in reference to Pope Sixtus IV, who commissioned the chapel itself.) The task took four years, and it's said that, for many years afterward, Michelangelo couldn't read anything without holding it over his head. The result, however, was the greatest artwork of the Renaissance. A pair of binoculars helps greatly, as does a small mirror—hold it facing the ceiling and look down to study the reflection.

More than 20 years after his work on the ceiling, Michelangelo was called on again, this time by Pope Paul III, to add to the chapel's decoration by painting the *Last Judgment* on the wall over the altar.

By way of signature on this, his last great fresco, Michelangelo painted his own face on the flayed-off human skin in St. Bartholomew's hand. ■TIP→ **The chapel is entered through the Musei Vaticani, and lines are slightly shorter after 2:30 (reservations are always advisable)—except free Sundays, which are extremely busy and when admissions close at 12:30.** ⊠ *Musei Vaticani, Vatican* ⊕ *www.museivaticani. va* ✉ *€20 (part of the Vatican Museums)* ☉ *Closed Sun.* Ⓜ *Ottaviano.*

Giardini Vaticani (*Vatican Gardens*)
GARDEN | Neatly trimmed lawns and flower beds extend over the hills behind St. Peter's Basilica, an area dotted with some interesting structures and other, duller ones that serve as office buildings. The Vatican Gardens occupy almost 40 acres and include a formal Italian garden, a flowering French garden, a romantic English landscape, and a small forest.

There's also the little-used Vatican railroad station, which now houses a museum of coins and stamps made in the Vatican, and the Torre di San Giovanni (Tower of St. John), restored by Pope John XXIII as a retreat for work and now used as a residence for distinguished guests. To visit the gardens, join a 45-minute open-bus tour (no stops). Garden visits must be booked online. ⊠ *Vatican City, Vatican* ☎ *06/69883145 tour info* ⊕ *www.museivaticani.va* ✉ *€40 for 45-minute open-bus tour (includes admission to the Musei Vaticani)* ☉ *Closed Sun.* Ⓜ *Ottaviano.*

★ **Musei Vaticani** (*Vatican Museums*)
ART MUSEUM | Other than the pope and his papal court, the occupants of the Vatican are some of the most famous artworks in the world. The Vatican Palace, residence of the popes since 1377, consists of an estimated 1,400 rooms, chapels, and galleries. The pope and his household occupy only a small part; most of the rest is given over to the Vatican Library and Museums.

Continued on page 124

HEAVENS ABOVE:
THE SISTINE CEILING

Forming lines that are probably longer than those waiting to pass through the Pearly Gates, hordes of visitors arrive at the Sistine Chapel daily to view what may be the world's most sublime example of artistry

Michelangelo: *The Creation of Adam*, Sistine Chapel, The Vatican, circa 1511.

Michelangelo's Sistine Ceiling. To paint this 12,000-square-foot barrel vault, it took four years, 343 frescoed figures, and a titanic battle of wits between the artist and Pope Julius II. While in its typical fashion, Hollywood focused on the element of agony, not ecstasy, involved in the saga of creation, a restoration of the ceiling, completed in 1994, and the installation of LEDs for better illumination, completed in 2018, have revolutionized our appreciation of the masterpiece of masterpieces.

By Martin Bennett

View of the Cappella Sistina

MICHELANGELO'S
MISSION IMPOSSIBLE

Designed to match the proportions of Solomon's Temple described in the Old Testament, the Sistine Chapel is named after Pope Sixtus VI, who commissioned it as a place of worship for himself and as the venue where new popes could be elected. Before Michelangelo, the barrel-vaulted ceiling was an expanse of azure fretted with golden stars. Then, in 1504, an ugly crack appeared. Bramante, the architect, managed do some patchwork using iron rods, but when signs of a fissure remained, the new Pope Julius II summoned Michelangelo to cover it with a fresco 135 feet long and 44 feet wide.

Taking in the entire span of the ceiling, the theme connecting the various scenes in this painted universe is seemingly mankind's need for redemption. The majestic panel depicting the Creation of Adam leads through the stages of the Fall and the expulsion from Eden to the tragedy of Noah found naked and mocked by his own sons. Witnessing all from the side and end walls, a chorus of ancient Prophets and Sibyls peers anxiously forward, awaiting the Redeemer who will come to save both the Jews and the Gentiles.

APOCALYPSE NOW

The sweetness and pathos of his *Pietà*, carved by Michelangelo only ten years earlier, have been left behind. The new work foretells an apocalypse, its congregation of doomed sinners facing the wrath of heaven through hanging, beheading, crucifixion, flood, and plague. Michelangelo, by nature a misanthrope, was already filled with visions of doom thanks to the fiery orations of Savonarola, whose thunderous preachments he had heard before leaving his hometown of Florence. Vasari, the 16th-century art historian, coined the word *terribilità* to describe Michelangelo's tension-ridden style, a rare case of a single word being worth a thousand pictures.

Michelangelo wound up using a condensed "Reader's Digest" version of the stories from Genesis, with the dramatis personae overseen by a punitive and terrifying God. In real life, poor Michelangelo answered to a flesh-and-blood taskmaster who was almost as vengeful: Pope Julius II. Less vicar of Christ than latter-day Caesar, he was intent on uniting Italy under the power of the Vatican and was eager to do so by any means, including riding into pitched battle. Yet this "warrior pope" considered his most formidable adversary to be Michelangelo. Applying a form of blackmail, Julius threatened to wage war on Michelangelo's Florence, to which the artist had fled after Julius canceled a commission for a grand papal tomb unless Michelangelo agreed to return to Rome and take up the task of painting the Sistine Chapel ceiling.

MICHELANGELO, SCULPTOR

A sculptor first and foremost, however, Michelangelo considered painting an inferior genre—"for rascals and sissies" as he put it. Second, there was the sheer scope of the task, leading Michelangelo to suspect he'd been set up by a rival, Bramante, chief architect of the new St. Peter's Basilica. As Michelangelo was also a master architect, he regarded this fresco commission as a Renaissance mission-impossible. Pope Julius's powerful will prevailed—and six years later the work of the Sistine Ceiling was complete. Irving Stone's famous novel *The Agony and the Ecstasy*—and the granitic 1965 film that followed—chart this epic battle between artist and pope.

THINGS ARE LOOKING UP

To better view the ceiling, bring binoculars or even just a mirror (to prevent your neck from becoming bent like Michelangelo's). Note that photos are not permitted. Admission and entry to the Sistine Chapel is only through the Musei Vaticani (Vatican Museums). To avoid crowds, visit at lunchtime or during the papal blessings and public audiences held in St. Peter's Square. Alternatively, book the Prime Experience Tour, which starts one hour before the museums open, or purchase the Extra Hours–Sistine Chapel ticket, which allows time in the chapel after the museums close.

SCHEMATIC OF THE SISTINE CEILING

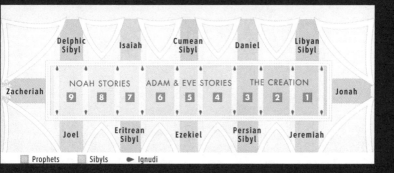

Delphic Sibyl — Isaiah — Cumean Sibyl — Daniel — Libyan Sibyl

Zacheriah

NOAH STORIES — ADAM & EVE STORIES — THE CREATION

9 8 7 6 5 4 3 2 1

Jonah

Joel — Eritrean Sibyl — Ezekiel — Persian Sibyl — Jeremiah

■ Prophets   ■ Sibyls   ➤ Ignudi

PAINTING THE BIBLE

The ceiling's biblical symbols were ideated by three Vatican theologians, Cardinal Alidosi, Egidio da Viterbo, and Giovanni Rafanelli, along with Michelangelo. As for

the ceiling's painted "framework," this quadratura alludes to Roman triumphal arches because Pope Julius II was fond of mounting "triumphal entries" into his conquered cities (in imitation of Christ's procession into Jerusalem on Palm Sunday).

THE CENTER PANELS

Prophet turned art-critic or, perhaps doubling as ourselves, the ideal viewer, Jonah the prophet (painted at the altar end) gazes up at the Creation, or Michelangelo's version of it.

1 The first of three scenes taken from the Book of Genesis: God separates Light from Darkness.

2 God creates the sun and a craterless, pre-Galilean moon, while the panel's other half offers an unprecedented rear view of the Almighty creating the vegetable world.

3 In the panel showing God separating the Waters from the Heavens, the Creator tumbles towards us as in a self-made whirlwind.

4 Pausing for breath, next admire probably Western Art's most famous image—God giving life to Adam.

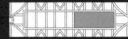

Adam's rib leads to the sixth panel.

6 In a sort of diptych divided by the trunk of the Tree of Knowledge of Good and Evil, Michelangelo retells the Temptation and the Fall.

illustrating Man's fallen nature, the last three panels narrate, in un-chronological order, the Flood. In the first Noah offers a pre-Flood sacrifice of thanks.

8 Damaged by an explosion in 1794, next comes Michelangelo's version of Flood itself.

Finally, above the monumental Jonah, you can just make out the small, wretched figure of Noah, lying drunk—in pose, the shrunken anti-type of the majestic Adam five panels down the wall.

THE CREATION OF ADAM

Michelangelo's Adam was partly inspired by the Creation scenes Michelangelo had studied in the sculpted doors of Jacopo della Quercia in Bologna and Lorenzo Ghiberti's Doors of Paradise in Florence. Yet in Michelangelo's version Adam's hand hangs limp, waiting God's touch to impart the spark of life. Facing his Creation, the Creator—looking a bit like the pagan god Jupiter—is for the first time ever depicted as horizontal, mirroring the biblical "in his own likeness." Decades after its completion, a crack began to appear, amputating Adam's fingertips.

Believe it or not, the most famous fingers in Western art are the handiwork, at least in part, of one Domenico Carnevale.

Tips on Touring the Vatican Museums

Remember that the Vatican's museum complex is humongous: only after walking through what seems like miles of galleries do you see the entrance to the Sistine Chapel (which cannot be entered from St. Peter's Basilica directly). Most people—especially those who rent an audio guide and must return it to the main desk—tour the complex, see the Sistine, then trudge back to the main museum entrance, itself a 15-minute walk from St. Peter's Square.

However, there is an "insider" exit directly from the Sistine Chapel to St. Peter's Basilica. Look for the "tour groups only" door on the right as you face the rear of the chapel and, when a group exits, go with the flow and follow them. This will deposit you on the porch of St. Peter's Basilica. While

this has served as a sly trick for years, if a guard is on watch you may not be able to slip in so smoothly. Also note that if you run to the Sistine Chapel, using the "shortcut" exit into the basilica, you will have missed the rest of the Vatican Museum collection.

Another possibility is to visit in the evening. This experiment began in 2009 and has been running intermittently ever since, with the Vatican opening on Friday and Saturday evening until 8 pm (final entry at 6:30), March–October. While the major hits, like the Sistine Chapel, are usually open during these special evenings, many more off-the-beaten-path rooms and galleries are not. Reservations are required (and possible to secure online at ⊕ *www.museivaticani.va*).

Beyond the glories of the Sistine Chapel, the collection is extraordinarily rich: highlights include the great antique sculptures (including the celebrated *Apollo Belvedere* in the Octagonal Courtyard and the *Belvedere Torso* in the Hall of the Muses); the Stanze di Raffaello (Raphael Rooms), with their famous gorgeous frescoes; and the Old Master paintings, such as Leonardo da Vinci's beautiful (though unfinished) *St. Jerome in the Wilderness*, some of Raphael's greatest creations, and Caravaggio's gigantic *Deposition in the Pinacoteca* ("Picture Gallery").

For those interested in guided visits to the Vatican Museums, tours start at €40, including entrance tickets, and can also be booked online. Other offerings include a regular two-hour guided tour of the Vatican gardens; call or check online to confirm. For more information, call ☏ *06/69884676* or go to ⊕ *www.museivaticani.va*. For

information on tours, call ☏ *06/69883145* or ☏ *06/69884676;* visually impaired visitors can arrange tactile tours by calling ☏ *06/69884947.* ✉ *Viale Vaticano, near intersection with Via Leone IV, Vatican* ☏ *06/69883145* ⊕ *www.museivaticani. va* 🎫 *€20* ⊗ *Closed Sun. and church holidays* Ⓜ *Cipro–Musei Vaticani or Ottaviano–San Pietro.*

Necropoli Vaticana (*Vatican Necropolis*) **CEMETERY** | With advance notice you can take a 1½-hour guided tour in English of the Vatican Necropolis, under the Basilica di San Pietro, which gives a rare glimpse of early Christian Roman burial customs and a closer look at the tomb of St. Peter. Apply via the contact form online, by fax, or in person (the entrance to the office is on the left of the Bernini colonnade), specifying the number of people in the group (all must be age 15 or older), preferred language, preferred time, available dates, and your contact information in

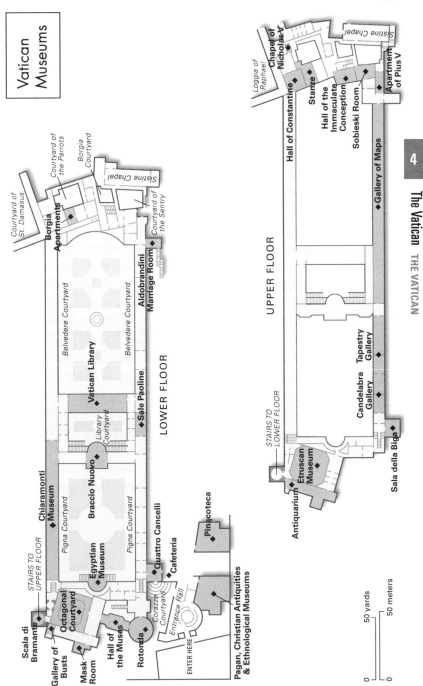

Vatican Museums

Courtyard of St. Damasus

Courtyard of the Parrots

Borgia Courtyard

Borgia Apartments

Sistine Chapel

Courtyard of the Sentry

Aldobrandini Marriage Room

Belvedere Courtyard

Vatican Library

Belvedere Courtyard

LOWER FLOOR

Sale Paoline

Library Courtyard

Chiaramonti Museum

Braccio Nuovo

Pigna Courtyard

Egyptian Museum

Pigna Courtyard

Quattro Cancelli

Cafeteria

Pinacoteca

STAIRS TO UPPER FLOOR

Scala di Bramante

Octagonal Courtyard

Gallery of Busts

Mask Room

Hall of the Muses

Rotonda

Corazze Courtyard

Entrance Hall

ENTER HERE

Pagan, Christian Antiquities & Ethnological Museums

Loggia of Raphael

Chapel of Nicholas V

Sistine Chapel

Stanze

Hall of Constantine

Hall of the Immaculate Conception

Sobieski Room

Apartment of Pius V

Gallery of Maps

UPPER FLOOR

STAIRS TO LOWER FLOOR

Antiquarium

Etruscan Museum

Candelabra Gallery

Tapestry Gallery

Sala della Biga

4

The Vatican THE VATICAN

50 yards

50 meters

0

Meet the Pope

Piazza di San Pietro is the scene of large papal audiences, as well as special commemorations, masses, and beatification ceremonies. When he's in Rome, the pope makes an appearance every Sunday at noon at the window of the Vatican Palace. He addresses the crowd and blesses all present, a ceremony that lasts about 10 to 15 minutes. The pope also holds general audiences in the square on Wednesday morning at about 9:15 am; a ticket is usually necessary for a seat, but even with a ticket you will have to arrive early, as about 40,000 people attend every week—sometimes many more for special occasions—and everyone must pass through security. The general audience lasts between an hour and an hour and a half. In the winter and inclement weather, the audience is held in a hall adjacent to the basilica (Aula Paolo Sesto), which houses far fewer people than the square.

For admission to an audience, apply for free tickets in advance, indicating your preferred date, number of tickets, and your contact information during your stay in Rome at the Prefettura della Casa Pontifice, either by email (✉ ordinanze@pontifical-isdomus.va), fax (☎ 06/69885863), or by mail (✉ Prefettura della Casa Pontificia, 00120 Città del Vaticano). You must pick up your tickets at the office through the Portone di Bronzo (Bronze Door) at the end of the right-hand colonnade. Note that in August no official tickets are issued; you just have to show up early and hope to get a seat.

Rome. Each group will have about 12 participants. Visits are not recommended for those with mobility issues or who are claustrophobic. ✉ Ufficio Scavi, Vatican ☎ 06/69885318, 06/69873017 reservations ⊕ www.scavi.va 🎟 €13 ⊗ Closed Sun. and Roman Catholic holidays ⚠ Reservations required Ⓜ Ottaviano.

★ **Piazza San Pietro**

PLAZA/SQUARE | Mostly enclosed within high walls that recall the papacy's stormy history, the Vatican opens the spectacular arms of Bernini's colonnade to embrace the world only at St. Peter's Square, scene of the pope's public appearances and another of Bernini's masterpieces. The elliptical Piazza di San Pietro was completed in 1667—after only 11 years' work—and holds about 100,000 people.

Surrounded by a pair of quadruple colonnades, the piazza is gloriously studded with 140 statues of saints and martyrs. At its center is the 85-foot-high Egyptian obelisk, which was brought to Rome by Caligula in AD 37 and moved here in 1586 by Pope Sixtus V. The famous Vatican post offices can be found on both sides of St. Peter's Square and inside the Vatican Museums complex. ■TIP→ **The main information office is just left of the basilica as you face it.** ✉ Piazza di San Pietro, Vatican ⊕ www.vaticanstate.va Ⓜ Ottaviano.

Borgo

Between the Vatican and the once-moated bulk of Castel Sant'Angelo—erstwhile mausoleum of Emperor Hadrian and now an imposing relic of medieval Rome—is the old Borgo neighborhood, whose workaday charm has largely succumbed to gentrification. Be wary of the tourist-trap lunch spots and souvenir shops right outside the Vatican walls.

Sights

Castle Sant'Angelo

CASTLE/PALACE | **FAMILY** | Standing between the Tiber and the Vatican, this circular castle has long been one of Rome's most distinctive landmarks. Opera lovers know it well as the setting for the final scene of Puccini's *Tosca*. Started in AD 135, the structure began as a mausoleum for the emperor Hadrian and was completed by his successor, Antoninus Pius. From the mid-6th century the building became a fortress, a place of refuge for popes during wars and sieges.

Its name dates to AD 590, when Pope Gregory the Great, during a procession to plead for the end of a plague, saw an angel standing on the summit of the castle, sheathing his sword. Taking this as a sign that the plague was at an end, the pope built a small chapel at the top, placing a statue next to it to celebrate his vision—thus the name, Castel Sant'Angelo.

In the rooms off the Cortile dell'Angelo, look for the Cappella di Papa Leone X (Chapel of Pope Leo X), with a facade by Michelangelo. In the Pope Alexander VI courtyard, a wellhead bears the Borgia coat of arms. The stairs at the far end of the courtyard lead to the open terrace for a view of the Passetto, the fortified corridor connecting Castel Sant'Angelo with the Vatican. In the *appartamento papale* (papal apartment), the Sala Paolina (Pauline Room) was decorated in the 16th century by Perino del Vaga and assistants with lavish frescoes of scenes from the Old Testament and the lives of St. Paul and Alexander the Great. ✉ *Lungotevere Castello 50, Prati* ☎ *06/6819111 central line, 06/6896003 tickets* ⊕ *www. castelsantangelo.beniculturali.it* ☞ *€13* ⊗ *Closed Mon.* Ⓜ *Lepanto.*

Ponte Sant'Angelo

BRIDGE | Angels designed by Baroque master Bernini line the most beautiful of central Rome's 20-odd bridges. Bernini himself carved only two of the angels (those with the scroll and the crown of thorns), both of which were moved to the church of Sant'Andrea delle Fratte shortly afterward at the behest of the Bernini family. Though copies, the angels on the bridge today convey forcefully the grace and characteristic sense of movement—a key element of Baroque sculpture—of Bernini's best work.

Originally built in AD 133–134, the Ponte Elio, as it was originally called, was a bridge over the Tiber to Hadrian's Mausoleum. Pope Gregory changed the bridge's name after he had a vision of an angel sheathing its sword to signal the ending of the plague of 590. In medieval times, continuing its sacral function, the bridge became an important element in funneling pilgrims toward St. Peter's. As such, in 1667 Pope Clement IX commissioned Bernini to design 10 angels bearing the symbols of the Passion, turning the bridge into a sort of Via Crucis. ✉ *Between Lungotevere Castello and Lungotevere Altoviti, Borgo* Ⓜ *Ottaviano.*

🍴 Restaurants

Many tourists think the area around the Vatican is rip-off central when it comes to drinking and dining. Although there are an overwhelming number of tourist "trap-torias," the Borgo area, just outside the Vatican walls, is home to some genuinely good restaurants off the usual tourist radar.

★ Chorus Café

$$ | **MODERN ITALIAN** | Tucked away above the Auditorium della Conciliazione, this glamorous restaurant/lounge with sky-high ceilings, marble walls, and plush seating feels like something out of Paolo Sorrentino's award-winning film *La Grande Bellezza*. Renowned bartender Massimo d'Addezio shakes up creative cocktails, like a twist on a French 75 made with yuzu, while the kitchen whips up delicious modern Italian

4

The Vatican BORGO

Did You Know?

Designed to be Hadrian's tomb, the Castel Sant'Angelo was originally topped by a marble-sheathed tumulus and crowned by a gigantic bronze of the emperor in his chariot.

cuisine. **Known for:** top-notch cocktails; sumptuous surroundings; DJ sets on the weekends. $ *Average main: €23* ✉ *Auditorium della Conciliazione, Via della Conciliazione 4, Borgo* ☎ *335/1449655* 🌐 *www.choruscafe.it* ⏲ *Closed Sun. and Mon.* [M] *Ottaviano.*

Ristorante Arlù

$$$ | **MODERN ITALIAN** | This tiny family-run restaurant has changed a lot since it first opened in 1959 as a simple trattoria. Today you'll still find classic Roman dishes on the menu, but it's worth trying original creations like salmon marinated in Aperol with avocado and savory panna cotta or the homemade ravioli stuffed with ricotta and topped with octopus confit. **Known for:** historic family-run restaurant; elegant decor; creative and classic dishes. $ *Average main: €28* ✉ *Borgo Pio 135, Borgo* ☎ *06/68689936* 🌐 *www.ristorantearlu.it* [M] *Ottaviano.*

Taverna Angelica

$$$ | **MODERN ITALIAN** | The Borgo area near St. Peter's Basilica hasn't been known for culinary excellence, but Taverna Angelica was one of the first refined restaurants in this part of town. The dining room is small, which allows the chef to create a menu that's inventive without being pretentious. **Known for:** eclectic Italian dishes; high-quality cuisine; ravioli with salt cod in arrabbiata oil spiced with red chili. $ *Average main: €26* ✉ *Piazza Amerigo Capponi 6, Borgo* ☎ *06/6874514* 🌐 *www.tavernaangelica.com* ⏲ *Closed Mon.* [M] *Ottaviano.*

Coffee and Quick Bites

Hedera

$ | **ICE CREAM** | **FAMILY** | Set in a historical, ivy-covered building in the Piazza del Catalone, with its famous fountain for pilgrims, this charming gelato shop makes its products according to tradition, with just the essentials: milk, cream, sugar, and eggs—usually all from organic farms. Its sorbetti are also classic, consisting of just water, sugar, and 51% minimum of fruit. **Known for:** soft brioche with mocha coffee granita; Calabrian truffles, hazelnut gelato balls with a liquid chocolate center; seasonal fruit gelato. $ *Average main: €4* ✉ *Borgo Pio 179, Borgo* ☎ *06/6832971* 🌐 *www.hederaroma.it* [M] *Ottaviano.*

Hotels

Just east of the Vatican, the Borgo area has a certain medieval charm but can be overwhelming—filled with both tourists and the tourist traps that love them. That said, there are a few appealing and atmospheric hotels here, and you can't beat the location if the focus of your visit is seeing the Vatican sights.

Hotel Atlante Star

$$$ | **HOTEL** | The rooftop garden terrace with a center-stage view of St. Peter's Basilica is just one reason to stay here; proximity to the Vatican and superb shopping is another. **Pros:** all rooms have robes and amenity kits; panoramic roof garden and terrace is open from morning to night; restaurant serves sophisticated cuisine with beautiful views. **Cons:** some rooms are nicer than others; one of the elevator is on the small side and a bit slow; some furniture and fixtures are in need of upgrading. $ *Rooms from: €230* ✉ *Via Vitelleschi 34, Borgo* ☎ *06/686386* 🌐 *www.atlantehotels.com* 🛏 *65 rooms* 🍴 *Free Breakfast* [M] *Ottaviano.*

Hotel Sant'Anna Roma

$ | **HOTEL** | Set in the shadow of St. Peter's, this small hotel is a good value, with simply decorated, ample guest rooms that feature wood-beam ceilings, parquet floors, and comfy beds. **Pros:** street is a pedestrian-only zone; beds are comfy; staff are friendly. **Cons:** no on-site bar or restaurant, and many

nearby restaurants are tourist traps; the neighborhood is dead at night; they can charge extra for a late checkout. $ *Rooms from: €120* ✉ *Borgo Pio 133, Borgo* ☎ *06/68801602* 🌐 *www.santanna-hotel.net* 🛏 *20 rooms* 🍴 *Free Breakfast* [M] *Ottaviano.*

Residenza Paolo VI

$$$$ | **HOTEL** | Set in a former monastery—still an extraterritorial part of the Vatican—abutting Bernini's colonnade of St. Peter's Square, the Paolo VI (pronounced "Sesto," a reference to Pope Paul VI) is unbeatably close to St. Peter's, with comfortable and quiet guest rooms. **Pros:** direct views of St. Peter's from the rooftop terrace; quiet rooms; lovely staff and service. **Cons:** some rooms are really small; bathrooms are a tight space; far away from Rome's historical attractions. $ *Rooms from: €302* ✉ *Via Paolo VI 26, Borgo* ☎ *06/684870* 🌐 *www.residenzapaolovi.com* 🛏 *35 rooms* 🍴 *Free Breakfast* [M] *Ottaviano.*

Shopping

Borgo is your destination for religious relics.

Savelli Arte e Tradizione

SOUVENIRS | Here you'll find a fully stocked selection of religious gifts: everything from rosaries and crosses to religious artwork and Pope Francis memorabilia. Founded in 1898, this family business provides a place for pilgrims to pick up a souvenir from the Holy See and also specializes in mosaics. The store has another location at the Self-Service Restaurant in Piazza del Sant'Uffizio 6/7. It's closed on Sunday afternoon. ✉ *Via Paolo VI 27–29, Borgo* ☎ *06/68307017* 🌐 *savellireligious.com* [M] *Ottaviano.*

Prati

Outside the Vatican walls, but slightly upriver from the Borgo neighborhood, Prati is coming into its own as a foodie destination.

Restaurants

Carter Oblio

$$ | **MODERN ITALIAN** | Chef Ciro Alberto Cucciniello studied economics, pivoted to cooking, and then cut his teeth at renowned restaurants in Italy and abroad before opening this intimate eatery with a Nordic-inspired design. He plays with smoke and fire to create artful dishes like pasta with Genovese sauce, smoked mackerel, wild fennel, and blue goat cheese, and he elevates humble ingredients like carrots to the level of culinary masterpieces. **Known for:** beautifully presented and creative dishes; reasonably priced tasting menus; sleek Nordic design. $ *Average main: €22* ✉ *Via Giuseppe Gioachino Belli 21, Prati* ☎ *391/4649097* 🌐 *www.carteroblio.com* 🕓 *Closed Mon.* [M] *Lepanto.*

Del Frate

$$ | **MODERN ITALIAN** | This impressive wine bar pairs modern decor with creative cuisine and three dozen wines available by the glass. There are some fantastic seasonal specialties, but you can also get cheeses, smoked meats, and composed salads. **Known for:** shares space with one of Rome's noted wine shops; daily aperitivo with a nice selection of wines by the glass; wide selection of after-dinner drinks, including mezcal and amari (bitter cordial). $ *Average main: €24* ✉ *Via degli Scipioni 118, Prati* ☎ *06/3236437* 🌐 *www.enotecadelfrate.it* 🕓 *Closed 2 wks in Aug.* [M] *Ottaviano.*

★ Enoteca La Torre Villa Laetitia

$$$$ | **MODERN ITALIAN** | In the Villa Laetitia, a boutique hotel owned by the Fendi family, this gorgeous restaurant has soaring ceilings, a crystal chandelier, and Art Nouveau motifs. The elegant setting provides the perfect backdrop for creative, flavorful dishes by Domenico Stile, one of Rome's youngest two-Michelin-starred chefs. **Known for:** one of the most beautiful restaurants in Rome; flavorful, creative cuisine; creative wine pairings. [$] *Average main: €40* ✉ *Villa Laetitia, Lungotevere delle Armi 23, Prati* ☎ *06/45668304* 🌐 *www.enotecalatorreroma.com* 🕒 *Closed Mon. and Tues.* [M] *Lepanto.*

Freni e Frizioni Draft

$ | **PIZZA** | If you fancy a cocktail with your pizza, head to this hip pizzeria created by the team behind the award-winning bar, Freni & Frizioni, in Trastevere. Six of the eatery's 18 taps are used for beer; the rest dispense cocktails that have been pre-batched and carbonated, resulting in perfectly blended, easy-to-serve drinks. **Known for:** cocktails on draft; Roman-style pizza; sleek, minimalist design. [$] *Average main: €12* ✉ *Via Sforza Pallavicini 12, Prati* ☎ *388/1832577* 🌐 *www.freniefrizioni.com* [M] *Ottaviano.*

Hostaria da Cesare

$$ | **ROMAN** | With wood-paneled walls, white tablecloths, and formally attired waiters, the vibe is old school at this Prati standby, so it's no surprise that the menu emphasizes culinary tradition. Homemade pasta with meat sauce is the primo to order; marinated anchovies and sardines or raw oysters quell seafood cravings, and thick Florentine steaks satisfy meat lovers. **Known for:** fresh, local ingredients; Roman and Tuscan specialties; extensive menu with lots of options. [$] *Average main: €20* ✉ *Via Crescenzio 13, Prati* ☎ *06/6861227* 🌐 *www.ristorantecesare.com* 🕒 *Closed 3 weeks in Aug.* [M] *Lepanto.*

Il Simposio di Costantini

$$$ | **MODERN ITALIAN** | At the most upscale wine bar in town, you come for the vino but return for the food. Everything here is appropriately *raffinato* (refined): raw and marinated fish; spaghetti with clams; and risotto with braised radicchio, mullet, and goat cheese mousse. **Known for:** favorite among locals; elegant atmosphere; seafood-heavy menu. [$] *Average main: €30* ✉ *Piazza Cavour 16, Prati* ☎ *06/3241489* 🌐 *www.ilsimposioroma.it* 🕒 *Closed Sun. and 2 wks in Aug.* [M] *Lepanto.*

La Zanzara

$$$ | **INTERNATIONAL** | This bright, modern establishment functions as a bar, café, and restaurant all in one, with plenty of indoor and outdoor seating. Salads, pastas, steaks, and seafood run the international gamut, but the beef burger is a standout. **Known for:** bacon cheeseburger; artisanal Italian beers; large grill for freshly cooked meats. [$] *Average main: €26* ✉ *Via Crescenzio 84, Prati* ☎ *06/68392227* 🌐 *www.lazanzararoma.com* [M] *Ottaviano.*

Ristorante Sinatra

$$ | **MODERN ITALIAN** | Named in homage to the Italian-American crooner, this intimate restaurant has a refined yet casual atmosphere, with wine bottles lining the walls, black-and-white photographs of jazz musicians, and vintage touches like rotary telephones. Although the menu emphasizes Italian classics, there are a few surprises, including focaccia with Spanish pata negra ham and raw shrimp in the *cacio e pepe* (pasta prepared with a pecorino-cheese sauce and black pepper). **Known for:** charming vintage setting; eclectic menu; live music. [$] *Average main: €18* ✉ *Via Fabio Massimo 68, Prati* ☎ *06/3219657* 🌐 *www.ristorante-sinatra.business.site* 🕒 *Closed Sun.* [M] *Lepanto.*

Romanè

$$ | ROMAN | Impresario chef Stefano Callegari's casual restaurant excels at reimagining nostalgic dishes, as evidenced by the fettuccine al tortellino, which transforms the classic tortellini in brodo into a rich primo of homemade fettuccine cooked in broth and topped with mortadella, prosciutto, Parmigiano-Reggiano, and nutmeg. Order à la carte, or opt for one of the affordable tasting menus, which include an appetizer, primo, secondo, side dish, and dessert. **Known for:** fettuccine al tortellino; Roman culinary traditions, including quinto quarto; laid-back, homey vibe. $ *Average main: €15* ✉ *Via Cipro 106, Prati* ☎ *340/7845281* ⊕ *www.romaneviacipro106.it* Ⓜ *Cipro.*

Sant'Isidoro Pizza & Bolle

$ | PIZZA | FAMILY | More upscale than a typical pizzeria but casual enough for a weeknight, this establishment pairs its pies with sparkling wines instead of beer. Opt for a classic pizza, or go with an innovative option, like one topped with stracciatella, raw shrimp, lemon peel, and mint. **Known for:** wide selection of sparkling wines; creative pizzas; chic modern design. $ *Average main: €14* ✉ *Via Oslavia 41, Prati* ☎ *06/89822607* ⊕ *www.pizzaebolle.it* Ⓜ *Lepanto.*

Sorpasso

$$ | MODERN ITALIAN | FAMILY | The focus at this happening spot is on using excellently sourced products to make simple but wonderful food. In the morning and afternoon, stop in for freshly baked sweet treats; in the evening, when people spill out into the street with cocktails in hand, come for an aperitivo or a hearty meal. **Known for:** meat and cheese board; strozzapretti (a short pasta) served with eggplant, pistachio, and chili bread crumbs; juicy steaks. $ *Average main: €15* ✉ *Via Properzio 31-33, Prati* ☎ *06/89024554* ⊕ *sorpasso.info/home-page* ☉ *Closed Sun. and Aug.* Ⓜ *Ottaviano.*

Tavola Bottiglieria con Cucina

$$ | MODERN ITALIAN | Exposed brick walls and tables made from up-cycled parquet flooring or white marble are among the design elements at this welcoming bistro founded by two surfer brothers. With the exception of *primi* (pastas) and burgers, all of the dishes can be ordered as full-size options or small portions that let you taste your way through the menu. **Known for:** convivial atmosphere; industrial-chic design; creative takes on Italian classics. $ *Average main: €20* ✉ *Via Fabio Massimo 91, Prati* ☎ *06/3211178* ⊕ *www.tavolaristorante.com* ☉ *Closed Tues.* Ⓜ *Ottaviano.*

☕ Coffee and Quick Bites

Al Settimo Gelo

$ | ICE CREAM | FAMILY | The unusual flavors of gelato scooped up here include cinnamon and ginger and fig with cardamom and walnut, but the classics also get rave reviews. Ask for a taste of the *passito* flavor, if it's available; it's inspired by the popular sweet Italian dessert wine. **Known for:** organic Sicilian lemon sorbetto; homemade whipped cream; completely gluten-free shop. $ *Average main: €5* ✉ *Via Vodice 21/a, Prati* ☎ *06/3725567* ⊕ *www.alsettimogelo.it* ☉ *Closed Mon. and 1 wk in Aug.* Ⓜ *Lepanto.*

★ Bonci Pizzarium

$ | PIZZA | FAMILY | This tiny storefront by famed pizzaiolo Gabriele Bonci is the city's most famous place for pizza *al taglio* (by the slice). It serves more than a dozen versions, from the standard margherita to slices piled high with prosciutto and other tasty ingredients. **Known for:** Rome's best pizza al taglio; over a dozen flavors; long lines. $ *Average main: €5* ✉ *Via della Meloria 43, Prati* ☎ *06/39745416* ⊕ *www.bonci.it* ☉ *Closed Mon.* Ⓜ *Cipro.*

Re-bio

$ | **CAFÉ** | **FAMILY** | This friendly spot, a stone's throw from the Musei Vaticani, serves super-fresh, organic, made-to-order sandwiches, poke bowls, and salads. Seating is limited. **Known for:** vegetarian and vegan options; smoothies and fresh juices; handy location. [S] *Average main: €9* ✉ *Via Germanico 59, Prati* ☎ *06/39746510* ⊕ *www.rebio.it* ⊘ *No dinner Sun.–Wed.* [M] *Ottaviano.*

Hotels

Here you'll find small, friendly hotels that don't break the bank.

Hotel al San Pietrino

$ | **HOTEL** | This simple budget hotel on the third floor of a 19th-century palazzo offers rock-bottom rates and is just a five-minute walk from the Vatican. **Pros:** heavenly rates near the Vatican; air-conditioning and Wi-Fi; free parking nearby. **Cons:** a couple of Metro stops from the centro storico; flat pillows and basic bedding; no bar. [S] *Rooms from: €98* ✉ *Via Giovanni Bettolo 43, Prati* ☎ *06/3700132* ⊕ *www.hotelsanpietrino.it* ⤳ *11 rooms* |⊚| *No Meals* [M] *Ottaviano.*

Hotel dei Mellini

$$ | **HOTEL** | On the west bank of the Tiber between the Spanish Steps and St. Peter's Basilica (a ten-minute stroll from Piazza del Popolo and the nearest Metro station), this modern luxury hotel is removed from the chaos of the centro storico. **Pros:** spacious and spotless rooms; breakfast served until 11 am; free bicycles to use based on availability. **Cons:** not for those who want to be in the center of the action; few dining options right nearby; spotty cell service. [S] *Rooms from: €149* ✉ *Via Muzio Clementi 81, Prati* ☎ *06/324771* ⊕ *www.hotelmellini.com* ⤳ *81 rooms* |⊚| *Free Breakfast* [M] *Lepanto, Flaminio.*

★ Mama Shelter Roma

$$ | **HOTEL** | **FAMILY** | The first Italian outpost of the French brand, Mama Shelter, this hip hotel features a funky design with lots colors and patterns and playful touches like graphic ceilings painted by French street artist Beniloys and vintage pinball machines you can play. **Pros:** sex-positive and LGBTQ+ friendly; programming like beer tastings and weekend brunch; relaxing area with a pool, sauna, and gym. **Cons:** €25 cleaning fee for pets; breakfast buffet costs €22; a bit far from most of the major sights. [S] *Rooms from: €149* ✉ *Via Luigi Rizzo 20, Prati* ☎ *06/94538900* ⊕ *www.mamashelter.com/roma* ⤳ *217 rooms* |⊚| *No Meals* [M] *Cipro.*

Nightlife

BARS

Emerald's Bar

COCKTAIL BARS | This classy cocktail bar a few blocks from the Vatican makes you feel transported to a cozy salon in New York or London. In addition to some original creations, the bartenders make reliably good classics, including excellent dirty martinis. The kitchen stays open until midnight, so it's also a good spot for a late bite. ✉ *Via Crescenzio 91C, Prati* ☎ *06/88654275* ⊕ *www.emeraldsbar.it* [M] *Ottaviano.*

LIVE MUSIC

Alexanderplatz Jazz Club

LIVE MUSIC | The excellent musical programming and the black-and-white-checker floors at Rome's most important live jazz and blues club evoke Harlem's 1930s jazz halls. The bar and restaurant are always busy, so reservations are suggested. ✉ *Via Ostia 9, Prati* ☎ *06/86781296, 349/9770309 WhatsApp* ⊕ *www.alexanderplatzjazz.com* [M] *Ottaviano.*

Fonclea

LIVE MUSIC | Situated just around the corner from Castel Sant'Angelo, Fonclea jams with live music—from jazz and Latin American to R&B and '60s cover bands—every night of the week. Entry is free. ✉ *Via Crescenzio 82/a, Prati* ☎ *06/6896302* ⊕ *www.fonclea.it* Ⓜ *Ottaviano.*

Shopping

DEPARTMENT STORES

Coin

DEPARTMENT STORE | **FAMILY** | Department stores aren't the norm in Italy, but Coin comes close with its large selection of upscale accessories; cosmetics; and clothing for men, women, and children. Searching for a pressure-driven espresso machine, a simpler stove-top Bialetti model, or a mezzaluna? You can find these and other high-quality, stylish housewares, too. There are 10 branches of this store around Rome, including a smaller one at Termini station. ✉ *Via Cola di Rienzo 173, Prati* ☎ *06/36004298* ⊕ *www.coin.it* Ⓜ *Lepanto, Ottaviano.*

FOOD AND WINE

★ Castroni

FOOD | Opening its flagship shop near the Vatican in 1932, this gastronomic paradise has long been Rome's port of call for decadent delicacies from around the globe; there are now 13 locations throughout the city. Jonesing expats and study-abroad students pop in for local sweets, 300 types of tea, and even good old-fashioned Betty Crocker red velvet cake mix. If you need a pick-me-up, try the house-roasted espresso, which is some of the best coffee in Rome. ✉ *Via Cola di Rienzo 196/198, Prati* ☎ *06/6874383* ⊕ *www.castronicoladirienzo.com* Ⓜ *Lepanto.*

SHOES AND ACCESSORIES

Il Sellaio di Serafini

LEATHER GOODS | For more than 70 years, saddler artisan Ferruccio Serafini handmade some of Rome's best leather bags, shoes, and belts—accessories beloved by the likes of Marlon Brando, Elizabeth Taylor, and the Kennedy brothers in the 1960s. Today, the family business is run by Francesca, Ferruccio Serafini's youngest daughter. Choose from the premade stock, or select your style and your leather and have something custom made. You can also bring vintage leather items in for repairs. ✉ *Via Caio Mario 14, Prati* ☎ *06/3211719* ⊕ *www.serafinipelletteria.it* Ⓜ *Ottaviano.*

PIAZZA NAVONA, CAMPO DE' FIORI, AND THE JEWISH GHETTO

Updated by
Natalie Kennedy

◉ Sights	🍴 Restaurants	🛏 Hotels	💼 Shopping	🌙 Nightlife
★★★★★	★★★☆☆	★★★★★	★★★★☆	★★★★☆

NEIGHBORHOOD SNAPSHOT

MAKING THE MOST OF YOUR TIME

Start at Campo de' Fiori, where the popular market takes place every morning, Monday through Saturday. The cobblestone streets that stretch out from the square are lined with an enchanting combination of artisans' workshops, sophisticated boutiques, and characteristic cafés. Wind your way west through the Jewish Ghetto, the historic home of Rome's once-vibrant Jewish community (and a good place for lunch). Don't miss the area around the Portico d'Ottavia, with some of the city's most atmospheric ruins.

Heading north will take you across busy Corso Vittorio Emanuele. Duck into the piazza of Santa Maria Sopra Minerva, which contains Rome's most delightful Baroque conceit, Bernini's 17th-century elephant obelisk memorial, and pop into the church, which has the only Gothic interior in Rome. Straight ahead is one of the wonders of the world: the ancient Pantheon, with that postcard icon, Piazza Navona, just a few blocks to the west. You could spend about five hours exploring, not counting breaks—but taking breaks is what this area is all about.

TOP REASONS TO GO

Piazza Navona: Rome's exuberant Baroque is on display in this glorious piazza. Savor both Bernini's fountain and Borromini's church of Sant'Agnese.

Caravaggio: Marvel at the play of light and dark in three of the finest paintings by 17th-century Rome's rebel artist at the church of San Luigi dei Francesi.

The Pantheon: Gaze up to the heavens through the dome of this ancient temple—is this the world's only architecturally perfect building?

Campo de' Fiori: Stroll through the morning market for a taste of the sweet life.

Portico d'Ottavia: This famed ancient landmark casts a spell over Rome's Jewish Ghetto.

GETTING HERE

■ Piazza Navona and Campo de' Fiori are an easy walk from the Vatican or Trastevere and a half-hour stroll from the Spanish Steps. From Termini or the Vatican, take Bus No. 40 Express or the No. 64 to Largo Torre Argentina; then walk 10 minutes to either piazza. Bus No. 116 winds from Via Veneto past the Spanish Steps to Campo de' Fiori.

■ From the Vatican or the Spanish Steps, it's a 30-minute walk to the Jewish Ghetto, or take the No. 40 Express or the No. 64 bus from Termini station to Largo Torre Argentina.

OFF THE BEATEN PATH

■ The market at Campo de' Fiori attracts the most visitors, but on the weekends Romans head to the Mercato Campagna Amica on Via di San Teodoro. This true farmers' market attracts producers from around the Lazio region to sell local cheese like the hard-to-find *marzolino* cheese, fresh produce, bread made from stoneground wheat, and *salumi* (cured meats) galore. A small kitchen near the back door whips up lunch with seasonal ingredients for about €8, and there is ample outdoor seating.

The area around Piazza Navona, Campo de' Fiori, and the Jewish Ghetto, also known as the Campo Marzio (Field of Mars) for its martial past, is beautiful, atmospheric, and lively. It's a neighborhood that's worth getting lost in, featuring cobblestone side streets and artisans' shops just around the corner from the piazzas, as well as tourist-packed sights and the establishments that cater to them.

Piazza Navona

In terms of sheer sensual enjoyment—from ornate palaces to mouthwatering restaurants and cozy bars to charming stores—it's tough to top this area of Rome. Just a few blocks (and some 1,200 years) separate the two showstoppers: Piazza Navona and the Pantheon. The first is an extraordinarily beautiful Baroque piazza that serves as the open-air salon for this quarter of Rome. Across Corso di Rinascimento is the Pantheon, the grandest extant building from ancient Rome, topped by the world's largest unreinforced concrete dome. Near the same massive hub, Bernini's delightful elephant obelisk proves that small can also be beautiful.

 Sights

Museo Napoleonico
SPECIALTY MUSEUM | Opulent, velvet-and-crystal salons in the Palazzo Primoli hauntingly capture the fragile charm of early-19th-century Rome and contain a specialized and rich collection of Napoléon memorabilia, including a bust by Canova of the general's sister, Pauline Borghese. You may well ask why this outpost of Napoléon is in Rome, but in 1798 the French emperor sent his troops to Rome, kidnapping Pope Pius VII and proclaiming his young son the King of Rome—though it all ultimately came to naught. ⊠ *Palazzo Primoli, Piazza di Ponte Umberto I, Piazza Navona* ☎ *06/0608* ⊕ *www.museonapoleonico. it* ⊘ *Closed Mon.* Ⓜ *Bus Nos. 70, 30, 81, 628, and 492.*

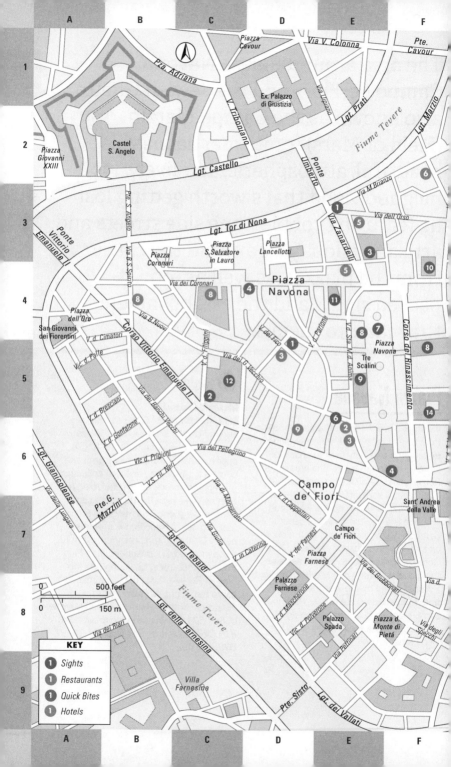

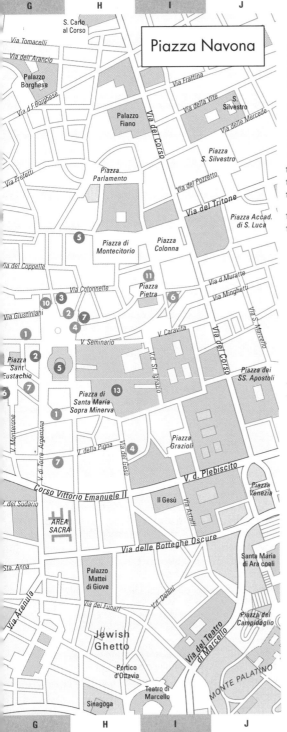

Piazza Navona

Sights ▼

1 Museo Napoleonico E3
2 Oratorio dei Filippini C5
3 Palazzo Altemps E3
4 Palazzo Massimo alle
   Colonne F6
5 Pantheon G5
6 Piazza di Pasquino................. E5
7 Piazza Navona E4
8 San Luigi dei Francesi............. F5
9 Sant'Agnese in Agone E5
10 Sant'Agostino F4
11 Santa Maria della Pace........... E4
12 Santa Maria in
   Vallicella/Chiesa Nuova........... C5
13 Santa Maria sopra Minerva...... H5
14 Sant'Ivo alla Sapienza F5

Restaurants ▼

1 Armando al Pantheon............. G5
2 Cul de Sac E6
3 Da Francesco D5
4 Enoteca Corsi H6
5 Il Convivio Troiani E3
6 La Campana F2
7 La Ciambella........................ G6
8 La Fraschetta di
   Castel Sant'Angelo B4
9 La Montecarlo D6
10 La Rosetta G4
11 Osteria dell'Ingegno............... I4

Quick Bites ▼

1 Bar del Fico......................... D5
2 Cremeria Monteforte.............. G5
3 Fiocco di Neve G4
4 Gelateria Del Teatro D4
5 Giolitti H3
6 Sant'Eustachio il Caffè........... G5
7 Tazza d'Oro H4
8 Tre Scalini E4

Hotels ▼

1 Albergo Santa Chiara G6
2 Antico Albergo del Sole
   al Pantheon......................... H4
3 G-Rough Hotel E6
4 Hotel Abruzzi H5
5 Hotel Genio......................... E4
6 9 Hotel Cesàri I4
7 The Pantheon
   Iconic Rome Hotel,
   Autograph Collection.............. G5
8 Relais Palazzo Taverna............ C4

Oratorio dei Filippini

LIBRARY | Housed in a Baroque master-work by Borromini, this former religious residence named for Saint Philip Neri, founder in 1551 of the Congregation of the Oratorians, now contains Rome's Archivio Storico. Like the Jesuits, the Oratorians—or Filippini, as they were commonly known—were one of the religious orders established in the mid-16th century as part of the Counter-Reformation. Neri, a man of rare charm and wit, insisted that the members of the order—most of them young noblemen whom he had recruited personally—not only renounce their worldly goods, but also work as common laborers in the construction of Neri's great church of Santa Maria in Vallicella.

The Oratory itself, built between 1637 and 1662, has a gently curving facade that is typical of Borromini, who insisted on introducing movement into everything he designed. The inspiration here is that of arms extended in welcome to the poor. The building houses the Vallicelliana Library founded by Philip Neri, and the courtyard is usually accessible during the library's opening hours. Otherwise, guided visits, usually in the mornings, can be booked by email. ⊠ *Piazza della Chiesa Nuova (Corso Vittorio Emanuele), Piazza Navona* ☎ *06/6893868* ✎ *b-vall.didattica@ beniculturali.it* ⊗ *Closed Sat. and Sun.*

★ Palazzo Altemps

CASTLE/PALACE | Containing some of the world's finest ancient Roman statues, Palazzo Altemps is part of the Museo Nazionale Romano. The palace's sober exterior belies a magnificence that appears as soon as you walk into the majestic courtyard, studded with statues and covered in part by a retractable awning. The restored interior hints at the Roman lifestyle of the 16th–18th centuries while showcasing the most illustrious pieces from the Museo Nazionale, including the collection of the Ludovisi noble family.

In the frescoed salons you can see the *Galata Suicida,* a poignant sculptural work portraying a barbarian warrior who chooses death for himself and his wife, rather than humiliation by the enemy. Another highlight is the large Ludovisi sarcophagus, magnificently carved from marble. In a place of honor is the *Ludovisi Throne,* which shows a goddess emerging from the sea and being helped by her acolytes. For centuries this was heralded as one of the most sublime Greek sculptures, but, today, at least one authoritative art historian considers it a colossally overrated fake. Look for the framed explanations of the exhibits that detail (in English) how and exactly where Renaissance sculptors, Bernini among them, added missing pieces to the classical works.

In the lavishly frescoed loggia stand busts of the Caesars. In the wing once occupied by early-20th-century poet Gabriele d'Annunzio (who married into the Altemps family), three rooms host the museum's Egyptian collection. ⊠ *Piazza di Sant'Apollinare 46, Piazza Navona* ☎ *06/684851* ⊕ *museonazionaleromano. beniculturali.it* ⊠ *€8; €12 combined ticket includes three other Museo Nazionale Romano sites over one week (Crypta Balbi, Palazzo Massimo alle Terme, and Museo delle Terme di Diocleziano)* ⊗ *Closed Mon.*

Palazzo Massimo alle Colonne

CASTLE/PALACE | Following the shape of Emperor Domitian's Odeon arena, a curving, columned portico identifies this otherwise inconspicuous palace on a traffic-swept bend of Corso Vittorio Emanuele. In the 1530s, Renaissance architect Baldassare Peruzzi built this palace for the Massimo family, after their previous dwelling had been destroyed during the Sack of Rome. (High in the papal aristocracy, they claimed an ancestor who had been responsible for the defeat of Hannibal.)

Every year on the feast of Pentecost, rose petals flutter down the oculus of the Pantheon.

If you visit on March 16, you'll be able to go upstairs to visit the family chapel in commemoration of a miracle performed here in 1583 by St. Philip Neri, who is said to have recalled a young member of the family, one Paolo Massimo, from the dead (expect a line). Any other day of the year, though, you'll only be able to view the private residence from the outside. The palazzo's name comes from the columns of the ancient Odeon; one is still visible in the square at the back of the palazzo. ✉ *Corso Vittorio Emanuele II 141, Piazza Navona.*

★ Pantheon

RELIGIOUS BUILDING | The city's best-preserved ancient building, this former Roman temple is a marvel of architectural harmony and proportion. It was entirely rebuilt by the emperor Hadrian around AD 120 on the site of a Pantheon (from the Greek: *pan,* all, and *theon,* gods) erected in 27 BC by Augustus's right-hand man and son-in-law, Agrippa.

The most striking thing about the Pantheon is not its size, immense though it is, nor even the phenomenal technical difficulties posed by so massive a construction; rather, it's the remarkable unity of the building. The diameter described by the dome is exactly equal to its height. It's the use of such simple mathematical balance that gives classical architecture its characteristic sense of proportion and its nobility. The opening at the apex of the dome, the *oculus,* is nearly 30 feet in diameter and was intended to symbolize the "all-seeing eye of the heavens." On a practical note, this means when it rains, it rains inside: look out for the drainage holes in the floor.

Although little is known for sure about the Pantheon's origins or purpose, it's worth noting that the five levels of trapezoidal coffers (sunken panels in the ceiling) represent the course of the five then-known planets and their concentric spheres. Ruling over them is the sun, represented symbolically and literally by the 30-foot-wide eye at the top. The heavenly symmetry is further paralleled by the coffers: 28 to each row, the number of lunar cycles. In the center of each would have shone a small bronze star. Down below, the seven large niches were occupied not by saints, but, it's thought, by statues of Mars, Venus, the deified Caesar, and the other "astral deities," including the moon and sun, the "sol invictus." (Academics still argue, however, about which gods were most probably worshipped here.)

One of the reasons the Pantheon is so well preserved is that it was consecrated as a church in AD 608. (It's still a working church today.) No building, church or not, though, escaped some degree of plundering through the turbulent centuries of Rome's history after the fall of the empire. In 655, for example, the gilded bronze covering the dome was stripped. The Pantheon is also one of the city's important burial places. Its most famous tomb is that of Raphael (between the second and third chapels on the left as you enter). Mass takes place on Sunday and on religious holidays at 10:30; it's open to the public, but you are expected to arrive before the beginning and stay until the end. General access usually resumes at about 11:30. You can buy tickets online in advance, which requires registering for an account, but it is better than waiting in the long line at the door. Each reservation can book up to 25 tickets. ■TIP➜ **On the first Sunday of every month, visitors can enter for free.** ✉ *Piazza della Rotonda, Piazza Navona* ☎ *06/6830 0230* ⊕ *www.museiitaliani.it* 💳 *€5; audio guide €8.50.*

Piazza di Pasquino

PLAZA/SQUARE | This tiny piazza takes its name from the figure in the corner, the remnant of an old Roman statue depicting Menelaus. The statue underwent a name change in the 16th century when Pasquino, a cobbler or barber (and part-time satirist), started writing comments around the base. The habit caught on; soon everyone was doing it. The most

loquacious of Rome's "talking statues," its lack of arms or face is more than made up for with the modern-day commentary that is still anonymously posted on the wall behind the weathered figure. ✉ *Piazza di Pasquino, Piazza Navona.*

★ Piazza Navona

PLAZA/SQUARE | Always camera-ready, this beautiful plaza has Bernini sculptures, three gorgeous fountains, and a magnificently Baroque church (Sant'Agnese in Agone), all built atop the remains of a Roman athletics track. Pieces of the arena are still visible near the adjacent Piazza Sant'Apollinare, and the ancient spirit of entertainment lives on in the buskers and artists who populate the piazza today.

The piazza took on its current look during the 17th century, after Pope Innocent X of the Pamphilj family decided to make over his family palace (now the Brazilian embassy and an ultra-luxe hotel) and its surroundings. Center stage is the Fontana dei Quattro Fiumi, created for Innocent by Bernini in 1651. Bernini's powerful figures of the four rivers represent the longest rivers of the four known continents at the time: the Nile (his head covered because the source was unknown); the Ganges; the Danube; and the Plata (the length of the Amazon was then unknown). Popular legend has it that the figure of the Plata—the figure closest to Sant'Agnese in Agone—raises his hand before his eyes because he can't bear to look upon the church's "inferior" facade designed by Francesco Borromini, Bernini's rival.

If you want a café with one of the most beautiful, if pricey, views in Rome, grab a seat at Piazza Navona. Just be aware that all the restaurants here are heavily geared toward tourists, so while it's a beautiful place for a coffee, you can find cheaper, more authentic, and far better meals elsewhere. ✉ *Piazza Navona.*

★ San Luigi dei Francesi

CHURCH | San Luigi's Contarelli Chapel (the fifth and last chapel on the left, toward the main altar) is adorned with three stunningly dramatic works by Caravaggio (1571–1610), the Baroque master of the heightened approach to light and dark. They were commissioned for the tomb of Mattheiu Cointerel in one of Rome's French churches (San Luigi is St. Louis, patron saint of France). The inevitable coin machine will light up his *Calling of Saint Matthew, Saint Matthew and the Angel*, and *Martyrdom of Saint Matthew* (seen from left to right), and Caravaggio's mastery of light takes it from there.

When painted, they caused considerable consternation among the clergy of San Luigi, who thought the artist's dramatically realistic approach was scandalously disrespectful. A first version of the altarpiece was rejected; the priests were not particularly happy with the other two, either. Time has fully vindicated Caravaggio's patron, Cardinal Francesco del Monte, who secured the commission for these works and staunchly defended them. ■ TIP→ **This church regularly enforces the rule of covered knees and shoulders, and turns away those who do not abide.** ✉ *Piazza di San Luigi dei Francesi, Piazza Navona* ☎ *06/688271* ⊕ *saintlouis-rome.net.*

Sant'Agnese in Agone

CHURCH | The quintessence of Baroque architecture, this church has a facade that is a wonderfully rich mélange of bell towers, concave spaces, and dovetailed stone and marble. It's the creation of Francesco Borromini (1599–1667), a contemporary and rival of Bernini. Next to his new Pamphilj family palace, Pope Innocent X had the adjacent chapel expanded into this full-fledged church. The work was first assigned to the architect Rainaldi. However, Donna Olimpia, the pope's famously domineering sister-in-law, became increasingly impatient with how the work was going and

brought in Borromini, whose wonderful concave entrance has the magical effect of making the dome appear much larger than it actually is.

The name of this church comes from the Greek *agones*, the source of the word *navona* and a reference to the agonistic competitions held here in Roman times. The saint associated with the church is Agnes, who was martyred here in the piazza's forerunner, the Stadium of Domitian. As she was stripped nude before the crowd, her hair miraculously grew to maintain her modesty before she was killed. The interior is a marvel of modular Baroque space and is ornamented by giant marble reliefs sculpted by Raggi and Ferrata. ✉ *Via di Santa Maria dell'Anima, 30/A, Piazza Navona* ☎ *06/68192134* ⊕ *www.santagneseinagone.org* ⊙ *Closed Mon.* Ⓜ *Bus Nos. 87, 40, and 64.*

★ Sant'Agostino

CHURCH | This basilica set atop a steep staircase between Piazza Navona and the Pantheon houses several treasures. In the first chapel on the left is Caravaggio's celebrated *Madonna of the Pilgrims*, which scandalized all of Rome for depicting a kneeling pilgrim all too realistically for the era's tastes, with dirt on the soles of his feet and the Madonna standing in a less-than-majestic pose in a dilapidated doorway. Pause at the third column on the left of the nave to admire Raphael's blue-robed *Isaiah*, said to be inspired by Michelangelo's prophets on the Sistine ceiling (Raphael, with the help of Bramante, had taken the odd peek at the master's original against strict orders of secrecy). Directly below is Sansovino's Leonardo-influenced sculpture, *St. Anne and the Madonna with Child*.

As you leave, in a niche just inside the door, is the sculpted *Madonna and Child*, known to the Romans as the "Madonna del Parto" (of Childbirth) and piled high with ex-voto offerings giving thanks for the safe deliveries of children. The artist was Jacopo Tatti, also sometimes confusingly known as Sansovino after his master. ⊠ *Piazza Sant'Agostino, Piazza Navona* ☎ *06/68801962.*

Santa Maria della Pace

CHURCH | In 1656, Pietro da Cortona (1596–1669) was commissioned by Pope Alexander VII to enlarge the tiny Piazza della Pace in front of the 15th-century church of Santa Maria so that it could accommodate the carriages of its wealthy parishioners. His architectural solution was to design a new church facade complete with semicircular portico, demolish a few buildings here and there to create a more spacious approach, add arches to give architectural unity to the piazza, and then complete it with a series of bijou-size palaces. The result was one of Rome's most delightful little architectural set pieces.

Within are several great Renaissance treasures. Raphael's fresco above the first altar on your right depicts the *Four Sibyls*—almost exact replicas of Michelangelo's, if more relaxed. The fine decorations of the Cesi Chapel, second on the right, were designed in the mid-16th century by Sangallo. Opposite is Peruzzi's wonderful fresco of the *Madonna and Child*. The octagon below the dome is something of an art gallery in itself, with works by Cavalliere Arpino, Orazio Gentileschi, and others; Cozzo's *Eternity* fills the lantern above.

Behind the church is its cloister, designed by Bramante (architect of St. Peter's) as the very first expression of High Renaissance style in Rome. In addition to an exhibit space for contemporary art, the cloister has a lovely coffee bar. ⊠ *Via Arco della Pace 5, Piazza Navona* ☎ *06/68804038* Ⓜ *Bus Nos. 87, 40, and 64.*

Santa Maria in Vallicella/Chiesa Nuova

CHURCH | This church, sometimes known as Chiesa Nuova (New Church), is most famous for its three magnificent altarpieces by Rubens. It was built toward the end of the 16th century at the urging of Philip Neri and, like Il Gesù, is a product of the fervor of the Counter-Reformation. It has a sturdy Baroque interior, all white and gold, with ceiling frescoes by Pietro da Cortona depicting a miracle reputed to have occurred during the church's construction: the Virgin and strong-armed angels hold up the broken roof to prevent it from crashing down upon the congregation. Note that the church closes daily from 12 pm–5 pm. ⊠ *Piazza della Chiesa Nuova, Corso Vittorio Emanuele II, Piazza Navona* ☎ *06/6875289* ⊕ *www.vallicella. org.*

★ Santa Maria sopra Minerva

CHURCH | The name of the church reveals that it was built *sopra* (over) the ruins of a temple of Minerva, the ancient goddess of wisdom. Erected in 1280 by Dominicans along severe Italian Gothic lines, it has undergone a number of more or less happy interior restorations. Certainly, as the city's major Gothic church, it provides a refreshing contrast to Baroque flamboyance. Have a €1 coin handy to illuminate the Cappella Carafa in the right transept; the small investment is worth it to better see Filippino Lippi's (1457–1504) glowing frescoes featuring a deep azure expanse of sky and musical angels hovering around the Virgin.

Under the main altar is the tomb of St. Catherine of Siena, one of Italy's patron saints and a major destination for faithful locals who drop written prayers on her final resting place. Left of the altar you'll find Michelangelo's *Risen Christ* and the tomb of the gentle artist Fra Angelico. Bernini's unusual and little-known monument to the Blessed Maria Raggi is on the fifth pier of the left-hand aisle.

In front of the church, Bernini's *Elephant and Obelisk* is perhaps the city's most charming sculpture. An inscription on the base references the church's ancient patroness, reading something to the effect that it takes a strong mind to sustain solid wisdom. ⊠ *Piazza della*

Minerva, Piazza Navona ☎ *06/792257* 🌐 *www.santamariasopraminerva.it.*

Sant'Ivo alla Sapienza

CHURCH | This eccentric Baroque church, probably Borromini's best, has one of Rome's most delightful "domes"—a dizzying spiral said to have been inspired by a bee's stinger. The apian symbol is a reminder that the church was commissioned by the Barberini pope Urban VIII (a swarm of bees figure on the Barberini family crest), although it was completed by Alexander VII. The interior, open only for three hours on Sunday morning, is worth a look, especially if you share Borromini's taste for complex mathematical architectural idiosyncrasies. "I didn't take up architecture solely to be a copyist," he once said. Sant'Ivo is certainly the proof. ✉ *Corso del Rinascimento 40, Piazza Navona* 🌐 *www.sivoallasapienza.eu* 🕑 *Closed Mon.–Sat., July, and Aug.*

🍴 Restaurants

The narrow, cobblestone *vicoli* (alleys) around Piazza Navona have everything from casual pizzerias, where hurried waiters scribble your bill on a paper tablecloth, to the city's most revered gastronomic temples, with star chefs, inventive cuisine, and decidedly higher bills placed on the fine damask tablecloths.

The area around the Pantheon is full of classic, old-school trattorias and midrange to upscale restaurants, including many with tables set in gorgeous piazzas that could double as opera sets. You'll feel the grandeur of Rome here, sometimes with prices to match.

★ Armando al Pantheon

$$ | **ROMAN** | In the shadow of the Pantheon, this small family-run trattoria, open since 1961, delights tourists and locals alike. There's an air of authenticity to the Roman staples here, and the quality of the ingredients and the cooking mean booking ahead through the website is a must. **Known for:** beautifully executed traditional Roman cooking; spaghetti alla gricia (with guanciale, pecorino cheese, and black pepper); reservation list that opens 30 days at a time. [$] *Average main: €16* ✉ *Salita dei Crescenzi 31, Piazza Navona* 🌐 *www.armandoalpantheon.it* 🕑 *Closed Sun. and Aug.*

★ Cul de Sac

$ | **WINE BAR** | This popular wine bar a stone's throw from Piazza Navona is among the city's oldest and has a book-length selection of wines from Italy, France, the Americas, and elsewhere. It offers great value and pleasant service and is a lovely spot for a light late lunch or an early dinner when most restaurants aren't open yet. **Known for:** great wine list (and wine bottle–lined interior); eclectic Italian and Mediterranean fare; relaxed atmosphere and outside tables. [$] *Average main: €14* ✉ *Piazza di Pasquino 73, Piazza Navona* ☎ *06/68801094* 🌐 *www.enotecaculdesacroma.it.*

Da Francesco

$$ | **ROMAN** | **FAMILY** | For good, hearty, Roman cuisine in an area filled with mediocre touristy restaurants, head to this trattoria that's been on the scene since the late 1950s. Stick with the classics, perhaps starting off with a mixed salumi plate featuring Parma ham and buffalo mozzarella before moving on to a *primi* (first course)—the amatriciana (with tomato sauce, guanciale, and pecorino cheese) is one of the standouts. **Known for:** authentic and informal atmosphere; outside tables in summer; truffle topped pasta alla gricia. [$] *Average main: €18* ✉ *Piazza del Fico 29, Piazza Navona* ☎ *06/6864009* 🌐 *www.dafrancesco.it.*

Enoteca Corsi

$ | **ITALIAN** | Although this old-school, centro storico trattoria has been renovated, you wouldn't know it, and that's part of its charm. At lunchtime, it's often packed with a mix of civil servants from the nearby government offices, construction workers, and in-the-know tourists enjoying classic pastas, octopus salad,

An *alimentari* is a specialty food shop. Visit one to stock up on lunch or picnic fixings; some will give you samples to taste.

and *secondi* (second courses) such as roast veal with peas. **Known for:** casual atmosphere; Roman specialties; brusque but friendly service. $ *Average main: €14* ✉ *Via del Gesù 88, Piazza Navona* ☎ *06/6790821* ⊕ *www.enotecacorsi. com* ⊗ *Closed Sun. and 3 wks in Aug. No dinner Sat.*

★ Il Convivio Troiani

$$$$ | **MODERN ITALIAN** | The three Troiani brothers—Angelo in the kitchen and Giuseppe and Massimo presiding over the dining room and wine cellar—have been quietly redefining the experience of Italian *alta cucina* (haute cuisine) since 1990 at this well-regarded establishment in a tiny, nondescript alley north of Piazza Navona. The service is attentive without being overbearing, and the wine list is exceptional. **Known for:** fine dining in elegant surroundings; inventive modern Italian cooking with exotic touches; amazing wine cellar and a great sommelier. $ *Average main: €65* ✉ *Vicolo dei Soldati 31, Piazza Navona* ☎ *06/6869432* ⊕ *www.ilconviviotroiani.it* ⊗ *Closed Sun. and 1 wk in Aug. No lunch.*

★ La Campana

$$ | **ROMAN** | **FAMILY** | Thought to be the oldest restaurant in Rome (a document dates it back to 1518), La Campana is well-liked for its honest Roman cuisine and its old-school, slightly upscale feel—think white tablecloths and unflappable waiters in black tie who have been there since the beginning of time. This is the place to have one of the best *coda alla vaccinara* (oxtail stew) in Rome, along with other specialties like saltimbocca and pasta *all'amatriciana* (a classic Roman tomato sauce with bacon-like pork cheek). **Known for:** old-school elegance; traditional Roman cooking; fantastic oxtail stew. $ *Average main: €18* ✉ *Vicolo della Campana 18, Piazza Navona* ☎ *06/6875273* ⊕ *www.facebook. com/ristorantelacampana* ⊗ *Closed Mon.* Ⓜ *Spagna.*

La Ciambella

$$$ | **ITALIAN** | A large glass wall to the kitchen and massive skylight in the dining room hint at the contemporary leanings of this restaurant built atop the ruins of the Baths of Agrippa behind the Pantheon. The emphasis here is on high-quality ingredients and classic Italian culinary traditions interpreted for modern diners. **Known for:** elegant setting in a great location near the Pantheon; sophisticated Italian cuisine; expert wine pairings. $ Average main: €35 ⊠ Via dell'Arco della Ciambella 20, Piazza Navona ☎ 06/6832930 ⊕ www.la-ciambella.it ♥ Closed Tues. and Wed.

La Fraschetta di Castel Sant'Angelo

$ | **ROMAN** | **FAMILY** | Fraschetta is the name given to one of the casual, boisterous countryside spots just outside Rome, where the menu focuses on porchetta, the Italian version of roast pork. This is a city-styled version of such an establishment, and the atmosphere is typical, with waiters yelling across the room and frequently breaking into song. **Known for:** jovial informal atmosphere; great value; excellent porchetta, of course. $ Average main: €12 ⊠ Via del Banco di Santo Spirito 20, Piazza Navona ☎ 06/68307661 ⊕ www.facebook.com/lafraschettadicastelsantangelo ♥ Closed Sun. No lunch Aug.

La Montecarlo

$ | **PIZZA** | **FAMILY** | The crusts on the pizza at this casual, perennially popular spot just off the Piazza Navona are superthin and charred around the edges a little—the sign of a good wood-burning oven. This is one of a few pizzerias open for both lunch and dinner, and it's busy day and night. **Known for:** charred thincrust pizza; outside tables; great value in a central location. $ Average main: €12 ⊠ Vicolo Savelli 13, Piazza Navona ☎ 06/6861877 ⊕ www.lamontecarlo.it ♥ Closed Mon. and 3 wks in Aug.

La Rosetta

$$$$ | **SEAFOOD** | Chef-owner Massimo Riccioli may have taken the nets and fishing gear off the walls of the trattoria he inherited from his parents, but this is still widely known as the place to go in Rome for first-rate seafood. The experience here includes friendly staff and undeniably high-quality fish, but be prepared for simple preparations and high prices. **Known for:** elegant restaurant (jackets required for men); first-rate fish and seafood; tagliolini pasta with shrimp. $ Average main: €75 ⊠ Via della Rosetta 9, Piazza Navona ☎ 06/6861002 ⊕ www.larosetta.com ♥ Closed Mon. and 2 wks in Aug. 🎩 Jacket required.

Osteria dell'Ingegno

$$ | **MODERN ITALIAN** | This casual, trendy place—vibrant with colorful paintings by local artists—is a great spot to enjoy an ancient piazza while savoring a glass of wine or a gourmet meal. The simple but innovative menu includes dishes like Roman artichokes with baccalà, beef tagliata (sliced grilled steak) with a redwine reduction, and a perfectly cooked duck breast with red fruit sauce. **Known for:** a mix of traditional and inventive pastas; a great spot both for aperitifs and/or a meal; outdoor seating with views of ancient ruins. $ Average main: €22 ⊠ Piazza di Pietra 45, Piazza Navona ☎ 06/6780662 ⊕ www.osteriadellingegno.com ♥ Closed Mon.

☕ Coffee and Quick Bites

Bar del Fico

$ | **ITALIAN** | **FAMILY** | Everyone in Rome knows Bar del Fico, located right behind Piazza Navona, so if you want to hang out with the locals, come here for a drink or something to eat at any time of day or night. In the mornings, chess players sit at tables outside under the shade of the fig tree that gives the bar its name; after sunset, the bar is packed with people sipping cocktails. **Known for:** outside tables in a pretty square; Italian-style brunch;

buzzy atmosphere. [S] *Average main:* *€12* ✉ *Piazza del Fico 26, Piazza Navona* ☎ *06/68891373* ⊕ *www.bardelfico.com.*

Cremeria Monteforte

$ | **ICE CREAM** | **FAMILY** | Immediately beside the Pantheon is this gelateria, which is well known for its flavors, like mango, pistachio, and chocolate chip. The chocolate *sorbetto*—an icier version of gelato, made without the dairy—is also excellent, and even better with a dollop of whipped cream on top. **Known for:** artisan gelato; fast, friendly service; large scoops for a fair price. [S] *Average main: €4* ✉ *Via della Rotonda 22, Piazza Navona* ☎ *06/6867720* ⊘ *Closed Mon. and mid-Dec.–mid-Jan.*

Fiocco di Neve

$ | **ICE CREAM** | **FAMILY** | The gelato is certainly excellent—the chocolate chip and After Eight (mint chocolate chip) flavors are delicious—but this small spot is also known for its *affogato di zabaione* (hot espresso poured over a small scoop of creamy marsala wine ice cream). Look for intriguing seasonal gelato flavors like pear-cinnamon. **Known for:** delicious gelato; interesting seasonal flavors; great location near the Pantheon. [S] *Average main: €4* ✉ *Via del Pantheon 51, Piazza Navona* ☎ *06/96006762* ⊕ *www.facebook.com/FioccodiNeveRoma.*

★ Gelateria Del Teatro

$ | **ICE CREAM** | **FAMILY** | In a window next to the entrance of this renowned gelateria, you can see the fresh fruit being used to create the day's flavors, which highlight the best of Italy—from Amalfi lemons to Alban hazelnuts. In addition to traditional options, look for interesting combinations like raspberry and sage or white chocolate with basil. **Known for:** sublime gelato; seasonal, all natural ingredients; charming location on a cobblestone street. [S] *Average main: €3* ✉ *Via dei Coronari 65/66, Piazza Navona* ☎ *06/45474880* ⊕ *www.gelateriadelteatro.it.*

★ Giolitti

$ | **ICE CREAM** | **FAMILY** | Open since 1900, Giolitti near the Pantheon is Rome's old-school gelateria par excellence. Pay in advance at the register by the door; take your receipt to the counter; and choose from dozens of flavors, including chocolate, cinnamon, and pistachio. **Known for:** excellent gelato; old-school setting; wide selection of flavors. [S] *Average main: €3* ✉ *Via degli Uffici del Vicario 40, Piazza Navona* ☎ *06/6991243* ⊕ *www.giolitti.it.*

Sant'Eustachio il Caffè

$ | **CAFÉ** | **FAMILY** | Frequented by tourists and government officials from the nearby Senate alike, this café is considered by many to make Rome's best coffee. Take it at the counter Roman-style—servers are hidden behind a huge espresso machine, where they vigorously mix the sugar and coffee to protect their secret method for the perfectly prepared cup (if you want yours without sugar here, ask for it *senza zucchero*). **Known for:** gran caffè (large sugared espresso); old-school Roman coffee bar vibe; 1930s interior. [S] *Average main: €3* ✉ *Piazza Sant'Eustachio 82, Piazza Navona* ☎ *06/68802048* ⊕ *www.caffesanteustachio.com.*

Tazza d'Oro

$ | **CAFÉ** | On the east corner of the piazza, in front of the Pantheon, this has been the place for serious coffee drinkers for nearly 80 years—there are no tables or frills, but there is a no-nonsense attitude when it comes to the dark coffee roasts that are perfect for espresso. Consider indulging in a *granita di caffè con panna* (coffee ice with whipped cream). **Known for:** coffee roasted on-site; gleaming retro interior; granita di caffè con panna. [S] *Average main: €3* ✉ *Via degli Orfani 86, Piazza Navona* ☎ *06/6789792* ⊕ *www.tazzadorocoffeeshop.com* ▭ *No credit cards.*

Tre Scalini

$ | **ICE CREAM** | **FAMILY** | The sidewalk tables of this café and its restaurant annex offer a grandstand view of all the action of the Piazza Navona. This is the place that invented the *tartufo,* a luscious chocolate ice-cream specialty. **Known for:** tables on the square with unmatched fountain views; decadent ice cream covered with a chocolate shell and whipped cream; sticker-shock prices for table service. $ *Average main: €10 ⊠ Piazza Navona 30, Piazza Navona* ☎ *06/6879148* ⊕ *www.ristorante-3scalini.com.*

 Hotels

Thanks to its Baroque palazzos, Bernini fountains, and outdoor cafés, Piazza Navona is one of Rome's most popular squares. The nearby Pantheon area, equally as beautiful with a few more quiet back alleys, offers great restaurants and shops. Hotels in this area offer postcard views of Rome and personalized service.

Albergo Santa Chiara
$$$$ | **HOTEL** | Guests choose this hotel, run by members of the same family for 200 years, not only for its prime location, but also its welcoming staff, top-notch service, and comfy beds. **Pros:** near the Pantheon and Santa Maria sopra Minerva; free Wi-Fi; lovely sitting area in front, overlooking the piazza. **Cons:** some rooms are on the small side; design is a bit basic given the higher price point; street-side rooms can be noisy. $ *Rooms from: €310 ⊠ Via Santa Chiara 21, Piazza Navona* ☎ *06/6872979* ⊕ *www.albergo-santachiara.com* ⇆ *96 rooms* ❍ *Free Breakfast.*

Antico Albergo del Sole al Pantheon
$$$$ | **HOTEL** | The granddaddy of Roman hotels and one of the oldest in the world—the doors first opened in 1467—this charming property is adjacent to the Pantheon and right in the middle of the lovely Piazza della Rotonda. **Pros:** larger rooms for groups available in an annex building; rich breakfast buffet; fabulous location. **Cons:** rooms are a bit small; complicated free Wi-Fi; not all

rooms have views. $ *Rooms from: €530 ⊠ Piazza della Rotonda 63, Piazza Navona* ☎ *06/6780441* ⊕ *www.hotelsolealpantheon.com* ⇆ *27 rooms* ❍ *Free Breakfast.*

G-Rough Hotel
$$$$ | **HOTEL** | With decor elements such as original wood-beamed ceilings, retro tiles, rich fabrics, contemporary art, and furniture that nods to 1930s and '40s Italian design, there's a hipster feel to this hotel inside a 17th-century palazzo around the corner from Piazza Navona. **Pros:** organic continental breakfast; free welcome drink at the hotspot bar; intriguing experience packages. **Cons:** rooms facing Piazza Pasquino can be noisy; no real reception area; consciously cool decor might be too overdone for some. $ *Rooms from: €550 ⊠ Piazza Pasquino 69, Piazza Navona* ☎ *06/68801085* ⊕ *g-rough.com* ⇆ *10 rooms* ❍ *Free Breakfast.*

Hotel Abruzzi
$$$ | **HOTEL** | This friendly, comfortable, family-run hotel has relatively gentle rates for such a prime location—directly in front of the Pantheon. **Pros:** magnificent Pantheon views; the piazza is a hot spot; sizable bathrooms. **Cons:** area can be somewhat noisy; breakfast is at a bar next door; elevator doesn't go to ground floor. $ *Rooms from: €280 ⊠ Piazza della Rotonda 69, Piazza Navona* ☎ *06/97841351* ⊕ *www.hotelabruzzi.it* ⇆ *26 rooms* ❍ *Free Breakfast* Ⓜ *Spagna.*

Hotel Genio
$$ | **HOTEL** | Just off the beautiful Piazza Navona, this aging but pleasant hotel has a lovely rooftop terrace that's the perfect place to enjoy a cappuccino or a glass of wine while taking in the view. **Pros:** breakfast buffet is abundant; moderate prices for the area; nice views from terrace. **Cons:** rooms facing the street can be noisy; spotty Wi-Fi; some furnishings need to be updated. $ *Rooms from: €190 ⊠ Via Giuseppe Zanardelli 28, Piazza Navona* ☎ *06/6833781* ⊕ *www.hotelgenioroma.it* ⇆ *60 rooms* ❍ *Free Breakfast.*

9 Hotel Cesàri

$$$$ | HOTEL | On a pedestrian-only street near the Pantheon, this lovely little hotel has an air of warmth and serenity, as well as a rooftop bar with great views of Rome. **Pros:** prime location; thoughtfully updated interiors; beautiful rooftop bar. **Cons:** two-night minimum; the area can be a bit noisy; rooftop bar not open in winter. $ *Rooms from: €350* ✉ *Via di Pietra 89/a, Piazza Navona* ☎ *06/6749701* ⊕ *www.9-hotel-cesari-rome.it* 🛏 *51 rooms* |⊚| *No Meals* Ⓜ *Barberini.*

The Pantheon Iconic Rome Hotel, Autograph Collection

$$$$ | HOTEL | A member of Marriott's Autograph Collection, this boutique hotel is a sleek retreat in the center of the action. **Pros:** modern design and amenities; exceptionally professional staff; Marriott Bonvoy members can redeem points. **Cons:** some rooms lack external views; no spa or gym; design might be considered a bit cold and corporate. $ *Rooms from: €600* ✉ *Via di Santa Chiara 4A, Piazza Navona* ☎ *06/87807070* ⊕ *www.thepantheonhotel.com* 🛏 *79 rooms* |⊚| *No Meals.*

Relais Palazzo Taverna

$$$ | HOTEL | This small, boutique-style hotel has reasonable rates considering its location—namely, a side street behind the lovely Via dei Coronari and right around the corner from Piazza Navona. **Pros:** centrally located; spacious accommodations; free Wi-Fi. **Cons:** staff on duty only until 5 pm (though can be contacted after-hours in an emergency); some rooms are showing wear and tear; walls are thin, so rooms can be noisy. $ *Rooms from: €210* ✉ *Via dei Gabrielli 92, Piazza Navona* ☎ *06/20398064* ⊕ *www.relaispalazzotaverna.com* 🛏 *11 rooms* |⊚| *No Meals* Ⓜ *Spagna.*

 Nightlife

In and around Piazza Navona, you can find anything from sophisticated cafés and flirty cocktail bars to dance clubs and outdoor chess games. Expect to be easily understood, as there is a high concentration of international guests mingling with Romans over a drink.

BARS

Enoteca al Parlamento Achilli

WINE BAR | The proximity of this traditional *enoteca* (wine bar) to Montecitorio, the Italian Parliament building, makes it a favorite with journalists and politicos, who often stop in for a glass of wine after work. But it's the tantalizing smell of truffles from the snack counter, where a sommelier waits to organize your tasting, that will probably lure you inside. There's also a celebrated restaurant where you can book a table and enjoy a parade of elegant Italian plates. Don't forget to check out the wine shop, too. ✉ *Via dei Prefetti 15, Piazza Navona* ☎ *06/6873446* ⊕ *achilli.restaurant.*

La Grande Bellezza Rooftop at Eitch Borromini

BARS | Rome has no shortage of gorgeous rooftop terrace bars, but this one—nestled amid cupolas and bell towers atop the Eitch Borromini hotel—is exceptional. Seats along the edge look down on Bernini's famed fountain in Piazza Navona. The chic white couches are almost always filled with well-heeled Romans, making sunset reservations essential. ✉ *Eitch Borromini, Via di Santa Maria dell'Anima, 30, Piazza Navona* ☎ *06/68215459* ⊕ *www.eitchborromini.com* ⊘ *Closed Nov.–Mar.*

Terrace Bar of the Hotel Raphaël

BARS | Want a peek at Rome's rooftops from atop an iconic, wisteria-draped palazzo? Head to the small terrace bar at the Hotel Raphaël, noted for its bird's-eye view of the campaniles and palazzi of Piazza Navona. This is one of Rome's most romantic spots, so booking a table (and being prepared for the relatively high prices) is advised. ✉ *Hotel Raphaël, Largo Febo 2, Piazza Navona* ☎ *06/682831* ⊕ *www.biohotelraphael.com.*

Vinoteca Novecento

WINE BAR | Salami-and-cheese tasting menus and a seemingly unlimited selection of wines, Prosecco, vini santi, and grappe are highlights of this lovely (albeit tiny) enoteca with a very old-fashioned vibe. Inside, it's standing-room only; in good weather, you can sit outside at an oak barrique on a quiet cobblestone street leading to one of Rome's prettiest small squares. ✉ *Piazza delle Coppelle 47, Piazza Navona* ☎ *06/6833078.*

DANCE CLUBS

Sharivari

DANCE CLUB | Here, a labyrinth of rooms contains a bistro and champagnerie, which are stocked with delicious delicacies and sought-after vintages, and a nightclub with two dance floors featuring every genre of music—from electronic and underground, to hip-hop, lounge, and international. ✉ *Via di Torre Argentina 78, Piazza Navona* ☎ *06/68806936* ⊕ *www.sharivari.it.*

 Performing Arts

FILM

Nuovo Olimpia

FILM | Just off Via del Corso in the center of the city, the somewhat basic two-screen Nuovo Olimpia is *the* cinema for Rome's international community, showing new-release films and Indie flicks in their original languages with Italian subtitles. ✉ *Via in Lucina 16/b, Piazza Navona* ☎ *06/88801283* ⊕ *www.circuitocinema.com* 🎟 *€8.50 Sat. and Sun., €6.50 Mon.–Fri.*

THEATER

English Theatre of Rome

THEATER | The oldest English-language theater group in town has a repertoire of original and celebrated plays. Performances are usually held at the intimate

70-seat Teatro Arciliuto. ✉ *Piazza Montevecchio 5, Piazza Navona* ☎ *346/3612209* ⊕ *rometheatre.org.*

 Shopping

The area around Piazza Navona is filled with vintage boutiques and tiny artisan shops; unique gifts such as marbled Florentine stationery or hand-blown Murano glass can be found here. You'll also find some classic wooden Italian playthings at the toy shops in this central area.

BEAUTY

Antica Erboristeria Romana

HEALTH & BEAUTY | Complete with hand-labeled wooden drawers holding more than 200 varieties of herbs, flowers, and tinctures, Antica Erboristeria Romana has maintained its old-world apothecary feel (it's the oldest shop of its kind in Rome, dating back to 1752). The shop stocks an impressive array of teas and herbal infusions, more than 700 essential oils, bud derivatives, and powdered extracts. ✉ *Via Torre Argentina 15, Piazza Navona* ☎ *06/6879493* ⊕ *www.anticaerboristeriaromana.it.*

BOOKS

Otherwise Bookshop

BOOKS | **FAMILY** | This fiercely independent bookstore with neon signs and bursting shelves stocks English-language best sellers as well as vintage postcards and used Italian books. It also regularly hosts chats with authors and has a particularly charming children's book section focused on all things Rome. ✉ *Via del Governo Vecchio, 80, Piazza Navona* ☎ *06/6879825* ⊕ *www.instagram.com/otherwisebookshop.*

CLOTHING

Davide Cenci

CLOTHING | Thanks to immaculate tailoring and custom-designed clothing, Davide Cenci is an Italian fashion powerhouse. Although the store features high-quality men's and women's clothing for every occasion, the label is most famous for its opulent cashmere, sailing sportswear, and trench coats. Attention to detail and customer service are hallmarks here: its clothiers will tailor most anything to fit your body like a glove and then have it delivered to your hotel within three days. ✉ *Via Campo Marzio 1–7, Piazza Navona* ☎ *06/6990681* ⊕ *www.davidecenci.com.*

Le Tartarughe

CLOTHING | A familiar face at the city's fashion shows, designer Susanna Liso, a Rome native, mixes raw silks or cashmere and fine merino wool to create captivating, enveloping garments that sometimes feature seductive or playful elements. Both her haute-couture and ready-to-wear lines are much loved by Rome's elite. ✉ *Via Piè di Marmo 17, Piazza Navona* ☎ *06/6792240* ⊕ *www. letartarughe.eu.*

Morgana

CLOTHING | When strolling down Via del Governo Vecchio, a street popular for funky and edgy clothing boutiques, you can't help but stop and stare at this shop's windows, where the family-run business displays some of its best hippie-chick and bridal-chic gowns, as well as Japanese Noh theater inspired coats. The highly original and highly coveted clothes are carefully crafted and hand-painted with one-of-a-kind designs. ✉ *Via del Governo Vecchio 27, Piazza Navona* ☎ *334/7960281.*

Replay

CLOTHING | Sitting in the shadow of the Pantheon, Replay has jeans and T-shirts with that little extra Italian kiss that makes everything fashionable and casual-chic rather than sloppy. Denim styles range from punk to hip-hop, though there are also some jeans with more traditional cuts. ✉ *Via della Rotonda 24, Piazza Navona* ☎ *06/68301212* ⊕ *www.replay.it.*

SBU

CLOTHING | SBU stands for Strategic Business Unit, a hip menswear label created by the Perfetti brothers in 1993. Just as their last name suggests, the jeans, casual clothing, shoes, and other sportswear sold here are just plain *perfetti.* Set in a 19th-century former draper's workshop, this is the store where Rome's VIPs buy their soft and supple vintage low-cut Japanese denim. The label also does well among A-listers in Paris, London, and Los Angeles. ✉ *Via di San Pantaleo 68–69, Piazza Navona* ☎ *06/68802547* ⊕ *www.sbu.it.*

Vestiti Usati Cinzia

CLOTHING | Vintage-clothes hunters, costume designers, and stylists alike love browsing through the racks at this fun, inviting shop, which is stocked wall-to-wall with funky 1960s and '70s apparel. There's definitely no shortage of goofy sunglasses, flower-power bell-bottoms, embroidered hippie tops, psychedelic boots, and other trippy merchandise from the days of peace and love. ✉ *Via del Governo Vecchio 45, Piazza Navona* ☎ *06/6832945* ⊕ *cinziavestitiusati.word-press.com.*

FOOD AND WINE

Moriondo e Gariglio

CANDY | **FAMILY** | Dating from 1850 and adhering strictly to family recipes passed on from generation to generation, this shop makes some of Rome's finest chocolate delicacies and other sweet treats. The selection of more than 80 confections includes everything from dark-chocolate truffles to marrons glacés. The chocolates shaped like every letter of the alphabet are perennial favorites, though. ✉ *Via Piè di Marmo 21, Piazza Navona* ☎ *06/6990856* ⊕ *moriondoegariglio.com.*

HOUSEWARES AND HOME DECOR

★ INOR dal 1952

HOUSEWARES | For more than 50 years, INOR dal 1952 has served as a trusted friend for Romans in desperate need of an exclusive wedding gift, delicate stemware, or oh-so-perfect china place settings for a fancy Sunday lunch. Entrance is via a secluded 15th-century courtyard and up a flight of stairs. The store specializes in work handcrafted by the silversmiths of Pampaloni and Bastianelli in Florence. ⊠ *Via della Stelletta 23, Piazza Navona* ☎ *06/6878579* ⊕ *www.inor.it.*

Murano Più

GLASSWARE | If you can't make it to Venice to shop for its famous handblown glassware, your next best option is to visit Murano Più, where items include vases, tableware, chandeliers, and jewelry. Each piece is handcrafted by a master glassblower using ancient techniques kept alive by artisans since 1291. ⊠ *Corso Rinascimento 53/55, Piazza Navona* ☎ *06/68808038* ⊕ *www.murano-roma.com/en.*

Society Limonta

HOUSEWARES | Have decorator envy? Head to the flagship store for Limonta, one of Italy's most prestigious and historical textile brands. Here, everything from table linens to duvet covers is made using the rarest and most sought-after fabrics in soft, calming colors. Look for comfy robes and other loungewear as well. ⊠ *Piazza di Pasquino 4, Piazza Navona* ☎ *06/6832480* ⊕ *www.societylimonta.com.*

Tebro

HOUSEWARES | First opened in 1867 and listed with the Associazione Negozi Storici di Roma (Association of Historic Shops of Rome), Tebro is a classic Roman department store that specializes in high-quality linens and sleepwear. You can even find those 100-percent-cotton, waffle-weave bath sheets that are synonymous with luxe Italian hotels. ⊠ *Via dei Prefetti 48, Piazza Navona* ☎ *06/6873441* ⊕ *www.tebro.it.*

JEWELRY

Co.Ro. Jewels

JEWELRY & WATCHES | Architects Giulia Giannini and Costanza De Cecco craft jewelry inspired by Italy's most beautiful structures. Available in silver and gold, standout designs from the contemporary brand include bold curved earrings in the shape of the Pantheon's internal dome, and delicate rings based on Venetian arches. ⊠ *Via della Scrofa, 52, Piazza Navona* ☎ *06/48930454* ⊕ *corojewels.com.*

Massimo Maria Melis

JEWELRY & WATCHES | Drawing heavily on ancient Roman and Etruscan designs, the jewelry from former costume designer Massimo Maria Melis will carry you back in time. Working with 21-carat gold, he often incorporates antique coins in many of his exquisite bracelets and necklaces. Some of his pieces are done with an ancient technique, much loved by the Etruscans, in which tiny gold droplets are fused together to create intricately patterned designs. ⊠ *Via dell'Orso 57, Piazza Navona* ☎ *06/6869188* ⊕ *www.massimomariamelis.com.*

Quattrocolo

JEWELRY & WATCHES | Dating from 1938, this shop showcases exquisite, antique, micro-mosaic jewelry painstakingly crafted in the style perfected by the masters at the Vatican mosaic studio. The small works were beloved by cosmopolitan clientele of the Grand Tour age and offer modern-day shoppers a taste of yesteryear's grandeur. You'll also find 18th- and 19th-century cameos and beautiful engraved stones, one-of-a-kind rings from the 1960s and '70s, as well as contemporary jewelry. ⊠ *Via della Scrofa 48, Piazza Navona* ☎ *06/68801367* ⊕ *www.quattrocolo.com.*

STATIONERY

★ Cartoleria Pantheon dal 1910

STATIONERY | Instead of sending a postcard home, why not send a letter written on sumptuous, handmade, Amalfi paper purchased from this shop? It also sells hand-bound leather journals in an extraordinary array of colors and sizes. There are two locations in the neighborhood. ⊠ *Via della Maddalena 41, Piazza Navona* ☎ *06/6795633* ⊕ *www.cartoleriapantheon.it.*

Manufactus

SPECIALTY STORE | One of Rome's preferred shops for those who appreciate exquisite writing materials specializes hand-bound leather journals but also sells such items as wax seals, presses for paper embossing, Venetian glass pens, and ink stamps. There are three other locations on Via della Rotonda, Piazza Navona, and Via dei Coronari. ✉ *Via del Pantheon 50, Piazza Navona* ☎ *06/6875313* ⊕ *www.manufactus.it.*

TOYS

Al Sogno

TOYS | FAMILY | This Navona jewel, around since 1945, is crammed top to bottom with artistic, well-crafted puppets, dolls, masks, stuffed animals, and other toys for children of all ages that encourage imaginative (and low-tech) play and learning. ✉ *Piazza Navona 53, corner of Via Agonale, Piazza Navona* ☎ *06/6864198* ⊕ *www.alsogno.com.*

La Città del Sole

TOYS | FAMILY | Chock-full of educational, fair-trade, and eco-friendly toys, puzzles, gadgets, books that share shelf space with retro and vintage favorites, La Città del Sole is a child-friendly delight. Items are arranged by age group, and the staffers are knowledgeable. ✉ *Via della Scrofa 65, Piazza Navona* ☎ *06/68803805* ⊕ *www.cittadelsole.it.*

Campo de' Fiori

In the morning, Campo de' Fiori, an evocative piazza ringed by medieval palazzi, is the site of a popular market—a bustling and beloved centro storico institution, where bag-toting *nonnas* shop for daily provisions side by side with people from tour groups browsing for souvenirs. In the evening and until well past midnight, the square is a hotspot, where young Romans and visitors alike patronize outdoor bars and restaurants.

 Sights

Chiesa del Gesù

CHURCH | With an overall design by Vignola and a facade and dome by Della Porta, the first Jesuit church in Rome influenced the city's ecclesiastical architecture for more than a century. Consecrated in 1584—after the Council of Trent (1545–63) solidified the determination of the Roman Catholic Church to push back against northern Europe's Reformed Protestants—Il Gesù also became the prototype for Counter-Reformation churches throughout not only Italy but also Europe and the Americas.

Although low lighting underplays the brilliance of everything, the inside of the church drips with gold and lapis lazuli, gold and precious marbles, and gold and more gold. The interior was initially left plain to the point of austerity; when it was finally fully embellished 100 years later, no expense was spared to inspire believers with pomp and majesty. The most striking element is the ceiling, where frescoes swirl down from on high and merge with painted stucco figures at the base. The artist Baciccia achieved extraordinary effects, especially over the nave in the *Triumph of the Holy Name of Jesus*. Here, the figures representing evil who are being cast out of heaven seem to hurtle down onto the observer.

The founder of the Jesuit order himself is buried in the Chapel of St. Ignatius, in the left-hand transept. This is surely one of the most sumptuous altars in Rome, though as is typical of Baroque decoration, which is renowned for its illusions, the enormous globe of lapis lazuli that crowns the alter is really only a shell of lapis over a stucco base. Note, too, architect Carlo Fontana's heavy, bronze altar rail, which is in keeping with the surrounding opulence. ✉ *Via degli Astalli 16, Campo de' Fiori* ☎ *06/697001* ⊕ *www.chiesadelgesu.org.*

Galleria Spada

ART MUSEUM | In this neighborhood of huge, austere palaces, Palazzo Spada strikes an almost frivolous note, with its pretty ornament-encrusted courtyard and its upper stories covered with stuccoes and statues. Although the palazzo houses an impressive collection of Old Master paintings, it's most famous for its trompe-l'oeil garden gallery, a delightful example of the sort of architectural games that rich Romans of the 17th century found irresistible.

Even if you don't go into the gallery, step into the courtyard and look through the glass window of the library to the colonnaded corridor in the adjacent courtyard. You'll see—or seem to see—a statue at the end of a 26-foot-long gallery, seemingly quadrupled in depth in a sort of optical telescope that takes Renaissance's art of perspective to another level. In fact the distance is an illusion: the corridor grows progressively narrower and the columns progressively smaller as they near a statue, which is just 2 feet tall. The Baroque period is known for its special effects, and this is rightly one of the most famous. It was long thought that Borromini was responsible for the ruse; it's now known that it was designed by an Augustinian priest, Giovanni Maria da Bitonto.

Upstairs is a seignorial picture gallery with the paintings shown as they would have been, hung one over the next clear to the ceiling. Outstanding works include Brueghel's *Landscape with Windmills,* Titian's *Musician,* and Andrea del Sarto's *Visitation.* Look for the fact sheets that have descriptive notes about the objects in each room. ⊠ *Piazza Capo di Ferro 13, Campo de' Fiori* ☎ *06/6874896* ⊕ *galleriaspada.cultura.gov.it* ⌨ *€6; free the first Sun. of the month* ⊗ *Closed Tues.*

★ Palazzo Farnese

CASTLE/PALACE | Rome's most beautiful Renaissance palace is fabled for its Galleria Carracci, whose ceiling is to the Baroque age what the Sistine Chapel ceiling is to the Renaissance. The Farnese family rose to great power and wealth during the Renaissance, in part because of the favor Pope Alexander VI showed to the beautiful Giulia Farnese. The massive palace was begun when, with Alexander's aid, Giulia's brother became cardinal; it was further enlarged on his election as Pope Paul III in 1534.

The uppermost frieze decorations and main window overlooking the piazza are the work of Michelangelo, who also designed part of the courtyard, as well as the graceful arch over Via Giulia at the back. The facade on Piazza Farnese has geometrical brick configurations that have long been thought to hold some occult meaning. When looking up at the palace, try to catch a glimpse of the splendid frescoed ceilings, including the Galleria Carracci vault painted by Annibale Carracci between 1597 and 1604.

The Carracci gallery depicts the loves of the gods, a supremely pagan theme that the artist painted in a swirling style that announced the birth of the Baroque. Other opulent salons are among the largest in Rome, including the Salon of Hercules, which has an impressive replica of the ancient *Farnese Hercules.* The French Embassy, which occupies the palace, offers tours (in English) on Monday, Wednesday, and Friday; book at least a few weeks (and up to eight months) in advance through the website, and bring a photo ID. ⊠ *French Embassy, Servizio Culturale, Piazza Farnese 67, Campo de' Fiori* ☎ *06/686011* ⊕ *www.visite-palazzo-farnese.it* ⌨ *€15* ⊗ *Closed Tues., Thurs., Sat., and Sun.*

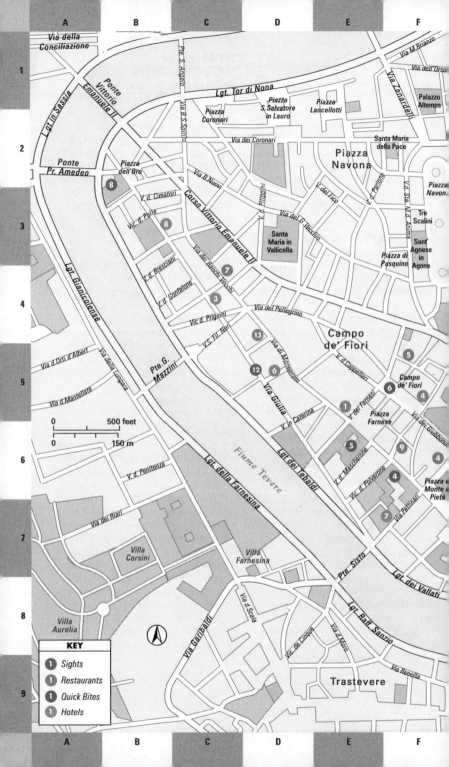

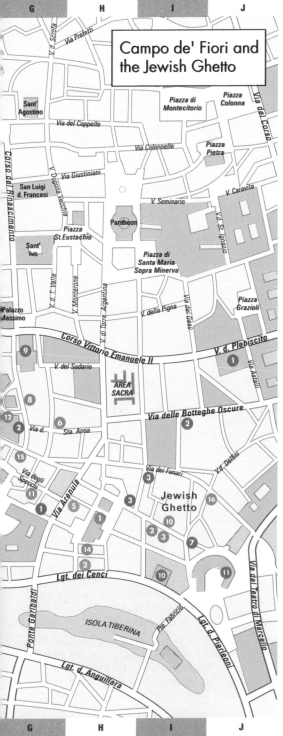

Campo de' Fiori and the Jewish Ghetto

157

Piazza Navona, Campo de' Fiori, and the Jewish Ghetto CAMPO DE' FIORI

Sights ▼

1 Chiesa del Gesù J5
2 Crypta Balbi I6
3 Fontana delle Tartarughe I6
4 Galleria Spada F6
5 Palazzo Farnese E6
6 Piazza Campo de' Fiori F5
7 Portico d'Ottavia I7
8 San Giovanni Battista
   dei Fiorentini...................... B3
9 Sant'Andrea della Valle G5
10 Sinagoga.............................. I8
11 Teatro di Marcello J8
12 Via Giulia............................ D5

Restaurants ▼

1 Al Pompiere H7
2 Ba'Ghetto............................ I7
3 BellaCarne........................... I7
4 Dar Filettaro a Santa Barbara..... F6
5 Ditirambo F5
6 Emma Pizzeria....................... G6
7 Il Pagliaccio C4
8 Il Sanlorenzo G5
9 L'Angolo Divino..................... F6
10 Nonna Betta......................... I7
11 Open Baladin........................ G7
12 Pesci Fritti G6
13 Pierluigi D4
14 Piperno Ristorante................. H7
15 Roscioli Salumeria con
    Cucina............................... G6
16 Vecchia Roma....................... J7

Quick Bites ▼

1 Bar Gelateria Alberto Pica........ G7
2 Fatamorgana Centro Storico G6
3 Pasticceria Boccione H7

Hotels ▼

1 Casa di Santa Brigida E5
2 citizenM.............................. H8
3 D.O.M. Hotel Roma C4
4 Hotel Campo de' Fiori F5
5 Hotel Chapter Roma................ H7
6 Hotel de' Ricci D5
7 Hotel Ponte Sisto F7
8 Relais Giulia B3

Piazza Campo de' Fiori

MARKET | **FAMILY** | A bustling marketplace in the morning (Monday through Saturday from 8 to 2) and a trendy meeting place the rest of the day and night, this piazza has plenty of down-to-earth charm. Just after lunchtime, all the fruit and vegetable vendors disappear, and this so-called *piazza trasformista* takes on another identity, becoming a circus of bars particularly favored by study-abroad students, tourists, and young expats. Brooding over the piazza is a hooded statue of the philosopher Giordano Bruno, who was burned at the stake here in 1600 for heresy, one of many victims of the Roman Inquisition. ⊠ *Intersection of Via dei Baullari, Via Giubbonari, Via del Pellegrino, and Piazza della Cancelleria, Campo de' Fiori.*

San Giovanni Battista dei Fiorentini

CHURCH | Imbued with the supreme grace of the Renaissance, this often-overlooked church dedicated to Florence's patron saint, John the Baptist, stands in what was the heart of Rome's Florentine colony, where residents included the goldsmiths, bankers, and money changers who contributed to the building of the church. Talented goldsmith and sculptor Benvenuto Cellini of Florence, known for both his genius and his vindictive nature, lived nearby.

Although the church was designed by Sansovino, Raphael (yes, he was also an architect) was among those who competed for this commission. The interior is the perfect Renaissance space, one so harmonious that it seems to be a 3-D Raphael painting. Borromini executed a splendid altar for the Falconieri family chapel in the choir. He's buried under the dome, despite the fact that those who committed suicide normally were refused a Christian burial. ⊠ *Via Acciaioli 2, Piazza dell'Oro, Campo de' Fiori* ☎ *06/68892059* ⊕ *sangiovannibattistadeifiorentini.it.*

Sant'Andrea della Valle

CHURCH | Topped by the highest dome in Rome after St. Peter's (designed by Maderno), this imposing 17th-century church is remarkably balanced in design. Fortunately, its facade, which had turned a sooty gray from pollution, has been cleaned to a near-sparkling white. Use one of the handy mirrors to examine the early-17th-century frescoes by Domenichino in the choir vault and those by Lanfranco in the dome. One of the earliest ceilings done in full Baroque style, its upward vortex was influenced by Correggio's dome in Parma, of which Lanfranco was also a citizen. (Bring a few coins to light the paintings, which can be very dim.) The three massive paintings of St. Andrew's martyrdom are by Mattia Preti (1650–51). Richly marbled and decorated chapels flank the nave, and in such a space, Puccini set the first act of *Tosca*. ⊠ *Piazza Vidoni 6, Corso Vittorio Emanuele II, Campo de' Fiori* ☎ *06/6861339* ⊕ *santandrea.teatinos.org.*

★ Via Giulia

STREET | Straight as a die and still something of a Renaissance-era diorama, Via Giulia was the first street in Rome since ancient times to be deliberately planned. It was named for Pope Julius II (of Sistine Chapel fame), who commissioned it in the early 1500s as part of a scheme to open up a grandiose approach to St. Peter's Basilica. Although the pope's plans were only partially completed, Via Giulia became an important thoroughfare in Renaissance Rome. It's still, after more than four centuries, the address of choice for Roman aristocrats, despite a recent, controversial addition: a large parking lot along one side of the street (creating it meant steamrolling through ancient and medieval ruins underneath).

A stroll around and along Via Giulia reveals elegant palaces and churches, including one, **San Eligio**, on the little side street Via di Sant'Eligio, that was designed by Raphael himself. Note also the **Palazzo Sacchetti** (✉ *Via Giulia 66*), with an imposing stone portal and an interior containing some of Rome's grandest staterooms; it remains, after 300 years, the private quarters of the Marchesi Sacchetti. The forbidding brick building that housed the **Carceri Nuove (New Prison)** (✉ *Via Giulia 52*), Rome's prison for more than two centuries, now contains the offices of the Direzione Nazionale Antimafia. Near the bridge that arches over Via Giulia's southern end is the church of **Santa Maria dell'Orazione e Morte** (Holy Mary of Prayer and Death), with stone skulls on its door. These are a symbol of a confraternity that was charged with burying the bodies of the unidentified dead found in the city streets.

Designed by Borromini and home, since 1927, to the Hungarian Academy, the **Palazzo Falconieri** (✉ *Via Giulia 1* ☎ *06/68896700*) has Borromini-designed salons and loggia that are sporadically open as part of guided tours; call for information. The falcon statues atop its belvedere are best viewed from around the block, along the Tiber embankment. Remnant of a master plan by Michelangelo, the arch over the street was meant to link massive **Palazzo Farnese,** on the east side of Via Giulia, with the building across the street and a bridge to the Villa Farnesina, directly across the river. Finally, on the right and rather green with age, dribbles that star of many a postcard, the **Fontana del Mascherone.** ✉ *Via Giulia, between Piazza dell'Oro and Piazza San Vincenzo Palloti, Campo de' Fiori.*

🍴 Restaurants

Campo de' Fiori is home to one of Rome's largest open-air produce markets and is historically the secular crossroads of the city: even in ancient Rome, pilgrims gathered here to eat, drink, and be merry. Today's shoppers at the market and the surrounding *forno* (bakeries) include local chefs who come to find inspiration and ingredients for dishes on their menus.

Dar Filettaro a Santa Barbara

$ | **ITALIAN** | The window reads "Filetti di Baccalà," but the official name of this small restaurant that specializes in one thing—deliciously battered and deep-fried fillets of salt cod—is Dar Filettaro a Santa Barbara. If it's in season, be sure to try the *puntarelle* (crisp chicory) tossed with garlic and anchovy dressing. **Known for:** piping hot filetti di baccalà; functional "hole-in-the-wall" interior; tables outside on the pretty square. [$] *Average main: €8* ✉ *Largo dei Librari 88, Campo de' Fiori* ☎ *06/6864018* 🌐 *www.facebook.com/FilettiDiBaccala* 🕒 *Closed Sun. and Aug. No lunch.*

Ditirambo

$$ | **ITALIAN** | Don't let the country-kitchen feel fool you. This little spot off of Campo de' Fiori goes a step beyond the ordinary with constantly changing offbeat takes on Italian classics. **Known for:** cozy and casual; hearty meat and pasta dishes; perfectly grilled octopus and other seafood dishes. [$] *Average main: €18* ✉ *Piazza della Cancelleria 74, Campo de' Fiori* ☎ *06/6871626* 🌐 *www.ristoranteditirambo.it* 🕒 *No lunch Mon. Closed Aug.*

★ Emma Pizzeria

$$$ | **ROMAN** | **FAMILY** | Smack in the middle of the city, with the freshest produce right outside its door, this pizzeria features pies made with dough by Rome's renowned family of bakers, the Roscriolis. The menu also offers a good selection of pastas, mains, and local Lazio wines. **Known for:** light, airy, and casual; thin-crust Roman pizza; tasty fritti (classic fried Roman pizzeria appetizers). [$] *Average main: €25* ✉ *Via Monte della Farina 28–29, Campo de' Fiori* ☎ *06/64760475* 🌐 *www.emmapizzeria.com.*

Il Pagliaccio

$$$$ | **MODERN ITALIAN** | Some of the most innovative interpretations of fine Roman cookery can be found in this starkly chic

restaurant on a backstreet between upscale Via Giulia and the Campo de' Fiori. Chef Anthony Genovese was born in France to Calabrese parents and spent time cooking in Japan and Thailand, so his dishes make use of nontraditional spices, ingredients, and preparations—garnering him a loyal following and multiple accolades. **Known for:** elaborate tasting menus; fine dining in elegant surroundings; discreet location. $ *Average main: €110* ⊠ *Via dei Banchi Vecchi 129a, Piazza Navona* ☎ *06/68809595* ⊕ *www.ristoranteilpagliaccio.com* ⊘ *Closed Sun., Mon., and Aug. No lunch Tues.–Fri.*

Il Sanlorenzo

$$$$ | **SEAFOOD** | A gorgeous space, with chandeliers and soaring original brickwork ceilings, is the setting for one of Rome's best seafood restaurants. Order à la carte, or if you're hungry, the eight-course tasting menu (given the quality of the fish, a relative bargain at €90), which might include cuttlefish-ink tagliatelle with mint, artichokes, and roe or shrimp from the island of Ponza with rosemary, bitter herbs, and porcini mushrooms. **Known for:** top-quality fish and seafood; spaghetti con ricci (sea urchins); elegant surroundings. $ *Average main: €70* ⊠ *Via dei Chiavari 4/5, Campo de' Fiori* ☎ *06/6865097* ⊕ *www.ilsanlorenzo.it* ⊘ *Closed 2 wks in Aug. No lunch Mon.*

L'Angolo Divino

$ | **WINE BAR** | There's something about this cozy wine bar that makes it feel as if it's in a small traditional village instead of a bustling metropolis. The walls are lined with a tempting array of bottles from around the Italian peninsula, and the counter is stocked with cheese and salumi that can be sliced and piled on plates to order. **Known for:** excellent wine selection and advice; cozy atmosphere; late-night snacks. $ *Average main: €14* ⊠ *Via dei Balestrari 12, Campo de' Fiori* ☎ *06/6864413* ⊕ *www.angolodivino.it* ⊘ *Closed 2 wks in Aug.*

Open Baladin

$$ | **BURGER** | The craft beer movement has taken hold in Italy, and this hip, sprawling space tucked down a tiny side road near Campo de' Fiori is headed up by the Baladin beer company. Staff members take their jobs—and brews—seriously, and they're helpful with recommendations from the more than 40 choices on tap and the over 100 options in bottles. **Known for:** great craft beer; hand-cut potato chips with pecorino cheese; modern gastropub atmosphere. $ *Average main: €15* ⊠ *Via degli Specchi 6, Campo de' Fiori* ☎ *06/6838989* ⊕ *www.baladin.it/open-baladin-roma.*

Pesci Fritti

$$ | **SOUTHERN ITALIAN** | This cute jewel box of a restaurant sits on the ruins of the ancient Theatre of Pompey just behind Campo de' Fiori (note the curve of the street). Step inside, and the whitewashed walls with touches of pale sea blue will make you feel like you've escaped to the Mediterranean coast for seafood favorites. **Known for:** fried fish and seafood choices; spaghetti with clams; cozy setting. $ *Average main: €18* ⊠ *Via di Grottapinta 8, Campo de' Fiori* ☎ *06/68806170* ⊕ *pescifritti.business.site* ⊘ *Closed Mon. and Aug.*

★ Pierluigi

$$$$ | **SEAFOOD** | This chic seafood restaurant is a fun spot on balmy summer evenings, where elegant diners sip crisp white wine at tables out on the pretty Piazza de' Ricci. The carpaccio selection is exquisite, but there is also a large selection of pastas extravagantly topped with white truffles. **Known for:** top-quality fish and seafood; tables on the pretty pedestrianized piazza; elegant atmosphere with great service. $ *Average main: €45* ⊠ *Piazza de' Ricci 144, Campo de' Fiori* ☎ *06/6868717* ⊕ *www.pierluigi.it.*

★ Roscioli Salumeria con Cucina

$$ | **WINE BAR** | The shop in front of this wine bar will beckon you in with top-quality comestibles like hand-sliced cured ham from Italy and Spain, more than 300 cheeses, and a dizzying array of wines—but venture farther inside to try an extensive selection of unusual dishes and interesting takes on the classics. There are tables in the cozy wine cellar downstairs, but try and bag a table at the back on the ground floor (reserve well ahead; Roscioli is very popular). **Known for:** extensive wine list; arguably Rome's best spaghetti alla carbonara; unrivaled prosciutto selection. $ *Average main: €22* ✉ *Via dei Giubbonari 21, Campo de' Fiori* ☎ *06/6875287* ⊕ *www.salumeriaroscioli.com* ☺ *Closed 1 wk in Aug.*

 Coffee and Quick Bites

Bar Gelateria Alberto Pica

$ | **ICE CREAM** | **FAMILY** | Here, gelato production is artisanal, and the selection of seasonal *sorbetti* and *cremolate* (the latter is similar to sorbetto but made with the fruit pulp, rather than just fruit juice) is diverse. Although the gelateria got contemporary makeover for its 50th birthday, it offers the same old-fashioned treats that the family has been serving for decades. **Known for:** sleek bar without losing its old-school attitude; brusque owners who keep the lines moving; riso a cannella gelato (cinnamon rice pudding). $ *Average main: €4* ✉ *Via della Seggiola 12, Campo de' Fiori* ☎ *06/6868405* ⊕ *facebook.com/bargelateriaalbertopica* ☺ *Closed Sun. and 2 wks in Aug.*

Fatamorgana Centro Storico

$ | **ICE CREAM** | **FAMILY** | The highest-quality ingredients go into the gelato here, and the flavors range from the traditional to the wonderfully unique (think Gorgonzola or tobacco and chocolate). The fruit flavors are always in season. **Known for:** quality gelato; seasonal fruit flavors; beloved local brand. $ *Average main:*

€4 ✉ *Via dei Chiavari 37, Campo de' Fiori* ☎ *06/88818437* ⊕ *www.gelateriafatamorgana.com* ☺ *Closed 1 wk in Aug.*

 Hotels

If you want to be in the *cuore of Roma vecchia* (or "heart of Old Rome"), there's no better place than Campo de' Fiori, a gorgeous piazza with lively merchants, outdoor cafés, and bars. There are standout luxury options but not all the budget hotels are as lovely as their surroundings: many are cramped and could use updating, though their rooftop views are eternally enticing.

Casa di Santa Brigida

$ | **B&B/INN** | The friendly sisters of Santa Brigida oversee simple, straightforward, and centrally located accommodations in one of Rome's loveliest convents, with a rooftop terrace overlooking Palazzo Farnese. **Pros:** insider papal audience tickets; large library and sunroof; free Wi-Fi. **Cons:** weak air-conditioning; no TVs in the rooms (though there is a common TV room); payment at structure only. $ *Rooms from: €50* ✉ *Piazza Farnese 96, entrance around the corner at Via Monserrato 54, Campo de' Fiori* ☎ *06/68892596* ⊕ *www.casabrigidaroma.it* ⤳ *20 rooms* ❖ *Free Breakfast.*

D.O.M Hotel Roma

$$$$ | **HOTEL** | In an old convent on Via Giulia, one of Rome's romantic ivy-covered streets, the D.O.M (Deo Optimo Maximo) is an ultrachic luxury hotel that resembles an aristocratic *casa nobile*. **Pros:** complimentary Acqua di Parma toiletries; heated towel racks; hip decor in historic setting. **Cons:** an armed guard at the anti-terrorism headquarters opposite the hotel may be off-putting for some; delicious but expensive cocktails; standard rooms are small for a five-star hotel. $ *Rooms from: €550* ✉ *Via Giulia 131, Campo de' Fiori* ☎ *06/6832144* ⊕ *www.domhotelroma.com* ⤳ *18 rooms* ❖ *Free Breakfast.*

Hotel Campo de' Fiori

$$$$ | HOTEL | This handsome, ivy-draped hotel is a romantic refuge in the heart of Campo de' Fiori. **Pros:** set on a gorgeous small square close to the action of the main campo; panoramic rooftop terrace; well-stocked library where one can relax and read. **Cons:** rooms are on the small side and could use updating; some apartments are too close to the area's noisy bar scene; can get pricey in high season. [$] *Rooms from: €420* ✉ *Via del Biscione 6, Campo de' Fiori* ☎ *06/68806865* 🌐 *www.hotelcampodefiori.com/en* 🛏 *25 rooms* 🍴 *Free Breakfast.*

Hotel de' Ricci

$$$$ | HOTEL | This intimate boutique hotel from the team behind the Pierluigi restaurant is a top spot for wine lovers. **Pros:** excellent wine cellar and cigar lounge; great location on a quiet street; perks include complimentary aperitivo and priority reservations at Pierluigi. **Cons:** there's a charge of €50 per day to bring pets; there is a weekend crowd for the brunch; no spa or gym. [$] *Rooms from: €680* ✉ *Via della Barchetta 14, Campo de' Fiori* ☎ *06/6874775* 🌐 *www.hotelderricci.com* 🛏 *8 rooms* 🍴 *No Meals.*

Hotel Ponte Sisto

$$$ | HOTEL | Situated in a remodeled Renaissance palazzo with one of the prettiest patio-courtyards in Rome, this hotel is a relaxing retreat close to Campo de' Fiori and Trastevere. **Pros:** rooms with views (and some with balconies and terraces); great location between Trastevere and Campo de' Fiori; beautiful courtyard garden. **Cons:** street-side rooms can be noisy; some upgraded rooms are small and not worth the price difference; a/c is controlled centrally and requires a call to the front desk to adjust. [$] *Rooms from: €260* ✉ *Via dei Pettinari 64, Campo de' Fiori* ☎ *06/6863100* 🌐 *www.hotelponte-sisto.it* 🛏 *106 rooms* 🍴 *Free Breakfast.*

Relais Giulia

$$$ | HOTEL | In a 15th-century palazzo on one of the city's oldest streets, Relais Giulia is a classic Roman Renaissance boutique hotel with sophisticated modern furnishings and fixtures. **Pros:** good value for the area; great location in between Campo de' Fiori and Trastevere; thoughtful amenities. **Cons:** Wi-Fi can be patchy; some rooms and facilities could use updating; keyless entry system takes getting used to. [$] *Rooms from: €270* ✉ *Via Giulia 93, Campo de' Fiori* ☎ *06/95581300* 🌐 *www.relaisgiuliahotel.it* 🛏 *13 rooms* 🍴 *Free Breakfast.*

🍸 Nightlife

With plenty of college bars, Campo de' Fiori is Rome's magnet for the study-abroad scene and young Romans. The lounge-style restaurants that line the square are also popular posts for people-watching with a spritz in hand after dark.

BARS

Il Goccetto

WINE BAR | Specializing in the vintages produced by smaller vineyards from Sicily to Venice, this historical wine bar also has a menu of Italian delicacies (meats and cheeses) that likewise represents the entire Italian peninsula. The burrata with sun-dried tomatoes is a perennial favorite. The tiny bar is well designed but is always busy and never accepts reservations. If all the seats are taken, you might be able to sip wine on the step outside while taking in the snippets of Roman life passing by. ✉ *Via dei Banchi Vecchi 14, Campo de' Fiori* ☎ *06/99448583* 🌐 *www.ilgoccetto.com.*

Jerry Thomas Speakeasy

COCKTAIL BARS | One of just a handful of hidden bars in Rome, this intimate bar looks like a Prohibition-era haunt and serves the kind of classic cocktails you find in New York speakeasies. It's seating

---

room only, so reservations must be made online in advance. Upon booking, you'll receive a password via email. Since it is a private club, the bar stays open late but patrons need to pay the €5 yearly membership fee once they arrive for the first time. Serious cocktail aficionados can also purchase specialty bitters and mixology tools at the Emporium across the alley from the drinks spot. ✉ *Vicolo Cellini 30, Campo de' Fiori* ☎ *340/7332980 WhatsApp only* ⊕ *www.thejerrythomasproject.it.*

The Sofa Bar Restaurant & Roof Terrace

BARS | The romantic rooftop terrace at I Sofà has a 360-degree view of the Eternal City, so it's no surprise that it's a prime spot for a late-afternoon cocktail (weather permitting). The bar takes its name from the historic stone benches carved into the wall at the entrance to the Hotel St. George. Head downstairs in the cooler months for a wide selection of craft beers on tap inside the Hotel Indigo. ✉ *Hotel Indigo Rome—St. George, Via Giulia 62, Campo de' Fiori* ☎ *06/68661846* ⊕ *www.isofadiviagiulia.com.*

 Performing Arts

THEATER

★ **Teatro Argentina**

THEATER | The 18th-century Teatro Argentina evokes glamour and sophistication with its velvet upholstery, large crystal chandeliers, and beautifully dressed theatergoers, who come to see international productions of stage and dance performances. ✉ *Largo di Torre Argentina 52, Campo de' Fiori* ☎ *06/684000314* ⊕ *www.teatrodiroma.net.*

 Shopping

Campo de' Fiori, one of Rome's most captivating piazzas, comes to life early in the morning, when merchants theatrically sell their best tomatoes, salumi, artichokes, blood oranges, herbs, and spices. The labyrinthine streets branching off the square are crowded with small shops with offerings to suit any budget.

ANTIQUES

Nardecchia

ANTIQUES & COLLECTIBLES | Since the 1950s, the Nardecchia family has been in the business of selling beautiful 19th-century prints, old photographs, and watercolors that depict Rome in centuries past. Can't afford an 18th-century etching? The store has beautiful postcards, too. ✉ *Via del Monserrato 106, Campo de' Fiori* ☎ *06/6869318* ⊕ *www.facebook.com/nardecchiastampe.*

CHILDREN'S CLOTHING

Rachele

CHILDREN'S CLOTHING | **FAMILY** | This charming shop near the Piazza Campo de' Fiori sells original and whimsical handmade children's clothing. If you're looking for something truly unique, Rachele (the Swedish owner and designer) makes only two of everything for tykes up to age 12. Your children can make a statement with any of her cute pants, trapeze skirts, or rainbow-color tops. ✉ *Vicolo del Bollo 6–7, Campo de' Fiori* ☎ *329/6481004* ⊕ *www.facebook.com/racheleart.*

CLOTHING

★ **L'Archivio di Monserrato**

CLOTHING | Tailored jackets with exotic trims, dresses in eclectic prints and bold colors, and smart linen suits are some of the offerings at this airy, spacious boutique curated by Soledad Twombly (daughter-in-law of painter Cy Twombly). In addition to her original designs, look for a sophisticated mix of antique Turkish and Indian textiles, jewelry, shoes, and small housewares picked up on her travels. ✉ *Via di Monserrato 150, Campo de' Fiori* ☎ *06/45654157* ⊕ *www.soledadtwombly.com.*

JEWELRY

Delfina Delettrez

JEWELRY & WATCHES | When your great-grandmother is Adele Fendi, it's not surprising that creativity runs in your genes. Young Roman designer Delfina Delettrez creates edgy gold and silver jewelry that might incorporate anything from bone and glass to diamonds and pearls. Although colorful pieces shaped like lips, eyes, or even fingers have a 1980s surrealist feel, items such as delicate gold chain necklaces or earrings designed to hold earbuds are oh-so contemporary. ⌂ *Via di Monserrato, 24A, Campo de' Fiori* ☎ *06/68134105* ⊕ *www. delfinadelettrez.com.*

SHOES, HANDBAGS, AND LEATHER GOODS

★ Chez Dede

SPECIALTY STORE | Husband-and-wife duo Andrea Ferolla and Daria Reina (he's a fashion illustrator, she's a photographer) curate a selection of clothes, bags, vintage jewelry, books, home decor, and anything else you might need in this cult favorite lifestyle-concept shop. Their signature fabric bags are designed to go from the plane straight to the beach club, and they regularly release collectible items featuring Ferolla's whimsical illustrations. ⌂ *Via di Monserrato 35, Campo de' Fiori* ☎ *06/83772934* ⊕ *www. chezdede.com.*

Ibiz

LEATHER GOODS | In business since 1972, this family team creates colorful, stylish leather handbags, belts, keychains, and sandals near Piazza Campo de' Fiori. Choose from the premade collection, or order something in the color of your choice; their workshop is visible in the boutique. ⌂ *Via dei Chiavari 39, Campo de' Fiori* ☎ *06/68307297* ⊕ *ibizroma.it.*

★ Maison Halaby

HANDBAGS | Lebanese designer and artist Gilbert Halaby was featured in fashion magazines like *Vogue* and created jewelry for Lady Gaga before giving up the rat race and opening his own shop, where the ethos is all about slow fashion. His boldly colored leather handbags incorporate suede, python, fringe, raffia, or jeweled handles, and his silk scarves are printed with his original watercolors, some of which are also on sale. The small, homey boutique—with a velvet sofa and lots of books, plants, and art by Halaby himself—is mainly open by appointment, but if you pass by, ring the bell, and if Gilbert is there, he might just invite you in for coffee or Campari. ⌂ *Via di Monserrato 21, Campo de' Fiori* ☎ *06/96521585* ⊕ *www.facebook.com/ HALABY.OFFICIAL.*

The Jewish Ghetto

Established by papal decree in the 16th century, the Jewish Ghetto was, by definition, a closed community whose inhabitants lived under lock and key until Italian unification in 1870. In 1943–44, the already small Jewish population was decimated by deportations.

Today, most of Rome's Jews live outside the Ghetto, but the area around the city's Great Synagogue is still the community's spiritual and cultural home. That heritage permeates its small commercial district of Judaica shops, kosher bakeries, and restaurants. Note, however, that most businesses here observe the Jewish Sabbath, so it's a relative ghost town on Saturday.

Tight, teeming alleys run down into the Ghetto from Giacomo della Porta's unmistakable Fontana delle Tartarughe (Turtle Fountain). A visit to the turn-of-the-20th-century synagogue, with its museum dedicated to the history of Jewish Rome, is a must for understanding the Ghetto. Afterward, stroll Via Portico d'Ottavia and see its namesake structure in the center of the district. The east end of the street leads down to a path past the 1st-century Teatro di Marcello.

At the center of the Jewish Ghetto you'll find Portico d'Ottavia, which was Rome's fish market in the Middle Ages.

The Tiber River separates the Ghetto and Trastevere, with the lovely Isola Tiberina (Tiber Island) in the middle. You can cross the river here via the Ponte Fabricio, the oldest bridge in Rome.

 ## Sights

Crypta Balbi

RUINS | The fourth component of the magnificent collections of the Museo Nazionale Romano, this museum is unusual because it represents several periods of Roman history. The crypt is part of the Balbus Theater complex (13 BC), and other parts of the complex are from the medieval period, up through the 20th century. Though the interior lacks the lingering opulence of some other Roman sites, the written explanations accompanying the well-lit exhibits are excellent, and this museum is a popular field trip for teachers and school groups. Note that recent restoration works have resulted in closures here; check for updates before visiting. ✉ *Via delle Botteghe Oscure 31, Jewish Ghetto* ☎ *06/684851* ⊕ *museonazionaleromano.beniculturali.it/crypta-balbi* ✉ *€8 Crypta Balbi only; €12 includes three other Museo Nazionale Romano sites over a 1-wk period (Palazzo Altemps, Palazzo Massimo, Museo Diocleziano)* ⊙ *Closed Mon.* Ⓜ *Bus Nos. 64 and 40, Tram No. 8.*

Fontana delle Tartarughe

FOUNTAIN | **FAMILY** | Designed by Giacomo della Porta in 1581 and sculpted by Taddeo Landini, this fountain, set in pretty Piazza Mattei, is one of Rome's most charming. Its focal point consists of four bronze boys, each grasping a dolphin spouting water into a marble shell. Bronze turtles just out of reach of the boys' hands drink from the upper basin. The turtles were added in the 17th century by Bernini. ✉ *Piazza Mattei, Jewish Ghetto.*

Portico d'Ottavia

RUINS | Looming over the Jewish Ghetto, this huge portico, with a few surviving columns, is one of the area's most picturesque set pieces, with the church of Sant'Angelo in Pescheria built right into its ruins. Named by Augustus in honor of his sister Octavia, it was originally 390 feet wide and 433 feet long; encompassed two temples, a meeting hall, and a library; and served as a kind of grandiose entrance foyer for the adjacent Teatro di Marcello.

In the Middle Ages, the cool marble ruins of the portico became Rome's *pescheria* (fish market). A stone plaque on a pillar (it's a copy as the original is in the Musei Capitolini) states in Latin that the head of any fish surpassing the length of the plaque was to be cut off "up to the first fin" and given to the city fathers or else the vendor was to pay a fine of 10 gold florins. The heads, which were used to make fish soup, were considered a great delicacy. ⊠ *Via Portico d'Ottavia 29, Jewish Ghetto* ☎ *06/0608.*

Sinagoga

RELIGIOUS BUILDING | This synagogue has been the city's largest Jewish temple, and a Roman landmark with its distinctive aluminum dome, since its construction in 1904. The building also houses the Jewish Museum, with displays of precious ritual objects and exhibits that document the uninterrupted presence of a Jewish community in the city for nearly 22 centuries. Until the 16th century, Jews were esteemed citizens of Rome. Among them were bankers and physicians to the popes, who had themselves given permission for the construction of synagogues. But, in 1555, during the Counter-Reformation, Pope Paul IV decreed the building of the walls of the Ghetto, confining the Jews to this small flood-prone area and imposing restrictions, some of which continued to be enforced until 1870. For security reasons, entrance is via guided visit only, and tours in English are available twice a day but should be booked online ahead of time. Entrance to the synagogue is through the museum on Via Catalana. ⊠ *Lungotevere de' Cenci 15, Jewish Ghetto* ☎ *06/68400661* ⊕ *www.*

museoebraico.roma.it ⊠ *€11* ⊙ *Museum closed Sat. and Jewish holidays.*

Teatro di Marcello

RUINS | Begun by Julius Caesar and completed by the emperor Augustus in 13 BC, this theater could house around 14,000 spectators. Like other Roman monuments, it was transformed into a fortress during the Middle Ages. During the Renaissance, it was converted into a residence by the Savelli, one of the city's noble families. Today, only the archaeological park around the theater is open to the public, with its picturesque walkway that curves past the ruins and links to the Portico d'Ottavia. In summer, the small park becomes a magical venue for open-air classical music concerts. ⊠ *Via del Teatro di Marcello, Jewish Ghetto* ☎ *06/87131590 concert info* ⊕ *www.tempietto.it.*

🍴 Restaurants

Across Via Arenula from Campo de' Fiori, the Ghetto is home to Europe's oldest Jewish population, who have lived in Rome for more than 2,000 years. There are excellent restaurants along its enchanting main drag, Via del Portico d'Ottavia, and in the backstreets that wind between the river, Via Arenula, and Piazza Venezia.

Al Pompiere

$$$ | ROMAN | The nondescript entrance on a narrow side street leads upstairs to the main dining room of this neighborhood favorite, where those in the know enjoy dining on classic Roman fare under arched, frescoed ceilings. Fried zucchini flowers, Roman-Jewish style artichokes, battered salt cod, and gnocchi are all consistently excellent, and the menu has some nice, historic touches, like a beef-and-citron stew from an ancient Roman recipe of Apicius. **Known for:** traditional elegant setting; ricotta and sour cherry tart; fettuccine al limone. $ *Average main: €25* ⊠ *Via Santa Maria dei Calderari 38,*

Jewish Ghetto ☎ *06/6868377* ⊕ *www. alpompiereroma.com* ⊘ *Closed Tues. and Aug. No dinner Sun.*

★ Ba'Ghetto

$$ | ITALIAN | FAMILY | This well-established hot spot on the Jewish Ghetto's main promenade has pleasant indoor and outdoor seating. The kitchen is kosher (many places featuring Roman Jewish fare are not) and is known for its Judeo-Roman meat dishes mixed with Middle Eastern recipes. **Known for:** carciofi alla giudia (deep-fried artichokes) and other Roman-Jewish specialties; casual family atmosphere; tables on the pedestrianized street. $ *Average main: €22* ⊠ *Via del Portico d'Ottavia 57, Jewish Ghetto* ☎ *06/68892868* ⊕ *www.baghetto.com* ⊘ *Dinner Fri. and lunch Sat. are strictly for those who observe Shabbat with advance payment.*

BellaCarne

$$ | ROMAN | *Bellacarne* means "beautiful meat," and that's the focus of the menu here (though it's also what a Jewish Italian grandmother might say while pinching her grandchild's cheek). The kosher kitchen makes its own pastrami, but the setting is more fine dining than deli. **Known for:** pastrami; shabbat menu; outside seating on a lively pedestrianized street. $ *Average main: €19* ⊠ *Via Portico d'Ottavia 51, Jewish Ghetto* ☎ *06/6833104* ⊕ *www.bellacarne.it* ⊘ *No dinner Fri. No lunch Sat. except limited Shabbat seating that must be pre-paid.*

Nonna Betta

$$ | ROMAN | This neighborhood institution serves all the Roman-Jewish classics. Like most of the starters, the *carciofi alla giudia* (Jewish-style artichokes) are outstanding, and a perfect meal might also include the carbonara, which incorporates dried beef instead of guanciale, or the semolina gnocchi baked in a terra-cotta ramekin. **Known for:** casual and busy atmosphere; vegetarian carbonara with zucchini; outside seating. $ *Average*

Roman Jewish Cuisine

Variations on cured pork, such as guanciale, prosciutto, and pancetta, are signature flavorings for Roman dishes. When Jewish culinary culture started intermingling with Roman, it was discovered that Jewish cooks used *alici* (anchovies) to flavor dishes the way Romans used cured pork. For excellent-quality anchovies, check out the Jewish *alimentari* (food shops) in the Ghetto.

main: *€17* ⊠ *Via del Portico d'Ottavia 16, Jewish Ghetto* ☎ *06/68806263* ⊕ *www. nonnabetta.it* ⊘ *Closed Tues.*

Piperno Ristorante

$$ | ROMAN | *The* place to go for Rome's extraordinary carciofi alla giudia, Piperno has been in business since 1860. The location, up a tiny hill in a piazza tucked away behind the palazzi of the Jewish Ghetto, lends the restaurant a rarefied air. **Known for:** old-school elegance; great fish dishes; fried stuffed zucchini flowers. $ *Average main: €23* ⊠ *Monte dei Cenci 9, Jewish Ghetto* ☎ *06/68806629* ⊕ *www.ristorantepiperno.it* ⊘ *Closed Mon. and Aug. No lunch Tues.–Fri., no dinner Sun.*

Vecchia Roma

$$ | SEAFOOD | Though the frescoed dining rooms are lovely, when the weather is good, the choice place to dine is out on the piazza, beneath big white umbrellas and in the shadow of Santa Maria in Campitelli. Seafood is the specialty, and simple southern Italian preparations, such as grilled calamari with Sicilian tomatoes, are excellent no-fail choices. **Known for:** large portions; fresh fruit sorbets; some of the best outdoor seating in the city. $ *Average main: €22* ✉ *Piazza Campitelli 18, Jewish Ghetto* ☎ *06/6864604* 🌐 *www.facebook.com/VecchiaRoma.Ristorante* 🕒 *Closed Sun. and 1 wk in Aug.*

Coffee and Quick Bites

Pasticceria Boccione

$ | **BAKERY** | **FAMILY** | This tiny, old-school bakery famed for its Roman-Jewish sweet specialties is easy to spot because there is always a line snaking out the door. Service is brusque, choices are few, what's available depends on the season, and when it's sold out, it's sold out. **Known for:** ricotta and cherry tarts; pizza ebraica ("Jewish pizza," a dense baked sweet rich in nuts and raisins); no frills and no seats. $ *Average main: €6* ✉ *Via del Portico d'Ottavia 1, Jewish Ghetto* ☎ *06/6878637* 🕒 *Closed Sat.*

Hotels

Chapter Roma

$$$$ | **HOTEL** | The edgy, of-the-moment design at this boutique hotel juxtaposes plush midcentury Italian furnishings with street art murals and industrial touches. **Pros:** trendy design; coworking space available; lively rooftop bar in summer. **Cons:** no gym; no spa; rooms below the bar can be noisy. $ *Rooms from: €380* ✉ *Via di Santa Maria de' Calderari 47, Jewish Ghetto* ☎ *06/89935351* 🌐 *www.chapter-roma.com* 🛏 *47 rooms* 🍴 *Free Breakfast.*

citizenM

$$$ | **HOTEL** | A cheerful hotel with irreverent art that overlooks Tiber Island, citizenM's first Italian property has a young sensibility and is located close to Rome's most ancient attractions. **Pros:** great location with easy access to Trastevere; tasty breakfast with specialty coffee; intimate rooftop terrace. **Cons:** limited menu that's heavy on bar food; not all rooms have river views; soundproofed but set on the busy Lungotevere artery with lots of traffic outside. $ *Rooms from: €260* ✉ *Lungotevere de' Cenci 5–8, Jewish Ghetto* ☎ *06/85871180* 🌐 *citizenm.com* 🛏 *162 rooms* 🍴 *No Meals.*

Performing Arts

CLASSICAL MUSIC

Il Tempietto

FESTIVALS | Music festivals and intimate concerts are organized throughout the year in otherwise inaccessible sites, such as the Teatro di Marcello, the Church of San Nicola in Carcere, and Villa Torlonia. Music covers the entire scope from classical to contemporary. ✉ *Piazza Campitelli 9, Jewish Ghetto* ☎ *348/7804314* 🌐 *www.tempietto.it.*

Chapter 6

TREVI AND PIAZZA DI SPAGNA

6

Updated by
Erica Firpo

Sights	Restaurants	Hotels	Shopping	Nightlife
★★★★★	★★★★★	★★★★★	★★★★★	★☆☆☆☆

NEIGHBORHOOD SNAPSHOT

MAKING THE MOST OF YOUR TIME

This neighborhood is chock-full of postcard-worthy sights, including the Spanish Steps, the Trevi Fountain, and the Victor Emanuel monument (Il Vittoriano), which means a long, rewarding walk alongside plenty of fellow visitors. Consider starting early or taking an evening stroll, when many of the area's must-sees (including the Trevi Fountain) are illuminated.

Shoppers flock to Via del Corso, though in recent years the street has been given over mostly to multinational chains. Poke through backstreets instead; Rome's swankiest boutiques and designers are on Via dei Condotti, Via del Babuino, and the surrounding streets.

TOP REASONS TO GO

Trevi Fountain: Iconic would be an understatement as this is the Elvis of waterworks—overblown, flashy, and reliably thronged by legions of fans.

The Spanish Steps: Saunter seductively up the world's most celebrated stairway—everyone's doing it.

The Ceiling of San Ignazio: Stand beneath the stupendous ceiling of Rome's most splendiferous Baroque church, and, courtesy of painter-priest Fra Andrea Pozzo, be transported heavenward.

Fabulous palazzos: Visit the Palazzo Doria Pamphilj and the Palazzo Colonna for an intimate look at the homes of Rome's 17th-century aristocrats.

Luxe shopping on Via dei Condotti and Via del Babuino: You can flit effortlessly from Bulgari to Gucci to Valentino to Ferragamo.

GETTING HERE

■ Piazza di Spagna is a short walk from Piazza del Popolo and the Pantheon. One of Rome's handiest subway stations, Spagna (Metro A), is tucked just left of the steps. Bus No. 119 (from Piazza del Popolo and Piazza Venezia) passes above, stopping at Piazza Trinità dei Monti. The Trevi Fountain lies about a 10-minute walk south of Piazza di Spagna.

PAUSE HERE

■ Buzzing Piazza di Spagna is characterized by its thoroughfares packed with shoppers. Slip away from the crowds by strolling down Via Margutta, a street that has long been synonymous with artists and is still full of galleries and studios.

■ Film buffs who prefer cinema to paintings can pay homage at house number 51, where Gregory Peck's character lived in the film *Roman Holiday*.

In both spirit and in fact, this area is grandiose. The overblown Vittoriano monument, the labyrinthine palaces of Rome's surviving aristocracy, and the diamond-draped denizens of Via Condotti all embody the exuberant ego of a city at the center of its own universe. Here's where you'll see ladies in fur as you walk through a thousand snapshots while climbing the famous Spanish Steps.

If Rome has a Main Street, it's Via del Corso, which is often jammed with Roman teenagers, in from the city's outlying districts for a ritual stroll that resembles a strutting migration of lemmings in blue jeans. Along this thoroughfare it's easy to forget that the gray and stolid atmosphere comes partially from the enormous palaces lining both sides of the street. Many were built over the past 300 years by princely families who wanted to secure front-row seats for the frantic antics of Carnevale, which once sent horses racing down the street from Piazza del Popolo to Piazza Venezia. Beyond the chaste entrances of these structures, however, are some of Rome's grandest 17th- and 18th-century treasures, including ornate golden ballrooms and Old Master paintings.

Trevi

Via del Corso begins at the noisy, chaotic Piazza Venezia, presided over by the Altare della Patria (Altar of the Nation)— also known as Il Vittoriano, or, less piously, "the typewriter" or "the wedding cake." Sitting grandly off the avenue are the Palazzo Doria Pamphilj and the Palazzo Colonna, two of the city's great art collections housed in magnificent family palaces. Follow the crowd north and you will see the great Baroque confection at the top of everyone's sightseeing list, the Trevi Fountain. Since pickpockets favor this tourist-heavy spot, be particularly aware as you withdraw that wallet to find a few coins.

172

👁 Sights

★ Monumento a Vittorio Emanuele II, or Altare della Patria (*Victor Emmanuel II Monument, or Altar of the Nation*)

MONUMENT | The huge white mass known as the "Vittoriano" is an inescapable landmark that has been likened to a giant wedding cake or an immense typewriter. Present-day Romans joke that you can only avoid looking at it if you are standing on it, but at the beginning of the 20th century, it was the source of great civic pride. Built to honor the unification of Italy and the nation's first king, Victor Emmanuel II, it also shelters the eternal flame at the tomb of Italy's Unknown Soldier, killed during World War I. Alas, to create this elaborate marble behemoth and the vast surrounding piazza, its architects blithely destroyed many ancient and medieval buildings and altered the slope of the Campidoglio (Capitoline Hill), which abuts it.

The underwhelming exhibit inside the building tells the history of the country's unification. The Vittoriano has a rooftop terrace, however, that offers the best panoramic views of Rome. ⊠ *Entrances on Piazza Venezia, Piazza del Campidoglio, and Via di San Pietro in Carcere, Trevi* ☎ *06/0608* ⊕ *vive.cultura.gov.it* ☑ *Main building free; €17 for the terrace* Ⓜ *Colosseo.*

Palazzo Bonaparte

ART MUSEUM | First designed by Giovanni Antonio De' Rossi for the Marquis of Aste in the 17th century, this Renaissance palace is better known as the home of Letizia Bonaparte, who purchased the elegant building in 1818. Napoleon's mother, who lived here until her death in 1836, was fond of sitting on the curious covered green balcony that wraps around a corner of the first floor. The stately home overlooks the Vittoriano and Palazzo Venezia, as well as the nonstop motion of Rome's busiest piazza. Palazzo Bonaparte is open for temporary exhibits, and has hosted the works of blockbuster artists like Vincent Van Gogh and M. C. Escher, among others. ⊠ *Piazza Venezia, 5, Trevi* ☎ *06/8715111* ⊕ *www.mostrepalazzobonaparte.it* ☑ *From €17.50 for exhibits.*

★ Palazzo Colonna

CASTLE/PALACE | Rome's grandest private palace is a fusion of 17th- and 18th-century buildings that have been occupied by the Colonna family for more than 20 generations. The immense residence faces Piazza dei Santi Apostoli on one side and the Quirinale (Quirinal Hill) on the other—with a little bridge over Via della Pilotta linking to gardens on the hill—and contains an art gallery that's open to the public on Saturday morning or by guided tour on Friday morning.

The gallery is itself a setting of aristocratic grandeur; you might recognize the Sala Grande as the site where Audrey Hepburn meets the press in *Roman Holiday.* An ancient red marble *colonna* (column), which is the family's emblem, looms at one end, but the most spectacular feature is the ceiling fresco of the Battle of Lepanto painted by Giovanni Coli and Filippo Gherardi beginning in 1675. Adding to the opulence are works by Poussin, Tintoretto, and Veronese, as well as portraits of illustrious members of the family, such as Vittoria Colonna, Michelangelo's muse and longtime friend.

It's worth paying an extra fee to take the guided, English-language gallery tour, which will help you navigate through the array of madonnas, saints, goddesses, popes, and cardinals to see Annibale Carracci's lonely *Beaneater,* spoon at the ready and front teeth missing. The gallery also has a café with a pleasant terrace. ⊠ *Via della Pilotta, 17, Trevi* ☎ *06/6784350* ⊕ *www.galleriacolonna.it* ☑ *€15 for gallery and gardens, €25 to also visit the Princess Isabelle Apartment, €30 for a guided tour on Friday* 🕐 *Closed Sun.–Thurs.* ☞ *Friday for guided tour only* Ⓜ *Barberini.*

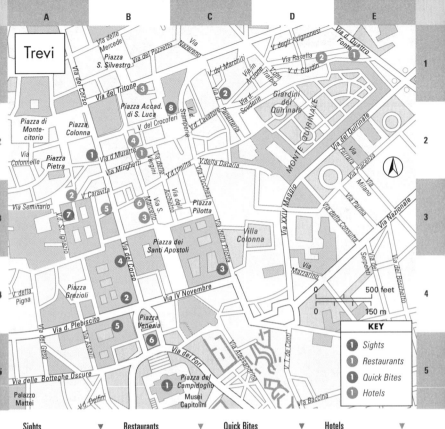

Trevi

KEY

- 1 *Sights*
- 1 *Restaurants*
- 1 *Quick Bites*
- 1 *Hotels*

Sights	▼
1 Monumento a Vittorio Emanuelle II, or Altare della Patria **B5**	
2 Palazzo Bonaparte **B4**	
3 Palazzo Colonna **C4**	
4 Palazzo Doria Pamphilj.................. **B4**	
5 Palazzo Venezia......... **B5**	
6 Piazza Venezia **B5**	
7 Sant'Ignazio **A3**	
8 Trevi Fountain **C2**	

Restaurants	▼
1 Baccano **B2**	
2 Da Sabatino **A3**	
3 L'Antica Birreria Peroni **B3**	

Quick Bites	▼
1 Gelateria Venchi **B2**	
2 Il Gelato di San Crispino **C1**	

Hotels	▼
1 Hotel Barberini **E1**	
2 Hotel Julia **D1**	
3 Hotel Tritone............. **B1**	
4 Maalot Roma............ **B2**	
5 Singer Palace **B3**	
6 Six Senses Rome **B3**	

★ Palazzo Doria Pamphilj

CASTLE/PALACE | Like the Palazzo Colonna and the Galleria Borghese, this dazzling 15th-century palace provides a fantastic glimpse of aristocratic Rome. It passed through several hands before becoming the property of the Pamphilj family, who married into the famous seafaring Doria family of Genoa in the 18th century. The family still lives in part of the palace.

The understated beauty of the graceful facade, designed by Gabriele Valvassori in 1730 and best admired from the opposite side of the street, barely hints at the interior's opulent halls and gilded galleries, which are filled with Old Master works. The 550 paintings here include three by Caravaggio: *St. John the Baptist, Mary Magdalene,* and the breathtaking *Rest on the Flight to Egypt.* Off the eye-popping Galleria degli Specchi (Gallery of Mirrors)—a smaller version of the one at Versailles—are the famous Velázquez *Pope Innocent X,* considered by some historians to be the greatest portrait ever painted, and the Bernini bust of the same Pamphilj pope.

A delightful audio guide is included in the ticket price and is narrated by the current heir, Prince Jonathan Doria Pamphilj, who divulges intimate family history. Plan to stay for lunch, or at least pause for a coffee, at the fashionable Caffè Doria, with elegant tables set out in the palace's peaceful cloisters. ⊠ *Via del Corso, 305, Trevi* ☎ *06/6797323* ⊕ *www.doriapamphilj.it* ⊠ *€16* ⊘ *Closed the 3rd Wed. of the month* ⌂ *Reservations required* Ⓜ *Barberini.*

Palazzo Venezia

CASTLE/PALACE | Rome's first great Renaissance palace, the centerpiece of an eponymous piazza, was originally built for Venetian cardinal Pietro Barbo (who eventually became Pope Paul II), but it was repurposed in the 20th century by Mussolini, who harangued crowds with speeches from the balcony over its finely carved door. Lights were left on through the night during his reign to suggest that the fascist leader worked without pause.

The palace is now open to the public, and highlights include frescoes by Giorgio Vasari, an Algardi sculpture of Pope Innocent X, and decorative art exhibits. The loggia has a pleasant view over the tranquil garden courtyard, which seems a million miles away from the chaos of Piazza Venezia on the other side of the building. The ticket price includes an audio guide. ⊠ *Via del Plebiscito, 118, Trevi* ☎ *06/69994388* ⊕ *vive.cultura.gov.it/en/palazzo-venezia* ⊠ *€15 for the palazzo, €2 extra for exhibit, gardens are free.*

Piazza Venezia

PLAZA/SQUARE | Piazza Venezia stands at what was the beginning of the ancient Via Flaminia, a historic Roman road leading northeast across Italy to the Adriatic Sea. From this square, Rome's geographic heart, all distances from the city are calculated.

The piazza was transformed at the turn of the 20th century when much older ruins were destroyed to make way for a modern capital city (and a massive monument to unified Italy's first king). The female bust near the church of San Marco in the southwest corner of the piazza is a fragment of a statue of Isis, now known to the Romans as Madama Lucrezia. It is one of the city's "talking statues" on which anonymous poets hung verses pungent with political satire.

The Via Flaminia remains a vital artery. The part leading from Piazza Venezia to Piazza del Popolo is now known as Via del Corso, after the horse races (*corse*) that were run here during the wild Roman carnival celebrations of the 17th and 18th centuries. It also happens to be one of Rome's busiest shopping streets. ⊠ *Piazza Venezia, Trevi.*

★ Sant'Ignazio

CHURCH | Rome's second Jesuit church, this 17th-century landmark set on a Rococo piazza harbors some of the city's

A sculptural masterpiece from the Baroque era, the Trevi Fountain is also a cultural icon, appearing in countless works of art, literature, and movies.

most magnificent trompe l'oeils. To get the full effect of the illusionistic ceiling by priest-artist Andrea Pozzo, stand on the small yellow disk set into the floor of the nave. The heavenly vision that seems to extend upward almost indefinitely represents the *Allegory of the Missionary Work of the Jesuits*. It's part of Pozzo's cycle of works in this church exalting the early history of the Jesuit order, whose founder was the reformer Ignatius of Loyola. The saint soars heavenward, supported by a cast of thousands, creating a jaw-dropping effect that was fully intended to rival that of the glorious ceiling by Baciccia in the nearby mother church of Il Gesù. Be sure to have coins handy for the machine that switches on the lights so you can marvel at the false dome, which is actually a flat canvas—a trompe l'oeil trick Pozzo used when the architectural budget drained dry.

Scattered around the nave are several awe-inspiring altars; their soaring columns, gold-on-gold decoration, and gilded statues are pure splendor.

Splendid, too, are the occasional sacred music concerts performed by choirs from all over the world. Look for posters by the main doors, or check the website for more information. ⊠ *Piazza S. Ignazio, Trevi* ⊹ *Via del Caravita 8A* ☎ *06/6794406* ⊕ *santignazio.gesuiti.it.*

★ Trevi Fountain

FOUNTAIN | FAMILY | Alive with rushing waters commanded by an imperious sculpture of Oceanus, the Fontana di Trevi has been all about theatrical effects from the start; it is an aquatic marvel in a city filled with them. The fountain's unique drama is largely due to its location: its vast basin is squeezed into the tight confluence of three little streets (the *tre vie*, which may give the fountain its name), with cascades emerging as if from the wall of Palazzo Poli.

The dream of a fountain emerging full force from a palace was first envisioned by Bernini and Pietro da Cortona from Pope Urban VIII's plan to rebuild an older fountain, which had earlier marked the end point of the Acqua Vergine, an

Rome's Fountains

Anyone who has thrown a coin backward over their shoulder into the Fontana di Trevi to ensure a return to Rome appreciates the magic of the city's fountains. From the magnificence of the Fontana dei Quattro Fiumi in Piazza Navona to the graceful caprice of the Fontana delle Tartarughe in the Jewish Ghetto, the water-spouting sculptures seem as essential to their piazzas as the cobblestones and ocher buildings that surround them.

Rome's original fountains date back to ancient times, when they were part of the city's remarkable aqueduct system. But from AD 537 to 1562, the waterworks were in disrepair, and the fountains lay dry and crumbling. Romans were left to draw their water from the Tiber and from wells.

During the Renaissance, the popes brought running water back to the city as a means of currying political favor. To mark the restoration of the Virgin Aqueduct, architect Giacomo della Porta designed 18 unassuming, functional fountains. Each consisted of a large basin with two or three levels of smaller basins in the center, which were built and placed throughout the city at points along the water line.

Although nearly all of della Porta's fountains remain, their spare Renaissance design is virtually unrecognizable. With the Baroque era, most were elaborately redecorated with dolphins, obelisks, and sea monsters. Of this next generation of fountaineers, the most famous is Gian Lorenzo Bernini. Bernini's writhing, muscular creatures of myth adorn most of Rome's most visible fountains, including the Fontana di Trevi (perhaps named for the three streets, or "tre vie," that converge at its piazza); the Fontana del Nettuno, with its tritons, in Piazza Barberini; and, in Piazza Navona, the Fontana dei Quattro Fiumi, whose hulking figures represented the four great rivers of the known world: the Nile, the Ganges, the Danube, and the Plata.

The most common type of fountain in Rome, however, is a kind rarely noted by visitors: the small, inconspicuous drinking fountains that burble away from side-street walls, old stone niches, and fire hydrant–like installations on street corners. You can drink this water, and many of these *fontanelle* even have pipes fitted with a little hole from which water shoots up for easier drinking when you press your hand under the main spout.

To combine the glorious Roman fountain with a drink of water, head to Piazza di Spagna, where the Barcaccia fountain is outfitted with spouts on the bow from which you can wet your whistle—but be sure to stay outside the rim. In a bid to better protect its fantastic fountains, the mayor of Rome has instituted steep fines for anyone who dares to step into the water.

aqueduct created in 18 BC by Agrippa. Three popes later, under Pope Clement XIII, Nicola Salvi finally broke ground with his winning design. Unfortunately, Salvi did not live to see his masterpiece of sculpted seashells, roaring sea beasts, and diva-like mermaids completed; he caught a cold and died while working in the culverts of the aqueduct 11 years before the fountain was finished in 1762.

Everyone knows the famous legend that if you throw a coin into the Trevi Fountain you will ensure a return trip to the Eternal City, but not everyone knows how to do it the right way. You must toss a coin with your right hand over your left shoulder, with your back to the fountain. One coin means you'll return to Rome; two, you'll return *and* fall in love; three, you'll return, find love, and marry. The fountain grosses some €600,000 a year, with every cent going to the Italian Red Cross, which is why Fendi was willing to fully fund the Trevi's recent restoration.

Tucked away in a little nearby alley is the Vicus Caprarius (⊠ *Vicolo del Puttarello 25*), a small museum where visitors can pay €8 for a guided tour that descends into a subterranean area that gives a glimpse at the water source that keeps the fountain running. ⊠ *Piazza di Trevi, Trevi* Ⓜ *Barberini.*

Restaurants

Baccano

$$$ | **BRASSERIE** | There are plenty of options for good food at reasonable prices around the Trevi Fountain, but this Paris-inspired brasserie—open for lunch, dinner, and everything in between—is a great bet. Although it emphasizes seafood, the extensive menu has something for everyone, from salads to pasta and entrées. **Known for:** oyster bar; excellent carbonara; classic international cocktails. $ *Average main: €28* ⊠ *Via delle Muratte, 23, Trevi* ☎ *06/69941166* ⊕ *www.baccanoroma.com* Ⓜ *Barberini.*

Da Sabatino

$$$ | **ITALIAN** | At this traditionally Roman, family-owned restaurant with picturesque outdoor tables, you can dig into classic Italian fares like veal meatballs, pasta all'amatriciana, and tartufo. The cozy piazza, where the restaurant is located, is just a little ways off of Via del Corso. **Known for:** picture-perfect outdoor dining in a beautiful, cozy piazza; pasta all'amatriciana; daily fish specialties. $ *Average main: €30* ⊠ *Piazza S. Ignazio, 169, Trevi* ☎ *06/6797821* ⊕ *dasabatino.it* Ⓜ *Spagna.*

L'Antica Birreria Peroni

$ | **NORTHERN ITALIAN** | With its long wooden tables, hard-back booths, and free-flowing beer, this Art Nouveau–style, circa-1906 restaurant in a 16th-century palazzo evokes a kitsch Munich beer hall. There is a full Italian menu, but hearty sausages or goulash make a nice break from pasta and tomato sauce, and this is one of the few places in the historic center where you can fill up on protein for very few euros. **Known for:** German dishes; casual, convivial atmosphere; close to the Trevi Fountain. $ *Average main: €10* ⊠ *Via di San Marcello, 19, Trevi* ☎ *06/6795310* ⊕ *www.anticabirreriaperoni.net* ⊗ *Closed Sun.*

☕ Coffee and Quick Bites

Gelateria Venchi

$ | **ITALIAN** | **FAMILY** | Established in 1878, Venchi is one of Italy's premier confectioners, and you'll see the brand all over the country. At this brick-and-mortar shop, you can buy chocolate as well as gelato, made fresh daily. **Known for:** free-flowing melted chocolate; creamy gelato flavors; packaged candies. $ *Average main: €5* ⊠ *Via del Corso, 335, Trevi* ☎ *06/69797790* Ⓜ *Spagna.*

Il Gelato di San Crispino

$ | **ICE CREAM** | **FAMILY** | Many people say this place—which is around the corner from the Trevi Fountain and had a cameo in the movie *Eat, Pray, Love*—serves the best gelato in Rome. Creative flavors like black fig, chocolate rum, Armagnac, and ginger-cinnamon all incorporate top-notch ingredients, and the shop is known for keeping its gelato hidden under metal covers to better preserve the quality. **Known for:** seasonal fruit flavors; offering only cups and no cones; wine-based gelato. [$] *Average main: €4* ✉ *Via della Panetteria, 42, Trevi* ☎ *06/69489518* 🌐 *www.ilgelatodisancrispino.it* [M] *Barberini.*

Hotels

Hotel Barberini
$$ | **HOTEL** | This elegant four-star hotel, housed in a 19th-century palazzo near Piazza Barberini, has old-world luxury and charm an easy distance from the Metro, the Trevi Fountain, and sophisticated Via Veneto. **Pros:** beautiful views from the rooftop terrace; on a quiet side street close to several important attractions; great value for the area. **Cons:** some rooms are on the small side; light sleepers may hear the Metro at night; beds are a bit hard. [$] *Rooms from: €180* ✉ *Via Rasella, 3, Trevi* ☎ *06/4814993* 🌐 *hotel-barberini.com/it* 🛏 *35 rooms* 🍴 *Free Breakfast* [M] *Barberini.*

Hotel Julia
$$$ | **HOTEL** | This small hotel, situated on a small cobblestone street just behind Piazza Barberini and a short walk to the Trevi Fountain, offers relatively spacious rooms that won't break the bank. **Pros:** safe neighborhood; convenient to sights and transportation; moderate prices for a central area. **Cons:** some street noise at night; very basic accommodations; some rooms are dark and cramped. [$] *Rooms from: €300* ✉ *Via Rasella, 29, Trevi* ☎ *06/83652440* 🌐 *www.hoteljulia.it* 🛏 *30 rooms* 🍴 *Free Breakfast* [M] *Barberini.*

Hotel Tritone
$$ | **HOTEL** | This trusty hotel offers modern accommodations steps from the majestic Trevi Fountain and close to great shopping. **Pros:** walking distance to major attractions; modern decor; friendly staff. **Cons:** rooms can be noisy despite soundproofing; breakfast isn't very exciting; spotty Wi-Fi. [$] *Rooms from: €140* ✉ *Via del Tritone, 210, Trevi* ☎ *06/69922575* 🌐 *www.tritonehotel.com* 🛏 *43 rooms* 🍴 *Free Breakfast* [M] *Barberini.*

Maalot Roma
$$$$ | **HOTEL** | This boutique property inside the former residence of opera composer Gaetano Donizetto aims to be a restaurant with rooms above rather than a hotel with a restaurant below. **Pros:** chic design with original art; great food at Don Pasquale restaurant; central location just steps from the Trevi Fountain. **Cons:** some rooms look directly onto the McDonald's across the street; no spa; service can be a bit slow. [$] *Rooms from: €750* ✉ *Via delle Murate, 78, Trevi* ☎ *06/878087* 🌐 *www.hotelmaalot.com* 🛏 *30 rooms and suites* 🍴 *Free Breakfast* [M] *Barberini.*

Singer Palace
$$$$ | **HOTEL** | Located steps from the bustling southern end of Via del Corso, Singer Palace is a boutique hotel that offers convenient access to Rome's cultural and commercial hubs, making it an ideal base for exploring the city's famous landmarks and indulging in shopping along Via del Corso. **Pros:** convenient location for sightseeing; charming rooftop terrace; beautiful Art Deco–inspired interiors. **Cons:** rooms on the smaller side; rooms on Via del Corso can be noisy; no gym. [$] *Rooms from: €460* ✉ *Via Alessandro Specchi, 10, Trevi* ☎ *06/6976161* 🌐 *singer-palacehotel.com* 🛏 *30 rooms and suites* 🍴 *Free Breakfast* [M] *Spagna.*

Six Senses Rome

$$$$ | **HOTEL** | Six Senses is known for a focus on 360-degree wellness and the brand's first Roman property is a delight: a luxurious, tranquil retreat in the center of one of the city's busiest neighborhoods, allowing guests to be in the middle of it all while opting out of the usual cacophony of the city center. **Pros:** lovely rooftop terrace and views from suites; free guest access to the Roman baths at the spa; discreet professional staff focused on guest experience. **Cons:** super luxury price point; concierge focused on unique experiences rather than traditional Rome tours; subdued spa-like setting not for everyone. $ *Rooms from: €1155* ✉ *P.za S. Marcello, Trevi* ☎ *06/86814000* ⊕ *sixsenses.com/en/hotels/rome* ⤴ *96 rooms and suites* ¶◎¶ *Free Breakfast.*

 Performing Arts

FILM

Multisala Barberini

FILM | One of the most commercial and central theaters in the city, Barberini is guaranteed to have at least one film on offer in its original language. It is the best and most comfortable place to watch the latest Italian films and international blockbusters (without dubbing), or view a recorded opera or ballet on one of its screens. ✉ *Piazza Barberini 24/26, Trevi* ☎ *06/40419403* ⊕ *multisala.barberini.18tickets.it* Ⓜ *Barberini.*

Shopping

BOOKS AND STATIONERY

Ex Libris

BOOKS | Founded in 1931, one of Rome's oldest and largest antiquarian bookshops has a distinctive selection of scholarly and collectible books from the 16th to 20th century. In addition to rare and early editions on art and architecture, music and theater, and literature and humanities, the shop sells maps and prints. ✉ *Via dell' Umiltà 77/a, Trevi* ☎ *06/6791540* ⊕ *www.exlibrisroma.it* Ⓜ *Barberini.*

CERAMICS AND DECORATIVE ARTS

Le 4 Stagioni

CERAMICS | If you're looking to purchase some traditional Italian pottery, Le 4 Stagioni has a colorful selection of glazed pots, vases, and charming ceramic-flower wall ornaments made by well-known manufacturers such as Faenza, Capodimonte, Vietri, and Deruta. All can be shipped internationally if you can't quite fit the gorgeous bowls and platters in your suitcase. ✉ *Via dell'Umiltà 30/b, Trevi* ☎ *06/69941029* Ⓜ *Barberini.*

Piazza di Spagna

Extending just east of Via del Corso, but miles away in style, Piazza di Spagna and its surrounding streets are where Rome's elite shop and gallery hop. The piazza's main draw remains the 18th-century Spanish Steps, which connect the ritzy shops at the bottom of the hill with the ritzy hotels (and one lovely church) at the top. The reward for climbing the *scalinata* (staircase) is a dizzying view of central Rome. Because the steps face west, the views are especially good around sunset.

Sights

★ Ara Pacis Augustae

(*Altar of Augustan Peace*)

MONUMENT | This pristine monument sits inside one of Rome's contemporary architectural landmarks: a gleaming, rectangular, glass-and-travertine structure designed by American architect Richard Meier. It overlooks the Tiber on one side and the ruins of the marble-clad Mausoleo di Augusto (Mausoleum of Augustus) on the other and is a serene, luminous oasis right in the center of Rome.

This altar itself dates from 13 BC and was commissioned to celebrate the Pax

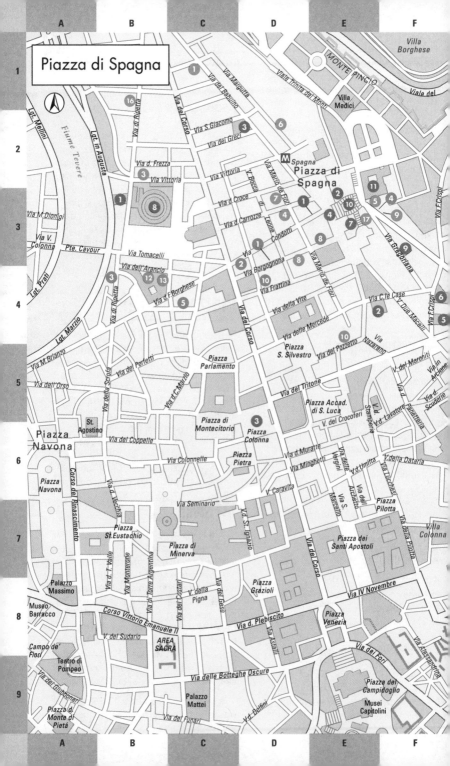

Sights ▼

1 Ara Pacis Augustae **B3**
2 Basilica di Sant'Andrea delle Fratte **E4**
3 Colonna di Marco Aurelio **D5**
4 Fontana della Barcaccia **E3**
5 Gagosian Gallery **F4**
6 Galleria d'Arte Moderna................. **F4**
7 Keats-Shelley Memorial House **E3**
8 Mausoleo di Augusto **B3**
9 Palazzo Zuccari........... **F3**
10 The Spanish Steps....... **E3**
11 Trinità dei Monti.......... **E2**

Restaurants ▼

1 Caffè Romano **D3**
2 Ginger Spagna **D3**
3 Il Marchese **B4**
4 Imàgo **F3**
5 Matricianella............. **C4**
6 Moma **I3**
7 Orma **I1**
8 Ristorante Nino **E3**
9 Settimo................... **G2**
10 Vynique **D4**

Quick Bites ▼

1 Antico Caffè Greco **D3**
2 Babington's Tea Rooms................ **E3**
3 Caffè Canova-Tadolini......... **D2**

Hotels ▼

1 Babuino 181 .... **C1**
2 Baglioni Hotel Regina............. **H2**
3 Bulgari Hotel Roma..... **B2**
4 Crossing Condotti....... **D3**
5 The Hassler............... **E3**
6 Hotel Art **D2**
7 Hotel Condotti........... **D3**
8 Hotel Croce di Malta ... **D3**
9 Hotel de la Ville **F3**
10 Hotel dei Borgognoni **E4**
11 Hotel Eden............... **G2**
12 Hotel Vilòn **B4**
13 J.K. Place Roma **B4**
14 La Residenza **H2**
15 Marriott Grand Hotel Flora **H1**
16 Palazzo Ripetta.......... **B1**
17 Scalinata di Spagna..... **E3**
18 Sofitel Roma Villa Borghese **G2**
19 W Rome.................. **H2**
20 The Westin Excelsior, Rome **H2**

KEY

● Sights
● Restaurants
● Quick Bites
● Hotels

0 — 500 feet
0 — 150 m

Romana, the era of peace ushered in by Augustus's military victories. When viewing it, keep in mind that the spectacular reliefs would have been painted in vibrant colors, now long gone. The reliefs on the short sides portray myths associated with Rome's founding and glory; those on the long sides display a procession of the imperial family. Although half of his body is missing, Augustus is identifiable as the first full figure at the procession's head on the south-side frieze; academics still argue over exact identifications of most of the figures. Be sure to check out the small downstairs museum, which hosts rotating exhibits on Italian culture, with themes ranging from design to film. ⊠ *Lungotevere in Augusta, at the corner of Via Tomacelli, Piazza di Spagna* ☎ *06/0608* ⊕ *www. arapacis.it* ⊠ *€12, €13 when there is an exhibition* ⚠ *Reservations essential for groups of 11 to 25 persons* Ⓜ *Flaminio.*

Basilica di Sant'Andrea delle Fratte
CHURCH | Two of Bernini's original angels that decorated the Ponte Sant'Angelo are found here, on either side of the high altar. The door in the right aisle leads into one of Rome's hidden gardens, where orange trees bloom in the cloister. Borromini's fantastic contributions—the dome and a curious bell tower with its droop-winged angels looking out over the city—are best seen from Via di Capo le Case, across Via dei Due Macelli. ⊠ *Via di Sant'Andrea delle Fratte 1, at Via della Mercede, Piazza di Spagna* ☎ *06/6793191* ⊕ *www.madonnadelmiracolo.it* Ⓜ *Spagna.*

Colonna di Marco Aurelio
MONUMENT | Inspired by Trajan's Column, this 2nd-century-AD column is composed of 27 blocks of marble covered in reliefs recounting Marcus Aurelius's victory over the Germanic tribes. A bronze statue of St. Paul, which replaced the original effigy of the emperor and his wife Faustina in the 16th century, stands at the top. The column is the centerpiece of Piazza Colonna. ⊠ *Piazza Colonna, Piazza di Spagna.*

Fontana della Barcaccia
(*Leaky Boat Fountain*)
FOUNTAIN | FAMILY | At the foot of the Spanish Steps, this curious, leaky boat fountain is fed by Rome's only surviving ancient aqueduct, the Acqua Vergine. The sinking ship design is a clever solution to low water pressure and was created by Pietro Bernini, with the help of his son, the prolific sculptor Gian Lorenzo Bernini. The project was commissioned by Barberini Pope Urban VIII, and the bees and suns on the boat are symbols of the Barberini family. Looking for more symbolism, some insist that the Berninis intended the fountain to be a reminder that this part of town was often flooded by the Tiber; others claim that it represents the Ship of the Church; and still others think that it marks the presumed site of the emperor Domitian's water stadium in which sea battles were reenacted in the glory days of the Roman Empire. ⊠ *Piazza di Spagna* Ⓜ *Spagna.*

Gagosian Gallery
ART GALLERY | This is the Roman outpost of Larry Gagosian's global art empire. Taking residence in a 1920s bank building, Gagosian brings an international crowd with highly anticipated exhibits and blockbuster showcases of megastars such as Cy Twombly, Damien Hirst, and Jeff Koons. ⊠ *Via Francesco Crispi 16, Piazza di Spagna* ☎ *06/42086498* ⊕ *www. gagosian.com* ☉ *Closed Sun. and Mon.* Ⓜ *Spagna.*

★ Galleria d'Arte Moderna
ART MUSEUM | Located in a former monastery, this small museum displays an impressive capsule collection of modern art, with an emphasis on Italian artists. The permanent collection is too large to be displayed at once, so exhibits rotate, displaying paintings, drawings, prints, and sculptures by the most famous names of the 19th and 20th centuries, including Giorgio de Chirico, Mario Mafai, Scipione, Gino Severini, and Giorgio Morandi. ⊠ *Via Francesco Crispi 24,*

Piazza di Spagna ☎ 06/0608 ⊕ www. galleriaartemodernaroma.it ⊠ €9; €11.50 if there's a special exhibit ⊙ Closed Mon. Ⓜ *Spagna.*

Keats-Shelley Memorial House

HISTORIC HOME | Sent to Rome in a last-ditch attempt to treat his consumptive condition, English Romantic poet John Keats—celebrated for such poems as "Ode to a Nightingale" and "Endymion"—lived in this house at the foot of the Spanish Steps. At the time, this was the heart of Rome's colorful bohemian quarter, an area favored by English expats. He took his last breath here on February 23, 1821, and is now buried in the Non-Catholic Cemetery in Testaccio. On a visit to his final home, you can see his death mask, though local authorities had all his furnishings burned after his death as a sanitary measure. You'll also find a quaint collection of memorabilia of other English literary figures of the period—Lord Byron, Percy Bysshe Shelley, Joseph Severn, and Leigh Hun—and an exhaustive library of works on the Romantics. ⊠ *Piazza di Spagna 26 ☎ 06/6784235 ⊕ ksh.roma.it ⊠ €6 ⊙ Closed Sun.* Ⓜ *Spagna.*

Mausoleo di Augusto

MONUMENT | One of Ancient Rome's largest circular tombs, the Mausoleum of Augustus celebrates the glory of Emperor Augustus, Julius Caesar's successor. Though today's mausoleum is brick and stone, the structure was originally covered in marble and travertine, with evergreen trees planted on top, a colossal statue of the emperor at the summit, and a pair of bronze pillars inscribed with his achievements at the entrance. The mausoleum's innermost sepulchral chamber housed the ashes of several members of the Augustan dynasty, but it was subsequently raided and the urns were never found.

Between the 13th and 20th centuries, the mausoleum was a garden, an amphitheater that hosted jousting tournaments, and a concert hall, which Mussolini tore down in 1936 in a bid to restore the monument to its imperial glory. His plans were interrupted by World War II, after which the mausoleum was all but abandoned until a recent restoration reopened it to the public.

Reservations are booked online; however, it is currently closed and slated to reopen with the 2025 Jubilee Year. Check the website for up-to-date details. ⊠ *Piazza Augusto Imperatore, Piazza di Spagna ☎ 06/0608 ⊕ www.mausoleodiaugusto.it ⊠ €5 ⊙ Closed Mon.* Ⓜ *Spagna.*

Palazzo Zuccari

CASTLE/PALACE | This amusing palazzo was designed in 1591 by noted painter Federico Zuccari (1540–1609), who frescoed the first floor of his custom-built home. Typical of the outré Mannerist style of the period, the two windows and the main door are designed to look like monsters with mouths gaping wide. Zuccari—whose frescoes adorn many Roman churches, including Trinità dei Monti just up the block—sank all his money into his new home, dying in debt before his curious memorial, as it turned out to be, was completed.

Today, it is home to the German state-run Bibliotheca Hertziana, a prestigious fine-arts library. Access is reserved for scholars, but the pristine facade can be admired for free. Leading up to the quaint Piazza della Trinità del Monti, the nearby Via Gregoriana is quite charming and has long been one of Rome's most elegant addresses, home to such residents as 19th-century French painter Ingres; Valentino also had his first couture salon here. ⊠ *Via Gregoriana 30, Piazza di Spagna ☎ 06/69993201 Bibliotheca Hertziana ⊕ www.biblhertz.it/en/home ⌂ The Bibliotheca occasionally offers guided tours. Otherwise, request a visit by email.* Ⓜ *Spagna.*

Did You Know?

The Spanish Steps—often called simply *la scalinata*, or "the staircase"—and the Piazza di Spagna from which they ascend both get their names from the Spanish Embassy to the Holy See.

★ The Spanish Steps

OTHER ATTRACTION | FAMILY | The iconic Spanish Steps (often called simply *la scalinata,* or "the staircase," by Italians) and the Piazza di Spagna from which they ascend both get their names from the Spanish Embassy to the Vatican on the piazza—even though the staircase was built with French funds by an Italian in 1723. In honor of a diplomatic visit by the King of Spain, the hillside was transformed by architect Francesco de Sanctis with a spectacular piece of urban planning to link the church of Trinità dei Monti at the top with the Via Condotti below.

In an allusion to the church, the staircase is divided by three landings (beautifully lined with potted azaleas from mid-April to mid-May). Bookending the bottom of the steps are beloved holdovers from the 18th century, when the area was known as the "English Ghetto": to the right, the Keats-Shelley House and to the left, Babington's Tea Rooms—both beautifully redolent of the era of the Grand Tour.

For weary sightseers who find the 135 steps too daunting, there is an elevator at Vicolo del Bottino 8, next to the Metro entrance. (Those with mobility problems should be aware that there is still a small flight of stairs after, however, and that the elevator is sporadically closed for repair.) At the bottom of the steps, Pietro Bernini's splendid 17th-century Barcaccia Fountain still spouts drinking water from the ancient aqueduct known as the Aqua Vergine. ⌂ *Plazza di Spagna, Piazza di Spagna* Ⓜ *Spagna.*

Trinità dei Monti

CHURCH | Standing high above the Spanish Steps, this 16th-century church has a rare double-tower facade, suggestive of late–French Gothic style; in fact, the French crown paid for the church's construction. Today, it is known primarily for its dramatic location and magnificent views. The obelisk in front is from 2nd or 3rd century AD, and was originally a centerpiece to an imperial villa. ⌂ *Piazza della Trinità dei Monti, Piazza di Spagna* ☎ *06/6794179* ⊕ *trinitadeimonti.net* Ⓜ *Spagna.*

🍴 Restaurants

During the day, the area around the Spanish Steps is a hotbed of tourists, shoppers, and office workers. It gets significantly quieter at night and, as a result, it's easy to fall into tourist traps and overpriced hotel dining.

Caffè Romano

$$$ | ECLECTIC | With *orario continuato,* or nonstop operating hours (noon till late at night), this sleek spot in the Hotel d'Inghilterra caters to jet-setters and hotel guests. The creative global menu can mean international misfires, so it's best to select from among the authentic Northern Italian meat and Southern Italian seafood dishes such as boar with polenta, seafood soup, or classic pastas. **Known for:** enviable outdoor seating; truffle pasta; signature Caesar salad with prawns. Ⓢ *Average main: €28* ⌂ *Hotel d'Inghilterra, Via Borgongna 4M, Piazza di Spagna* ☎ *06/69981500* ⊕ *collezione. starhotels.com* Ⓜ *Spagna.*

Ginger Spagna

$$ | MODERN ITALIAN | FAMILY | A luminous contemporary bistro with skylights illuminating white walls, this all-day eatery offers diverse delights with a healthy focus, from acai bowls and juices to organic pancakes, salads, sandwiches, pizza and pasta, plus a curated wine selection. There is a nearby location on Via del Corso and another near the Pantheon. **Known for:** vegetarian, vegan, and dairy-free options; organic and homemade baguettes for panini; tasty fruit bowls. Ⓢ *Average main: €20* ⌂ *Via Borgognona, 43, Piazza di Spagna* ☎ *06/69940836* ⊕ *gingersaporiesalute.com* Ⓜ *Spagna.*

★ Il Marchese

$$ | **ITALIAN** | This rustic-meets-glamorous bistro attracts locals for its flawless execution of Roman classics (many served photogenically in metal cooking pans) as well as original dishes. Its bar is known among amaro connoisseurs for having the largest selection in Rome, and the bitter liquors are the stars of the expertly crafted cocktail menu. **Known for:** beautiful design; well-executed classics; extensive selection of amaros and great cocktails. [$] *Average main: €18* ✉ *Via di Ripetta 162, Piazza di Spagna* ☎ *06/90218872* 🌐 *www.ilmarcheseroma.it* [M] *Spagna.*

Imàgo

$$$$ | **MODERN ITALIAN** | Excellence is at the forefront of everything at Imàgo, the Michelin-starred restaurant inside the legendary Hotel Hassler, now headed by young star chef Andrea Antonini. You can order à la carte, but this is the place to splurge on a tasting menu. **Known for:** tempting tasting menus; innovative creations inspired by all of Italy; sweeping city views from rooftop terrace. [$] *Average main: €50* ✉ *Hotel Hassler, Piazza Trinità dei Monti 6, Piazza di Spagna* ☎ *06/69934726* 🌐 *www.hotelhasslerroma.com* ⏲ *Closed Sun. and Mon. No lunch* [M] *Spagna.*

Matricianella

$$$ | **ITALIAN** | Family-owned neighborhood staple with its quintessentially Roman wooden tables and checkered tablecloths, Matricianella charms with hearty Roman dishes and a biblical wine list. Try any of the Roman pasta trifecta—amatriciana, cacio e pepe, and carbonara—or other classics like crispy fried artichokes or saltimbocca alla romana (thin veal slices with prosciutto and sage). **Known for:** rustic charm; classic Roman dishes; extensive wine list. [$] *Average main: €30* ✉ *Via del Leone, 4, Piazza di Spagna* ☎ *06/6832100* 🌐 *www.matricianella.it* ⏲ *Closed Sun.* [M] *Spagna.*

★ Moma

$$$ | **MODERN ITALIAN** | In front of the American embassy and a favorite of the design *trendoisie*, Michelin-starred Moma attracts well-heeled businessmen at lunch but turns into a more intimate affair for dinner. The kitchen turns out hits as it creates *alta cucina* (haute cuisine) made using Italian ingredients sourced from small producers. **Known for:** pasta with a twist; creative presentation; affordable fine dining. [$] *Average main: €25* ✉ *Via San Basilio 42, Piazza di Spagna* ☎ *06/42011798* 🌐 *www.ristorantemoma.it* ⏲ *Closed Sun. No lunch Sat.* [M] *Barberini.*

Orma

$$$$ | **FUSION** | Helmed by Colombian-Italian chef Roy Caceres, Orma boasts a modern mix of inventive gastronomy, sleek wooden interiors, and attentive service. The rotating prix fixe menus offer delicacies like egg tortelli stuffed with pig head and drizzled with roasted onion broth. **Known for:** inventive Michelin-starred cuisine; wine pairing; beautiful Scandinavian-inspired interior design. [$] *Average main: €140* ✉ *Via Boncompagni, 31, Piazza di Spagna* ☎ *06/8543182* 🌐 *www.ormaroma.it* ⏲ *Closed Sun. and Mon. No lunch* [M] *Popolo.*

Ristorante Nino

$$$ | **ITALIAN** | A favorite among international journalists and the rich and famous since the 1930s, this rustic, Tuscan-styled restaurant does not seem to have changed at all over the decades. Its menu is meat-focused with many Tuscan classics: try the *bistecca di costa all'arrabbiata*, a flavorful rib-eye steak cooked with chili and garlic. **Known for:** warm crostini spread with pâté; upscale old-school Italian vibe; ribollita (Tuscan bean soup). [$] *Average main: €26* ✉ *Via Borgognona 11, Piazza di Spagna* ☎ *06/6786752* 🌐 *ristorantenino.it* ⏲ *Closed Sun. and Aug.* [M] *Spagna.*

Settimo

$$$ | **ITALIAN** | Crowning the Sofitel Rome Villa Borghese hotel, this chic restaurant serves fancy takes on Rome's *cucina povera* (peasant cooking) in a chic space with graphic punches of color. The terrace offers fantastic views that stretch from Villa Borghese to the dome of St. Peter's, but the interior dining room, with its floor-to-ceiling windows and terrazzo-inspired floors, is lovely, too. **Known for:** amped-up version of classic Roman recipes; colorful, modern design; terrace with great views. Ⓢ *Average main: €26* ✉ *Sofitel Rome Villa Borghese, Via Lombardia 47, Piazza di Spagna* ☎ *06/478021* ⊕ *www.settimoristorante.it* Ⓜ *Barberini.*

★ Vynique

$$ | **MODERN ITALIAN** | This sleek wine bar and restaurant is just a short walk from the Spanish Steps, and its modern design looks the part among the fashion-forward streets. However, its unique focus is that its owners collaborate with the Regionale del Lazio (the state within which Rome sits) to showcase Lazio's regional products—from the cheeses to the wines to the bottled water—in its menu. **Known for:** chic contemporary style; excellent carbonara; extensive list of local wines. Ⓢ *Average main: €18* ✉ *Via Frattina 94, Piazza di Spagna* ☎ *06/98184507* ⊕ *vynique.it* ⊙ *Closed Mon.* Ⓜ *Spagna.*

☕ Coffee and Quick Bites

Antico Caffè Greco

$ | **CAFÉ** | The red-velvet chairs and marble tables of one of Rome's oldest cafés have seen the likes of Byron, Shelley, Keats, Goethe, and Casanova. Locals love basking in the more than 260 years of history held within its dark-wood walls lined with antique artwork; tourists appreciate its location amid the shopping madness of upscale Via Condotti. **Known for:** lavish historic design; perfect espresso; crystal goblets and high prices to match. Ⓢ *Average main: €12* ✉ *Via dei Condotti 86,* *Piazza di Spagna* ☎ *06/6791700* ⊕ *antico-caffegreco.eu* Ⓜ *Spagna.*

Babington's Tea Rooms

$$ | **BRITISH** | Located at the base of the Spanish Steps, this family-run English-style tea house has catered to the refined tea and scone cravings of travelers since 1893. The blends are carefully designed and can be brought to your homey table accompanied by a tower of tiny sandwiches, a fully loaded salad, or a risotto dish. **Known for:** unique (and pricey) loose leaf teas; homemade scones; cozy, historic atmosphere. Ⓢ *Average main: €20* ✉ *Piazza di Spagna 23–25* ☎ *06/6786027* ⊕ *www.babingtons.com/it* ⊙ *Closed Tues.* Ⓜ *Spagna.*

Caffè Canova-Tadolini

$ | **CAFÉ** | On chic Via del Babuino, the former studio of Neoclassical sculptor Antonio Canova and his student, Adamo Tadolini, is now an atmospheric spot for coffee, snack, or lunch. Opt for the budget-friendly option of taking your coffee at the bar while admiring the enormous plaster copies of the maestros' work, or pay more for table service and sit amid vast sculptures. **Known for:** museum-like setting; respectable aperitivo snacks for the price; slow and serious service. Ⓢ *Average main: €5* ✉ *Via del Babuino 150/A, Piazza di Spagna* ☎ *06/32110702* ⊕ *www.canovatadolini.com* Ⓜ *Spagna.*

Hotels

If being right in the heart of Rome's shopping district and within walking distance of major sights is a priority, Piazza di Spagna is the place to stay. Here, you'll find a wide range of accommodations—from exclusive boutique hotels with over-the-top amenities to moderately priced urban bed-and-breakfasts and *pensioni* (guesthouses) with clean, comfortable rooms.

Babuino 181

$$$ | **HOTEL** | On chic Via del Babuino, known for its high-end boutiques, jewelry stores, and antiques shops, this discreet and stylish hotel is an ideal pied-à-terre, with spacious rooms spread over two historic buildings. **Pros:** spacious suites; luxury Frette linens; iPhone docks and other handy in-room amenities. **Cons:** rooms can be a bit noisy; breakfast is nothing special; annex rooms feel removed from service staff. $ *Rooms from: €261 ⊠ Via del Babuino 181, Piazza di Spagna ☎ 06/32295295 ⊕ www.romeluxurysuites.com/it/babuino-181 ⤲ 25 rooms* ⫶○⫶ *Free Breakfast* Ⓜ *Flaminio, Spagna.*

Baglioni Hotel Regina

$$$$ | **HOTEL** | The former home of Queen Margherita of Savoy, the Baglioni Hotel Regina, which enjoys a prime spot on the Via Veneto, is still a favorite among today's jet-setters. **Pros:** chic decor; luxury on-site spa; excellent on-site restaurant and bar. **Cons:** internal rooms overlook air-conditioning ducts; extra charge for breakfast à la carte; location isn't as prestigious as it once was. $ *Rooms from: €650 ⊠ Via Veneto 72, Piazza di Spagna ☎ 06/421111 ⊕ www.baglionihotels.com/rome ⤲ 117 rooms* ⫶○⫶ *No Meals* Ⓜ *Barberini.*

Bulgari Hotel Roma

$$$$ | **HOTEL** | Nestled within Piazza Augusto Imperatore, Bulgari Hotel Roma is an architectural gem born from a meticulous four-year restoration of a historic edifice. **Pros:** great location in the historic center; large rooftop with views; visually striking and luxurious spa. **Cons:** ultra-luxury price point; underwhelming breakfast; sidestreet-facing rooms have no view. $ *Rooms from: €1710 ⊠ Piazza Augusto Imperatore, 17, Piazza di Spagna ☎ 06/36080400 ⊕ www.bulgarihotels.com/it_IT/rome ⤲ 114 rooms and suites* ⫶○⫶ *Free Breakfast* Ⓜ *Spagna.*

Crossing Condotti

$$$$ | **B&B/INN** | Located blocks away from Piazza di Spagna, Crossing Condotti is a chic, apartment-style escape in an 18th-century palazzo that comes with a curated pantry and a cozy library lounge. **Pros:** great location in Piazza di Spagna side streets; extremely quiet thanks to reinforced windows; excellent concierge service. **Cons:** no nightlife in neighborhood; no gym; no elevator. $ *Rooms from: €340 ⊠ Via Mario de' Fiori, 28, Piazza di Spagna ☎ 06/69920633 ⊕ www.crossingcondotti.it ⤲ 11 rooms and suites* ⫶○⫶ *Free Breakfast* Ⓜ *Spagna.*

★ The Hassler

$$$$ | **HOTEL** | When it comes to million-dollar views, the best place to stay in the whole city is the Hassler, so it's no surprise many of the rich and famous (Tom Cruise, Jennifer Lopez, and the Beckhams among them) are willing to pay top dollar for a room at this exclusive hotel atop the Spanish Steps. **Pros:** prime location and panoramic views; exceptional service; sauna access included with each reservation. **Cons:** VIP rates (10% VAT not included); gym and wellness area is tiny; rooms are updated on a rolling basis, leaving some feeling dated. $ *Rooms from: €1400 ⊠ Piazza Trinità dei Monti 6, Piazza di Spagna ☎ 06/699340, 800/223–6800 in U.S. ⊕ www.hotelhasslerroma.com ⤲ 87 rooms and suites* ⫶○⫶ *Free Breakfast* Ⓜ *Spagna.*

Hotel Art

$$ | **HOTEL** | High-fashion Rome meets chic contemporary art gallery at this hotel on Via Margutta, "the street of painters." As you glide through the stylish lobby and other public spaces, the smart furnishings and unique fixtures feel positively eclectic, but the color-coordinated guest rooms have been done in a more standard contemporary style (sleek wood headboards accented with handmade Florentine leather, puffy white comforters, bathrobes, and high-speed Internet). **Pros:** ultra-hip art gallery feel; free access

to the fitness center with sauna and Turkish baths; comfortable beds. **Cons:** glass floors are noisy at night; courtyard bar crowd may keep you awake; interior needs a refresh. [$] *Rooms from: €195* ✉ *Via Margutta 56, Piazza di Spagna* ☎ *06/328711* 🌐 *www.gruppouna.it/esperienze/hotel-art-by-the-spanish-steps* 🛏 *46 rooms* 🍴 *Free Breakfast* [M] *Spagna.*

Hotel Condotti

$$ | **B&B/INN** | Near the most expensive shopping street in Rome, Via Condotti, and one block from the Spanish Steps, this delightful little hotel is all about peace, comfort, and location. **Pros:** soundproof rooms with terraces; individual climate control; gorgeous decor. **Cons:** small rooms; tiny elevator; annex rooms on a different street without front desk support. [$] *Rooms from: €140* ✉ *Via Mario de' Fiori 37, Piazza di Spagna* ☎ *06/6794661* 🌐 *www.hotelcondotti.com* 🛏 *87 rooms* 🍴 *Free Breakfast* [M] *Spagna.*

Hotel Croce di Malta

$$ | **HOTEL** | This is a cheerful and reliable hotel in the side streets of Piazza di Spagna that offers great value for money. **Pros:** great location and price; air-conditioning; relaxing terraces. **Cons:** no extra services; slightly outdated interiors; smaller, spartan-like rooms. [$] *Rooms from: €142* ✉ *Via Borgognona 28, Piazza di Spagna* ☎ *06/6795482* 🌐 *www.crocemalta.com* 🛏 *25 rooms* 🍴 *Free Breakfast* [M] *Spagna.*

★ **Hotel de la Ville**

$$$$ | **HOTEL** | Occupying a prime position atop the Spanish Steps, this glamorous sister property of the beloved Hotel de Russie near the Piazza del Popolo has as a Grand Tour–inspired design featuring antiques, custom wallpaper stamped with Piranesi prints, and plenty of silk. **Pros:** must-visit rooftop bar with panoramic views; prestigious location atop the Spanish Steps; pampering spa uses signature made-in-Italy organic products. **Cons:** some rooms are a bit small for the price; service can be a bit slow at the bar; no pets allowed. [$] *Rooms from: €1400* ✉ *Via Sistina 69, Piazza di Spagna* ☎ *06/977931* 🌐 *www.roccofortehotels.com* 🛏 *104 rooms and suites* 🍴 *Free Breakfast* [M] *Spagna.*

Hotel dei Borgognoni

$$ | **HOTEL** | Travelers who love peace and tranquility appreciate the position of this chic hotel set in a prestigious palazzo from the 1800s. **Pros:** free in-room Wi-Fi; some rooms have private balconies or terraces; free use of bicycles. **Cons:** some rooms are small for the price; cramped bathrooms; breakfast lacks variety. [$] *Rooms from: €200* ✉ *Via del Bufalo 126, Piazza di Spagna* ☎ *06/69941505* 🌐 *www.hotelborgognoni.com* 🛏 *51 rooms* 🍴 *Free Breakfast* [M] *Barberini.*

★ **Hotel Eden**

$$$$ | **HOTEL** | At what was once a favorite haunt of Ingrid Bergman, Ginger Rogers, and Fellini, dashing elegance, exquisite decor, and stunning vistas of Rome combine with true Italian hospitality. **Pros:** gorgeous rooftop terrace restaurant; tranquil spa facilities; 24-hour room service. **Cons:** breakfast not included (and very expensive, at €50); gym is standard but small; some rooms overlook an unremarkable courtyard. [$] *Rooms from: €1260* ✉ *Via Ludovisi 49, Piazza di Spagna* ☎ *06/478121* 🌐 *www.dorchestercollection.com/en/rome/hotel-eden* 🛏 *98 rooms and suites* 🍴 *No Meals* [M] *Spagna.*

★ **Hotel Vilòn**

$$$$ | **HOTEL** | Set in a 16th-century mansion annexed to Palazzo Borghese and tucked behind a discreet entrance, this intimate hotel might be Rome's best-kept secret. **Pros:** gorgeous design; attentive staff; fantastic location. **Cons:** not much communal space; no spa or gym; some rooms are a bit small. [$] *Rooms from: €780* ✉ *Via dell'Arancio 69, Piazza di Spagna* ☎ *06/878187* 🌐 *www.hotelvilon.com* 🛏 *18 rooms and suites* 🍴 *Free Breakfast* [M] *Spagna.*

J.K. Place Roma

$$$$ | **HOTEL** | Set in what was once an architecture school and featuring gorgeous modern design, this intimate hotel is a stone's throw from the Mausoleum of Augustus and not far from the Spanish Steps and Piazza del Popolo. **Pros:** stellar staff are eager to please; excellent meals at rooftop lounge; complimentary minibar. **Cons:** no fitness center; not all rooms have a balcony; some rooms are on the small side. [$] *Rooms from: €800* ✉ *Via Monte d'Oro 30, Piazza di Spagna* ☎ *06/982634* 🌐 *jkroma.com* 🛏 *27 rooms and suites* 🍴 *Free Breakfast* [M] *Spagna.*

La Residenza

$$$ | **HOTEL** | This cozy hotel in a converted town house near Via Veneto is very popular with American travelers thanks to its location close to the embassy, American-style breakfast, and helpful staff. **Pros:** free breakfast buffet; spacious rooms with balconies; charming decor. **Cons:** the building's exterior doesn't compare to its interior; disappointing views out windows; rooms are in need of restyling. [$] *Rooms from: €254* ✉ *Via Emilia 22/24, Piazza di Spagna* ☎ *06/4880789* 🌐 *www.laresidenzaroma.com* 🛏 *27 rooms* 🍴 *Free Breakfast* [M] *Spagna.*

Marriott Grand Hotel Flora

$$$$ | **HOTEL** | Not only is this handsome hotel at the top of Via Veneto and next to the Villa Borghese park something of a beacon on the Rome landscape, but its standard of excellence is among the highest in the Eternal City, and its guest rooms are among the largest. **Pros:** convenient location and pleasant staff; spectacular view from the terrace; fitness center and spa. **Cons:** sometimes the noise from Via Veneto drifts in; crowded with businessmen and big tour groups; service is hit or miss. [$] *Rooms from: €420* ✉ *Via Veneto 191, Piazza di Spagna* ☎ *06/4820359* 🌐 *www.marriott.com* 🛏 *155 rooms and suites* 🍴 *No Meals* [M] *Barberini, Spagna.*

Palazzo Ripetta

$$$$ | **HOTEL** | Originally a 17th-century convent for orphaned girls, Palazzo Ripetta is now a stylish hotel designed by Fausta Gaetani, featuring vibrant upholstery, abstract art, and colorful Murano glass fixtures. **Pros:** spacious, beautifully designed rooms; great hangout spaces including lounge bar and rooftop; delicious food. **Cons:** no terraces; courtyard can be noisy; no spa or gym. [$] *Rooms from: €740* ✉ *Via di Ripetta 231, Piazza del Popolo* ☎ *06/3231144* 🌐 *www.palazzoripetta.com* 🛏 *78 rooms and suites* 🍴 *Free Breakfast* [M] *Popolo.*

Scalinata di Spagna

$$$ | **B&B/INN** | Perched atop the Spanish Steps, this charming boutique hotel is so popular that it's often booked far in advance. **Pros:** friendly and helpful concierge; fresh fruit in guest rooms; free Wi-Fi throughout. **Cons:** hike up the hill to the hotel; small rooms; no porter and no elevator. [$] *Rooms from: €257* ✉ *Piazza Trinità dei Monti 17, Piazza di Spagna* ☎ *06/45686150* 🌐 *www.hotelscalinata.com* 🛏 *30 rooms* 🍴 *Free Breakfast* [M] *Spagna.*

Sofitel Roma Villa Borghese

$$$$ | **HOTEL** | Set in a refurbished 1902 Victorian palace, the Sofitel—which has a long-standing good reputation with business travelers—exudes old-world elegance with modern-design sensibility. **Pros:** luxury lodging off the main drag (but not far from it); first-rate concierge and porter; luminous updated guest rooms. **Cons:** rooms are on the smaller side; prominent business clientele and quiet location might make it too low-key for some; tiny fitness center. [$] *Rooms from: €510* ✉ *Via Lombardia 47, Piazza di Spagna* ☎ *06/478021* 🌐 *sofitel-rome.com* 🛏 *78 rooms and suites* 🍴 *Free Breakfast* [M] *Spagna.*

W Rome

$$$$ | **HOTEL** | On a quiet street between Via Veneto and the Spanish Steps, the W Rome brings a calculated cool to an upscale old-world area. **Pros:** craft cocktails; rooftop pool and lounge area;

live music and a popular brunch add to the buzz. **Cons:** 24/7 energy not for everyone; no spa; live music can be a pain. [$] *Rooms from: €549* ✉ *Via Liguria 26–36, Piazza di Spagna* ☎ *06/894121* 🌐 *www.marriott.com* 🛏 *162 rooms and suites* 🍴 *Free Breakfast* [M] *Barberini.*

The Westin Excelsior, Rome

$$$$ | HOTEL | FAMILY | Ablaze with lights at night, this seven-layer-cake hotel—topped off by its famous cupola—is popular with visiting diplomats (who might be headed to the U.S. Embassy across the street), celebrities, and American conference groups. **Pros:** elegant period furnishings and decor; health club and indoor pool; historic restaurant. **Cons:** worn floors distract from ornate furnishings; some bathrooms are small; decor is grand but due for a makeover. [$] *Rooms from: €472* ✉ *Via Veneto 125, Piazza di Spagna* ☎ *06/47081* 🌐 *www.marriott.com* 🛏 *281 rooms and 35 suites* 🍴 *No Meals* [M] *Barberini, Spagna.*

Nightlife

After 9 pm, Piazza di Spagna holds the title for being the quietest area in the *centro storico* (historic center). Don't expect a party here, but do come to seek out some lovely *enoteche*, or wine bars.

BARS

Antica Enoteca

WINE BAR | Piazza di Spagna's historic wine bar literally corners the market on prime people-watching. Cozy up to the counter to sip a drink under the charming frescoes, or snag a coveted outdoor table. In addition to a vast selection of wine, Antica Enoteca has delectable antipasti, perfect for a snack or a light lunch, as well as a full menu of pastas and pizzas. ✉ *Via della Croce 76/b, Piazza di Spagna* ☎ *06/6790896* 🌐 *www.anticaenoteca.com* [M] *Spagna.*

Café Doney at the Westin Excelsior

COCKTAIL BARS | Nattily dressed businesspeople and harried tourists enjoy signature martinis at the street-side Café Doney, Via Veneto's grand dame, in front of the Westin Excelsior. The outdoor tables offer prime people-watching, while the seats inside are set under impossibly sparkly chandeliers amongst impeccable Italian design. ✉ *Westin Excelsior, Via Vittorio Veneto 125, Piazza di Spagna* ☎ *06/47082783* 🌐 *www.restaurantdoney.com.*

Il Marchese

COCKTAIL BARS | With high bar stools and midnight blue accents, Il Marchese feels every bit the sophisticated Roman nightcap hot spot. It was the first amaro bar in Europe, stocking more than 500 labels of the bitter, herbal liqueur, which can be served straight or mixed into creative cocktails. Pop in for a tapas-style aperitivo, or stay for dinner and watch the chef "shop" from his market of gourmet Italian ingredients that takes up part of the space. ✉ *Via di Ripetta 162, Piazza di Spagna* ☎ *06/90218872* 🌐 *www.ilmarcheseroma.it* [M] *Spagna.*

Il Palazzetto Wine Bar

WINE BAR | This rooftop wine bar and restaurant wins the prize for the perfect aperitivo spot, with excellent drinks and appetizers, as well as a breathtaking view of the comings and goings on the Spanish Steps. Reach it by climbing the monumental staircase that it overlooks, or getting a lift from the elevator inside the Spagna Metro station. ✉ *Il Palazzetto, Vicolo del Bottino 8, Piazza di Spagna* ✥ *The main entrance is a small gate at the top of the Spanish Steps* ☎ *342/1507215* 🌐 *www.hotelhasslerroma.com/en/il-palazzetto* [M] *Spagna.*

Shopping

The Piazza di Spagna area is considered to be the heart and soul of shopping in Rome, with international chains and luxury brands alongside independent shops. If your budget isn't big enough to binge at the high-end fashion houses along Via dei Condotti and Via del Babuino, try

Via dei Condotti is named for the conduits that once carried water to the Baths of Agrippa. Today, it's flooded by shoppers eager to browse in its high-end stores.

the more moderate stores down Via del Corso, where young Romans shop for jeans and inexpensive, trendy clothes. As you move toward Piazza del Popolo, you'll find more antiques shops and art galleries tucked away on Via Margutta.

ANTIQUES
Galleria Benucci
ANTIQUES & COLLECTIBLES | With carved and gilded late-Baroque and Empire period furniture and paintings culled from the noble houses of Italy's past, Galleria Benucci is a literal treasure trove. An establishment favored by professionals from Europe and abroad, this conservative gallery next to a former sculpture studio has an astonishing selection of objects in a hushed atmosphere where connoisseurs will find the proprietors only too happy to discuss their latest finds. ⊠ *Via del Babuino 150/C, Piazza di Spagna* ☎ *06/36002190* Ⓜ *Spagna.*

BEAUTY
Castelli Profumerie
FRAGRANCES | This fragrance shop has been in the business of heavenly scents for more than 50 years. In addition to offering an array of labels like Acqua di Parma, Bois 1920, Bond No. 9, and Comme des Garçons, the store has courteous, multilingual staffers who know the merchandise, making a shopping experience here a lot more pleasant than a dash through duty-free. There are three locations around the city: two on Via Frattina and one on Via Oslavia in the Prati neighborhood. ⊠ *Via Frattina 54, Piazza di Spagna* ☎ *06/6790339* ⊕ *www. profumeriecastelli.com* Ⓜ *Spagna.*

Pro Fumum
FRAGRANCES | Started in 1996, Pro Fumum (also seen as Pro Fvmvm) is a cult classic in Italian fragrance design. Each of its 35 unisex scents comes with a poem that describes the intention of the artisans. The philosophy here is that smell can trigger memories more powerfully than any photo, so the pricey-but-worth-it fragrances are created to evoke experiences like walking through a forest or listening to a thundering Roman fountain. ⊠ *Via Ripetta*

248, Piazza di Spagna ☎ *06/3200306*
⊕ *www.profumum.com* Ⓜ *Spagna.*

BOOKS AND STATIONERY

Anglo-American Book Co

BOOKS | FAMILY | With more than 40,000 books in English and shelves that are stuffed from floor-to-ceiling with both British and American editions, this large, friendly shop has been a mecca for English-language reading material in Rome for more than 60 years. The bilingual staff always goes the extra mile to find what you need, whether you're a study-abroad student looking for an art history or archaeology textbook or you're a visitor searching for a light read for the train. ✉ *Via della Vite 27, Piazza di Spagna* ☎ *06/6795222* ⊕ *www.facebook.com/AngloAmericanBookCoRoma* Ⓜ *Spagna.*

★ Pineider

STATIONERY | This outfit has been making exclusive stationery since 1774. The first Rome shop opened at the request of the royal household, and this is where the city's aristocratic families still come for engraved wedding invitations and timeless visiting cards. It also sells desk accessories, wallets, and briefcases made using the best Florentine leather. ✉ *Via del Leoncino 25, Piazza di Spagna* ☎ *06/6795884* ⊕ *www.pineider.com* Ⓜ *Spagna.*

CHILDREN'S CLOTHING

Mettimi Giù

CHILDREN'S CLOTHING | FAMILY | Taking its name from the common childhood demand "put me down," this shop has been styling the littlest Romans for more than three decades. It's stocked with European brands to outfit children from head to toe, plus all the toys, bags, and adorable accessories a tiny tot can tote. There are two neighboring storefronts: one for ages 0–3 and the other for ages 4–14. ✉ *Via Dei Due Macelli 56 and 59/e, Piazza di Spagna* ☎ *06/6789761* ⊕ *www.mettimigiu.it/en-gb* Ⓜ *Spagna.*

Piccadilly

CHILDREN'S CLOTHING | FAMILY | Specializing in timeless styles for the youngest Romans (ages 0–16) since 1932, Piccadilly is bursting with Liberty-print floral frocks, bloomers, scalloped collars, and dress shorts with suspenders. It's known for its special occasion–worthy clothes and impeccable tailoring. ✉ *Via Sistina 92, Piazza di Spagna* ☎ *3473785274* ⊕ *www.instagram.com/piccadillybabyroma* Ⓜ *Spagna.*

CLOTHING

★ Brioni

CLOTHING | Founded in 1945, Brioni is hailed for its impeccably crafted menswear. Italy's best tailors create bespoke suits to exacting standards, measured to the millimeter and completely personalized from a selection of more than 5,000 spectacular fabrics. A single made-to-measure wool suit will take a minimum of 32 hours to make. The brand's prêt-à-porter line is also praised for peerless cutting and stitching. Past and present clients include Clark Gable, Barack Obama, and, of course, James Bond. ✉ *Via Condotti 21A, Piazza di Spagna* ☎ *06/6783428* ⊕ *www.brioni.com* Ⓜ *Spagna.*

Dolce & Gabbana

CLOTHING | Dolce and Gabbana met in 1980 when both were assistants at a Milan fashion atelier, and they opened their first store in 1982. With a modern aesthetic that screams sex appeal, the brand has always thrived on excess and is known for its bold, creative designs. The Rome store has a glass ceiling above a sparkling chandelier to allow natural light to spill in, illuminating the marble floors, antique brass accents, and the latest lines for men, women, and children. ✉ *Via Condotti 49–51, Piazza di Spagna* ☎ *06/69924999* ⊕ *www.dolcegabbana.com* Ⓜ *Spagna.*

The Piazza di Spagna area is the heart and soul of shopping in Rome, with everything from luxury chains and art and antiques galleries to indie boutiques and souvenir stands.

Eddy Monetti

CLOTHING | Eddy Monetti, which began as a hat shop in Naples more than 130 years ago, is known for classic, upscale men's jackets, sweaters, slacks, and ties made out of wool, cotton, and cashmere. Sophisticated and pricey, the store carries a range of stylish British- and Italian-made pieces. ✉ *Via Borgognona 36, Piazza di Spagna* ☎ *06/6794117* ⊕ *www.eddymonetti.com* Ⓜ *Spagna.*

Elena Mirò

CLOTHING | Elena Mirò is a high-end brand that offers curvy women sophisticated, beautifully feminine clothes in sizes 46 (U.S. size 12, U.K. size 14) and up. There are several locations in Rome, including one on Via Nazionale. ✉ *Via Frattina 11, Piazza di Spagna* ☎ *06/6784367* ⊕ *www.elenamiro.com* Ⓜ *Spagna.*

Fendi

CLOTHING | Fendi has been a fixture of the Roman fashion landscape since "Mamma" Fendi first opened shop with her husband in 1925. With an eye for genius, she hired Karl Lagerfeld, whose furs and runway antics made him one of the most influential designers of the 20th century and brought international acclaim to Fendi. More recently, the atelier has gotten new life in the Italian press for its "Fendi for Fountains" campaign, which included funding the restoration of Rome's Trevi Fountain, and for moving its global headquarters to a striking Mussolini-era building known as the "square Colosseum" in the city's EUR neighborhood. The flagship store in Rome is on the ground floor of Palazzo Fendi. Upper floors contain the brand's seven private suites (the first ever Fendi hotel), and the rooftop is home to Zuma, a modern Japanese restaurant with an oh-so-cool bar that has sweeping views across the city. ✉ *Largo Carlo Goldoni 420, Piazza di Spagna* ☎ *06/33450896* ⊕ *www.fendi.com* Ⓜ *Spagna.*

Galassia

CLOTHING | If you're the type who dares to be different and prefers funky statement clothes and accessories, you'll love the edgy selection here. Look for classy, avant-garde men's and women's styles by A-list designers that include Rick Owens, Gaultier, Westwood, Issey Miyake, and Yamamoto. ⊠ *Via Frattina 20, Piazza di Spagna* ☎ *06/6797896* ⊕ *www.galassia-roma.com* Ⓜ *Spagna.*

Giorgio Armani

CLOTHING | One of the most influential designers of Italian haute couture, Giorgio Armani is world-famous for dazzling evening gowns and iconic suits in clean, fluid silhouettes. The flagship store is the best place to find pieces that range from exotic runway-worthy masterpieces to more wearable collections emphasizing casual Italian elegance with just the right touch of whimsy and sexiness. ⊠ *Via dei Condotti 76, Piazza di Spagna* ☎ *06/6991460* ⊕ *www.armani.com* Ⓜ *Spagna.*

Gucci

CLOTHING | Guccio Gucci opened his first leather shop selling luggage in Florence in 1921, and, more than 100 years later, the success of the double-G trademark is unquestionable. Tom Ford joined as creative director in 1994, helping the fashion house move into a new era that refreshed the label's aesthetic with reinterpretations of old-school favorites like horsebit loafers and Jackie Kennedy scarves. Now helmed by Sabato de Sarno, Gucci remains a fashion must for virtually every A-list celebrity. ⊠ *Via Condotti 8, Piazza di Spagna* ☎ *06/6790405* ⊕ *www.gucci.com* Ⓜ *Spagna.*

★ Patrizia Pepe

CLOTHING | Patrizia Pepe first emerged on the scene in Florence in 1993 with an aesthetic that's both minimalist and bold. Jackets with oversize lapels, playful pleats, mesmerizing mesh, and the occasional feathered poof set the designs apart. Spending time in the shop of this relative newcomer to the Italian fashion scene gives you the opportunity to pick up an item or two before the brand becomes the next fast-tracked craze. ⊠ *Via Frattina 5, Piazza di Spagna* ☎ *06/6781851* ⊕ *www.patriziapepe.com* Ⓜ *Spagna.*

Prada

CLOTHING | Mario Prada founded the Italian luggage brand in 1913, but it has been his granddaughter, Miuccia, who updated the designs into the timeless investment pieces of today. You'll find the Rome store more service-oriented than the New York City branches—a roomy elevator delivers you to a series of thickly carpeted salons where a flock of discreet assistants will help you pick out dresses, shoes, lingerie, and fashion accessories. The men's store is located at Via Condotti 88/90, while the women's is down the street at 92/95. ⊠ *Via dei Condotti 88/90 and 92/95, Piazza di Spagna* ☎ *06/6790897* ⊕ *www.prada.com* Ⓜ *Spagna.*

Schostal

CLOTHING | A Piazza di Spagna fixture since 1870, this was once the go-to shop for corsets, petticoats, stockings, and bonnets. Today, it's the place to stop for essential basics that are increasingly difficult to find, like fine-quality shirts, underwear, and handkerchiefs made of wool and pure cashmere at affordable prices. ⊠ *Via della Fontanella di Borghese 29, Piazza di Spagna* ☎ *06/6791240* ⊕ *www.schostaloriginals.com* Ⓜ *Spagna.*

Valentino

CLOTHING | Valentino fills most of Piazza di Spagna, where the designer lived for decades in a lovely palazzo next to one of the multiple boutiques showcasing his eponymous designs with a romantic edginess—think studded heels or prêt-à-porter evening gowns worthy of the Oscars. Rock stars and other music lovers can also have their Valentino guitar straps personalized when they buy one at this enormous boutique. ⊠ *Piazza di Spagna 38* ☎ *06/94515710* ⊕ *www.valentino.com* Ⓜ *Spagna.*

Versace

CLOTHING | Versace's Rome flagship is a gem of architecture and design, with Byzantine-inspired mosaic floors, futuristic interiors with transparent walls, and merchandise that has a sexy rocker-Gothic-underground vibe. Here you'll find apparel, accessories, and home furnishings in designs every bit as flamboyant as Donatella and Allegra (Gianni's niece). ⊠ *Via di San Sebastianello, 12, Piazza di Spagna* ☎ *06/6784600* ⊕ *www.versace. com* Ⓜ *Spagna.*

Zegna Boutique

CLOTHING | For more than 100 years, Ermenegildo Zegna has been a powerhouse of men's clothing in terms of both construction and fabric. Indeed, to ensure a high standard of quality, Zegna prefers to produce all the wool fabric it uses. Suits here start from €2,000, with the top of the line, known as "couture," costing considerably more. Although there are also lines of sportswear and accessories, this really is the place to splurge on a formal, tailored suit. ⊠ *Via Borgognona, 7E, Piazza di Spagna* ☎ *06/69940678* ⊕ *www.zegna. com* Ⓜ *Spagna.*

DEPARTMENT STORES

★ **La Rinascente**

DEPARTMENT STORE | FAMILY | Set in a dazzling, seven-story space, Italy's best-known department store is packed topped to bottom with luxury goods, from cosmetics, handbags, and accessories to ready-to-wear designer sportswear to kitchen items and housewares. Even if you're not planning on buying anything, the basement excavations of a Roman aqueduct and the roof terrace bar with its splendid view are well worth a visit. There's also a location at Piazza Fiume. ⊠ *Via del Tritone 61, Piazza di Spagna* ☎ *02/91387388* ⊕ *www.rinascente.it* Ⓜ *Barberini.*

FOOD AND WINE

Buccone

WINE/SPIRITS | A landmark wineshop inside the former coach house of a noble Roman family, Buccone has shelves that stretch impressively from floor to ceiling and are packed with wines and spirits ranging in price from a few euros to several hundred for rare vintages. The historical atmosphere has been preserved in the original wood-beam ceiling, long marble counter, and antique till. You can also buy jams, pasta, and packaged candy—perfect for inexpensive gifts. Consider booking (a week in advance) a guided wine tasting that features highlights from many of Italy's important wine-producing regions. ⊠ *Via di Ripetta 19/20, Piazza di Spagna* ☎ *06/3612154* ⊕ *www.enotecabuccone.com* Ⓜ *Piazza del Popolo.*

HOME DECOR

Frette

HOUSEWARES | Always timeless and luxurious, sometimes colorful or even playful—there is nothing like Frette's bed collections. The retailer has been a leader in sumptuous linens and towels for the home and the hotel industry since 1860, and sinking into its sophisticated cotton, satin, percale, or silk sheets is the perfect way to end the day. Complete your bedtime experience with pajamas and a gorgeous silk robe. ⊠ *Piazza di Spagna 11* ☎ *06/6790673* ⊕ *www.frette. com* Ⓜ *Spagna.*

JEWELRY

Bulgari

JEWELRY & WATCHES | Bulgari (also seen as Bvlgari) is to Rome what Tiffany is to New York and Cartier is to Paris. The jewelry giant has developed a reputation for meticulous craftsmanship melding noble metals with precious gems. In the middle of the 19th century, the great-grandfather of the current Bulgari brothers began working as a silver jeweler in his native Greece and is said to have moved to Rome with less than 1,000 lire in his pocket. This store's temple-inspired interior pays homage to the jeweler's ties to both places. ⊠ *Via dei Condotti 10, Piazza di Spagna* ☎ *06/696261* ⊕ *www. bulgari.com* Ⓜ *Spagna.*

LINGERIE
La Perla

LINGERIE | La Perla was founded in Bologna in 1954 and is now the global go-to for beautifully crafted lingerie and glamorous underwear for that special night, a bridal trousseau, or just to spoil yourself on your Roman holiday. If you like decadent finery that is both stylish and romantic, with plenty of well-placed frills, you will find something here to make you feel like a goddess. There are silk boxers for gents, too. ⊠ *Via Bocca di Leone 28, Piazza di Spagna* ☎ *06/69941934* ⊕ *www. laperla.com* Ⓜ *Spagna.*

Lingerie D'Elia

LINGERIE | The sisters who run this discreet store near the Spanish Steps were raised by their tailor father and developed a love of luxe fabrics early on. A fixture in Rome for nearly four decades, Lingerie D'Elia specializes in silky loungewear, and is rumored to be where Princess Diana shopped for made-in-Italy lace-trimmed nightgowns. ⊠ *Via Sistina, 119, Piazza di Spagna* ☎ *06/4881909* ⊕ *www. lingeriedelia.com* Ⓜ *Spagna.*

Marisa Padovan

SWIMWEAR | The place to go for unique, handmade-in-Rome bathing suits, Marisa Padovan has been sewing for Hollywood starlets like Audrey Hepburn and the well-heeled women of the Eternal City for more than 50 years. Choose from ready-to-wear coverups or suits trimmed with Swarovski crystals and polished turquoise stones or have the staff help you design a bespoke bikini or one-piece. The chic, cheery boutique also sells daughter Flavia's line of velvet trousers, knit ponchos, silk dresses, and cashmere coverups that make it easy to transition from a day by sea to an evening on the town. ⊠ *Via delle Carrozze, 81, Piazza di Spagna* ☎ *06/6793946* ⊕ *www.marisapadovan.com* Ⓜ *Spagna.*

MALLS
Galleria Alberto Sordi

MALL | This gorgeous covered shopping arcade on the Piazza Colonna was envisioned in the late 19th century, but not opened to the public until 1922. A Neoclassical palazzo with a brilliant stained-glass ceiling, the indoor mall is home to individual boutiques with both big and small names. ⊠ *Piazza Colonna, Piazza di Spagna* ⊕ *galleriaalbertosordi. com* Ⓜ *Barberini.*

SHOES, HANDBAGS, AND LEATHER GOODS
★ Braccialini

HANDBAGS | Founded in 1954 by Florentine stylist Carla Braccialini and her husband, Robert, this outfit makes bags that are authentic works of art in bright colors and delightful shapes, such as London black cabs or mountain chalets. The adorably quirky tote bags have picture-postcard scenes of luxury destinations made of brightly colored appliquéd leather. Be sure to check out the eccentric Temi (Theme) creature bags; the snail-shaped version made out of python skin makes a true fashion statement. There is another location on Via dei Condotti. ⊠ *Via Frattina, 117, Piazza di Spagna* ☎ *342/0338947* ⊕ *www.braccialini.it* Ⓜ *Spagna.*

Fausto Santini

SHOES | Shoe lovers with a passion for minimalist design flock to Fausto Santini to get their hands on his nerdy-chic footwear with its statement-making lines. Santini has been in business since 1970 and caters to a sophisticated, avant-garde clientele looking for elegant, classic shoes with a kick and a rainbow color palette. An outlet at Via Cavour 106, named for Fausto's father, Giacomo, sells last season's shoes at a big discount. ⊠ *Via Frattina 120, Piazza di Spagna* ☎ *06/6784114* ⊕ *www. faustosantini.com* Ⓜ *Spagna.*

Fratelli Rossetti

SHOES | Fratelli Rossetti is an old-world company with modern aspirations. Although known for its classic leather mens' and womens' loafers, some of its recent offerings are slightly more playful, with oversized tassels, say, or contrasting colors. It also has lines of leather sandals and sneakers. There is another location on Via del Babuino. ⊠ *Via Borgognona 5/a, Piazza di Spagna* ☎ *06/6782676* ⊕ *www.fratellirossetti.com* Ⓜ *Spagna.*

Furla

HANDBAGS | Furla very well might be the best deal in Italian leather, selling high-quality purses and wallets at comparatively affordable prices. Be prepared to fight your way through crowds of passionate handbag lovers, all anxious to possess one of the delectable bags, wallets, or whimsical key chains in trendy sherbet hues or timeless bold color combos. ⊠ *Piazza di Spagna 22, Piazza di Spagna* ☎ *06/6797159* ⊕ *www.furla.com* Ⓜ *Spagna.*

Giuseppe Zanotti

SHOES | Giuseppe Zanotti creates sought-after women's and men's shoes ranging from pencil-thin stilettos (often with a bit of sparkle or other bling) to colorful loafers to couture sneakers. The footwear here is placed on a literal pedestal so the craftsmanship can be admired from all angles. ⊠ *Piazza di Spagna, 33, Piazza di Spagna* ☎ *06/69924220* ⊕ *www.giuseppezanotti. com* Ⓜ *Spagna.*

Salvatore Ferragamo

SHOES | Fans of the brand will think they have died and followed the white light when they enter the Ferragamo stores, where shoes and handbags are displayed on pillars like jewels. The Florentine design house also has ready-to-wear clothes, scarves, and ties. Men's styles are found at Via Condotti 65, women's at 73/74. Its splendid luxury Portrait Suites Hotel is on the upper floors. ⊠ *Via dei Condotti 65 and 73/74, Piazza di Spagna* ☎ *06/6781130* ⊕ *www.ferragamo.com* Ⓜ *Spagna.*

Sermoneta

HATS & GLOVES | Whether you're looking for fancy opera gloves or for a fashionable but warm pair to get you through the winter, Sermoneta has a vast selection. Browse through stacks of hand-stitched nappa leather, deerskin, and cashmere-lined capybara gloves in all colors. You can also head upstairs for a custom fitting, and then have your gloves personalized with your own initials, logos, or other designs. ⊠ *Piazza di Spagna 61, Piazza di Spagna* ☎ *06/6791960* ⊕ *www. sermonetagloves.it* Ⓜ *Spagna.*

Superga

SHOES | In business for more than 100 years and beloved by many Italians, Superga sells timeless sneakers in classic white or a rainbow of colors. The 2750 model has been worn by everyone from Kelly Brook to the Princess of Wales. There is another location on Via di Campo Marzio. ⊠ *Via delle Vite 86, Piazza di Spagna* ☎ *06/6787654* ⊕ *www.superga. com* Ⓜ *Spagna.*

★ Tod's

SHOES | Founded in the 1920s, Tod's has grown from a small family brand into a global powerhouse so wealthy that its owner Diego Della Valle donated €20 million to the Colosseum restoration project. The shoe baron is best known for his simple, classic, understated designs done in butter-soft leather, but his light, flexible Gommini line of driving shoes with rubber-bottomed soles are popular as well. This location sells menswear and men's shoes; womenswear and women's shoes are available at another location on Via dei Condotti. ⊠ *Via della Fontanella di Borghese 56a–57, Piazza di Spagna* ☎ *06/68210066* ⊕ *www.tods. com* Ⓜ *Spagna.*

Chapter 7

REPUBBLICA AND THE QUIRINALE

Updated by
Laura Itzkowitz

⊙ Sights	🍴 Restaurants	🛏 Hotels	🛍 Shopping	🍸 Nightlife
★★★★☆	★★★☆☆	★★★★☆	★★★☆☆	★★☆☆☆

NEIGHBORHOOD SNAPSHOT

MAKING THE MOST OF YOUR TIME

While slightly off Rome's bustling tourist path, this central (and well-connected) area has a number of intriguing sights, from the stunning sweep of Piazza della Repubblica and the excellent ancient art collection of the Palazzo Massimo alle Terme to the bones of the Capuchin Crypt and Bernini's breathtaking sculpture, the *Ecstasy of St. Teresa.* It's possible to walk the whole area, but this part of town is so well connected by bus and Metro that it's usually quicker to take public transport. When choosing a time of day to visit, remember that many churches (like Santa Maria della Vittoria, home of Bernini's *Saint Teresa* sculpture) close at midday, reopening around 3 or 4.

TOP REASONS TO GO

Bernini's *Ecstasy of St. Teresa*: Admire the worldly realism of Teresa's allegedly spiritual rapture. The star of the Cappella Cornaro, Santa Maria della Vittoria, Bernini's theatrical masterpiece is a cornerstone of the high Roman Baroque period.

Palazzo Barberini: Take in five centuries of art at one of Rome's greatest family palaces, where you can gape at Rome's biggest ballroom and Raphael's *La Fornarina.*

Palazzo Massimo alle Terme: See the spectacular Hellenistic *Boxer at Rest,* get your emperors straight in the portrait gallery, and marvel at breathtaking 2,000-year-old frescoes on the top floor.

Capuchin Crypt: Contemplate eternity in the creepy-yet-creative crypt under Santa Maria della Concezione, "decorated" with the skeletons of 4,000 monks, replete with fluted arches made of collarbones and arabesques of shoulder blades.

Piazza del Quirinale: Crowning the Quirinale—the loftiest of Rome's seven hills—is the Piazza del Quirinale, with spectacular views over the city, its horizon marked by "Il Cupolino," the dome of St. Peter's. Framing the vista are enormous ancient statues of Castor and Pollux, the Dioscuri (Horse-Tamers).

GETTING HERE

■ Located between Termini station and the Spanish Steps, this area is about a 15-minute walk from either. Bus No. 40 will get you from Termini to the Quirinale in two stops; from the Vatican take Bus No. 64. The very central Repubblica Metro stop is on the piazza of the same name.

PAUSE HERE

■ The small, verdant park across the street from the Piazza del Quirinale is a good spot to stop and take a break. In the center sits an equestrian statue of King Carlo Alberto, the king of Piedmont-Sardinia during the turbulent period of the Reunification of Italy. There are benches, and kids often play on the grass. If you happen to be in the area in the early evening, cross the street to see the spectacular sunset over Piazza del Quirinale and the rooftops of Rome.

Just northwest of the modern Termini station, this area offers an extraordinary Roman blend of old and new. The stretch from Piazza della Repubblica to Piazza Barberini swarms with professionals going in and out of office buildings, as the Quirinale, home to the president of Italy, buzzes with political activity. It's more than just a workaday area, though, with intriguing attractions ranging from the bizarre Capuchin Crypt to great Bernini sculptures.

Repubblica

Piazza della Repubblica was laid out to serve as a monumental gateway between the Termini rail station and the rest of the city. The piazza's main landmark, the vast ruins of the Terme di Diocleziano (Baths of Diocletian), were subsequently transformed into a Renaissance monastery and then, by Michelangelo's design, to the church of Santa Maria degli Angeli. The ancient treasures at Palazzo Massimo delle Terme, Bernini's spectacular Capella Cornaro, and, farther afield, the modern Museo d'Arte Contemporanea (MACRO) will always be vying for your attention.

 Sights

★ MACRO
ART MUSEUM | Formerly known as Rome's Modern and Contemporary Art Gallery, and before that as the Peroni beer factory, this redesigned industrial space has brought new life to the gallery and museum scene of a city hitherto hailed for its "then," not its "now." The collection here covers Italian contemporary artists from the 1960s through today. The goal is to bring current art to the public in innovative spaces and, not incidentally, to support and recognize Rome's contemporary art scene, which labors in the shadow of the city's artistic heritage. After a few days—or millennia—of dusty marble, it's a breath of fresh air. ■ TIP→ Check the website for occasional late-night openings and events. ✉ Via Nizza 138, Repubblica ☎ 06/696271 ⊕ www.museomacro.it ✆ Free ☾ Closed Mon. Ⓜ Castro Pretorio.

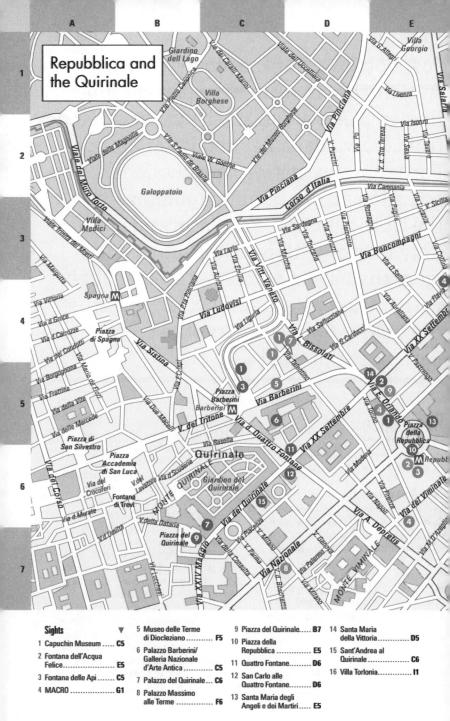

Republica and the Quirinale

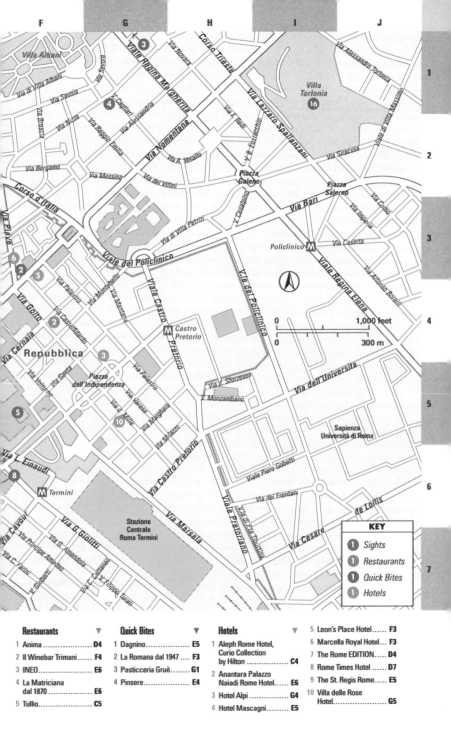

| F | G | H | I | J |

1
Villa Albani
Viale Regina Margherita
Villa Torlonia 🔟6️⃣
Via Alessandro Torlonia

2
Via Nomentana
Piazza Galeno
Piazza Salerno

3
Corso d'Italia
Viale del Policlinico
Policlinico Ⓜ
Viale Regina Elena

4
Via Goito
Repubblica ③
Viale del Policlinico
Castro Pretorio Ⓜ

5
Piazza dell'Indipendenza
Via d. Sforzesca
Via dell'Universitá
Sapienza Universitá di Roma

6
Termini Ⓜ
Viale Piero Gobetti
de Lollis

7
Via Cavour
Via G. Giolitti
Stazione Centrale Roma Termini
Via Marsala
Via Cesare

0 —— 1,000 feet
0 —— 300 m

Restaurants ▼	**Quick Bites** ▼	**Hotels** ▼	5 Leon's Place Hotel...... **F3**
1 Anima **D4**	1 Dagnino............ **E5**	1 Aleph Rome Hotel,	6 Marcella Royal Hotel... **F3**
2 Il Winebar Trimani **F4**	2 La Romana dal 1947 .... **F3**	Curio Collection	7 The Rome EDITION..... **D4**
3 INEO................. **E6**	3 Pasticceria Gruè......... **G1**	by Hilton **C4**	8 Rome Times Hotel **D7**
4 La Matriciana	4 Pinsere................ **E4**	2 Anantara Palazzo	9 The St. Regis Rome..... **E5**
dal 1870 .... **E6**		Naiadi Rome Hotel...... **E6**	10 Villa delle Rose
5 Tullio.................. **C5**		3 Hotel Alpi **G4**	Hotel................ **G5**
		4 Hotel Mascagni.......... **E5**	

Museo delle Terme di Diocleziano
(*Baths of Diocletian*)

RUINS | Though part of this ancient bath complex (the largest in the Roman world) is now the church of Santa Maria degli Angeli, and other parts were transformed into a Carthusian monastery or razed to make room for later urban development, a visit still gives you a sense of the scale and grandeur of this complex, which included a gymnasium, library, and public baths. Upon entering the church, you see the major structures of the baths, partly covered by 16th- and 17th-century overlay, some of which is by Michelangelo. The calm monastery cloister is filled with the Museo Nazionale Romano's collection of inscriptions; other rooms have pieces associated especially with remote Roman antiquity (think: huts), as well as archaeological finds from Rome's Republican and imperial periods, including a rare painted relief of the god Mithras. ⊠ *Viale Enrico de Nicola 78, Repubblica* ☎ *06/39967700* ⊕ *www.museonazionaleromano.beniculturali.it* 🎟 *€8, or €12 for a combined ticket including access to Crypta Balbi, Palazzo Massimo alle Terme, and Palazzo Altemps (valid for 1 wk)* ☽ *Closed Mon.* Ⓜ *Repubblica, Termini.*

★ Palazzo Massimo alle Terme

ART MUSEUM | The Museo Nazionale Romano, with items ranging from striking classical Roman paintings to marble bric-a-brac, has four locations: Palazzo Altemps, Crypta Balbi, the Museo delle Terme di Diocleziano, and this, the Palazzo Massimo alle Terme—a vast structure containing the great ancient treasures of the archaeological collection and also the coin collection. Highlights include the *Dying Niobid*, the famous bronze *Boxer at Rest*, and the *Discobolus Lancellotti*.

Among the museum's most intriguing attractions, however, are the ancient frescoes on view on the top floor. They're stunningly set up to "re-create" the look of the homes they once decorated, and

their colors are remarkably preserved. You'll see stuccoes and wall paintings found in the area of the Villa Farnesina (in Trastevere), as well as those depicting a garden in bloom and an orchard alive with birds that once covered the walls of cool sunken rooms at Empress Livia's villa in Prima Porta, just outside the city. ⊠ *Largo di Villa Peretti 2, Repubblica* ☎ *06/39967700* ⊕ *www.museonazionaleromano.beniculturali.it* 🎟 *€10, or €14 for a combined ticket including access to Crypta Balbi, Museo delle Terme di Diocleziano, and Palazzo Altemps (valid for 1 wk)* ☽ *Closed Mon.* Ⓜ *Repubblica, Termini.*

Piazza della Repubblica

PLAZA/SQUARE | Often the first view that spells "Rome" to weary travelers walking from Termini station, this round piazza was laid out in the late 1800s and follows the line of the caldarium of the vast ancient public baths, the Terme di Diocleziano. At its center, the exuberant Fontana delle Naiadi (Fountain of the Naiads) teems with voluptuous bronze ladies happily wrestling with marine monsters. The nudes weren't there when the pope unveiled the fountain in 1888—sparing him any embarrassment—but when the figures were added in 1901, they caused a scandal. It's said that the sculptor, Mario Rutelli, modeled them on the ample figures of two musical-comedy stars of the day. The colonnades now house the luxe hotel Anantara Palazzo Naiadi and various shops and cafés. ⊠ *Repubblica* Ⓜ *Repubblica.*

Santa Maria degli Angeli e dei Martiri

CHURCH | The curving brick facade on the northeast side of Piazza della Repubblica is one small remnant of the colossal Terme di Diocleziano, the largest and most impressive of the baths of ancient Rome. A gift to the city from Emperor Diocletian, the complex was completed in AD 306. In 1561 Michelangelo was commissioned to convert the vast *frigidarium,* the central hall of

The Rivalry of Bernini and Borromini

Even the famous feuding duos of Michelangelo and Raphael or Mozart and Salieri couldn't match the rivalry of Gian Lorenzo Bernini and Francesco Borromini. In a pitched battle of anything-you-can-do-I-can-do-better, these two Baroque masters transformed 17th-century Rome into a city of spectacle, the "theater of the entire world." Although it was Bernini who triumphed and Borromini who wound up taking his own life, the real winner was Rome itself—much of the city is a feast for the eyes that was cooked up by these two great artists.

United in genius, the two could not have been more different in fortune and character. Born within a year of each other at the turn of the 1600s, they spent decades laying out majestic squares, building precedent-shattering churches, all while attempting to outdo each other in Baroque bravado.

Bernini, perhaps the greatest showman of all time, exulted in Technicolor-hued theatricality; Borromini, the reclusive purist, pursued the pure light of geometry, although with an artisan's hankering for detail. Bernini grew into the famed lover and solid family man; Borromini seems not to have had any love life at all. Bernini became a smooth mingler with society's great and worthy ranks; Borromini remained the quirky outsider.

Bernini triumphed as the all-rounder, he of the *bel composto*—as in the Cornaro Chapel, where his talents as sculptor/architect/dramatist come stunningly together. Borromini was an architect, pure and simple. Throughout their lives, they tried to turn the tables—psychologically as well as architecturally—on each other, a struggle that ended with Borromini's tragic suicide.

Both men, however, fervently believed in the Baroque style and its mission to amaze, as well as edify. Thanks to the Counter-Reformation, the Catholic church discovered, and exploited, the effects of such Baroque techniques as chiaroscuro (light and dark) and trompe l'oeil (fool-the-eye). Bernini and Borromini also found ways to give sculpture movement. In Bernini's famed *Pluto and Persephone*, for example, the solid stone seems transmuted into living flesh—an effect previously thought possible only in paint. Together transforming the city into a "giant theater," the rivals thus became the principal dramaturges and stage managers of Baroque Rome.

the baths, into a church. His work was later altered by Vanvitelli in the 18th century, but the huge transept, which formed the nave in Michelangelo's plan, has remained. The eight enormous monolithic columns of red granite that support the great beams are the original columns of the tepidarium, 45 feet high and more than 5 feet in diameter. The great hall is 92 feet high. ✉ *Piazza della Repubblica, Repubblica* ☎ *06/4880812*

⊕ *www.santamariadegliangeliroma.it*
Ⓜ *Repubblica.*

★ **Santa Maria della Vittoria**
CHURCH | Designed by Carlo Maderno, this church is best known for Bernini's sumptuous Baroque decoration of the Cappella Cornaro (Cornaro Chapel, the last on the left as you face the altar), which houses his interpretation of divine love in the *Ecstasy of St. Teresa.*

Bernini's masterly fusion of sculpture, light, architecture, painting, and relief is a multimedia extravaganza, with the chapel modeled as a theater, and one of the key examples of the Roman High Baroque. The members of the Cornaro family meditate on the communal vision of the great moment of divine love before them: the swooning saint's robes appear to be on fire, quivering with life, and the white marble group seems suspended in the heavens as golden rays illuminate the scene. An angel assists as Teresa abandons herself to the joys of heavenly love. To modern eyes, Bernini's representation of the saint's experience may seem more earthly than mystical. As the visiting French dignitary Charles de Brosses put it in the 18th century, "If this is divine love, I know all about it." ✉ *Via XX Settembre 17, Largo Santa Susanna, Repubblica* ☎ *06/42740571* [M] *Repubblica.*

Villa Torlonia

CASTLE/PALACE | **FAMILY** | Built for aristocrats-come-lately, the Torlonia family—the Italian Rockefellers of the 19th century—this villa became Mussolini's residence and now serves as a public park. The Casino Nobile, the main palace designed by architect Giuseppe Valadier, is a grand, Neoclassical edifice, replete with a gigantic ballroom, frescoed salons, and a soaring temple-like facade. While denuded of nearly all their furnishings and art treasures, some salons have important remnants of decor, including the reliefs once fashioned by the father of Italian Neoclassical sculpture, Antonio Canova.

A complete contrast is offered by the Casina delle Civette (Little House of Owls), a hyper-charming example of the Liberty (Art Nouveau) style of the early 1900s. The gabled, fairy tale–like cottage-palace now displays majolica and stained-glass decorations, including windows with owl motifs—a stunning, oft-overlooked find for lovers of 19th-century decorative arts. Temporary exhibits are held in the small and elegant Il Casino dei Principi (The House of Princes), designed in part by Valadier. ✉ *Villa Torlonia, Via Nomentana 70, Repubblica* ☎ *06/0608* 🌐 *www.museivillatorlonia.it* 🎟 *€9 Casina delle Civette with exhibit, €14 Casino Nobile, Casino dei Principe and Casina delle Civette (with exhibit)* 🕒 *Closed Mon.* [M] *Policlinico.*

🍴 Restaurants

The areas around Piazza della Repubblica and Termini station aren't known as gastronomic hot spots, but they do have some classic Roman restaurants and wine bars.

Il Winebar Trimani

$$$ | **WINE BAR** | This wine bar is run by the Trimani family of wine merchants, whose shop next door has been in business for nearly two centuries. Hot food is served at lunch and dinner in the minimalist interior, and it is also perfect for an aperitif or an early supper (it opens for evening service at 6 pm). **Known for:** warmly lit second floor for sipping; torte salate (savory tarts); 5,000 wines from around the world. [$] *Average main: €30* ✉ *Via Cernaia 37/b, Repubblica* ☎ *06/4469630* 🌐 *www.trimani.com* 🕒 *Closed Sun. and 3 wks in Aug.* [M] *Castro Pretorio, Repubblica.*

★ **INEO**

$$$$ | **MODERN ITALIAN** | It's only a matter of time before this elegant restaurant inside the Anantara Palazzo Naiadi Hotel gets a Michelin star. With a chic, modern design, creative tasting menus by chef Heros De Agostinis, and special touches like a roving cart with a variety of delicious bread made in-house, this is a true five-star experience. **Known for:** gourmet tasting menus; globally influenced dishes; romantic ambiance. [$] *Average main: €48* ✉ *Anantara Palazzo Naiadi, Piazza della Repubblica 46, Repubblica* ☎ *06/489381* 🌐 *www.ineorestaurant.com* 🕒 *Closed Sun. and Mon.* [M] *Repubblica.*

Bernini vs. Borromini: A Mini-Walk

In Rome, you may become lost looking for the work of one rival, then suddenly find yourself gazing at the work of the other. As though an eerily twinned path was destined for the two giants, several of their greatest works are just a few blocks from each other.

A short street (Via Orlando) away from mammoth Piazza Repubblica stands Santa Maria della Vittoria, famed for Bernini's Cornaro Chapel. Out of favor with new anti-Barberini Pope Innocent X, Bernini was rescued by a commission from Cardinal Cornaro to build a chapel for his family. Here, as if in a "theater," sculpted figures of family members look down from two marble balconies on the Carmelite Saint Theresa of Avila being pierced by the arrow of the Angel of Divine Love, eyes shut in agony, mouth open in rapture.

Leave the church and head down Via Barberini to Piazza Barberini to see three of the largest bees you'll ever see. The Fountain of the Bees is Bernini's tribute to his arch-patron from the Barberini family, Pope Urban VIII. The bees were family emblems. Another Bernini masterstroke is the Triton Fountain in the center of Piazza Barberini. Turn left up Via delle Quattro Fontane. On your left is spectacular Palazzo Barberini,

where Bernini and Borromini worked together in an uneasy partnership. The wonderful winding staircase off to the right is the work of Borromini, while the other more conventionally angled staircase on the left is by Bernini, who also has a self-portrait hanging in the art gallery upstairs.

Borromini's prospects soon took a turn for the better thanks to the Barefoot Spanish Trinitarians, who commissioned him to design San Carlo alle Quattro Fontane, set at the crossroads up the road. One of the marvels of architecture, its dome—not much bigger than a down-turned bathtub—is packed immaculately throughout with hexagons, octagons, and crosses. In the adjoining cloister, revel in Borromini's rearrangement of columns, which transform what would be a conventional rectangle into an energetic octagon. Don't forget to stop and admire the church's facade.

On the same Via del Quirinale stands a famous Bernini landmark, the Jesuits' Sant'Andrea al Quirinale. With steps flowing out into the street, it could be viewed as Bernini's response to his rival's nearby masterpiece. Ironically, the commission for the Jesuit church was originally earmarked for Borromini (but transferred when Pope Alexander VII took over).

★ La Matriciana dal 1870

$$ | ROMAN | This old school Roman restaurant traces its roots back to 1870, when a woman from the town of Amatrice in northern Lazio arrived in Rome and started to cook her town's renowned bucatini all'amatriciana near Termini Station. Whether the story is true or a legend, this is indeed a great place to try the famous pasta and other Roman specialties in an elegant space with white tablecloths, plates emblazoned with the restaurant's name, and courteous and formally attired waiters. **Known for:** bucatini all'amatriciana; elegant, old school atmosphere; local favorite restaurant. $ *Average main: €20* ⊠ *Via del Viminale 44, Repubblica*

☎ *06/4881775* 🌐 *www.lamatriciana.it* 🕓 *Closed Sat.* [M] *Repubblica.*

Coffee and Quick Bites

Dagnino

$ | **BAKERY** | Hidden inside a covered arcade, this Sicilian pasticceria, which opened in 1955, has pastry cases filled with cannoli, cassata, cakes, and marzipan as well as savory items like sandwiches and arancini. Go for breakfast, and try the cornetto filled with ricotta and chocolate chips—this might be the only place in Rome where you can find it. **Known for:** Sicilian desserts; midcentury modern design; cornetti filled with ricotta and chocolate chips. [$] *Average main: €3* ✉ *Via Vittorio Emanuele Orlando 75, Repubblica* ☎ *06/4818660* 🌐 *www.dagnino.com* [M] *Repubblica.*

La Romana dal 1947

$ | **ICE CREAM** | **FAMILY** | In summer, the line at this gelateria stretches out the door and around the corner. Though it's a franchise that originated in Rimini, it's loved by Romans for its rich, creamy gelato made with organic milk, fresh fruit, nuts, and chocolate. **Known for:** reasonably priced; big portions; modern decor. [$] *Average main: €3* ✉ *Via XX Settembre 60, Repubblica* ☎ *06/42020828* 🌐 *www.gelateriaromana.com* [M] *Repubblica.*

Pasticceria Gruè

$ | **CAFÉ** | **FAMILY** | This chic, modern pasticceria and café run by a husband-and-wife team is the perfect place to stop for a quick lunch or something sweet near MACRO and Villa Torlonia. The panettone is award-winning, but it's far from the only thing worth trying—the cakes, petit-fours, macarons, and gelato are some of the best in Rome. **Known for:** panettone available year-round; award-winning bakery; light lunch fare. [$] *Average main: €8* ✉ *Viale Regina Margherita 95/99, Repubblica* ☎ *06/8412220* 🌐 *www.gruepasticceria.it* 🕓 *Closed Mon.*

Pinsere

$ | **PIZZA** | **FAMILY** | In Rome, you'll usually find either pizza *tonda* (round) or pizza *al taglio* (by the slice), but there's also pizza *pinsa*—an oval-shaped individual pie that's a little thicker than the classic Roman pizza. Pinsere is mostly a take-out shop, with people eating on the street for their lunch break, so it's the perfect quick meal. **Known for:** budget-friendly options; seasonal toppings; mortadella and pistachio pizzas. [$] *Average main: €6* ✉ *Via Flavia 98, Repubblica* ☎ *06/42020924* 🌐 *www.pinsereroma.it* 🕓 *Closed weekends and 2 wks in Aug.* [M] *Castro Pretorio.*

Hotels

With its beautiful piazza and fountain, Repubblica is the place to stay if you want to be near but not *too* near Termini station, Rome's central train hub. Though you'll find lodging here in all price ranges, rooms tend to be a better value in this part of town.

Anantara Palazzo Naiadi Rome Hotel

$$$$ | **HOTEL** | You'll experience exquisite service and pampering at this Neoclassical landmark on the Piazza della Repubblica built on the foundations of the Baths of Diocletian—it's now run by Anantara, a luxury hotel brand with roots in Thailand. **Pros:** top-notch concierge and staff; multiple romantic dining options; spa with both Asian and European-style treatments. **Cons:** food and beverages are expensive; beyond the immediate vicinity of many sights; rooms are a different style than public spaces. [$] *Rooms from: €750* ✉ *Piazza della Repubblica 47, Repubblica* ☎ *06/489381* 🌐 *www.anantara.com/en/palazzo-naiadi-rome* 🛏 *232 rooms* 🍴 *No Meals* [M] *Repubblica, Termini.*

Hotel Alpi

$$ | **HOTEL** | You'll feel right at home from the moment you waltz into this hotel, where high ceilings, elegant chandeliers,

white walls, and marble floors lend both elegance and warmth—all right around the corner from Termini station. **Pros:** clean and comfortable; lovely terraces for relaxing; boutique design and service. **Cons:** not all rooms are created equal; location is not very picturesque; you'll need to take transportation to most sights. $ *Rooms from: €130* ✉ *Via Castelfidardo 84, Repubblica* ☎ *06/4441235* ⊕ *www.hotelalpi.com* 🛏 *48 rooms* ⏹ *No Meals* Ⓜ *Castro Pretorio, Termini.*

Hotel Mascagni

$$ | **HOTEL** | **FAMILY** | On a side street around the corner from one of Rome's most impressive piazzas, this friendly hotel has polite and professional staff, public spaces styled with contemporary art, and guest rooms with wood fixtures and furnishings accentuated by warm colors. **Pros:** cozy library-style lobby; evening lounge serves light fare; special programs include a "Family Perfect" room option. **Cons:** elevator is too small and takes a while; breakfast options are basic; some bathrooms are smallish. $ *Rooms from: €200* ✉ *Via Vittorio Emanuele Orlando 90, Repubblica* ☎ *06/48904040* ⊕ *www.mascagnihotel-rome.it* 🛏 *40 rooms* ⏹ *Free Breakfast* Ⓜ *Repubblica.*

Leon's Place Hotel

$$$ | **HOTEL** | Just around the corner from Piazza della Repubblica, this extremely Instagrammable hotel has a lobby lounge with surrealist design elements, like lip-shaped sofas, and an interior courtyard done up in millennial pink. **Pros:** gourmet minibar; eye-catching design; top-quality toiletries. **Cons:** hotel bar is pricey; some rooms face the courtyard; some rooms lack windows. $ *Rooms from: €228* ✉ *Via XX Settembre 90/94, Repubblica* ☎ *06/890871* ⊕ *www.leonsplacehotel.it* 🛏 *56 rooms* ⏹ *No Meals* Ⓜ *Repubblica.*

Marcella Royal Hotel

$$$ | **HOTEL** | You can do your sightseeing from the rooftop terrace of the Marcella, a midsize hotel with the feel of a smaller, more intimate establishment, where staff go the extra mile to make your stay pleasant. **Pros:** all-day dining in the rooftop garden; helpful, friendly staff; large bathrooms with excellent water pressure. **Cons:** some rooms are in need of restyling; spotty internet; closet storage is minimal in some rooms. $ *Rooms from: €240* ✉ *Via Flavia 106, Repubblica* ☎ *06/42014591* ⊕ *www.marcellaroyalhotel.com* 🛏 *92 rooms* ⏹ *Free Breakfast* Ⓜ *Repubblica.*

The St. Regis Rome

$$$$ | **HOTEL** | Originally opened by César Ritz in 1894, this grande dame has a Belle Epoque lobby filled with classic and contemporary art, a ballroom with painstakingly restored ceiling frescoes, and an intimate library where you can sip a cup of tea or something stronger. **Pros:** houses the Roman location of international art gallery Galleria Continua; every room comes with 24/7 butler service; the library lounge serves a lovely afternoon tea. **Cons:** food and drinks are pricey; breakfast is not included; restaurant feels more like a lounge than a proper restaurant. $ *Rooms from: €800* ✉ *Via Vittorio E. Orlando 3, Repubblica* ☎ *06/47091* ⊕ *www.marriott.com* 🛏 *161 rooms* ⏹ *No Meals* Ⓜ *Repubblica.*

Villa delle Rose Hotel

$$ | **HOTEL** | When the Eternal City becomes too chaotic for you, head to this 19th-century palazzo retreat in a Roman villa just minutes from Termini Station. **Pros:** delightful garden with roses and bougainvillea; good value; free Wi-Fi. **Cons:** some rooms are small (ask for a larger one); elevator is cramped; decor could use revamping. $ *Rooms from: €125* ✉ *Via Vicenza 5, Repubblica* ☎ *06/4451788* ⊕ *www.villadellerose.it* 🛏 *37 rooms* ⏹ *Free Breakfast* Ⓜ *Termini.*

Performing Arts

OPERA

★ Teatro dell'Opera

OPERA | The company at this theater, a far younger sibling of La Scala in Milan and La Fenice in Venice, commands an audience during its mid-November–May season. In the hot summer months, it moves to the Terme di Caracalla for an outdoor opera series. As you might expect, the oft-preferred performance is *Aida*, for its spectacle, which once included real elephants. The company has lately taken a new direction, using projections atop the ancient ruins to create cutting-edge sets. ✉ *Piazza Beniamino Gigli 7, Repubblica* ☎ *06/481601, 06/4817003 tickets* ⊕ *www.operaroma.it* Ⓜ *Repubblica.*

👜 Shopping

In this neighborhood you'll find bookstores and souvenir shops, as well as various European clothing chains.

BOOKS AND STATIONERY

Libraccio

BOOKS | One of the best parts of Libraccio (part of the IBS chain of bookstores) is the wide variety of European cinema and music selections. Another perk is the discount the store dishes out on its stock of remainders and secondhand books. The shop also has a modest selection of English-language paperbacks and hardcovers. ✉ *Via Nazionale 254–255, Repubblica* ☎ *06/4885405* ⊕ *www.ibs.it* Ⓜ *Repubblica.*

CLOTHING

Esedra 58

CLOTHING | For gentlemen looking to bring home some Italian style, this family-run boutique under the arcades on Piazza della Repubblica is a must. You won't find designer names like Armani but rather small Italian producers like Gran Sasso, which makes high quality knits, and Camplin, which makes the original Royal Navy peacoat. The in-house tailor is available to make quick adjustments. ✉ *Piazza della Repubblica 58, Repubblica* ☎ *06/4814701* ⊕ *www.esedra58.it* Ⓜ *Repubblica.*

FOOD AND WINE

Trimani Vinai a Roma dal 1821

WINE/SPIRITS | In business since 1821, Trimani Vinai a Roma occupies an entire block near Termini Station with one of the city's largest selections of wines from all over the world, plus champagne, spumante, grappa, and sundry liqueurs. With thousands of bottles to choose from and knowledgeable wine stewards to consult, Trimani will give you the opportunity to explore Italy's diverse wine regions without leaving the city. It also offers gift boxes and will ship almost anywhere in the world. ✉ *Via Goito 20, Repubblica* ☎ *06/4469661* ⊕ *www.trimani.com* Ⓜ *Castro Pretorio, Repubblica.*

The Quirinale

Rome's highest hill, the Quirinale, has been home to ancient Roman senators, 17th- and 18th-century popes, and Italy's kings. West from Via Nazionale, the hill is set with various Baroque-era jewels, including masterpieces by Bernini and Borromini. Nearby stands Palazzo Barberini, a gorgeous 16th-century palace holding five centuries of masterworks.

Crowning the Piazza del Quirinale is the enormous Palazzo del Quirinale, built in the 16th century as a summer residence for the popes; it became the presidential palace in 1946. Outside on the piazza, you can watch the changing of the guard, an old-fashioned exercise in pomp and circumstance that takes place on Sunday at 4 pm (6 pm in summer).

As in Repubblica, you can find masterworks by Bernini here. Indeed, the artist and architect considered the church of Sant'Andrea al Quirinale to be one of his best.

Sights

Capuchin Museum

CEMETERY | Devoted to teaching visitors about the Capuchin order, this museum is mainly notable for its strangely touching and beautiful crypt under the church of Santa Maria della Concezione. The bones of some 4,000 friars are arranged in odd decorative designs around the shriveled and decayed remains of their kinsmen, a macabre reminder of the impermanence of earthly life. As one sign proclaims: "What you are, we once were. What we are, you someday will be."

Upstairs in the church, the first chapel on the right contains Guido Reni's mid-17th-century *Archangel St. Michael Trampling the Devil*. The painting caused great scandal after an astute contemporary observer remarked that the face of the devil bore a surprising resemblance to Pope Innocent X, archenemy of Reni's Barberini patrons. Compare the devil with the bust of the pope that you saw in the Palazzo Doria Pamphilj and judge for yourself. ⊠ *Via Veneto 27, Quirinale* ☎ *06/88803695* ⊕ *www.museoecriptacappuccini.it* ⊠ *€10* Ⓜ *Barberini.*

Fontana dell'Acqua Felice (*Fountain of Moses*)

FOUNTAIN | When Pope Sixtus V (Felice Peretti) completed the restoration of the Acqua Felice aqueduct toward the end of the 16th century, Domenico Fontana was commissioned to design its monumental fountain. Sculptors Leonardo Sormani and Prospero da Brescia had the unhappy task of executing the central figure of Moses; the comparison with Michelangelo's magnificent *Moses* in the church of San Pietro in Vincoli was inevitable, and the giant sculpture was widely criticized. But the new fountain served to position the formerly rustic Quirinale neighborhood as a thriving urban center. ⊠ *Piazza di San Bernardo, Repubblica* Ⓜ *Repubblica.*

Fontana delle Api (*Fountain of the Bees*)

FOUNTAIN | The upper shell and inscription of this fountain, which is decorated with the famous heraldic bees of the Barberini family, are from a fountain that Bernini designed for Pope Urban VIII; the rest was lost when the fountain was moved to make way for a new street. The inscription caused considerable uproar when the fountain was first built in 1644. It said that the fountain had been erected in the 22nd year of the pontiff's reign, although, in fact, the 21st anniversary of Urban's election to the papacy was still some weeks away. The last numeral was hurriedly erased, but to no avail—Urban died eight days before the beginning of his 22nd year as pope. The superstitious Romans, who had regarded the inscription as a foolhardy tempting of fate, were vindicated. ⊠ *Piazza Barberini, Quirinale* Ⓜ *Barberini.*

★ Palazzo Barberini/Galleria Nazionale d'Arte Antica

ART MUSEUM | One of Rome's most splendid 17th-century buildings is a Baroque landmark. The grand facade was designed by Carlo Maderno (aided by his nephew, Francesco Borromini), but when Maderno died, Borromini was passed over in favor of his great rival, Gian Lorenzo Bernini. The palazzo is now home to the Galleria Nazionale d'Arte Antica, with a collection that includes Raphael's *La Fornarina,* a luminous portrait of the artist's lover (a resident of Trastevere, she was reputedly a baker's daughter). Also noteworthy are Guido Reni's portrait of the doomed Beatrice Cenci (beheaded in Rome for patricide in 1599)—Hawthorne called it "the saddest picture ever painted" in his Rome-based novel, *The Marble Faun*—and Caravaggio's dramatic *Judith Beheading Holofernes.*

The showstopper here is the palace's Gran Salone, a vast ballroom with a ceiling painted in 1630 by the third (and too-often-neglected) master of the Roman Baroque, Pietro da Cortona. It

depicts the *Glorification of Urban VIII's Reign* and has the spectacular conceit of glorifying Urban VIII as the agent of Divine Providence, escorted by a "bomber squadron" (to quote art historian Sir Michael Levey) of huge Barberini bees, the heraldic symbol of the family. ⊠ *Via delle Quattro Fontane 13, Quirinale* ☎ *06/4814591* ⊕ *www.barberinicorsini. org* 🎫 *€12, includes Galleria Corsini* ⊘ *Closed Mon.* Ⓜ *Barberini.*

Palazzo del Quirinale

CASTLE/PALACE | Pope Gregory XIII started building this spectacular palace, now the official residence of Italy's president, in 1574. He planned to use it as a summer home, but less than 20 years later, Pope Clement VIII made the palace—safely elevated above the malarial miasmas shrouding the low-lying location of the Vatican—the permanent papal residence, which it remained until 1870. The palace underwent various expansions and alterations over time.

In 1870, when Italian troops under Garibaldi stormed Rome, making it the capital of the newly united Italy, the popes moved back to the Vatican, and the Palazzo del Quirinale became the official residence of the kings of Italy. After the Italian people voted out the monarchy in 1946, the palazzo passed to the presidency of the Italian Republic.

To go inside, you must prebook a guided tour (in Italian only, although materials in English can be purchased) and present an ID on entry. Outside the gates, you can see the changing of the military guard at 4 pm on Sunday (at 6 pm June through August). You might also glimpse the impressive presidential guard. ⊠ *Piazza del Quirinale, Quirinale* ☎ *06/46991* ⊕ *www.palazzo.quirinale.it* 🎫 *By tour only: €2.50 booking fee* ⊘ *Closed Mon. and Thurs.* ⚲ *Reservations must be made at least 5 days prior* Ⓜ *Barberini.*

Piazza del Quirinale

PLAZA/SQUARE | This strategic location atop the Quirinale has long been important. Indeed, it served as home of the Sabines in the 7th century BC—when they were deadly enemies of the Romans, who lived on the Campidoglio and Palatino (all of 1 km [½ mile] away). Today, it's the foreground for the presidential residence, Palazzo del Quirinale, and home to the Palazzo della Consulta, where Italy's Constitutional Court sits.

The open side of the piazza has a vista over the rooftops and domes of central Rome and St. Peter's. The Fontana di Montecavallo, or Fontana dei Dioscuri, has a statuary group of Dioscuri trying to tame two massive marble steeds that was found in the Baths of Constantine, which once occupied part of the Quirinale's summit. Unlike many ancient statues in Rome, this group survived the Dark Ages intact, becoming one of the city's great sights during the Middle Ages. The obelisk next to the figures is from the Mausoleo di Augusto (Tomb of Augustus) and was put here by Pope Pius VI in the late 18th century. ⊠ *Piazza del Quirinale, Quirinale* Ⓜ *Barberini.*

Quattro Fontane (*Four Fountains*)

VIEWPOINT | This intersection takes its name from its four Baroque fountains, which represent the Tiber (on the San Carlo corner), the Arno, Juno, and Diana. Despite the nearby traffic and the tightness of the sidewalk, it's worth taking in the views in all four directions from this point: to the southwest, as far as the obelisk in Piazza del Quirinale; to the northeast, along Via XX Settembre to the Porta Pia; to the northwest, across Piazza Barberini to the obelisk of Trinità dei Monti; and to the southeast, as far as the obelisk and apse of Santa Maria Maggiore. The prospect is a highlight of Pope Sixtus V's campaign of urban beautification and an example of Baroque influence on city planning. ⊠ *Intersection of Via*

The dome of San Carlo alle Quattro Fontane was designed by Borromini and is the centerpiece of the small church.

Quattro Fontane, Via XX Settembre, and Via del Quirinale, Quirinale Ⓜ *Barberini.*

San Carlo alle Quattro Fontane

CHURCH | Sometimes known as San Carlino because of its tiny size, this is one of Borromini's masterpieces. In a space no larger than the base of one of the piers of St. Peter's Basilica, he created a church that is an intricate exercise in geometric perfection, with a coffered dome that seems to float above the curves of the walls. Borromini's work is often bizarre, definitely intellectual, and intensely concerned with pure form. In San Carlo, he invented an original treatment of space that creates an effect of rippling movement, especially evident in the double-S curves of the facade. Characteristically, the interior decoration is subdued, in white stucco with no more than a few touches of gilding, so as not to distract from the form. Don't miss the cloister: a tiny, understated Baroque jewel, with a graceful portico and loggia above, echoing the lines of the church. ✉ *Via del Quirinale 23, Quirinale* ☎ *06/48907729* 🕑 *Closed Sun.* Ⓜ *Barberini.*

Sant'Andrea al Quirinale

CHURCH | Designed by Bernini, this small church is one of the triumphs of the Roman Baroque period. His son wrote that Bernini considered it his best work and that he used to come here occasionally, just to sit and contemplate. Bernini's simple oval plan, a classic form in Baroque architecture, is given drama and movement by the decoration, which depicts St. Andrew's martyrdom and ascension into heaven and starts with the painting over the high altar, up past the figure of the saint above, to the angels at the base of the lantern and the dove of the Holy Spirit that awaits on high. ✉ *Via del Quirinale 30, Quirinale* ☎ *06/4819399* ⊕ *www.santandrea. gesuiti.it* 🕑 *Closed Mon.* Ⓜ *Barberini.*

🍴 Restaurants

This area has lots of government offices, hotels, and museums, and the tourist traps and expense-account stalwarts that go with them. There are some reasonable standouts though.

★ Anima

$$$$ | **MODERN ITALIAN** | Paola Colucci, the self-taught chef of beloved local restaurant Pianostrada, has brought her refined approach to comfort food to this buzzy restaurant in the Rome EDITION hotel. Be sure to request a table in the garden and don't skip the focaccia—baked fresh and topped with delicious things like gorgonzola, pears, cinnamon, arugula, and mint—before moving on to the fresh pasta. **Known for:** pillowy focaccia topped with gourmet ingredients; superlative pastas; beautifully presented dishes. [$] *Average main: €38* ✉ *The Rome EDITION, Salita di S. Nicola da Tolentino, 14, Quirinale* ☎ *06/45249009* 🌐 *www.animaristoranteroma.it* [M] *Barberini.*

Tullio

$$$ | **TUSCAN** | Just off Piazza Barberini, this upscale trattoria has been serving Tuscan classics since 1950. It specializes in high-quality meat dishes, including prime cuts of beef, lamb, and veal. **Known for:** bistecca alla fiorentina (Tuscan porterhouse); tagliolini (ribbon pasta) with truffles; old-school style and brusque waiters. [$] *Average main: €32* ✉ *Via San Nicola da Tolentino 26, Quirinale* ☎ *06/4745560* 🌐 *www.tullioristorante.it* ⏲ *Closed Sun. and Aug.* [M] *Barberini.*

🛏 Hotels

Aleph Rome Hotel, Curio Collection by Hilton

$$$$ | **HOTEL** | Fashionable couples tend to favor the Aleph, a former bank–turned–luxury hotel, where the motto seems to be "more marble, everywhere." The abundant facilities include two pools (one in the spa and one on the roof), a cigar lounge, a cocktail bar, and two restaurants (one on the ground floor and one on the rooftop). **Pros:** free access to the spa for hotel guests; award-winning design; terrace with small pool. **Cons:** rooms are petite for the price; rooftop views don't showcase Rome's most flattering side; buffet breakfast not included. [$] *Rooms from: €448* ✉ *Via San Basilio 15, Piazza di Spagna* ☎ *06/4229001* 🌐 *alephrome.com* 🔑 *80 rooms and suites* 🍽 *No Meals* [M] *Barberini.*

Rome Times Hotel

$$$$ | **HOTEL** | This modern hotel has large, soundproofed rooms with contemporary furnishings, hardwood floors, and huge fluffy beds. **Pros:** late checkout if booked through site; free use of Samsung smartphone for calls and Internet during your stay; large bright bathrooms. **Cons:** lower floors can be noisy; rooms in the annex don't come with all the benefits of the main hotel; lighting in rooms is not optimal. [$] *Rooms from: €323* ✉ *Via Milano 42, Quirinale* ☎ *06/99345101* 🌐 *www.rometimeshotel.com* 🔑 *81 rooms* 🍽 *No Meals* [M] *Repubblica.*

★ The Rome EDITION

$$$$ | **HOTEL** | Set in a rationalist 1940s building that once housed the offices of the Banca Nazionale del Lavoro, this trendy lifestyle hotel by Ian Schrager and Marriott is one of the city's buzziest new places to stay. **Pros:** excellent dining and drinks; stylish interiors by renowned designer Patricia Urquiola; great location on a quiet street near Piazza Barberini. **Cons:** expensive; service can be hit or miss; some rooms are quite small. [$] *Rooms from: €696* ✉ *Salita di S. Nicola da Tolentino 14, Quirinale* ☎ *06/45249000* 🌐 *www.editionhotels.com* 🔑 *91 rooms* 🍽 *No Meals* [M] *Barberini.*

Chapter 8

VILLA BORGHESE AND ENVIRONS

8

Updated by
Laura Itzkowitz

⊙ Sights	🍴 Restaurants	🛏 Hotels	🛍 Shopping	🍸 Nightlife
★★★★☆	★★☆☆☆	★★★☆☆	★☆☆☆☆	★☆☆☆☆

NEIGHBORHOOD SNAPSHOT

MAKING THE MOST OF YOUR TIME

Explore this area on a clear day: the Villa Borghese park is at its best (and most bustling with strolling Italian families) on beautiful days, while the view from the top of the Pincio provides a stunning panorama over Rome's pastel rooftops. The Galleria Borghese, one of several museums within the Villa Borghese, is a Roman gem and a must-see for art lovers; just remember to book your tickets in advance (you can do so online), as walk-ins are rarely accommodated. After your "walk in the park," head down to Piazza del Popolo, one of Rome's loveliest piazzas, and duck into Santa Maria del Popolo for its gorgeous paintings by Baroque master Caravaggio—keeping in mind that, like many of Rome's churches, it closes in the middle of the day.

GETTING HERE

■ The Metro stop for Piazza del Popolo is Flaminio on Metro A. The Villa Giulia, the Galleria Nazionale d'Arte Moderna e Contemporanea, and the Bioparco in Villa Borghese are accessible from Via Flaminia, 1 km (½ mile) from Piazza del Popolo. Tram No. 19 stops at each.

■ Buses No. 160 and No. 628 connects Piazza del Popolo to Piazza Venezia. Bus No. 61 goes into Villa Borghese.

TOP REASONS TO GO

Piazza del Popolo: At the end of three of the *centro storico*'s (historic center's) most important streets—Via del Babuino, Via del Corso, and Via di Ripetta—the "People's Square" provides a front-row seat for some of Rome's best people-watching.

Villa Borghese: Drink in the fresh air in central Rome's largest park—stretches of green and plenty of leafy pathways encourage wandering, biking, or just chilling out.

The Pincio: Stroll through formal gardens in the footsteps of aristocrats out of a 19th-century fashion plate.

Santa Maria del Popolo: Marvel at the incredible realism of Caravaggio's gritty paintings in the Cerasi Chapel, then savor Raphael's Chigi Chapel.

Galleria Borghese: Appreciate the extravagant interior decor in one of Rome's most opulent—and pleasant—museums.

OFF THE BEATEN PATH

■ **Foro Italico.** Just across the river from the northernmost reaches of Flaminio lies the Foro Italico sports complex. A pet project of Mussolini, it's a classic example of Rationalist architecture. The impressive Stadio dei Marmi features a track dotted with 60 larger-than-life statues of athletes. There's also the tennis stadium, two pools, and the Olympic stadium, where soccer matches take place. ⊠ *Via del Foro Italico* 🚊 *Take Tram 2 to Mancini.*

It may not feel like it amid the centro storico's warren of cobblestone streets, but Rome is a very green city. All around the immediate city center are vast public parks, the most central of which is the city's giant green lung: the Villa Borghese park, where residents love to escape for some serious R&R. But don't think you can completely avoid sightseeing—three of Rome's most important museums are inside the park, and Piazza del Popolo, which has more than one art-crammed church, is close by.

Villa Borghese

Rome's Central Park, the Villa Borghese was laid out as a recreational garden in the early 17th century by Cardinal Scipione Borghese. The word "villa" was used to mean suburban estate, of the type developed by the ancient Romans and adopted by Renaissance nobles. Today's gardens cover a much smaller area—by 1630, the perimeter wall was almost 5 km (3 miles) long. At the end of the 18th century, Scottish painter Jacob More remodeled the gardens into the English style popular at the time.

In addition to the gloriously restored Galleria Borghese, the highlights of the park are Piazza di Siena, a graceful amphitheater, and the botanical garden on Via Canonica, where there is a pretty little lake as well as the Neoclassical faux–Temple of Aesculapius, the Biopark zoo, Rome's own replica of London's Globe Theatre, and the Villa Giulia museum.

The Carlo Bilotti Museum (⊕ www.museocarlobilotti.it) is particularly attractive for Giorgio de Chirico fans, and there is more modern art in the nearby Galleria Nazionale d'Arte Moderna e Contemporanea (⊕ www.lagallerianazionale.com). The 63-seat children's movie theater, Cinema dei Piccoli, shows films for adults in the evening. There's also Casa del Cinema (⊕ www.casadelcinema.it), which screens films and has a sleek indoor-outdoor café.

Sights

Bioparco

ZOO | FAMILY | This zoo has been remodeled along eco-friendly lines: there is now more space for the animals, most of which were brought from other zoos or born from animals already in captivity (rather than those snatched from the wild). There aren't any koalas, pandas, or polar bears, but there are big cats, elephants, chimpanzees, and local brown bears from Abruzzo, and other creatures. You'll also find the Reptilarium, the Bioparco Train, a picnic area next to the flamingos, and a farm. ⊠ *Piazzale del Giardino Zoologico 1, Villa Borghese* ☎ *06/3608211* ⊕ *www.bioparco.it* 🖙 *€18; €2 for Bioparco Train.*

★ Galleria Borghese

ART MUSEUM | It's toss-up as to which is more magnificent: the museum or the art that lies within it. The luxury-loving Cardinal Scipione Borghese had the museum custom built in 1612 as a showcase for his collection of both antiquities and more "modern" works, including those he commissioned from the masters Caravaggio and Bernini. Today, it's a monument to Roman interior decoration at its most extravagant.

One of the collection's most famous works is Canova's Neoclassical sculpture, *Pauline Borghese as Venus Victorious.* The next three rooms hold three key early Baroque sculptures: Bernini's *David*; *Apollo and Daphne*; and *The Rape of Persephone.* All were done when the artist was in his twenties and all illustrate his extraordinary skill. *Apollo and Daphne* shows the moment when, to aid her escape from the pursuing Apollo, Daphne is turned into a laurel tree. Leaves and twigs sprout from her fingertips as she stretches agonizingly away from Apollo. In *The Rape of Persephone,* Pluto has either just plucked Persephone (or Proserpina) from her flower-picking or is in the process of returning to Hades with

his prize. Note the realistic way his grip causes dimples in Persephone's flesh. This is the stuff that makes the Baroque exciting—and moving. Other Berninis on view include a large, unfinished figure called *Verità,* or *Truth.*

Room 8 contains six paintings by Caravaggio, the hotheaded genius who died at age 37. All of his paintings, even the charming *Boy with a Basket of Fruit,* have an undercurrent of darkness. The disquieting *Sick Bacchus* is a self-portrait of the artist who, like the god, had a fondness for wine. *David and Goliath,* painted in the last year of Caravaggio's life—while he was on the run, murder charges hanging over his head—includes his self-portrait in the head of Goliath. Upstairs, the Pinacoteca (Picture Gallery) boasts paintings by Raphael (including his moving *Deposition*), Pinturicchio, Perugino, Bellini, and Rubens. Probably the gallery's most famous painting is Titian's allegorical *Sacred and Profane Love,* a mysterious image with two female figures, one nude, one clothed. ∎TIP→ **Admission to the Galleria Borghese is by reservation only. Visitors are admitted in two-hour shifts 9–5. Prime-time slots sell out days in advance, so reserve directly (and early) through the museum's website.** ⊠ *Piazzale Scipione Borghese 5, off Via Pinciana, Villa Borghese* ☎ *06/32810 reservations, 06/8413979 info* ⊕ *www.galleriaborghese.beniculturali.it* 🖙 *€15, including €2 reservation fee; increased fee during temporary exhibitions* ⊙ *Closed Mon.* ⚹ *Reservations essential.*

★ Galleria Nazionale d'Arte Moderna e Contemporanea (*National Gallery of Modern Art*)

ART MUSEUM | This massive white Beaux-Arts building, built for the 1911 World Exposition in Rome, contains one of Italy's leading collections of 19th- and 20th-century works. It's primarily dedicated to the history of Italian modernism, examining the movement's development over the last two centuries, but

Principessa Pauline Borghese, Napoléon's sister, scandalized Europe by posing as a half-naked Venus for Canova; the statue is on view at the Galleria Borghese.

crowd-pleasers Monet, Rodin, Van Gogh, and Warhol put in appearances, and there's also an outstanding Dadaist collection. You can mix coffee and culture at the mid-century-inspired Caffè delle Arti in a columned alcove. ✉ *Viale delle Belle Arti 131, Villa Borghese* ☎ *06/32298221* ⊕ *www.lagallerianazionale.com* ✉ *€10* ☾ *Closed Mon.* Ⓜ *Flaminio.*

★ Museo Nazionale Etrusco di Villa Giulia
(*National Etruscan Museum*)
ART MUSEUM | The world's most outstanding collection of Etruscan art and artifacts is housed in Villa Giulia, built around 1551 for Pope Julius III. Among the team called in to plan and construct the villa were Michelangelo and fellow Florentine Vasari. Most of the actual work, however, was done by Vignola and Ammannati. The villa's *nymphaeum*—or sunken sculpture garden—is a superb example of a refined late-Renaissance setting for princely pleasures.

No one knows precisely where the Etruscans originated, but many scholars maintain they came from Asia Minor,

appearing in Italy about 2000 BC and creating a civilization that was a dazzling prelude to that of the ancient Romans. Among the most striking pieces are the terra-cotta statues, such as the *Apollo of Veii* and the serenely beautiful *Sarcophagus of the Spouses.* Dating from 530–500 BC, this couple (or *sposi*) look at the viewer with almond eyes and archaic smiles, suggesting an openness and joie de vivre rare in Roman art. Other highlights include the cinematic frieze from a later temple (480 BC) in Pyrgi, resembling a sort of Etruscan Elgin marbles in terra-cotta; the displays of Etruscan jewelry; and the beautiful gardens. ✉ *Piazzale di Villa Giulia 9, Villa Borghese* ☎ *06/3226571* ⊕ *www.museoetru.it* ✉ *€12* ☾ *Closed Mon.*

★ Pincio Promenade
VIEWPOINT | **FAMILY** | Redolent of the era of Henry James and Edith Wharton, the Pincian gardens have long been a classic setting for a walk. Grand Tourists—and even a pope or two—came here to see and be seen among the beau monde of

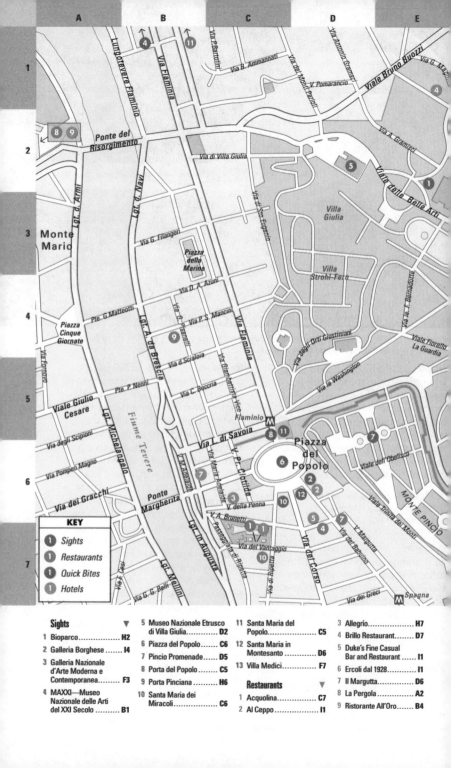

Sights ▼

1 Bioparco.................. H2
2 Galleria Borghese I4
3 Galleria Nazionale
  d'Arte Moderna e
  Contemporanea.......... F3
4 MAXXI—Museo
  Nazionale delle Arti
  del XXI Secolo B1
5 Museo Nazionale Etrusco
  di Villa Giulia............. D2
6 Piazza del Popolo........ C6
7 Pincio Promenade...... D5
8 Porta del Popolo........ C5
9 Porta Pinciana.......... H6
10 Santa Maria dei
   Miracoli.................. C6

11 Santa Maria del
   Popolo...................... C5
12 Santa Maria in
   Montesanto D6
13 Villa Medici.............. F7

Restaurants ▼

1 Acquolina................. C7
2 Al Ceppo I1
3 Allegrío.................... H7
4 Brillo Restaurant........ D7
5 Duke's Fine Casual
  Bar and Restaurant I1
6 Ercoli dal 1928.......... I1
7 Il Margutta................ D6
8 La Pergola A2
9 Ristorante All'Oro........ B4

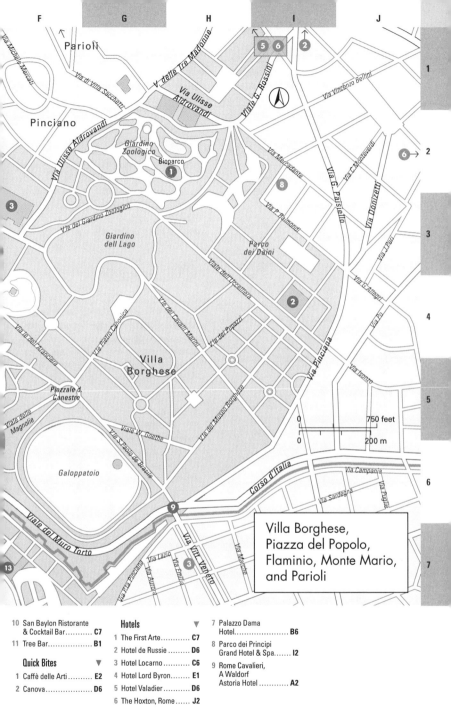

Villa Borghese,
Piazza del Popolo,
Flaminio, Monte Mario,
and Parioli

10 San Baylon Ristorante
   & Cocktail Bar........... **C7**
11 Tree Bar.................. **B1**

Quick Bites ▼

1 Caffè delle Arti **E2**
2 Canova.................. **D6**

Hotels ▼

1 The First Arte............ **C7**
2 Hotel de Russie **D6**
3 Hotel Locarno **C6**
4 Hotel Lord Byron........ **E1**
5 Hotel Valadier........... **D6**
6 The Hoxton, Rome...... **J2**

7 Palazzo Dama
   Hotel...................... **B6**
8 Parco dei Principi
   Grand Hotel & Spa....... **I2**
9 Rome Cavalieri,
   A Waldorf
   Astoria Hotel **A2**

Rome. Today, the Pincian terrace remains a favorite spot for locals taking a springtime Sunday stroll. The rather formal, early-19th-century style contrasts with the far more elaborate terraced gardens of Lucullus, the Roman gourmand who held legendary banquets here. Today, off-white marble busts of Italian Risorgimento heroes and artists line the pathways. Along with similar busts on the Gianicolo (Janiculum Hill), their noses have been targets of vandalism.

A stretch of ancient walls separates the Pincio from the southwest corner of Villa Borghese. From the balustraded terrace, you can look down at Piazza del Popolo and beyond, surveying much of Rome. Southeast of the Pincian terrace is the Casina Valadier (🌐 *www.casinavaladier.it*), a magnificently decorated Neoclassical building that contains an event space with glorious views. ✉ *Piazzale Napoleone I and Viale dell'Obelisco, Villa Borghese* [M] *Flaminio.*

Porta Pinciana (*Pincian Gate*)
NOTABLE BUILDING | FAMILY | Framed by two squat, circular towers, this gate was constructed at the beginning of the 5th century during a renovation of the 3rd century Aurelian Walls. Here you can see just how well the walls have been preserved and imagine hordes of Visigoths trying to break through them. Sturdy as they look, these walls couldn't always keep out the barbarians: Rome was sacked three times during the 5th century alone. ✉ *Piazzale Brasile, corner of Via Veneto and Corso d'Italia, Villa Borghese.*

Villa Medici (*The French Academy of Rome*)
HISTORIC HOME | Originally belonging to Cardinal Ferdinando I de' Medici, who also laid out the immaculate Renaissance garden to set off his sculpture collection, this villa was purchased by Napoléon to create the French Academy of Rome, opened in 1803, where artists could study Italian art and put it toward the (French) national good. You can visit during special exhibitions or take a guided tour to see the gardens and the incredibly picturesque garden facade, which is studded with Mannerist and Rococo sculpted reliefs and overlooks a loggia with a beautiful fountain devoted to Mercury. Some of the historic rooms have been restyled by Fendi and Paris-based designer India Mahdavi. ✉ *Viale della Trinità dei Monti 1, Villa Borghese* ☎ *06/6761200* 🌐 *www.villamedici.it* 🎫 *€10, exhibits; €14, includes guided tour of the gardens and historic rooms and exhibit* ⏲ *Closed Tues.* [M] *Spagna.*

🍴 Restaurants

One of Rome's two large parks borders the famed-but-faded Via Veneto, the former haunt of the Hollywood-on-the-Tiber scene. The upscale neighborhood is home to historic dining destinations as well as the café culture that formed the backdrop for those living *la dolce vita,* the sweet life.

Al Ceppo
$$$ | ITALIAN | The well-heeled, the business-minded, and those with refined palates frequent this outpost of tranquility. The owners hail from Le Marche, the region northeast of Rome that encompasses inland mountains and the Adriatic coastline, so dishes from their native region feature alongside seafood and meats ready to be grilled. **Known for:** grilled meat and fish; authentic Le Marche cuisine; excellent wine list. [$] *Average main: €30* ✉ *Via Panama 2, Villa Borghese* ☎ *06/8419696* 🌐 *www.ristorantealceppo.it* ⏲ *No lunch Mon. Closed 3 wks in Aug.*

Allegrío
$$ | ITALIAN | Though there's a full menu of pasta and mains, those in the know head to this restaurant on Via Veneto specifically for the award-winning pizza. The decor is a bit over-the-top and the prices are a little higher than at the average pizzeria,

but it's a great option in this neighborhood. **Known for:** award-winning Neapolitan pizza; Instagrammable decor; good craft beer selection. $ *Average main: €24* ✉ *Via Vittorio Veneto 14, Villa Borghese* ☎ *06/45543423* ⊕ *www.allegrio.com* Ⓜ *Barberini.*

Coffee and Quick Bites

Caffè delle Arti

$$$ | **CAFÉ** | Attached to the Galleria d'Arte Moderna, inside the Villa Borghese, this elegant café with a pretty terrace is a favorite all-day rendezvous both for Romans from nearby upscale Parioli and for visitors to the Villa Borghese park and museums. **Known for:** popular shaded terrace; good coffee and desserts; salads and sandwiches. $ *Average main: €25* ✉ *Galleria d'Arte Moderna, Via Gramsci 73, Villa Borghese* ☎ *06/32651236* ⊕ *www.facebook.com/caffedelleartiroma* ⊗ *No dinner in winter.*

🛏 Hotels

The area around the Villa Borghese gardens is a relaxing retreat from the hustle and bustle of the Eternal City. You won't get tired of waking up to views of the park.

Parco dei Principi Grand Hotel & Spa

$$$$ | **HOTEL** | The 1960s-era facade of this large, seven-story hotel designed by Gio Ponti contrasts with the turn-of-the-20th-century Italian court decor and the extensive botanical garden outside, resulting in a combination of traditional elegance and contemporary pleasure. **Pros:** quiet location on Villa Borghese; fitness room with wide variety of equipment; biosauna and sensory showers at spa. **Cons:** extra charge to use the pool; bathrooms could use an update; a bit of a hike to cafés and restaurants. $ *Rooms from: €450* ✉ *Via Gerolamo Frescobaldi 5, Villa Borghese* ☎ *06/854421* ⊕ *www.parcodeiprincipi.com* ⇥ *177 rooms* ⊚ *Free Breakfast.*

🎫 Performing Arts

FILM
Casa del Cinema

FILM | Casa del Cinema is Rome's hub for all things film, with multiple screening rooms, an exhibition space, and a room for filming interviews, plus a caffè and restaurant. Yearly programming includes new and retro films from its vast archives as well as many original-language films often showcased from several festivals, including Rome Film Fest. In summer, the cinema heads outdoors to show a wide array of movies. ✉ *Largo Marcello Mastroianni 1, Villa Borghese* ☎ *06/0608* ⊕ *www.casadelcinema.it.*

Cinema dei Piccoli (*Mickey Mouse Cinema*)

FILM | **FAMILY** | This quaint theater in the middle of the park has only 63 seats and plays children's films during the day and adult new releases at night. It opened in 1934, and many Romans still refer to it as "Casa di Topolino," thanks to the giant Mickey Mouse sign that appeared on the building until the 1970s. Warning to the very tall: leg room is minimal. ✉ *Viale della Pineta 15, Villa Borghese* ☎ *06/8553485* ⊕ *www.cinemadeipiccoli.it* ⇥ *€6 weekdays; €7.50 weekends.*

Piazza del Popolo

The formal garden terraces of the Pincio, on the southwestern side of Villa Borghese, give way to a stone staircase down to Piazza del Popolo (the People's Square). One of Rome's largest piazzas—and best people-watching spots—is very round, very explicitly defined, and very picturesque. It's also mercifully free of traffic.

Papal architect Giuseppe Valadier laid out this square around 1820 with twin churches at one end and the Porta del Popolo, Rome's northern city gate, at the other. Part of an earlier urban plan, the three streets to the south radiate straight as spokes to other parts of the city, forming the famed *tridente* that gives this neighborhood its nickname.

The center is marked with an Egyptian obelisk that was carved for Ramses II in the 13th century BC and today is guarded by four water-gushing lions and steps that mark the end of many a sunset *passeggiata* (stroll). The piazza's most fascinating pieces of art—including masterpieces by Raphael and Caravaggio—are hidden within the northeast corner's often-overlooked church of Santa Maria del Popolo, snuggled against the 400-year-old Porta del Popolo.

Sights

★ Piazza del Popolo
PLAZA/SQUARE | FAMILY | With its obelisk and twin churches, this immense square marks what was, for centuries, Rome's northern entrance, where all roads from the north converged and where visitors, many of them pilgrims, got their first impression of the Eternal City. The desire to make this entrance to Rome something special was a pet project of popes and their architects for more than three centuries. Although it was once crowded with fashionable carriages, the piazza today is a pedestrian zone. At election time, it's the scene of huge political rallies, and on New Year's Eve, Rome stages a mammoth alfresco party here. ⊠ *Piazza del Popolo* Ⓜ *Flaminio.*

Porta del Popolo (*City Gate*)
NOTABLE BUILDING | The medieval gate in the Aurelian walls was replaced by the current one between 1562 and 1565, by Nanni di Bacco Bigio. Bernini further embellished the inner facade in 1655 for the much-heralded arrival of Queen Christina of Sweden, who had abdicated her throne to become a Roman Catholic. ⊠ *Piazza del Popolo and Piazzale Flaminio, Piazza del Popolo* Ⓜ *Flaminio.*

Santa Maria dei Miracoli
CHURCH | A twin to Santa Maria in Montesanto, this church dedicated to Our Lady of the Miracles was built in the 1670s, started by Carlo Rainaldi and completed by Bernini and Carlo Fontana as an elegant frame for the entrance to Via del Corso from Piazza del Popolo. Inside, there is a gorgeous stucco designed by Bernini pupil Antonio Raggi. ⊠ *Via del Corso 528, Piazza del Popolo* ☎ *06/3610250* Ⓜ *Flaminio.*

★ Santa Maria del Popolo
CHURCH | Standing inconspicuously in a corner of the vast Piazza del Popolo, this church often goes unnoticed, but the treasures inside make it a must for art lovers. Bramante enlarged the apse, which was rebuilt in the 15th century on the site of a much older place of worship. Inside, in the first chapel on the right, you'll see some frescoes by Pinturicchio from the mid-15th century; the adjacent Cybo Chapel is a 17th-century exercise in decorative marble.

Raphael designed the famous Chigi Chapel, the second on the left, with vault mosaics—showing God the Father in Benediction—as well as statues of Jonah and Elijah. More than a century later, Bernini added the oval medallions on the tombs and the statues of Daniel and Habakkuk. Finally, the Cerasi Chapel, to the left of the high altar, holds two Caravaggios: *The Crucifixion of St. Peter* and *The Conversion of St. Paul.* Exuding drama and realism, both are key early Baroque works that show how "modern" 17th-century art can appear. Compare their style with the much more restrained and classically "pure" *Assumption of the Virgin* by Annibale Carracci, which hangs over the altar of the chapel. ⊠ *Piazza del Popolo 12, near Porta del Popolo, Piazza del Popolo* ☎ *06/3610836* ⊕ *www.agostiniani.it* Ⓜ *Flaminio.*

Santa Maria in Montesanto (*Church of the Artists*)

CHURCH | On the eastern side of the Piazza del Popolo, Santa Maria dei Miracoli's Baroque "twin church" was built in the 1660s–70s. It was originally designed by Carlo Rainaldi and finished by Carlo Fontana who was supervised by his brilliant teacher, Bernini (whose other pupils are responsible for the saints topping the facade). On the last Sunday of the month from October to June, a mass is held in tribute to artists, with live musical accompaniment, earning the church its nickname of the Church of the Artists. ✉ *Piazza del Popolo 18, Piazza del Popolo* ☎ *06/3610594* 🌐 *www.chiesadegliartisti.it* [M] *Flaminio.*

🍴 Restaurants

This high-traffic shopping and tourist zone has both casual pizzerias and upscale eateries, as well as classic cafés where you can have a restorative espresso and a light bite.

Acquolina

$$$$ | **MODERN ITALIAN** | This two-Michelin-starred restaurant turns out delicious and high-quality seafood dishes that surprise and evoke a sensory experience. Tortelli are served with cheese, black pepper, eel, and onion, and all the dishes are artfully presented. **Known for:** elaborate tasting menus; spaghetti with langoustines; sophisticated desserts. [$] *Average main: €200* ✉ *The First Arte, Via del Vantaggio 14, Piazza del Popolo* ☎ *06/3201590* 🌐 *www.acquolinaristorante.it* 🕒 *Closed Sun. and Mon.* ☞ *Tasting menus only* [M] *Flaminio.*

Brillo Restaurant

$$ | **ITALIAN** | The location near Piazza del Popolo makes Brillo especially convenient for lunch or dinner after shopping in the Via del Corso area. The menu is quite extensive, with fried starters, burgers, salads, pastas, grilled meats, and pizzas. **Known for:** squash blossom pizza; more than 400 types of wine; open late, ideal for an after-show meal. [$] *Average main: €19* ✉ *Via della Fontanella 12, Piazza del Popolo* ☎ *06/3243334* 🌐 *www.brillorestaurant.com* [M] *Flaminio.*

Il Margutta

$$ | **VEGETARIAN** | Parallel to posh Via del Babuino, Via Margutta was once a street of artists' studios (including Fellini's), and this chic vegetarian restaurant, with changing displays of modern art, sits on the far end of the now-gallery-lined street. It turns out tasty meat-free versions of classic Mediterranean dishes, as well as more daring concoctions. **Known for:** organic fruit and vegetable juices; gourmet vegetarian dishes; arty atmosphere. [$] *Average main: €16* ✉ *Via Margutta 118, Piazza del Popolo* ☎ *06/32650577* 🌐 *www.ilmargutta.bio* [M] *Flaminio.*

San Baylon Ristorante & Cocktail Bar

$$$ | **ITALIAN** | Inside the Palazzo Ripetta hotel, this all-day dining destination has a warm ambience, with marble-topped tables; velvet sofas; and archival maps, prints, and photos decorating the walls. Chef Marco Ciccotelli, who previously worked with Michelin-starred chef Fabio Ciervo, gets some inspiration from his native Abruzzo, with fresh house-made pasta and an emphasis on seasonal, local ingredients. **Known for:** warm, cozy ambience; delicious, unfussy cuisine; cocktail program designed in collaboration with the Jerry Thomas Project. [$] *Average main: €35* ✉ *Via di Ripetta 232, Piazza del Popolo* ☎ *06/3222381* 🌐 *www.sanbaylon.com* [M] *Flaminio.*

☕ Coffee and Quick Bites

Canova

$$ | **ITALIAN** | **FAMILY** | Esteemed director Federico Fellini, who lived around the corner on Via Margutta, used to come here all the time and even had an office in the back. His drawings and black-and-white stills from his films remain on display in the hallway that leads to the interior dining room, but the best place to sit for people-watching with a coffee, light lunch, or aperitivo is on the terrace out front. **Known for:** great people-watching; sandwiches and other light fare; Fellini's old hangout. Ⓢ *Average main: €15* ⊠ *Piazza del Popolo 16, Piazza del Popolo* ☎ *06/3612231* ⊕ *www.canovapiazzadel-popolo.it* Ⓜ *Flaminio.*

Hotels

While Piazza del Popolo is still quite close to the *centro* action, it's just removed enough to feel relaxing after a day of sightseeing. Here, amid high-end boutiques and galleries, you'll find several smart, stylish hotels.

The First Arte
$$$$ | HOTEL | Set in a 19th-century Neo-classical palace, this cozy boutique hotel was remodeled to feature high-tech, elegant guest rooms while keeping the core structure, including unique windows and tall ceilings, intact. **Pros:** fitness room with Technogym equipment; staff that is eager to please; more than 200 works of art on display from Galleria Mucciaccia. **Cons:** some rooms can be dark; rooftop bar can get quite crowded; no spa. Ⓢ *Rooms from: €500* ⊠ *Via del Vantaggio 14, Piazza del Popolo* ☎ *06/45617070* ⊕ *www.pavilionshotels.com/rome/the-firstarte* ⊅ *29 rooms* ⦿ *Free Breakfast* Ⓜ *Flaminio.*

★ Hotel de Russie
$$$$ | HOTEL | Occupying a 19th-century hotel that once hosted royalty, Picasso, and Cocteau, the Hotel de Russie is now the first choice in Rome for government bigwigs and Hollywood high rollers seeking ultimate luxury in a secluded retreat. **Pros:** big potential for celebrity sightings; well-equipped gym and world-class spa; excellent Stravinskij cocktail bar has outdoor tables on the Piazzetta Valadier. **Cons:** faster Internet comes at a fee; breakfast not included; very expensive.

Ⓢ *Rooms from: €1700* ⊠ *Via del Babuino 9, Piazza del Popolo* ☎ *06/328881* ⊕ *www.roccofortehotels.com* ⊅ *120 rooms* ⦿ *No Meals* Ⓜ *Flaminio.*

Hotel Locarno
$$$$ | HOTEL | Established in 1925, this hotel feels like an authentic time capsule of a more glamorous era. **Pros:** spacious rooms; complimentary bicycles; gym. **Cons:** some rooms are dark; cleaning fee of €40 per night for pets; food and drinks are expensive. Ⓢ *Rooms from: €390* ⊠ *Via della Penna 22, Piazza del Popolo* ☎ *06/3610841* ⊕ *www.hotellocarno.com* ⊅ *49 rooms* ⦿ *Free Breakfast* Ⓜ *Flaminio.*

Hotel Valadier
$$$ | HOTEL | Just a quick walk from the Spanish Steps, this hotel has captured the hearts of many travelers over the years. **Pros:** excellent American-style breakfast; marble and travertine bathrooms; discount if booking directly through website. **Cons:** pillows are flat and outdated; fitness room is small; rooms can be very dark and small. Ⓢ *Rooms from: €283* ⊠ *Via della Fontanella 15, Piazza del Popolo* ☎ *06/3611998* ⊕ *www.hotelvaladier.com* ⊅ *60 rooms* ⦿ *No Meals* Ⓜ *Flaminio.*

Nightlife

Like nearby Piazza di Spagna, Piazza del Popolo takes a turn for the quiet once the sun sets.

BARS
★ Stravinskij Bar at the Hotel de Russie
COCKTAIL BARS | The Stravinskij Bar, in the Hotel de Russie, is the best place to sample la dolce vita. Celebrities, blue bloods, and VIPs hang out in the gorgeous Piazzetta Valadier where mixed drinks and cocktails are well above par. There are also healthy smoothies and bites if you need to refuel. ⊠ *Hotel de Russie, Via del Babuino 9, Piazza del Popolo* ☎ *06/3288874* ⊕ *www.roccofortehotels.com* Ⓜ *Flaminio.*

🛒 Shopping

Borsalino Boutique

HATS & GLOVES | Considered by many to be the Cadillac of fedoras, the dashing version by Borsalino has been a staple of the fashionable Italian man since 1857, adorning the heads of many silver-screen icons, including Humphrey Bogart (who donned one in *Casablanca*) and Harrison Ford (as Indiana Jones). Few hats are made with such exacting care and attention, and the company's milliners still use machines that are more than 100 years old. Borsalino also has boutiques near the Pantheon and Piazza di Spagna. ✉ *Piazza del Popolo, 20, Piazza del Popolo* ☎ *06/3233353* ⊕ *www.borsalino.com* Ⓜ *Flaminio*.

⭐ Il Marmoraro

SPECIALTY STORE | This tiny shop is a holdout of Via Margutta's days as a street full of artists and artisans. Sandro Fiorentino's father opened the shop in 1969 (he carved plaques like the one that marks Federico Fellini's house up the street), and Sandro still engraves the marble by hand. The shop is packed full of plaques, many with clever phrases, which make a great souvenir. Sandro will also engrave a message of your choice upon request. ✉ *Via Margutta 53B, Piazza del Popolo* ☎ *335/6593612* Ⓜ *Spagna*.

Laura Urbinati

CLOTHING | Originally from Rome but now based in Milan, Laura Urbinati is a fashion designer whose swimwear has appeared on the pages of *Vogue, Elle, W,* and other magazines. At her namesake shop on a street just off Piazza del Popolo, you'll find colorful silk tops, pants, dresses, and skirts with bold prints and patterns in addition to the swimwear she's famous for. ✉ *Via dell'Oca 48, Piazza del Popolo* ☎ *06/3214345* ⊕ *www.lauraurbinati.com* Ⓜ *Flaminio*.

1903 Jewels

JEWELRY & WATCHES | At this little atelier on a side street off Via di Ripetta, Elisa Ruggieri and Ilaria Gozzi dream up sustainable jewelry in unconventional shapes (think: square or egg-shaped rings). They like to work with clients to create tailor-made jewelry, customizing pieces with precious and semi-precious stones. ✉ *Via Angelo Brunetti 26, Piazza del Popolo* ☎ *06/83084518* ⊕ *www.1903jewels.it* Ⓜ *Flaminio*.

Flaminio

The Flaminio neighborhood, in northern Rome near the Tiber, was the focus of urban renewal plans for many years. Renzo Piano's Auditorium Parco della Musica put the area on the map, and the MAXXI museum solidified the area as a destination.

👁 Sights

⭐ MAXXI—Museo Nazionale delle Arti del XXI Secolo (*National Museum of 21st-Century Arts*)

ART MUSEUM | Designed by the late Iraqi-British architect Zaha Hadid, this modern building plays with lots of natural light and has curving and angular lines, big open spaces, glass ceilings, and steel staircases that twist through the air—all meant to question the division between "within" and "without." The MAXXI hosts temporary exhibitions of art, architecture, film, and more. The permanent collection, displayed on a rotating basis, has more than 350 works from modern and contemporary artists, including Andy Warhol, Francesco Clemente, and Gerhard Richter. ✉ *Via Guido Reni 4/A, Flaminio* ☎ *06/3201954* ⊕ *www.maxxi.art* 💶 *€15* 🕐 *Closed Mon.* Ⓜ *Flaminio, then Tram No. 2 to Apollodoro*.

8

Villa Borghese and Environs FLAMINIO

🍴 Restaurants

Long a residential area, Flaminio is starting to come into its own, with new and interesting bars and restaurants opening.

★ Ristorante All'Oro
$$$$ | **MODERN ITALIAN** | At this sleek Michelin-starred restaurant inside the Hall Tailor Suite hotel, chef/owner Riccardo Di Giacinto and his wife Ramona make fine dining a fun and entertaining experience. Di Giacinto worked with Ferran Adrià in Spain and uses some of his techniques without veering too far into the territory of molecular gastronomy. **Known for:** playful riffs on Roman dishes; top-notch service; sleek, modern design. [$] *Average main: €38* ✉ *Via Giuseppe Pisanelli 25, Flaminio* ☎ *06/97996907* 🌐 *www.ristorantealloro.it* 🕒 *No lunch weekdays* [M] *Flaminio.*

Tree Bar
$$ | **CAFÉ** | As its name suggests, this place is, indeed, set amid lush greenery and decorated in tree-house style. Functioning as a bar, restaurant, and enoteca all at once, it's open for lunch and dinner as well as for apertivi and late-night drinks and brunch on weekends. **Known for:** organic wines; pasta e ceci (pasta with chickpeas); aperitivo served with snacks. [$] *Average main: €15* ✉ *Via Flaminia 226, Flaminio* ☎ *06/49773501* 🌐 *www.treebar.it* 🕒 *Closed Mon. in winter and a few days in Aug.*

🛏 Hotels

Palazzo Dama Hotel
$$$$ | **HOTEL** | This former Roman villa was once home to the Malaspina family, who hosted high society gatherings throughout the 18th century. **Pros:** drinks and bites available all-day in garden or main hall; Acqua di Parma toiletries; pool is open year-round. **Cons:** standard rooms are small with little storage space; room service is slow and portions are tiny; rooms can be noisy. [$] *Rooms from: €430* ✉ *Lungotevere Arnaldo da Brescia 2, Flaminio* ☎ *06/89565272* 🌐 *www.palazzodama.com* 🛏 *29 rooms* 🍴 *Free Breakfast* [M] *Flaminio.*

🍸 Nightlife

Metropolita
COCKTAIL BARS | Conveniently close to MAXXI and the Auditorium Parco della Musica, this hip lounge serves classic and creative cocktails as well as light bites in a two-story space with tables on the mezzanine and low sofas on the ground floor. The tapas-style menu is international, with offerings like guacamole and hummus in addition to the popular *maritozzo salato*, a savory version of the Roman bun filled with tuna instead of cream, and a few heartier options, including a burger. Food is served until 1 am every night, and brunch is available on weekends. ✉ *Piazza Gentile da Fabriano 2, Flaminio* ☎ *06/84381895* 🌐 *www.metropolita.it.*

🎟 Performing Arts

Accademia Filarmonica Romana (*Roman Philharmonic Academy*)
MUSIC | Founded in 1821, this musical institution is known for its symphonic and chamber-music concerts but also presents dance performances and musical theater productions in a variety of venues, including the Argentina Theater and the Teatro Olimpico. ✉ *Via Flaminia 118, Flaminio* ☎ *06/3201752* 🌐 *www.filarmonicaromana.org* [M] *Flaminio.*

Accademia Nazionale di Santa Cecilia (*National Academy of Santa Cecilia*)
CONCERTS | One of the oldest conservatories in the world (founded 1585) has a program of performances ranging from classical to contemporary and a lineup of world-renowned artists. The Renzo Piano–designed Auditorium Parco della Musica hosts Santa Cecilia's shows in its three music concert halls. ✉ *Viale Pietro de Coubertin 30,*

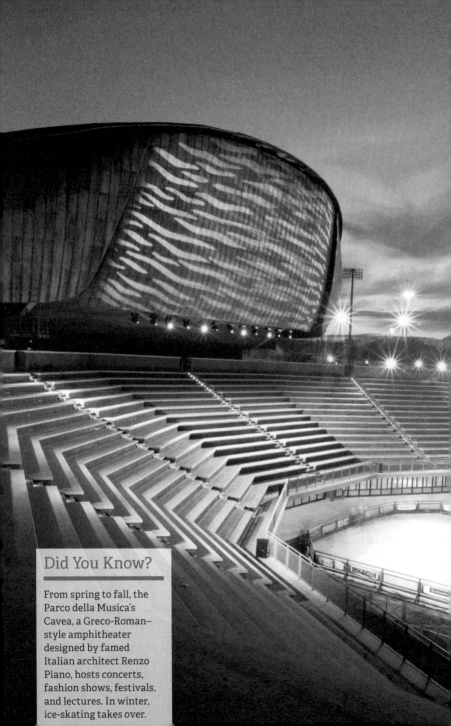

Did You Know?

From spring to fall, the Parco della Musica's Cavea, a Greco-Roman–style amphitheater designed by famed Italian architect Renzo Piano, hosts concerts, fashion shows, festivals, and lectures. In winter, ice-skating takes over.

Flaminio ☎ 06/80242501 ⊕ www.santa-cecilia.it Ⓜ Flaminio, then Tram No. 2 to Apollodoro.

★ **Auditorium Parco della Musica**

CONCERTS | Architect Renzo Piano conceived and constructed the Auditorium Parco della Musica, a futuristic complex made up of three enormous, pod-shaped concert halls, which have hosted some of the world's greatest music acts. The Sala Santa Cecilia is a massive hall for grand orchestra and choral concerts; the Sala Sinopoli is more intimately scaled for smaller troupes; and the Sala Petrassi was designed for alternative events. All three are arrayed around the Cavea (amphitheater), a vast outdoor Greco-Roman-style theater. The Auditorium also hosts seasonal festivals, including the Rome Film Fest. ✉ Viale Pietro de Coubertin 30, Flaminio ☎ 06/80241281 ⊕ www.auditorium.com Ⓜ Flaminio, then Tram No. 2 to Apollodoro.

Teatro Olimpico

THEATER | Part of Rome's theater circuit, the 1930s-era Teatro Olimpico is one of the main venues for cabaret, contemporary dance companies, visiting international ballet companies, and touring Broadway shows. ✉ Piazza Gentile da Fabriano 17, Flaminio ☎ 349/2378200 ⊕ www.teatroolimpico.it Ⓜ Flaminio, then Tram 2 to Mancini.

Monte Mario

In the northwest part of Rome, perched on the city's highest hill, the neighborhood of Monte Mario has fabulous views. Although not the easiest to get to by public transportation, the area has a few noteworthy restaurants and hotels.

🍴 Restaurants

This neighborhood is home to one of Rome's fanciest restaurants.

★ **La Pergola**

$$$$ | MODERN ITALIAN | Dinner here is a truly spectacular and romantic event, with incomparable views across the city matched by a stellar dining experience that includes top-notch service as well as sublimely inventive fare. The difficulty comes in choosing from among Michelin-starred chef Heinz Beck's alta cucina (high cuisine) specialties. **Known for:** fagotelli La Pergola stuffed with pecorino, eggs, and cream with guanciale and zucchini; award-winning wine list; weekend reservations that book up three months in advance. $ Average main: €75 ✉ Rome Cavalieri, A Waldorf Astoria Resort, Via Alberto Cadlolo 101, Monte Mario ☎ 06/35092152 ⊕ www.romecavalieri.com ⊘ Closed Sun. and Mon., 3 wks in Aug., and 3 wks in Jan. No lunch 🎩 Jacket required.

🛏 Hotels

Travelers looking for a relaxing getaway at a distance from the city center will appreciate staying in Monte Mario, but beware: the trip from the centro storico can take 20 to 30 minutes by car and as much as an hour on public transport, which is very limited in this area. Some hotels offer shuttles, but if you'd rather not rely on them or on taxi service, consider renting a car.

Rome Cavalieri, A Waldorf Astoria Hotel

$$$$ | RESORT | FAMILY | Set in a quiet residential neighborhood amid 15 acres of lush Mediterranean parkland, the Rome Cavalieri is a true hilltop oasis with magnificent views as well as three outdoor pools, one indoor pool, and a palatial spa. **Pros:** famed art collection, including a Tiepolo triptych from 1725; complimentary

shuttle to city center; impressive on-site restaurant. **Cons:** you definitely pay for the luxury of staying here—everything is expensive; outside the city center; not all rooms have great views. $ *Rooms from: €420* ⊠ *Via Alberto Cadlolo 101, Monte Mario* ☎ *06/3509* ⊕ *www.romecavalieri. com* ⇨ *370 rooms* ✦ *No Meals.*

Parioli

The elegant residential neighborhood of Parioli, north of the Villa Borghese, is home to some of the city's poshest hotels and restaurants. However, it's not especially convenient if you're planning to do any sightseeing.

 Restaurants

Duke's Fine Casual Bar and Restaurant

$$$ | AMERICAN | It dubs itself an American West Coast–style restaurant, and the decor is very Malibu beach house, with a patio out back. It opened in 1998 and feels a bit frozen in that time, but it's a nice change from eating Italian and everything is high quality. **Known for:** satisfying cravings for non-Italian food; homemade bread and biscuits; Asian-influenced cuisine. $ *Average main: €29* ⊠ *Viale Parioli 200, Parioli* ☎ *06/80662455* ⊕ *www.dukes.it* ⊘ *Closed Sun. and Mon.*

Ercoli dal 1928

$$$ | ITALIAN | The original location of Ercoli opened in Prati as a gourmet food store and this newer location has a deli counter where you can buy cheeses, cold cuts, smoked salmon, caviar, and other delicacies. What this location has that the other two don't is a vermouth bar—and during aperitivo hour (6 pm until 8 pm), classic cocktails and select small plates are 50% off. **Known for:** wide selection of cheese, cold cuts, and smoked fish; vermouth bar; great aperitivo. $ *Average main: €28* ⊠ *Viale Parioli, 184, Parioli* ☎ *06/8080084* ⊕ *www.ercoli1928.com.*

 Hotels

Rome's poshest residential neighborhood attracts a worldly international crowd that's happy to be away from the centro storico hubbub. Chic lodgings range from luxurious boutique hotels to trendy newcomers geared to more budget-conscious travelers. Public transportation is limited in this area, but some hotels offer shuttles to major attractions.

Hotel Lord Byron

$$$$ | HOTEL | With a serene location near the Villa Borghese Gardens and a country-manor feel, this family-run Art Deco retreat attracts an older, well-off international crowd. **Pros:** luxury bathrobes and slippers; gorgeous bar; huge bathrooms, some with soaking tubs. **Cons:** too far to walk to sights; not many cafés and shops in the area; cabs to the city center are expensive. $ *Rooms from: €350* ⊠ *Via Giuseppe de Notaris 5, Parioli* ☎ *06/3220404* ⊕ *www.lordbyronhotel. com* ⇨ *27 rooms* ✦ *Free Breakfast.*

The Hoxton, Rome

$$ | HOTEL | British brand The Hoxton's first foray into Italy is a design lover's dream filled with 1970s-inspired bespoke furniture, art tomes, and plants that transform the large lobby into intimate seating nooks perfect for socializing and coworking. **Pros:** stylish design; friendly staff; great food and drinks. **Cons:** far from main sights, with the closest Metro stop a mile away; rooms have little storage space for clothes; no gym or spa. $ *Rooms from: €189* ⊠ *Largo Benedetto Marcello 220, Parioli* ☎ *06/94502700* ⊕ *www.thehoxton.com/rome* ⇨ *192 rooms* ✦ *No Meals.*

TRASTEVERE AND MONTEVERDE

Updated by
Natalie Kennedy

⊙ Sights	🎭 Restaurants	🛏 Hotels	🛍 Shopping	🍸 Nightlife
★★★★★	★★★★☆	★★★☆☆	★★★☆☆	★★★★☆

NEIGHBORHOOD SNAPSHOT

MAKING THE MOST OF YOUR TIME

It's easy to get to Trastevere from Piazza Venezia: just take Tram No. 8 to the first stop on the other side of the river. You'll probably want to head right to the Piazza di Santa Maria in Trastevere, the heart of this lively area. Heading to the opposite side of Viale di Trastevere, though, is a treat many visitors miss. The cobblestone streets around Piazza in Piscinula and Via della Luce—locals peering down from balconies and the smell of fresh-baked bread floating from small shops—are much more reminiscent of how Trastevere used to be than the touristic area to the north.

Either way, remember that many of Trastevere's lovely small churches close, like others in Rome, in the afternoons. In the evenings, the neighborhood heats up with locals and students drinking, eating, and going for *passeggiate* (strolls)—a not-to-be-missed atmosphere.

TOP REASONS TO GO

Santa Maria in Trastevere: Tear yourself away from the ever-changing piazza scene outside to take in the gilded glory of one of the city's oldest and most beautiful churches, fabled for its medieval mosaics.

Isola Tiberina: Cross the river on the Ponte Fabricio—the city's oldest bridge—for a stroll on the paved shores of the adorable Tiber Island (and don't forget to detour for the lemon ices at La Grattachecca kiosk on the Lungotevere).

Nightlife: Trastevere has become one of Rome's hottest nighttime-scene arenas, where people often spill out into the streets from the many lively bars.

Get a feel for the Middle Ages: With cobblestone alleyways and medieval houses, the area around Trastevere's Piazza in Piscinula offers a magical dip into Rome's Middle Ages.

GETTING HERE

■ From the Vatican or Spanish Steps, expect a 30- to 40-minute walk to reach Trastevere. From Termini Station, take Bus No. 40 Express or No. 64 to Largo di Torre Argentina, where you can switch to Tram No. 8 to get to Trastevere. The H bus will also take you directly from the main station to Termini and then Monteverde.

■ If you don't feel like climbing the steep Gianicolo, take Bus No. 115 from Largo dei Fiorentini, then enjoy the walk down to the northern reaches of Trastevere, or explore the leafy residential area of Monteverde Vecchio on the other side of the hill. Monteverde is a 10-minute tram ride from Trastevere.

VIEWFINDER

■ Trastevere is one of Rome's most enchanting neighborhoods, full of photo-worthy moments around nearly every corner. The start of Vicolo del Cedro, at the intersection of Via della Scala, is particularly perfect for a close-up. The small pedestrian street is bursting with blooming plants and a mishmash of ochre buildings, strung with colorful, freshly washed laundry languidly rippling in the Italian breeze.

Trastevere ("beyond the Tiber") can feel a world apart from the rest of Rome, and, despite galloping gentrification, the bohemian neighborhood remains about the most tightly knit community in the city.

The inhabitants of Trastevere don't even call themselves Romans but rather Trasteverini, claiming that they, not the citizens east of the river, are the true remaining Romans. And although grand art awaits at Santa Maria in Trastevere, San Francesco a Ripa, and the Villa Farnesina, the neighborhood's greatest attraction is simply its atmosphere.

Perfectly picturesque piazzas, tiny winding medieval alleyways, and time-burnished Romanesque houses cast a frozen-in-history spell. Traditional shops line crooked streets that are peaceful during the day and alive with throngs of people at night. From here, a steep hike up stairs and along the road to the Gianicolo, Rome's second-highest hill, earns you a panoramic view of the city.

Farther uphill, along the No. 8 Tram line, Monteverde—with its sprawling parks and typical residential lanes—is a quiet contrast to the bustle of trendy Trastevere. This neighborhood has also become a destination in its own right for its growing culinary scene.

Trastevere

Sights

Gianicolo (*Janiculum Hill*)
VIEWPOINT | FAMILY | The Gianicolo is famous for its peaceful and pastel panoramic views of the city, a noontime cannon shot, the Fontana dell'Acqua Paola (affectionately termed "the big fountain" by Romans), and a monument dedicated to Giuseppe and Anita Garibaldi (the guiding spirit behind the unification of Italy in the 19th century, and his long-suffering wife). The view from the terrace, with the foothills of the Appennini in the background, is especially breathtaking at dusk. It's also a great view for dome-spotting along the city skyline, from the Pantheon to the myriad city churches. ⊠ *Via Servilia 43, Trastevere.*

Isola Tiberina (*Tiber Island*)
ISLAND | FAMILY | It's easy to overlook this tiny island in the Tiber, but you shouldn't. In terms of history and sheer loveliness, charming Isola Tiberina—shaped like a boat about to set sail—gets high marks. Cross onto the island via Ponte Fabricio, Rome's oldest remaining bridge, constructed in 62 BC. On the north side of the island crumbles the romantic ruin of the Ponte Rotto (Broken Bridge), which dates from 179 BC. Descend the steps

Did You Know?

From Gianicolo (Janiculum Hill), the views of the tightly knit, bohemian Trastevere neighborhood and Isola Tiberina (Tiber Island) are particularly enchanting at dusk.

to the lovely river embankment to see a Roman relief of the intertwined-snakes symbol of Aesculapius, the great god of healing.

In imperial times, Romans sheathed the entire island with marble to make it look like Aesculapius's ship, replete with a towering obelisk as a mast. Amazingly, a fragment of the ancient sculpted ship's prow still exists. You can marvel at it on the downstream end of the embankment. Today, medicine still reigns here. The island is home to the hospital of Fatebenefratelli (literally, "Do good, brothers"). Nearby is San Bartolomeo, built at the end of the 10th century by the Holy Roman Emperor Otto III and restored in the 18th century.

During summer, the island hosts an outdoor cinema while its rim is dotted with white tented bars and pop-up eateries. ⊠ *Rome* ✛ *Isola Tiberina can be accessed by Ponte Fabricio or Ponte Cestio.*

Palazzo Corsini

ART MUSEUM | A brooding example of Baroque style, the palace (once home to Queen Christina of Sweden) is across the road from the Villa Farnesina and houses part of the 16th- and 17th-century sections of the collection of the Galleria Nazionale d'Arte Antica. Among the star paintings in this manageably sized collection are Rubens's *St. Sebastian Healed by Angels* and Caravaggio's *St. John the Baptist*. Stop in if only to climb the 17th-century stone staircase, itself a drama of architectural shadows and sculptural voids. Behind, but separate from, the palazzo is the University of Rome's Orto Botanico, home to 3,500 species of plants, with various greenhouses around a stairway/fountain with 11 jets. ⊠ *Via della Lungara 10, Trastevere* ☎ *06/68802323 Galleria Corsini, 06/32810 Galleria Corsini tickets, 06/49917107 Orto Botanico* ⊕ *www.barberinicorsini.org* ☞ *€12 Galleria Corsini, including entrance to Palazzo Barberini within 20 days; €5 Orto Botanico* ⊗ *Closed Mon.*

Piazza di Santa Maria in Trastevere

PLAZA/SQUARE | FAMILY | At the very heart of the Trastevere *rione* (district) lies this beautiful piazza, with its elegant raised fountain and sidewalk cafés. The centerpiece is the 12th-century church of Santa Maria in Trastevere, first consecrated in the 4th century. Across countless generations, this piazza has seen the comings and goings of residents and travelers, as well as intellectuals and artists, who today often lounge on the steps of the fountain or eat lunch at an outdoor table at Sabatini's. At night, the piazza is the center of Trastevere's action, with street festivals, musicians, and the occasional mime vying for attention from the many people taking the evening air. ⊠ *Piazza di Santa Maria in Trastevere.*

Piazza in Piscinula

PLAZA/SQUARE | One of Trastevere's most historic and time-burnished squares (albeit one that's now a bit overrun by traffic), this piazza takes its name from ancient Roman baths on the site (*piscina* means "pool"). It's said that the tiny church of San Benedetto on the piazza was built on the home of Roman nobles in which St. Benedict lived in the 5th century. Opposite is the medieval Casa dei Mattei (House of the Mattei), where the rich and powerful Mattei family lived until the 16th century, when, after a series of murders on the premises, colorful legend has it that they were forced to move out of the district, crossing the river to build their magnificent palace close to the Jewish Ghetto. ⊠ *Piazza in Piscinula, Trastevere.*

San Crisogono

CHURCH | Dating from the 4th or 5th century, this might be Rome's first parish church. Its soaring medieval bell tower can best be seen from the little piazza flanking the church or from the other side of Viale di Trastevere. Inside, ring the bell of the room to the left of the apse to gain access to the underground area, where you can explore the ruins of the ancient basilica, discovered in 1907 beneath the "new" 12th-century structure. The eerie space is astonishingly large and dotted with gems like 8th-century frescoes, ancient marble sarcophagi, and even a 6th-century marble altar. ⊠ *Piazza Sidney Sonnino 44, Trastevere* ☏ *06/5810076* ⊠ *€3 for underground area.*

San Francesco a Ripa

CHURCH | The dedication of this church, which is in a quiet area south of Viale di Trastevere, refers to the fact that St. Francis of Assisi stayed nearby during a visit to Rome. The medieval church was rebuilt in the 17th century and houses one of Bernini's last works, the *Blessed Ludovica Albertoni.* It is perhaps Bernini's most hallucinatory sculpture, a dramatically lighted figure ecstatic at the prospect of entering heaven as she expires on her deathbed. The cell in which Saint Francis is said to have stayed (Il Santuario di San Francesco) is often visitable. If you're a fan of the 20th-century metaphysical painter Giorgio de Chirico, call ahead and ask to visit his tomb in a chapel that contains three of his works. ⊠ *Piazza di San Francesco d'Assisi 88, Trastevere* ☏ *06/5819020* ⊕ *www.sanfrancescoaripa.it.*

San Pietro in Montorio

CHURCH | Built by order of Ferdinand and Isabella of Spain in 1481 near the spot where medieval tradition believed St. Peter was crucified (the crucifixion site at the Vatican is much more probable), this church is a handsome and dignified edifice. It contains a number of well-known works, including, in the first chapel on the right, the *Flagellation* painted by the Venetian Sebastiano del Piombo from a design by Michelangelo, and *St. Francis in Ecstasy,* in the next-to-last chapel on the left, in which Bernini made one of his earliest experiments with concealed lighting effects.

The most famous work here, though, is the circular Tempietto (Little Temple) in the monastery cloister next door. This small sober building (it holds only 10 people and is a church in its own right) marks the spot where Peter was thought to have been crucified. Designed by Bramante (the first architect of the "new" St. Peter's Basilica) in 1502, it represents one of the earliest and most successful attempts to create an entirely classical building. The Tempietto is reachable via the Royal Spanish Academy next door. ⊠ *Piazza di San Pietro in Montorio 2 (Via Garibaldi), Trastevere* ☏ *06/5813940 San Pietro in Montorio, 06/5812806 Tempietto (Accademia di Spagna)* ⊕ *www.sanpietroinmontorio.it* ⊘ *Tempietto closed Mon.*

★ Santa Cecilia in Trastevere

CHURCH | This basilica commemorates the aristocratic St. Cecilia, patron saint of musicians. One of ancient Rome's most celebrated early Christian martyrs, she was most likely put to death by the Emperor Diocletian just before the year AD 300. After an abortive attempt to suffocate her in the baths of her own house (a favorite means of quietly disposing of aristocrats in Roman days), she was brought before the executioner. But not even three blows of the executioner's sword could dispatch the young girl. She lingered for several days, converting others to the Christian cause, before finally dying. In 1595, her body was exhumed— it was said to look as fresh as if she still breathed—and the heart-wrenching sculpture by eyewitness Stefano Maderno that lies below the main altar was, he insisted, exactly how she looked.

Time your visit in the morning to enter the cloistered convent to see what remains of Pietro Cavallini's *Last Judgment,* dating from 1293. It's the only major fresco in existence known to have been painted by Cavallini, a contemporary of Giotto. To visit the frescoes, ring the bell of the convent to the left of the church entrance between 10 am and 12 pm. ⊠ *Piazza di Santa Cecilia 22, Trastevere* ☏ *06/45492739* ⊕ *www.benedettinesantacecilia.it* ⊠ *Frescoes €2.50, underground €2.50 ⏲ Access to frescoes closed in the afternoon.*

★ Santa Maria in Trastevere

CHURCH | Built during the 4th century and rebuilt in the 12th century, this is one of Rome's oldest and grandest churches. It is also the earliest foundation of any Roman church to be dedicated to the Virgin Mary. The 18th-century portico draws attention to the facade's 800-year-old mosaics, which represent the parable of the Wise and Foolish Virgins. They enhance the whole piazza, especially at night, when the church front and bell tower are illuminated.

With a nave framed by a processional of two rows of gigantic columns (22 in total) taken from the ancient Baths of Caracalla, and an apse studded with gilded mosaics, the interior conjures the splendor of ancient Rome. Overhead is Domenichino's gilded ceiling (1617). The church's most important mosaics, Pietro Cavallini's six panels of the *Life of the Virgin,* cover the semicircular apse. Note the building labeled "Taberna Meritoria" just under the figure of the Virgin in the Nativity scene, with a stream of oil flowing from it; it recalls the legend that a fountain of oil appeared on this spot, prophesying the birth of Christ. Off the piazza's northern side is a street called Via delle Fonte dell'Olio in honor of this miracle. ✉ *Piazza Santa Maria in Trastevere, Trastevere* ☎ *06/5814802* 🌐 *www.santamariaintrastevere.it.*

★ Villa Farnesina

CASTLE/PALACE | Money was no object to the extravagant Agostino Chigi, a banker from Siena who financed many papal projects. His munificence is evident in this elegant villa, built for him in about 1511. Agostino entertained the popes and princes of 16th-century Rome, impressing his guests at riverside suppers by having his servants clear the table by casting the precious silver and gold dinnerware into the Tiber (indeed, nets were unfurled a foot or two beneath the water's surface to retrieve the valuable ware).

In the magnificent Loggia of Psyche on the ground floor, Giulio Romano and others created the frescoes from Raphael's designs. Raphael's lovely *Galatea* is in the adjacent room. On the floor above you can see the trompe-l'oeil effects in the aptly named Hall of Perspectives by Peruzzi. Agostino Chigi's bedroom, next door, was frescoed by Il Sodoma with the *Wedding of Alexander and Roxanne,* which is considered to be the artist's best work. The palace also houses the Gabinetto Nazionale delle Stampe, a treasure trove of old prints and drawings. ✉ *Via della Lungara 230, Trastevere* ☎ *06/68027268* 🌐 *www.villafarnesina.it* 🎫 *€12* ⏲ *Closed Sun.*

🍴 Restaurants

The streets of this hip expat enclave with working-class roots and bohemian appeal are lined with trattorias and full-to-capacity bars. The Gianicolo area, atop the hill, is more subdued, with breathtaking views.

★ Antico Arco

$$$ | **MODERN ITALIAN** | Founded by three friends with a passion for wine and fine food, Antico Arco attracts diners from Rome and beyond with its refined culinary inventiveness. The location on top of the Janiculum Hill makes for a charming setting, and inside, the dining rooms are plush, modern spaces, with whitewashed brick walls, dark floors, and black velvet chairs. **Known for:** changing seasonal menu; molten chocolate soufflé cake; extensive wine celler. [$] *Average main: €35* ✉ *Piazzale Aurelio 7, Trastevere* ☎ *06/5815274* 🌐 *anticoarco.it* ⏲ *Closed Tues.*

Baylon Cafe

$ | **CAFÉ** | With eclectic vintage decor, colorful mismatched tables and chairs, and free Wi-Fi, this low-key neighborhood hot spot lures lots of expats and

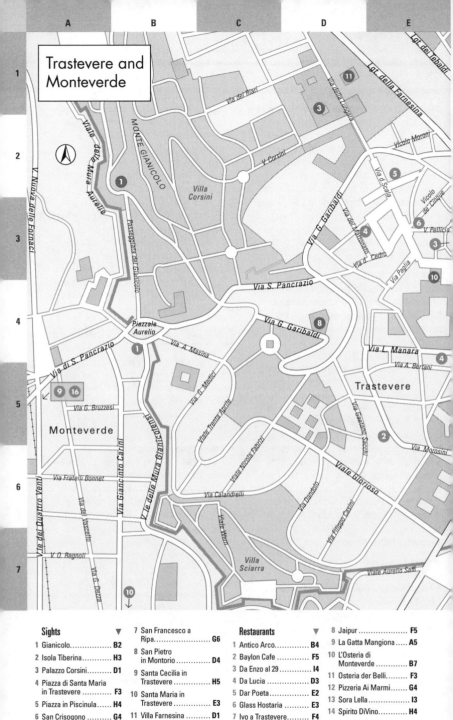

Trastevere and Monteverde

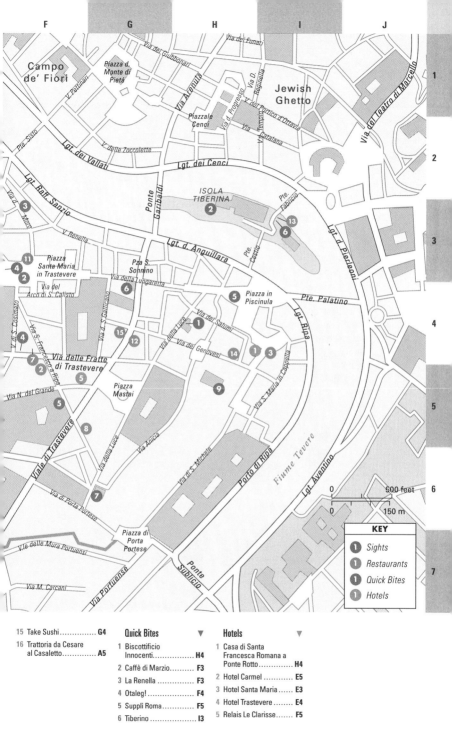

F G H I J

Via dei Funari

Campo de' Fiori

Via del Giubbonari

Piazza d. Monte di Pietá

Jewish Ghetto

Via Arenula

Via D. Reginella

Via del Progresso

Via del Portico d'Ottavia

Via S. Tempio/Gesú

Via Catalana

Piazzale Cenci

Via del Teatro di Marcello

1

Pte. Sisto

Lgt. dei Vallati

V. delle Zoccolette

Lgt. dei Cenci

2

Lgt. Raff. Sanzio

Via d. Moro

ISOLA TIBERINA 2

Ponte Garibaldi

Pte. Fabricio

13

6

V. Renella

Lgt. d. Anguillara

Pte. Cestio

Lgt. d. Pierleoni

3

11

Piazza Santa Maria in Trastevere

4

2

Pza S. Sonnino

Via della Lungaretta

6

Piazza in Piscinula 5

Pte. Palatino

V. d. S. Cosimato

Via del Arco di S. Calisto

Via della Luce

Via dei Salumi

Lgt. Ripa

4

Via d. S. Francesco a Ripa

Via d. S. Gallicano

15

12

Via dei Genovesi

14

1 3

4

7

Via delle Fratte di Trastevere

2

5

Piazza Mastai

9

Via S. Maria in Cappella

Via N. del Grande

5

Via della Luce

Via Anicia

8

Fiume Tevere

Lgt. Aventino

5

Viale di Trastevere

Via di S. Michele

Porto di Ripa

7

Via di Porta Portese

0 ——— 600 feet

0 ——— 150 m

6

Piazza di Porta Portese

V.le delle Mura Portuensi

Ponte Sublicio

KEY

1 Sights
1 Restaurants
1 Quick Bites
1 Hotels

7

Via M. Carcani

Via Portuense

American travelers. In the evenings, order an aperitivo and you can accompany it with a variety of small plates brought to you at minimal cost. **Known for:** lots of vegetarian and vegan options; lively dining terrace; prime people-watching. $ *Average main: €13* ✉ *Via di San Francesco a Ripa 151, Trastevere* ☎ *06/5814275* ⊕ *bayloncafe.business. site.*

★ Da Enzo al 29

$ | ROMAN | In the quieter part of Trastevere, the family-run Da Enzo is everything you would imagine a classic Roman trattoria to be. There are just a few tables, but diners from around the world line up to eat here—a testament to the quality of the food. **Known for:** cacio e pepe (pasta with pecorino-cheese sauce and black pepper), carbonara, and other Roman classics; boisterous, authentic atmosphere; small space with long waits. $ *Average main: €14* ✉ *Via dei Vascellari 29, Trastevere* ☎ *06/5812260* ⊕ *www. daenzoal29.com* ⊗ *Closed Sun. and 2 wks in Aug.*

Da Lucia

$ | ROMAN | FAMILY | There's no shortage of old-school trattorias in Trastevere, but this one has a strong following. Both locals and expats enjoy the brusque but "authentic" service and the hearty Roman fare; snag a table outside in warm weather for the true Roman experience of cobblestone-terrace dining. **Known for:** bombolotti (a tubular pasta) all'amatriciana; homemade gnocchi; involtini (beef rolls). $ *Average main: €14* ✉ *Vicolo del Mattonato 2, Trastevere* ☎ *06/5803601* ⊗ *Closed Mon.–Wed. and Aug.*

Dar Poeta

$ | PIZZA | FAMILY | Romans drive across town for great pizza from this neighborhood institution, which offers both thin-crust and thick-crust (*alta*) Neapolitan-style pies with any of the given toppings. It doesn't accept reservations, so arrive early or late, or expect to wait in line. **Known for:** "superformaggio" (i.e.,

cheese lover's) pizza; dessert calzone with Nutella and ricotta cheese; friendly service. $ *Average main: €13* ✉ *Vicolo del Bologna 45, Trastevere* ☎ *06/5880516* ⊕ *www.darpoeta.com.*

★ Glass Hostaria

$$$$ | MODERN ITALIAN | After 14 years in Austin, Texas, chef Cristina Bowerman returned to Rome to reconnect with her Italian roots, and her cooking is as innovative as the building she works in (Glass has received numerous recognitions for its design as well as its expertly executed cuisine). The menu, which changes frequently, features dishes like a standout steak tartare and lobster polenta with yuba. **Known for:** vegetarian tasting menu; plates inspired by Italy from north to south; more than 600 types of wine. $ *Average main: €40* ✉ *Vicolo del Cinque 58, Trastevere* ☎ *06/58335903* ⊕ *www. glasshostaria.it* ⊗ *Closed Mon., Tues., and 2 wks in July. No lunch Wed.–Fri.*

Ivo a Trastevere

$$ | PIZZA | FAMILY | This always-crowded pizzeria opens early and closes late, and in between it's packed with locals, tourists, and sports fans who know they can watch the Roma soccer team play on big, flat-screen TVs. The selection of pizzas is extensive, with delicious mains available as well. **Known for:** mixed-vegetables pizza; sports-friendly atmosphere; long, leisurely meals. $ *Average main: €16* ✉ *Via di San Francesco a Ripa 158, Trastevere* ☎ *06/5817082* ⊕ *ivoatrastevere.it* ⊗ *Closed Tues. and 2 wks in Jan. No lunch.*

Jaipur

$$ | INDIAN | Named after the Pink City in India, this restaurant serves high-quality curries in a large space just off the main Viale di Trastevere. It's a festive and fun destination if you're craving a change from Italian food. **Known for:** 10 varieties of chicken curry; tasting menus for two people; outside seating. $ *Average main: €16* ✉ *Via di San Francesco a Ripa 56,*

Trastevere ☎ 06/5803992 ⊕ www.risto-rantejaipur.com ⊗ No lunch Mon.

Osteria der Belli

$$ | **SEAFOOD** | **FAMILY** | You might overlook Osteria der Belli because of its proximity to the central square of Trastevere, Piazza Santa Maria in Trastevere—and that would be a crying shame. Leo, the owner, is Sardinian and has been running this place daily for over 35 years, and, while Roman dishes are on the menu, it excels at seafood and Sardinian cuisine. **Known for:** sea bass carpaccio; ravioli or fettuccine alla sarda (in a creamy mushroom sauce); large outdoor patio. $ Average main: €18 ⊠ Piazza di Sant'Apollonia 11, Trastevere ☎ 06/5803782 ⊗ Closed Mon. and 3 wks in Jan.

Pizzeria Ai Marmi

$ | **PIZZA** | **FAMILY** | This place is packed pretty much every night with diners munching on crisp pizzas that come out of the wood-burning ovens at top speed. It's best not to go during peak dining hours, so go early or late if you don't want to wait. **Known for:** excellent wood-oven pizzas; fried starters such as supplì (breaded fried rice balls); open until midnight for a late-night bite. $ Average main: €13 ⊠ Viale Trastevere 53, Trastevere ☎ 06/5800919 ⊕ www.facebook. com/aimarmi ⊗ Closed Wed. and 3 wks in Aug. No lunch.

Sora Lella

$$$ | **ROMAN** | The draw here—in addition to the wonderful food—is the fantastic setting on Isola Tiberina, the wondrously picturesque island set in the middle of the Tiber River between the Jewish Ghetto and Trastevere. As for the food, try the delicious prosciutto and mozzarella to start, and move on to classics like pasta all'amatriciana, meatballs in tomato sauce, or Roman baby lamb chops. **Known for:** stuffed calamari in white wine sauce; elegant setting; unique location. $ Average main: €26 ⊠ Via di Ponte Quattro Capi 16, Jewish Ghetto

☎ 06/6861601 ⊕ www.trattoriasoralella.it ⊗ Closed Sun. and 1 wk in Aug.

Spirito DiVino

$$ | **ITALIAN** | At this restaurant, you get to enjoy an evening of historical interest alongside an excellent meal. The building was constructed on the site of an 11th-century synagogue, and the spot is rich with history—several ancient sculptures, now in the Vatican and Capitoline museums, were unearthed in the basement in the 19th century. **Known for:** ancient Roman recipe for braised pork shoulder with apples and leeks; mostly organic ingredients; cavernous wine cellar in historic location. $ Average main: €18 ⊠ Via dei Genovesi 31 a/b, Trastevere ☎ 331/3342716 ⊕ www.ristorantespirito-divino.com ⊗ Closed Sun. and Aug. No lunch.

Take Sushi

$$ | **JAPANESE** | An increasingly familiar sight on the streets of Rome are all-you-can-eat Japanese restaurants, popular for their inexpensive prices—but Take Sushi couldn't be further from this concept. It's all about top-quality, authentic food here. **Known for:** uni nigiri (sea urchin roe); tasty algae salad; imported Japanese beer and sake. $ Average main: €24 ⊠ Viale di Trastevere 4, Trastevere ☎ 06/65810075 ⊕ www.take-sushi.it ⊗ Closed Mon.

☕ Coffee and Quick Bites

★ Biscottificio Innocenti

$ | **ITALIAN** | **FAMILY** | The scent of cookies wafts out into the street as you approach this family-run bakery, where a small team makes sweet treats the old-school way in a massive oven bought in the 1960s. There are dozens of varieties of baked goods, mostly sweet but some savory. **Known for:** old-school family-run bakery; dozens of varieties of baked goods; brutti ma buoni ("ugly but good") hazelnut cookies. $ Average main: €3 ⊠ Via della Luce 21, Trastevere ☎ 06/5803926 ⊕ www.facebook.com/

BiscottificioInnocenti ⏲ *Closed Sun. and 2 wks in Aug.*

Caffè di Marzio

$ | **CAFÉ** | Over a coffee or a cocktail, sit and gaze upon Santa Maria in Trastevere's glistening golden facade and the busy piazza rom a perch at Caffè di Marzio. The outdoor seating is the main selling point, but the interior is warm and welcoming, too. **Known for:** prime piazza views; sunny outdoor seating; American-style breakfast. [$] *Average main: €9* ✉ *Piazza di Santa Maria in Trastevere 15, Trastevere* ☎ *06/5816095* 🌐 *www.facebook.com/CaffeDiMarzio* ⏲ *Closed 3 wks in Jan.*

La Renella

$ | **PIZZA** | **FAMILY** | This no-frills pizzeria *al taglio* (by the slice) and bakery is hidden a few minutes away from Piazza Trilussa. As in many traditional bakeries, pizza is sold by weight, so get yours sliced to the size you want. **Known for:** classic Roman pizza from a wood-fired oven; no additives or animal fats; homemade breads and sweets. [$] *Average main: €6* ✉ *Via del Moro 15, Trastevere* ☎ *06/5817265* 🌐 *www.facebook.com/LaRenella.*

Otaleg!

$ | **ICE CREAM** | **FAMILY** | A slow wander through town for a scoop of gelato after lunch or dinner is a summer sport in Rome. Galley-sized Otaleg is a must in Trastevere, where gelato master Marco Radicioni dreams up concoctions like *croccante totale* (completely crunchy) with fiordilatte, toasted nuts, sesame, and honey, as well as perfectly distilled seasonal fruit sorbets made with produce from the nearby open-air market in Piazza San Cosimato. **Known for:** high-quality ingredients; creative flavors; neighborhood go-to. [$] *Average main: €5* ✉ *Via di San Cosimato, 14a, Trastevere* ☎ *338/6515450* 🌐 *www.otaleg.com.*

Supplì Roma

$ | **ROMAN** | **FAMILY** | Trastevere's best supplì (Roman-style rice croquettes) have been served at this hole-in-the-wall takeout spot since 1979. At lunchtime, the line spills out onto the street with locals who've come for the namesake treats, as well as fried baccalà fillets and stuffed zucchini flowers. **Known for:** old-fashioned baked pizza with spicy marinara sauce; gnocchi on Thursday (the traditional day for it in Rome); classic fried risotto ball with ragù or cacio e pepe. [$] *Average main: €6* ✉ *Via di San Francesco a Ripa 137, Trastevere* ☎ *06/5897110* 🌐 *www.suppliroma.it* ⏲ *Closed Sun. and 2 wks in Aug.*

Tiberino

$$ | **ITALIAN** | **FAMILY** | Named for the island that it sits on in the middle of the Tiber River, Tiberino is a historic café that has gotten a modern makeover. In the morning, stop in for a pastry topped with slivered almonds or a savory panino with mortadella and arugula. **Known for:** shady outdoor seating near the river; unique setting in the center of Rome's only island; freshly squeezed seasonal juice. [$] *Average main: €16* ✉ *Via di Ponte Quattro Capi, 18, Trastevere* ☎ *06/6877662* 🌐 *www.tiberinoroma.it* ⏲ *No dinner Sun.–Thurs.*

🛏 Hotels

Trastevere's village-within-a-city charm makes it an appealing place to stay. You'll find a mix of modern and moderate accommodations here, including converted convents and small family-run hotels.

Casa di Santa Francesca Romana a Ponte Rotto

$$ | **HOTEL** | In the heart of Trastevere but tucked away from the hustle and bustle of the medieval quarter, this comfortable, affordable hotel in a former monastery is centered on a lovely green courtyard and still has a chapel off the corridor. **Pros:** rates can't be beat; triple rooms for small groups; free breakfast. **Cons:** a bit far from Metro, but there are tram and bus stops nearby; few amenities besides TV room and reading room; main door

locks at midnight, requiring guests to ring the bell. $ *Rooms from: €140* ✉ *Via dei Vascellari 61, Trastevere* ☎ 06/5812125 🌐 *www.sfromana.it* ⇨ *37 rooms* ⦿ *Free Breakfast.*

Hotel Carmel

$$ | **HOTEL** | In the heart of Trastevere and across the Tiber from the main synagogue in the Jewish Ghetto is Rome's only kosher hotel, a friendly and budget-friendly place to stay. **Pros:** lovely dining terrace outside; kosher breakfast can be arranged for €5 extra per person per day; check-in starts at noon. **Cons:** no frills; air-conditioning is a bit weak; some rooms share a bath. $ *Rooms from: €130* ✉ *Via Goffredo Mameli 11, Trastevere* ☎ 06/5809921 🌐 *www.hotelcarmel.it* ⇨ *11 rooms* ⦿ *Free Breakfast.*

Hotel Santa Maria

$$$ | **HOTEL** | A Trastevere treasure with a pedigree going back four centuries, this ivy-covered, mansard-roofed, rosy-brick-red, erstwhile Renaissance-era convent—just steps away from the glorious Santa Maria in Trastevere church and a few blocks from the Tiber—has sweet and simple guest rooms: a mix of brick walls, "cotto" tile floors, oak furniture, and matching bedspreads and curtains. **Pros:** a quaint and pretty oasis in a central location; spacious rooms for groups; lovely rooftop terrace with views across the city. **Cons:** tricky to find; not the best value for money; church bells may wake light sleepers. $ *Rooms from: €250* ✉ *Vicolo del Piede 2, Trastevere* ☎ 06/5894626 🌐 *www.hotelsantamariatrastevere.it* ⇨ *20 rooms* ⦿ *Free Breakfast.*

Hotel Trastevere

$$ | **HOTEL** | This hotel captures the villagelike charm of the Trastevere district and offers basic, clean, comfortable rooms. **Pros:** good rates for location; convenient to tram and bus; friendly staff. **Cons:** rooms are a little worn around the edges; few amenities; standard rooms are quite small. $ *Rooms from: €180*

✉ *Via Luciano Manara 24/a, Trastevere* ☎ 06/5814713 🌐 *www.hoteltrastevere. net* ⇨ *14 rooms* ⦿ *Free Breakfast.*

Relais Le Clarisse

$$ | **B&B/INN** | Set within the former cloister grounds of the Santa Chiara order, with beautiful gardens, Le Clarisse makes you feel like a personal guest at a friend's villa, thanks to the comfortable size of the guest rooms and personalized service. **Pros:** spacious rooms with comfy beds; high-tech showers/tubs with good water pressure; complimentary high-speed Wi-Fi. **Cons:** this part of Trastevere can be noisy at night; check when booking as you may be put in neighboring building; no restaurant or bar. $ *Rooms from: €200* ✉ *Via Cardinale Merry del Val 20, Trastevere* ☎ 06/58334437 🌐 *www. leclarissetrastevere.com* ⇨ *17 rooms* ⦿ *Free Breakfast.*

Nightlife

Trastevere is no longer the rough-around-the-edges neighborhood where visitors once came for a glimpse of the "real" Rome. Years of gentrification have made this medieval "village in the city" a mecca for tourists and foreign students. Its nightlife is a fun mix of overflowing piazzas filled with creative buskers, busy pubs, and great hole-in-the-wall restaurants that are packed into the wee hours of the morning.

BARS

★ Freni e Frizioni

COCKTAIL BARS | This hipster hangout is great for a sunset aperitivo or for late-night socializing. Though the vibe is artsy and laid-back, the bartenders take their cocktails seriously—and have the awards to prove it. In warmer weather, the crowd overflows into the large terrazza overlooking the Tiber and the side streets of Trastevere. ✉ *Via del Politeama 4, Trastevere* ☎ 06/45497499 🌐 *www. freniefrizioni.com.*

Jerry Thomas Bar Room

COCKTAIL BARS | As much about the design as the drinks, this classic cocktail bar comes from the master mixologists behind Rome's most popular speakeasy. With mixed drinks, hard-to-find spirits, and a great selection of champagne, the upscale watering hole feels miles away from the packed alleyways of the rest of Trastevere. Reservations are essential and can be made online. ⊠ *Via del Moro, 10, Trastevere* ☎ *340/7332980* ⊕ *www. thejerrythomasproject.it/en/bar-room.*

Ombre Rosse

WINE BAR | Set on a private terrace overlooking Trastevere, Ombre Rosse bustles with expats and other regulars who appreciate the cocktail creations and the ever-lively atmosphere. On weekends, the outdoor patio is the perfect spot to enjoy an aperitivo and nibbles, before finishing off an evening with friends at the bar. ⊠ *Via Garibaldi 27/G, Trastevere* ☎ *06/45686620* ⊕ *ombrerosseintrastevere.it.*

Rivendita

WINE BAR | The full name is "Rivendita: Libri Teatro e Cioccolata" and that's exactly what you'll find in this charming hole-in-the-wall: books and chocolate. Open only in the evenings, the used-bookstore-bar combo offers wine, sweet cocktails, or coffee served in shot glass-sized cups of pure chocolate. ⊠ *Vicolo del Cinque 11/a, Trastevere* ☎ *06/58301868.*

PUBS

Ma Che Siete Venuti a Fa

PUB | Affectionately shortened to "Makke" by Romans, this tiny pub can't contain the number of beer lovers who flock here at all hours to indulge in a craft pint, or three. Patrons spill out onto the sidewalk behind Piazza Trilussa, sipping the carefully selected artisan brews that arrive from around the world. There is a rotating selection on the 16 taps, and an impressive list of bottled beer. ⊠ *Via Benedetta, 25, Trastevere* ☎ *06/42918213* ⊕ *football-pub.com.*

 Performing Arts

FILM

L'isola del Cinema

FILM FESTIVALS | Every summer from June until September, the gorgeous open-air Cinema d'Isola di Tiberina hosts its own film festival on Tiber Island. The 450-seat Arena Groupama unfolds its silver screen against the backdrop of the ancient Ponte Fabricio, while the 50-seat CineLab is set against Ponte Garibaldi facing Trastevere. There's a mix of international films in their original languages, documentaries, and new Italian films as well as talks with cinematic greats. Screenings usually start at 9:30 pm; admission is €6 for the Arena Groupama, €5 for CineLab. ⊠ *Isola Tiberina, Piazza San Bartolomeo all'Isola, Trastevere* ⊕ *www.isoladelcinema.com.*

THEATER

Teatro India

THEATER | Located in Marconi, close to Trastevere, Teatro India occupies a former soap factory and showcases the best in contemporary theater from local and visiting artists. Most shows are in Italian, but they have occasional English-language performances. ⊠ *Lungotevere Vittorio Gassman 1, Trastevere* ☎ *06/87752210* ⊕ *www.teatrodiroma.net* 🎟 *Tickets €25.*

Shopping

Not only is Trastevere filled with funky boutiques, but it's also home to the biggest open-air Sunday flea market in Rome. Although the neighborhood attracts a lot of tourist traffic and an international college-student crowd thanks to the bustling nightlife, it's also a local favorite for low-key shopping.

BOOKSTORES

Almost Corner Bookshop

BOOKS | Bursting at the seams with not an inch of space left on its shelves, this tiny little bookshop is a favorite meeting point for English speakers in Trastevere.

Irish owner Dermot O'Connell goes out of his way to find what you're looking for, and if he doesn't have it in stock he'll make a special order for you. The shop carries everything from popular best sellers to translated Italian classics, as well as lots of good books about Rome. ⊠ *Via del Moro 45, Trastevere* ☎ *06/5836942* ⊕ *www.facebook.com/ AlmostCornerBookshop.*

FOOD AND WINE
Antica Caciara Trasteverina

FOOD | Step inside this beloved deli for some of the freshest ricotta in town, as well as ham and salami, burrata cheese from Puglia, Parmigiano-Reggiano, Rome's famed pecorino, Sicilian ancho-vies, and local wines—all served with polite joviality. Although not everything can be imported to the United States, some of the savory delights can be vacuum-sealed in case you want to pack some Italian specialties in your suitcase. ⊠ *Via San Francesco a Ripa 140 a/b, Trastevere* ☎ *06/5812815* ⊕ *www.face-book.com/anticacaciaratrasteverina.*

HOME DECOR
Flake's Design & Arredo

HOME DECOR | Specializing in Italian handi-crafts, Flake's selects the best ceramics and small home décor items from all over the country. From elaborately designed platters from Deruta and hand-carved kitschy gnomes, there is something for every taste. However, the best sellers by far are the blue and white vintage enamel plates that are painted with Roman sayings. ⊠ *Via della Scala, 45, Trastevere* ☎ *06/5812846* ⊕ *shop.flakesarredo.com.*

MARKETS
Porta Portese

MARKET | FAMILY | One of the biggest flea markets in Italy welcomes shoppers in droves every Sunday from 7 am to 2 pm. Treasure seekers and bargain hunters love scrounging around the hundreds of tents for new and vintage clothing and accessories, antique furniture, used books, and other odds 'n' ends. Bring your haggling skills, and cash (preferably small bills—it'll work in your favor when driving a bargain); many stallholders don't accept credit cards, and the nearest ATM is a hike. ⊠ *Via Portuense and adjacent streets between Porta Portese and Via Ettore Rolli, Trastevere.*

SHOES AND ACCESSORIES
Marta Ray

ACCESSORIES | Ballet flats in every color of the rainbow and perfectly slouchy Italian leather handbags line the walls at Marta Ray. The boutique carries timeless accessories that never go out of style and have been carefully crafted to last many years of wear on the Roman cob-blestones. ⊠ *Via del Moro, 6, Trastevere* ☎ *06/5811108* ⊕ *martaray.it.*

SOUVENIRS
Elvis Lives

SOUVENIRS | FAMILY | The shop is a great bet for unexpected souvenirs—from accessories to home goods to stationery supplies—from your Roman holiday. Retro tube socks dedicated to pizza appreciation and mouth-watering puzzles featuring high-definition photos of plates of pasta are a few of the fun and funky tchotchkes on offer. ⊠ *Via di San Frances-co a Ripa, 27, Trastevere* ☎ *06/45509542* ⊕ *shop.elvislives.it.*

Monteverde

Southwest of Trastevere, adjacent to the expansive Villa Pamphili Park, Monte-verde is a residential area that's been getting more and more foot traffic from travelers in recent years. Tram 8, which connects all the way to central Piazza Venezia, makes it easy to reach its desti-nation-worthy dining spots.

🍴 Restaurants

La Gatta Mangiona
$$ | PIZZA | FAMILY | The pizza at this neighborhood spot is Roman-style—with a thin crust, charred on the edges. All the standard toppings are available, from margherita to buffalo mozzarella and prosciutto, but try one of the newfangled combinations like ricotta and pancetta and edible wildflowers. **Known for:** Thai pizza with tomato sauce, cheese, and spices; pizza-and-wine pairings; great craft beer selection. [$] *Average main: €15* ✉ *Via Federico Ozanam 30–32, Rome* ☎ *06/65346702* 🌐 *www.lagattamangiona.com* ⏲ *No lunch.*

L'Osteria di Monteverde
$$ | MODERN ITALIAN | FAMILY | Romans are starting to recognize Monteverde as a foodie hub, and this trattoria is one of the neighborhood's outstanding spots. The food ranges from the classics to carefully thought-out modern creations, but whatever you order, the quality of the produce shines. **Known for:** tagliolino (ribbon pasta) stuffed with duck; good selection of dessert wines; classic Roman tripe. [$] *Average main: €18* ✉ *Via Pietro Cartoni 163, Monteverde* ☎ *06/53273887* 🌐 *www.losteriadimonteverde.it* ⏲ *Closed 3 wks in Aug. No lunch Mon.*

Trattoria da Cesare al Casaletto
$$ | ROMAN | FAMILY | This beloved neighborhood trattoria does many things well, from the fried starters to the pastas to the meaty *secondi* (second course), so it's no surprise that it's won the hearts—and stomachs—of Romans all over town. The wine list is extensive, and the friendly waitstaff are happy to offer advice. **Known for:** stewed meatballs; hearty gnocchi with sugo alla coda alla vaccinara (tomato and oxtail sauce); outdoor seating on a leafy patio. [$] *Average main: €15* ✉ *Via del Casaletto 45, Monteverde* ☎ *06/536015* 🌐 *www.trattoriadacesare.it* ⏲ *Closed Wed.*

🍸 Nightlife

La Mescita Monteverde
WINE BAR | Taking over the space next to Villa Sciarra that once housed the Litro wine bar, the beloved drinking spot La Mescita opened its second location atop Monteverde. The wine selection is impressive, though you will only find Italian, French, and other international natural wines on the menu. In the summer, sit out in the garden and you'll feel a million miles from the hectic clamor of Rome. ✉ *Via Fratelli Bonnet, 5, Monteverde* ☎ *328/3970682* 🌐 *www.instagram.com/lamescitamonteverde.*

Chapter 10

AVENTINO AND TESTACCIO

Updated by
Natalie Kennedy

 Sights
★★☆☆☆

 Restaurants
★★★☆☆

 Hotels
★★★☆☆

Shopping
★☆☆☆☆

 Nightlife
★★★☆☆

NEIGHBORHOOD SNAPSHOT

MAKING THE MOST OF YOUR TIME

Travelers with limited time often see just one sight here: the Bocca della Verità, or "Mouth of Truth." There are other gems, though, including the Basilica di Santa Sabina, one of Rome's finest ancient churches, and, in Piazza dei Cavalieri di Malta, the Gran Priorato di Roma dell'Ordine di Malta, where a keyhole hides a special surprise.

Visit Testaccio in the evening, when locals take their *passeggiata* (stroll) and restaurants fill with diners. Admire the Piramide di Caio Cestio, and duck into the Cimitero Acattolico, or "Non-Catholic Cemetery," one of the most atmospheric spots in Rome.

In addition to the allure of its mix of ancient ruins and 19th-century architecture, Romans know that this is where to come for a good meal. The area is famed for its restaurants and has a unique culinary history that dates back to a time when the city's slaughterhouse sat at the edge of the neighborhood.

TOP REASONS TO GO

Santa Maria in Cosmedin: Test your truthfulness at the Bocca della Verità and swoon over St. Valentine's relics.

Cimitero Acattolico "Non-Catholic Cemetery": Full of flowering trees and friendly cats, this romantic graveyard even has an ancient Roman pyramid.

Gran Priorato di Roma dell'Ordine di Malta: Head to the compound of the Knights of Malta in Piazza Cavalieri di Malta to peek through the keyhole of a door and see a perfectly framed view of one of Rome's most famous landmarks.

Roseto Comunale: Overlooking the Circo Massimo, this seasonal rose garden offers a fitting and fragrant vestibule to Rome's most poetic hill.

Baths of Caracalla: South of the lovely Villa Celimontana Park are the imposing ruins of the Terme di Caracalla, once the second-largest bathing complex of the Roman world.

PAUSE HERE

■ The beating heart of Testaccio is its central square, Piazza Testaccio. Shaded by trees and ringed with benches, this is where locals of all ages meet in the afternoons and evenings to play soccer, eat a gelato, and swap stories. At the center of the square is the Fountain of the Anfore, designed by Pietro Lombardi in 1926 and restored and reinstated to its rightful spot after the historic daily market that was once held here moved to its new location in 2015.

GETTING HERE

■ It's a spectacular 20-minute walk through ancient ruins like the Circo Massimo to reach the Aventine Hill from either the Roman Forum or the Campidoglio. There's a Metro stop by the same name at the foot of Aventino, too. If you're coming from the Colosseum or Trastevere, take Tram No. 3; from the Spanish Steps, take Bus No. 160; from Termini, Bus No. 175. For Testaccio, use the Piramide (Ostiense) Metro stop.

Although Romans consider these neighborhoods central, they're just far enough off the beaten path to be little-known to visitors—and to have retained their unique character. If you have a little extra time, a visit to these areas allows a glimpse beyond the Rome of the Trevi Fountain and the Spanish Steps and into a more lived-in Eternal City—from the well-heeled, garden-filled residential quarter of Aventino to the traditional-yet-trendy riverside neighborhood of Testaccio.

Aventino

One of the seven hills on which the city was founded, the Aventine Hill enjoys a serenity that's hard to find elsewhere in Rome. Trills of birdsong win out over the din of traffic—appropriate, since the hill's name derives from the Latin *avis,* or bird. Indeed, legend says that the sighting of eagles was used by Romulus and Remus to determine the prime spot for the city's foundation. In the end, though, Romulus's site on the Palatine Hill won, and Remus's Aventino was abandoned. It would remain for centuries thereafter the hill of the plebs, who looked across the valley to the grandeur of Palatine Hill.

Today, however, this is a rarefied district where some villas still have their own bell towers, and private gardens are called "parks" without exaggeration. Like the emperors of old on Palatino, the fortunate residents here look out over the Circus Maximus and the Tiber, winding its way far below. The great views also famously include one through the peculiar keyhole at the gates to the headquarters of the Cavalieri di Malta (Knights of Malta).

 Sights

Basilica di San Saba

CHURCH | FAMILY | A former monastery, founded in the 7th century by monks fleeing Jerusalem following the Arab invasion, this is a major monument of Rome, though it takes on a subdued air thanks to its modern quiet surroundings in the upscale San Saba district. The serene but rustic interior harbors 10th-century frescoes, a famed Cosmatesque mosaic

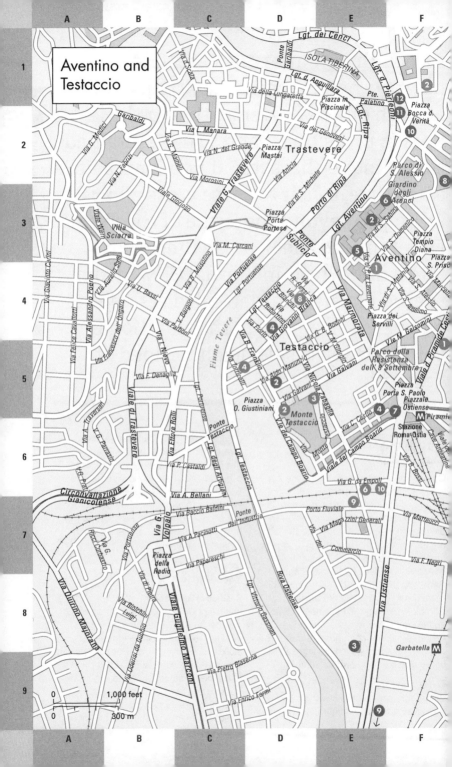

Aventino and Testaccio

ISOLA TIBERINA

Lgt. dei Cenci

Lgt. d. Anguillara

Ponte Garibaldi

Pte. Palatino

Lgt. d. Pierleoni

Lgt. Ripa

Piazza Bocca d. Verità

Piazza in Piscinula

Via della Lungaretta

Via dei Genovesi

2

12
11
10

Piazza Scala

Via L. Manara

Via N. del Grande

Piazza Mastai

Via G. Medici

Garibaldi

Via N. Fabrizi

Via G. Mameli

Via Morosini

Via Anicia

Via di S. Michele

Trastevere

Parco di S. Alessio

8

Giardino degli Aranci

Via di S. Sabina

6

2

Viale Glorioso

Viale Aurelio Saffi

Villa Sciarra

Via M. Carcani

Piazza Porta Portese

Via Portuense

Ponte Sublicio

Porto di Ripa

Lgt. Aventino

Via di S. Prisca

Via S. Domenico

Piazza Tempio Diana

Piazza S. Prisca

5

Aventino

1

Via di S. Melania

Via S. Alessio

Via Marcella

Via Giacinto Carini

Viale delle Mura

Via Alessandro Poerio

Via Francesco dell'Ongaro

Via Felice Cavallotti

Via B. Musolino

Via L. Bargoni

Via Paisoni

Via di Porta Lavernale

Piazza dei Servilli

Via S. Anselmo

1

Viale di Trastevere

Via M. Calsomini

Viale di Piramide Cestia

Via B. Franklin

Via I. Nievo

Via F. Denaglia

Lgt. Portuense

Via Florio

Via Aldo Manuzzi

Via G. B. Bodoni

Via Nicola Zabaglia

Via Galvani

Via Giovanni Branca

Via Zabaglia

Via A. Gessi

Via Beniamino Franklin

Via Luca della Robbia

Via Mastro Giorgio

Testaccio

8
4
4
4
2

Lgt. Testaccio

Parco della Resistenza dell' 8 Settembre

Piazza Porta S. Paolo

Piazzale Ostiense

M Piramide

1
4
7

Via M. Gelsomini

Via G. B. Bodoni

Via L. Cestio

Stazione Roma-Ostia

Via A. Traversari

Via V. G. Parravicini

Via G. Flaiano

Via Ettore Rolli

Via P. Castaldi

Via degli Argonauti

Lgt. Testaccio

Ponte Testaccio

Piazza O. Giustiniani

2

Monte Testaccio

2

3

Viale del Campo Boario

Monte Testaccio

Viale del Campo Boario

Via B. Bossi

Viale Aventino

Via della Piramide Cestia

Fiume Tevere

Circonvallazione Gianicolense

Via G. Volpato

Via P. Castaldi

Via A. Bellani

Lgt. Portuense

Ponte dell'Industria

Via Baccio Baldini

Via A. Pacinotti

Porto Fluviale

Via G. da Empoli

6 **10**

9

Via Magazzini Generali

Via Matteucci

Via G. Ricci Curbastro

Via G. Pomense

Piazza della Radio

Via Papareschi

Via di Pietra

Via Biatchini Luigi

Lgt. Vittorio Glassman

Riva Ostiense

Commercio

Via F. Negri

Viale Guglielmo Marconi

Via Oderisi da Gubbio

Via Pietra Blaserna

Via Enrico Fermi

Garbatella M

3

9

0   1,000 feet

0   300 m

10

Aventino and Testaccio AVENTINO

Map Labels

Parco Traiano
Colosseo
Viale Domus Aurea
Via Labicana
MONTE PALATINO
ROMAN FORUM (FORO ROMANO)
Via L. Vibenna
Via Ostilia
Via C. d'Africa
Parco del Celio
Via Annia
Circo Massimo
Via dei Cerchi
Via del Circo Massimo
Piazza Ugo la Malta
Via delle Terme Deciane
Via Terme Deciane
Via Fonte di Fauno
Basilica Santi Giovanni e Paolo
Viale delle Camene
Viale Aventino
Via di S.Gregorio
Via Celimontana
Basilica di Santo Stefano Retondo
Villa Celimontana
Via della Navicella
Via di Sant'Erasmo
Piazzale Metronio
Parco di Porta Capena
Via Aventina
Via B. Peruzzi
Via di S.Saba
Viale della Terme di Caracalla
Via Antoniana
Via Druso
Via Guido Baccelli
Via E. Rosa
Piazza G. L. Bernini
Via di Villa Pepoli
Via Guerrieri
Via delle Terme di Caracalla
Via di Porta San Sebastiano
Via Giotto
Viale di Porta Ardeatina
Via Fabio Massimo
Viale di Porta Ardeatina
Via Geronimo Dandini
Viale Marco Polo
Via Beltrami
Via dal Baccari
Piazza dei Partigiani
Villa Osio
Piazzale 12 Ottobre 1492
Via Palos
Via Benzoni
Via Antonio Pigafetta
Via della Moletta
Via Capitan Bavastro
Via P. Feilter
Via Camperio
Circonvallazione Ostiense
Via Cristoforo Colombo
Via Cafaro
Via Ignazio Persico

Sights ▼

1 Basilica di San Saba G5
2 Basilica di Santa Sabina........... E3
3 Centrale Montemartini E8
4 Cimitero Acattolico E5
5 Gran Priorato di Roma dell'Ordine di Malta. E3
6 Parco Savello / Giardino degli Aranci. F3
7 Piramide di Caio Cestio F5
8 Roseto Comunale..................... F2
9 San Paolo fuori le Mura............. E9
10 Santa Maria in Cosmedin........ F2
11 Tempio di Ercole Vincitore......... F2
12 Tempio di Portuno F1
13 Terme di Caracalla................. H4

Restaurants ▼

1 Aventina F4
2 Checchino dal 1887................ D5
3 Flavio al Velavevodetto D5
4 La Torricella C5
5 Marco Martini G4
6 Marigold E6
7 Numa al Circo...................... G3
8 Pizzeria Remo D4
9 Porto Fluviale...................... E7
10 Trattoria Pennestri.................. E6

Quick Bites ▼

1 Casa Manfredi G4
2 Mordi e Vai D5
3 Ruver Teglia Frazionata G3
4 Trapizzino D4

Hotels ▼

1 Hotel San Anselmo E4
2 Palazzo Velabro..................... F1

KEY

🔵 Sights
🔵 Restaurants
🔵 Quick Bites
🔵 Hotels

G   H   I   J

floor, and a hodgepodge of ancient marble pieces. ✉ *Piazza Gian Lorenzo Bernini 20, Aventino* ☎ *06/64580140* ⊕ *sansaba. gesuiti.it* Ⓜ *Circo Massimo.*

Basilica di Santa Sabina

CHURCH | FAMILY | This Early Christian basilica is stark and tranquil, showing off the lovely simplicity common to churches of its era. Although some of the side chapels were added in the 16th and 17th centuries, the essential form is as Rome's Christians knew it in the 5th century. Most striking are the 24 fluted Corinthian columns which line the classical interior. Once bright with mosaics, today the church has only one above the entrance door (its gold letters announce how the church was founded by Peter of Illyria, "rich for the poor," under Pope Celestine I). The beautifully carved, 5th-century cedar doors to the left of the outside entrance are the oldest of their kind in existence. ✉ *Piazza Pietro d'Illiria 1, Aventino* ☎ *06/579401* ⊕ *www.op.org/ the-basilica-of-santa-sabina* Ⓜ *Circo Massimo; Bus Nos. 60, 75, 81, 118, 160, 175, and 715; Tram No. 3.*

★ Gran Priorato di Roma dell'Ordine di Malta

RELIGIOUS BUILDING | FAMILY | Although the line to peek through the keyhole of a nondescript green door in the Gran Priorato, the walled compound of the Knights of Malta, sometimes snakes around Piazza dei Cavalieri di Malta, the enchanting view is worth the wait. Far across the city, you'll see the dome of St. Peter's Basilica flawlessly framed by the keyhole and tidily trimmed hedges that lie just beyond the locked door. The priory and the square are the work of Giovanni Battista Piranesi, an 18th-century engraver who is more famous for etching Roman views than for orchestrating them, but he fancied himself a bit of an architect and did not disappoint.

Founded in the Holy Land during the Crusades, the Knights of Malta is the world's oldest and most exclusive order of chivalry. The knights amassed huge tracts of land in the Middle East and were based on the Mediterranean island of Malta from 1530 until 1798, when Napoléon expelled them. In 1834, they established themselves in Rome, where ministering to the sick became their raison d'être. ■**TIP→ Private, guided tours of the Gran Priorato are usually offered on Friday morning, but you must prebook by email.** ✉ *Via Santa Sabina and Via Porta Lavernale, Rome* ✍ *visitorscentre@order-ofmalta.int* ⊕ *www.ordinedimaltaitalia. org/gran-priorato-di-roma* 🎫 *From €5 per person (min. of 10 people), plus the cost of the required guide, €80 in Italian, €100 in any other language. If a group has already formed, then anyone may join for the regular entry fee* ⊗ *Villa closed Jul., Aug., and Dec.* ⚠ *Reservations required* Ⓜ *Circo Massimo; Tram No. 3.*

Parco Savello / Giardino degli Aranci
(*The Orange Garden*)

GARDEN | Umbrella-like Roman pines line the pathway of Savello Park, an enchanting public garden atop the Aventine Hill. The towering trees lead the way to a mesmerizing belvedere of the Tiber and the city rooftops, offering views spanning from the Monument to Vittorio Emmanuele II all the way to St. Peter's. The park is named after the Savelli family who built a fortified palace on the spot in the late 13th century, but it is better known simply as the Giardino degli Aranci, or the Orange Garden, thanks to the numerous citrus trees that were planted here in honor of St. Dominic, the founder of the Dominican order who preached under an orange tree at the nearby cloister of Santa Sabina. The former fortress opened as a park in 1932, but there are still some traces of its more ancient past in the old walls opposite the church, where the outline of an old drawbridge

The Savello Park, or as it is known to Romans, the Orange Garden, provides a relaxing refuge from a day of sightseeing.

is still visible. ✉ *Piazza Pietro D'Illiria, Aventino* ☎ *06/67105457.*

Roseto Comunale

GARDEN | As suggested by the paths shaped like a menorah, this was once a Jewish cemetery. All but one tombstone was moved, and the space is now a municipal garden that is open during the few weeks in the warmer months when the roses are in bloom. The garden is laid out to reflect the history of roses from antiquity to the present day and features over 1,000 varieties. Its location also offers sweeping views across the old chariot track of the Circus Maximus. ✉ *Viale di Valle Murcia, Rome* ☉ *Closed July–late Apr.* Ⓜ *Circo Massimo. Bus Nos. 60, 81, 118, 160, 271, 628, and 715; Tram No. 3.*

★ Santa Maria in Cosmedin

CHURCH | **FAMILY** | One of Rome's oldest churches—built in the 6th century and restored in the late 19th century—is on the Piazza della Bocca della Verità, originally the location of the Forum Boarium, ancient Rome's cattle market and later

the site of public executions. Although the church has a haunting interior and contains the flower-crowned skull of St. Valentine, who is celebrated every February 14th, it plays second fiddle to the renowned artifact installed out in its portico.

The Bocca della Verità (Mouth of Truth) is in reality nothing more than an ancient drain cover, unearthed during the Middle Ages. Legend has it, however, that the teeth will clamp down on a liar's hand if they dare to tell a fib while holding their fingers up to the fearsome mouth. Hordes of tourists line up to take the test every day (kids especially get a kick out of it). ✉ *Piazza della Bocca della Verità 18, Rome* ☎ *06/6787759* ⊕ *www.cosmedin. org* Ⓜ *Circo Massimo.*

Tempio di Ercole Vincitore

TEMPLE | The round layout of the Temple of Hercules Victor led it to be mistakenly identified for centuries as the Temple of Vesta, which has a similar shape but really sits on the other side of Palatine Hill in the Roman Forum. Now called by its correct name, it was built in the 2nd century BC around the same time as its neighbor, the Tempio di Portuno. The little park around the temples was once ancient Rome's cattle market, but now has benches to rest weary feet. ⊠ *Piazza Bocca della Verità, Aventino* Ⓜ *Circo Massimo; Bus Nos. 60, 75, 81, 118, 160, 175, and 271; Tram No. 3.*

Tempio di Portuno

TEMPLE | A picture-perfect, if doll-house-size, Roman temple, this rectangular edifice from the 2nd century BC is built in the Greek style. Positioned in a bend in the Tiber River and long known as the Temple of Fortuna Virilis (Manly Fortune), it was appropriately dedicated to Portunus, the protector of ports. It now sits on a slip of greenery between two well-trafficked roads and owes its fine state of preservation to the fact that it was consecrated as a church in the 9th century. ⊠ *Piazza Bocca della Verità, Aventino* Ⓜ *Circo Massimo; Bus Nos. 60, 75, 81, 118, 160, 175, and 271; Tram No. 3.*

Terme di Caracalla (*Baths of Caracalla*)

RUINS | FAMILY | The Terme di Caracalla are some of Rome's most massive—yet least visited—ruins. Begun in AD 206 by the emperor Septimius Severus and completed by his son, Caracalla, the 28-acre complex could accommodate 1,600 bathers at a time. Along with an Olympic-size swimming pool and baths, the complex also had two gyms, a library, and gardens. The impressive baths depended on slave labor, particularly the unseen stokers who toiled in subterranean rooms to keep the fires roaring in order to heat the water.

Rather than a simple dip in a tub, Romans turned "bathing" into one of the most lavish leisure activities imaginable. A bath began in the sudatoria, a series of small rooms resembling saunas, which then led to the caldarium, a circular room that was humid rather than simply hot. Here a strigil, or scraper, was used to get the dirt off the skin. Next stop: the warm(-ish) tepidarium, which helped start the cool-down process. Finally, it ended with a splash around the frigidarium, a chilly swimming pool.

Although some black-and-white mosaic fragments remain, most of the opulent mosaics, frescoes, and sculptures have found their way into Rome's museums. Nevertheless, the towering walls and sheer size of the ruins give one of the best glimpses into ancient Rome's ambitions. A new portable video guide allows a glimpse of the past grandeur, with images and audio that describes how the ruins appeared centuries ago. If you're here in summer, don't miss the chance to catch an open-air opera or ballet in the baths, put on by the Teatro dell'Opera di Roma. ⊠ *Viale delle Terme di Caracalla 52, Rome* ☎ *06/39967702* ⊕ *www. coopculture.it* 🎫 *€8 (includes Villa dei Quintili and Tomba di Cecilia Metella); €17 includes video guide* 🕐 *Closed Mon.* Ⓜ *Circo Massimo.*

🍴 Restaurants

Although there are no eateries on the tree-lined streets of the Aventine Hill itself, you can take a stroll down to Viale Aventino to find a range of restaurants and cafés that cater to the international staff at the nearby United Nations office.

Aventina

$$ | ITALIAN | Cheese sprinkled with flower petals, jars of jewel-tone sauces, and dramatically lit salumi are just some of the high-quality products that dazzle behind Aventina's swanky deli counter. Everything is available to purchase and take away for a gourmet picnic, but the best way to sample the spread is as a *tagliere* (meat and cheese platter) in the contemporary dining room before moving on to the standout pasta dishes. **Known for:** exceptional salumi; game-meat main courses; savory maritozzi (Roman buns). 💲 *Average main: €16*

✉ *Viale della Piramide Cestia, 9, Aventino* ☎ *06/66594151* 🌐 *www.aventinaroma.com.*

Marco Martini

$$$$ | **ITALIAN** | In addition to innovative Italian-inspired cuisine and one Michelin star, this intimate restaurant has a lovely terrace bar as well as a romantic plant-draped dining room. Twirl your fork into a bowl of spaghetti with a delightful oyster, sausage, and turnip-top sauce, or save room for the lamb with butter anchovies and pistachios. **Known for:** whimsical garden setting; creative presentation; value-for-money tasting menu. [$] *Average main: €35* ✉ *Viale Aventino 121, Aventino* ☎ *06/45597350* 🌐 *www.marcomartinichef.com* ⏲ *Closed Sun. No lunch Sat.* [M] *Circo Massimo.*

Numa al Circo

$$ | **ITALIAN** | **FAMILY** | Circus Maximus was a place for sporting entertainment, and now, just a few minutes' walk from the ancient chariot track, Numa al Circo focuses on gastronomic spectacle. Carbonara pasta, melon-sized balls of mozzarella di bufala perched precariously atop massive platters of tomatoes, and traditional thin crust pizzas are the crowd favorites. **Known for:** nonstop hours from morning to night; raw artichoke and pecorino salad; figliata di bufala cheese ball. [$] *Average main: €15* ✉ *Viale Aventino, 20, Aventino* ☎ *06/64420669* 🌐 *www.numaalcirco.it* ⏲ *Closed Mon.*

Coffee and Quick Bites

Casa Manfredi

$ | **BAKERY** | Pastries rule supreme at this popular shop on Viale Aventino that imports French butter for the tasty creations. There are elegant cakes and tarts for indulgent occasions, but even the humble cornetti (Italy's spin on croissants) are elevated to everyday treats. **Known for:** pain au chocolat; excellent coffee; panettone cake in December. [$] *Average main: €8* ✉ *Viale Aventino, 91/93, Aventino* ☎ *06/97605892* 🌐 *www.casamanfredi.it.*

Ruver Teglia Frazionata

$ | **PIZZA** | Pizzamaker Antonio Ruver may be young but he has already spent years working alongside Rome's pizza master Gabriele Bonci. Now setting out on his own solo venture, Ruver specializes in pre-portioned pizza-by-the-slice. **Known for:** pre-portioned pizza by the slice; ragu topping; thin, crunchy base. [$] *Average main: €7* ✉ *Viale Aventino, 46, Aventino* 🌐 *www.instagram.com/ruver_tegliafrazionata* ⏲ *Closed Sun.*

Hotels

This affluent neighborhood full of trees, set on the Aventine Hill, attracts travelers looking for a green oasis slightly removed from the *centro storico* (historic center). Hotels take advantage of the extra space, with gardens and courtyards where you can enjoy a little R&R alfresco and where the only sounds you'll hear in the morning are bells from the basilica and birdsong.

Hotel San Anselmo

$$$ | **HOTEL** | Set in a *molto* charming garden atop the Aventine Hill, this refurbished 19th-century villa is a romantic retreat. **Pros:** free Wi-Fi; historic building with artful interior; garden where you can enjoy breakfast. **Cons:** some rooms are quite small; limited public transportation; no full restaurant. [$] *Rooms from: €220* ✉ *Piazza San Anselmo 2, Rome* ☎ *06/570057* 🌐 *www.aventinohotels.com/sananselmo* 🛏 *34 rooms* 🍴 *Free Breakfast* [M] *Circo Massimo.*

Palazzo Velabro

$$$$ | **HOTEL** | Overlooking the Arch of Janus and offering glimpses of Palatine Hill, boutique Palazzo Velabro combines timeless architecture and contemporary design in a quiet corner of the neighborhood. **Pros:** pet-friendly with a welcome goodie bag for pups; walkable to many of the main sights; terrace for outdoor

lounging. **Cons:** far from metro; gym is available but limited; service can be a bit slow. [$] *Rooms from: €350* ✉ *Via del Velabro, 16, Aventino* ☎ *06/97619197* 🌐 *www.palazzovelabro.it* 🛏 *32 rooms* 🍴 *No Meals.*

Performing Arts

OPERA

Terme di Caracalla Ballet and Opera
OPERA | In summer, the 3rd-century-AD Baths of Caracalla are the spectacular backdrop for the Teatro dell'Opera's ballet and opera series. *Aida* is the most sought-after performance, thanks to its melodramatic flair and amazing props. The impressive productions keep the traditional sonatas and musical numbers untouched while incorporating contemporary elements into each show, including stage design that sometimes uses projections atop the ancient ruins. ✉ *Viale delle Terme di Caracalla 52, Aventino* ☎ *06/481601* 🌐 *www.operaroma.it.*

Testaccio

Once considered to be on the periphery of the city, Testaccio is fast becoming a Roman destination in its own right—a must-visit for for those seeking an authentic neighborhood with relatively affordable Roman cuisine. Formerly a bit frayed on the edges, Testaccio has undergone a trendy revival and is sometimes hailed as Rome's new "Left Bank" district. Note, too, that locals claim that their neighborhood bleeds red and yellow, a reference to the colors of the A.S. Roma soccer team that has a raucous fan club located here.

Most of the area's buildings date from the late 19th-century, but nearly all were built on literal broken pots. The district takes its name from Monte Testaccio, a hill made up of 53 million discarded ancient Roman amphorae that were used to store oil, wine, and other goods loaded from the nearby Ripa, when Rome had a port and the Tiber was once a mighty river to an empire.

Sights

★ Centrale Montemartini
ART MUSEUM | A decommissioned early-20th-century power plant is now this intriguing exhibition space for the overflow of ancient art from the Musei Capitolini collection. Getting here is half the fun. A 15-minute walk from the heart of Testaccio will lead you past walls covered in street art to the urban district of Ostiense. Head southwest and saunter under the train tracks passing buildings adorned with four-story-high murals until you reach the often-uncrowded Centrale Montemartini, where Roman sculptures and mosaics are set amid industrial machinery and pipes.

Unusually, the collection is organized by the area in which the ancient pieces were found. Highlights include the former boiler room filled with ancient marble statues that once decorated Rome's private villas, such as the beautiful *Esquiline Venus*, as well as a large mosaic of a hunting scene. ■ **TIP→ A purchase of the Capitolini Card will allow entry into Musei Capitolini and Centrale Montemartini.** ✉ *Via Ostiense, 106, Rome* ☎ *06/0608* 🌐 *www.centralemontemartini.org* 🎟 *€11.50; admission included with the purchase of the Capitolini Card (€14.50)* 🕒 *Closed Mon.* [M] *Garbatella.*

★ Cimitero Acattolico (*Non-Catholic or Protestant Cemetery*)
CEMETERY | Built up against the ancient Aurelian Walls, this famed cemetery was intended for the interment of non-Catholics who were barred from burial within the city walls. Poetic souls seek out the tomb of John Keats, who tragically died in Rome after succumbing to consumption at age 25 in 1821. The headstone is famously inscribed, "Here lies one whose name was writ in

Did You Know?

The Piramide di Caio
Cestio was built as a tomb
for Gaius Cestius, in a
time when Romans were
fascinated by all things
Egyptian. When Rome
conquered Egypt in 30 BC,
several pyramids were
erected throughout the
city, but this is the only
one that remains.

water" (the poet requested that no name or dates should appear). Nearby is the place where Shelley's heart was buried, as well as the tombs of Goethe's son, the founder of the Italian Communist Party and vehement anti-Fascist Antonio Gramsci, and America's famed beat poet Gregory Corso.

The cemetery's quiet paths are lined with fruit trees and prowled by shy cats from a nearby animal sanctuary. The tranquil spot is far from morbid and quite easy to find: simply catch the Metro B from Termini station to the Piramide stop, which is just around the corner from the entrance to the cemetery. ⊠ *Via Caio Cestio, 6, Testaccio* ☎ *06/5741900* ⊕ *www.cemeteryrome.it* ✉ *€5 suggested donation* Ⓜ *Piramide; Buses Nos. 23, 30, 60, 75, 118, and 715; Tram No. 3.*

Piramide di Caio Cestio
MONUMENT | FAMILY | Once a part of the Aurelian Walls and now a part of the Cimitero Acattolico, this monumental tomb was designed in 12 BC for the immensely wealthy praetor, Gaius Cestius, in the form of a 120-foot-tall pyramid. According to an inscription, it was completed in a little less than a year. Though little else is known about the Roman official, he clearly had a taste for grandeur and liked to show off his travels to far parts of the nascent empire. The pyramid was restored in 2014 thanks to a €1 million donation from Japanese fashion tycoon Yuzo Yagi. Guided visits (when available) require a reservation but are usually on the second and fourth Saturday of each month. ⊠ *Piazzale Ostiense, Testaccio* ☎ *06/5743193* ⊕ *www.beniculturali.it/ luogo/piramide-di-caio-cestio* ⊘ *Closed Aug.* Ⓜ *Piramide; Bus Nos. 3, 30, 60, 75, 95, 118, 130, 175, and 719.*

San Paolo fuori le Mura
(*St. Paul's Outside the Walls*)
CHURCH | One of Rome's most significant churches is a couple of Metro stops farther down Via Ostiense from Testaccio. Built in the 4th century AD

by Constantine, over the site where St. Paul had been buried, the church was later enlarged, but in 1823 a fire burned it almost to the ground. Although the the location near the river can be dreary, and the outside lacks any real charm, the rebuilt St. Paul's is massive, second in size only to St. Peter's Basilica, and has a sort of monumental grandeur that follows the plans of the earlier basilica.

Highlights include the 272 roundels depicting every pope from St. Peter to Pope Francis (found below the ceiling, with spaces left blank for pontiffs to come) and the cloisters (€4), where you get a real sense of the magnificence of the original building. In the middle of the nave is the famous baldacchino created by sculptor Arnolfo di Cambio. ⊠ *Piazzale San Paolo, Via Ostiense 190, Testaccio* ☎ *06/69880800* ⊕ *basilicasanpaolo.org* ✉ *Basilica free; cloister €4* Ⓜ *Basilica San Paolo.*

🍴 Restaurants

This working-class neighborhood is where the old slaughterhouses once stood and where the butchers invented many of the (in)famous meat and offal dishes you can still find in authentic old-school restaurants. An influx of young people drawn by the area's unique blend of trendy and traditional has made this one of the Rome's most well known culinary destinations.

Checchino dal 1887
$$$ | ROMAN | Literally carved into the side of a hill made up of ancient shards of amphorae, this upscale, family-run establishment has an exceptional wine cellar and stellar contemporary cocktails that incorporate traditional local ingredients. One of the first restaurants to open near Testaccio's (now long-closed) slaughterhouse, it still serves classic offal dishes—though the white-jacketed waiters are happy to suggest other options. **Known for:** old-school Roman

Although the Basilica of St. Paul's Outside the Walls suffered a great fire in 1823, its original triumphal arch and marble tabernacle survived and remain to this day.

cooking; old-school Roman waiters; coda alla vaccinara (Roman-style oxtail). [$] *Average main: €25* ✉ *Via di Monte Testaccio 30, Rome* ☎ *06/5743816* 🌐 *www.checchino-dal-1887.com* ⏲ *Closed Mon. and Tues., Aug., and 2 wks in Jan.* [M] *Piramide.*

★ Flavio al Velavevodetto

$$ | **ROMAN** | It's everything you're looking for in a true Roman eating experience: authentic, in a historic setting, and filled with Italians eating good food at good prices. In this very *romani di Roma* (Rome of the Romans) neighborhood, surrounded by discos and bars, you can enjoy classic local dishes, from vegetable antipasto to cacio e pepe (said to be the best version in the city) and lamb chops. **Known for:** authentic Roman atmosphere and food; outdoor covered terrace in summer; polpette di bollito (fried breaded meatballs). [$] *Average main: €16* ✉ *Via di Monte Testaccio 97, Testaccio* ☎ *06/5744194* 🌐 *www.ristorantevelavevodetto.it* [M] *Piramide.*

La Torricella

$$ | **SEAFOOD** | **FAMILY** | This family-run institution has been serving seafood in the working-class Testaccio neighborhood for more than 40 years, and if you visit the local market early enough you might spot the owner selecting the freshest fish, which mainly arrives from Gaeta, south of Rome. The menu changes every day, but look for house specialties like *paccheri* (a very large, tubular pasta) with *totani* (baby calamari), pasta with *telline* (small clams), or the wondrously simple spaghetti with lobster. **Known for:** fresh, local seafood; relaxed but refined setting with outdoor seating; polpette di pesce al sugo (fish balls in tomato sauce). [$] *Average main: €18* ✉ *Via Evangelista Torricelli 2/12, Testaccio* ☎ *06/5746311* 🌐 *www.la-torricella.com* ⏲ *Closed Mon.* [M] *Piramide.*

★ Marigold

$ | **SCANDINAVIAN** | Run by a Danish-Italian duo, this hip restaurant has a Scandinavian-meets-Roman design and menu. It draws a young, international crowd who come for the sourdough, cinnamon buns, and veggie-forward dishes. **Known for:** sourdough breads and other baked goods; specialty coffee; minimalist Italian design. [$] *Average main: €13* ⊠ *Via Giovanni da Empoli, 37, Rome* ☎ *06/87725679* ⊕ *marigoldroma.com* ⊘ *Closed Mon. and Tues., 3 wks in Aug., and 2 wks in Dec. No dinner* Ⓜ *Ostiense.*

Pizzeria Remo

$ | **PIZZA** | **FAMILY** | Arrive promptly at 7 pm or expect to wait in line at this pizzeria favored by students and locals. There are no tablecloths or other nonessentials, just excellent classic Roman pizza and boisterous conversation. **Known for:** local crowds; fried appetizers; perfectly charred pizza crusts. [$] *Average main: €11* ⊠ *Piazza Santa Maria Liberatrice 44, Testaccio* ☎ *06/5746270* ▭ *No credit cards* ⊘ *Closed Sun. and 3 wks in Aug. No lunch* Ⓜ *Piramide.*

Porto Fluviale

$ | **ITALIAN** | Set in a structure so massive that it takes up the better part of a block on a street that's gone from gritty clubland to popular nightspot, Porto Fluviale is a bar, café, pizzeria, lunch buffet, and lively evening restaurant with a sprawling design that honors the area's industrial past. The menu is all-encompassing, too, with dishes that highlight cuisine from all over Italy. **Known for:** good cocktails; pizza from wood-burning oven; cicheti (Venetian-style tapas). [$] *Average main: €13* ⊠ *Via del Porto Fluviale 22, Testaccio* ☎ *06/5743199* ⊕ *www.portofluviale.com* Ⓜ *Piramide.*

Trattoria Pennestri

$$ | **ROMAN** | Sitting between Testaccio and Ostiense, Trattoria Pennestri manages to strike a careful balance between tradition and innovation. The thoughtful takes on Roman classics brighten up heavy dishes and add a more appetizing spin to some of the city's beloved entrails recipes. **Known for:** modern Roman cooking; duck breast with peaches and wine; uncommon wines. [$] *Average main: €17* ⊠ *Via Giovanni da Empoli, 5, Testaccio* ☎ *06/5742418* ⊕ *www.trattoriapennestri.it* ⊘ *Closed Mon. and two wks in Feb. No lunch Tues.–Thurs.* Ⓜ *Piramide.*

☕ Coffee and Quick Bites

★ Mordi e Vai

$ | **ITALIAN** | **FAMILY** | This family-run stall at what will forever be called the "New" Testaccio Market (it moved in 2012) sells the best sandwiches in town. Meatballs, tongue, tripe, and other Roman classics are generously smothered on fresh bread, and there is always a vegetarian option, too. **Known for:** alesso (slow-cooked beef) sandwiches; breaded meatballs; long lines at lunch time. [$] *Average main: €5* ⊠ *Testaccio Market Box 15, Via Beniamino Franklin, Rome* ☎ *347/6632731* ⊕ *www.facebook.com/mordievai* ⊘ *Closed Sun. No dinner.*

Trapizzino

$ | **ROMAN** | **FAMILY** | Stefano Callegari is one of Rome's most famous pizza makers, but at Trapizzino he's doing something a bit different. The name of the restaurant is derived from the Italian words for sandwich (*tramezzino*) and pizza, and the result is something like an upscale pizza pocket, stuffed on the spot with local specialties like chicken alla cacciatore, or *trippa* (tripe), or roast pumpkin, pecorino, and almonds. **Known for:** casual setting, with seating available next door; eggplant parmigiana and meatball sandwiches; Italian craft beer. [$] *Average main: €5* ⊠ *Via Giovanni Branca 88, Testaccio* ☎ *06/43419624* ⊕ *www.trapizzino.it* ⊘ *Closed 1 wk in Aug.* Ⓜ *Piramide.*

Nightlife

Even if it is a bit outside the meandering medieval alleyways of the historic center, Testaccio is a hotbed for the Eternal City's nightlife scene. The rowdy clubs that are dug into the side of Monte

Testaccio have lost some of their appeal in recent years as the trendier dance clubs moved to old warehouses even farther out to the edge of Rome, but this has left space for new wine bars and hip street-food stops.

BARS

L'Oasi della Birra

PUB | A long menu of imported brews make this a true beer oasis, although there are also good wines available by the bottle or the glass. Locals love the generous happy-hour buffet that runs from about 6 pm to 8 pm every day, but come early to snag one of the outdoor picnic tables that overlook the piazza. Best known as a low-key drinking spot, the bar also doubles as a specialty food store that stocks Italian jams, chocolates, and pastas. ⊠ *Piazza Testaccio 38/41, Testaccio* ☎ *06/5746122* ⊕ *www.facebook. com/EnotecaPalombi1917* Ⓜ *Piramide.*

Taverna Volpetti

WINE BAR | Most aperitivos tend to be more all-you-can-eat than refined pre-dinner stop, but that is not the case at Taverna Volpetti. The chic bistro-style wine bar and restaurant sources all its ingredients from the gourmet food store by the same name that sits just around the corner. The warm atmosphere, stellar wine list, and excellent cheese and salami make it the ideal place for a drink and a snack—or to stay put with a bottle and sip the night away. ⊠ *Via Alessandro Volta 8, Testaccio* ☎ *349/7186894* ⊕ *www. tavernavolpetti.it* Ⓜ *Piramide.*

★ Tram Depot

COCKTAIL BARS | A coffee stand by day and cocktail bar by night, this outdoor establishment began life as a city tram car back in 1903. Now the historic carriage has been converted to a kiosk permanently stationed on a park corner with retro tables and garden seating. A trendy crowd descends at sunset for an evening spritz, and seats are at a premium until

the wee hours of the morning. Since it is entirely outside, Tram Depot is mainly open in the warmer months of the year (April through November); but weather permitting, the kiosk stays open on the weekends year round. ⊠ *Via Marmorata 13, Testaccio* ☎ *380/6455154* ⊕ *www. facebook.com/TramDepotOfficial* Ⓜ *Piramide.*

Shopping

Testaccio is Rome's original foodie neighborhood, with plenty of specialty food and wine shops, as well as an abundance of great Roman eateries. But look between the traditional working-class storefronts and you will also find trendy boutiques and artisan shops.

FOOD

Emporio delle Spezie

FOOD | This itty-bitty specialty shop bursts with ingredients from every corner of the world. It specializes in high-quality spices, but you can also find dried goods like legumes, nuts, and rice. All are carefully scooped from the colorful glass jars that line the walls and measured out to your liking. ⊠ *Via Galvani 11, Testaccio* ☎ *327/8612655* ⊕ *www.emporiodellespezie.it* Ⓜ *Piramide.*

★ Volpetti

FOOD | A Roman institution for 50 years, Volpetti sells excellent cured meats and salami from its buzzing deli counter. The food selection also includes genuine buffalo-milk mozzarella, fresh pasta, Roman pecorino, olive oils, balsamic vinegars, and fresh bread. The rich aromas and flavors are captivating from the moment you enter the store—pull up a high stool and order a sampling platter with a glass of wine. It's also a great place for assembling gift baskets, and offers worldwide shipping. ⊠ *Via Marmorata 47, Testaccio* ☎ *375/5130898* ⊕ *www.volpetti.com* Ⓜ *Piramide.*

SOUVENIRS

Assemblea

CRAFTS | FAMILY | This modest shop is brimming with fantastic small gifts ranging from handmade ceramic volcanoes to tote bags crafted from vintage Italian silk. Assemblea finds artisans throughout the country and makes their quirky creations available in Rome, so every item featured is guaranteed to be made in Italy. ✉ *Via Alessandro Volta 22, Testaccio* ☎ *06/5747696* ⊕ *www.facebook.com/ assemblea22* Ⓜ *Piramide.*

Rome is More

SOUVENIRS | FAMILY | Romanesco is one of the more colorful Italian dialects and a lot gets lost in translation. This creative shop shills humorous mugs, tote bags, and magnets emblazoned with popular local phrases along with definitions not found in any dictionary. ✉ *Via Mastro Giorgio, 31, Testaccio* ☎ *06/97278712* ⊕ *www. romeismore.com.*

Chapter 11

ESQUILINO AND ENVIRONS

11

Updated by
Laura Itzkowitz

⊙ Sights	🍴 Restaurants	🛏 Hotels	🛍 Shopping	🌙 Nightlife
★★★☆☆	★★★☆☆	★★★☆☆	★★☆☆☆	★★☆☆☆

NEIGHBORHOOD SNAPSHOT

MAKING THE MOST OF YOUR TIME

Some of central Rome's least touristy and best-loved neighborhoods, these areas have a great deal to explore. With its bustling food market and multicultural shops, Esquilino represents a more modern Rome. Its rich street life has attracted numerous artists, actors, and filmmakers who often gather at some of the popular cafés in the neighborhood. With Termini at its center, it's also a bus and Metro hub for reaching other parts of Rome or hopping on a train for a day trip out of the city. Nearby Pigneto, with its hipster bars and street art, is also an example of the ever-evolving city.

San Giovanni is well worth the Metro trip to discover the Basilica of San Giovanni in Laterano, a cathedral that holds centuries of church history in its walls. This residential area also has great flea market shopping if you have the patience to browse.

For a bustling night out, head to San Lorenzo, home to the Sapienza University of Rome and the crowds of young students that go with it. And no visit to Rome is complete without a tour of the catacombs on the Appian Way, one of the ancient republic's earliest and most strategically placed roads, built in 312–264 BC.

TOP REASONS TO GO

Arcibasilica di San Giovanni in Laterano: Before the Holy See made the Vatican its permanent home, leaders of the Catholic Church made the Lateran buildings their primary residence for nearly 1,000 years.

Catacomb country: Be careful exploring the underground graves of the earliest Christians—one wrong turn and it may be days before you surface.

Porta Maggiore: This white travertine "great gate" is an essential stop for understanding Rome's ancient aqueduct culture.

VIEWFINDER

■ Fans of street art will find much to admire in San Lorenzo and Pigneto, as both neighborhoods have large-scale murals. There's a particularly impressive work across from the Soho House in San Lorenzo. In Pigneto, you'll find several murals on and around Via Fanfulla da Lodi. To learn more about this art and the neighborhoods they're in, you can take a street art tour with **Scooteroma** (⊕ *scooteroma.com*), which offers Vespa excursions around Rome.

GETTING HERE

■ The Esquilino Hill can be reached via the Vittorio Emanuele subway station, one stop from Termini station. Pigneto is easily reached by the Metro Line C. Metro Lines A and C meet at the San Giovanni stop.

Districts in the area just north of the Roman Forum and the Colosseum range from the bustling, multicultural Esquilino neighborhood to the hipster enclaves of Pigneto and San Lorenzo. Like many travelers, you'll probably at least pass through this area, either when coming into the Termini train station or when visiting the magnificent Basilica of San Giovanni in Laterano. Farther south, the evocative Via Appia Antica is dotted with ruins and catacombs.

Esquilino

Rome's most sprawling hill—the Esquilino—lies at the very edge of most tourist maps. Even imperial Rome could not have matched this minicosmopolis for sheer internationalism. Right around Termini, sons of the soil—the so-called "romani romani"—mingle with Chinese, Sri Lankans, Sikhs, and a hundred nationalities in between.

One highlight is the Nuovo Mercato Esquilino, a covered market hall where goods from the four corners of the Earth are bought and sold in a multitude of languages. The area also has the city's largest variety of restaurants and cheapest bed-and-breakfasts—just not the cobblestone atmosphere that most think of when they think of Rome.

Sights

Porta Maggiore (*Great Gate*)
RUINS | The massive, 1st-century-AD arch was built as part of the original Aqua Claudia and then incorporated into the walls hurriedly erected in the late 3rd century as Rome's fortunes began to decline. The great arch of the aqueduct subsequently became a *porta* (city gate) and gives an idea of the grand scale of ancient Roman public works. On the Piazzale Labicano side, to the east, is the curious Baker's Tomb, erected in the 1st century BC by a prosperous baker (predating both the aqueduct and the city walls); it's shaped like an oven to signal the deceased's trade. The site is now in the middle of a public transport node and is close to Rome's first tram depot (going back to 1889). ⊠ *Piazza di Porta Maggiore, Esquilino* Ⓜ *Tram No. 5, 14, or 19.*

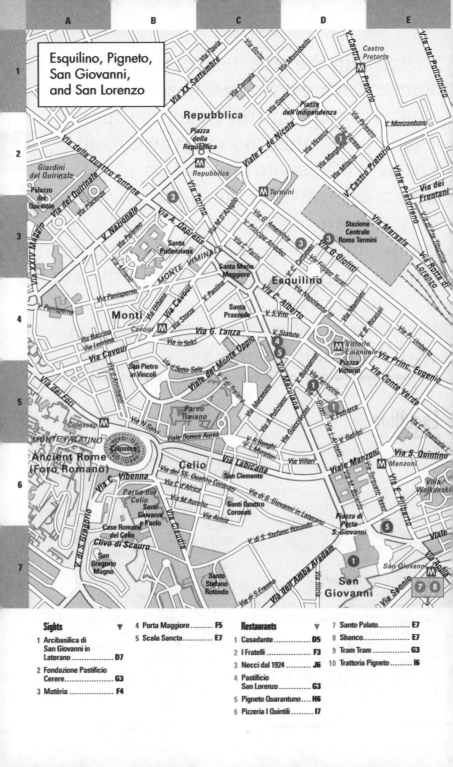

Esquilino, Pigneto,
San Giovanni,
and San Lorenzo

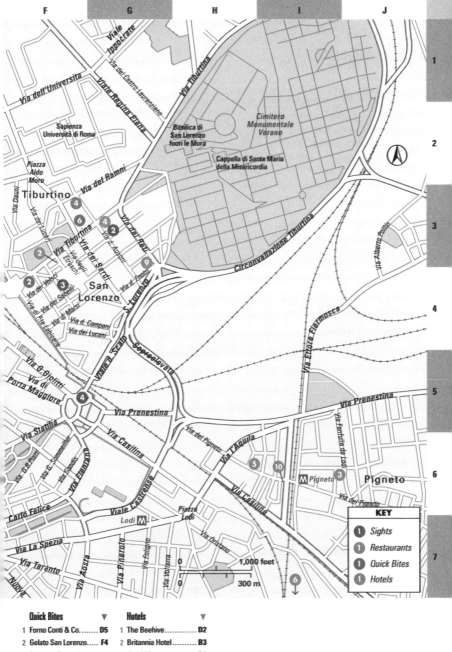

🍴 Restaurants

Casadante

$$ | **ITALIAN** | Set in what was once an industrial space, this cavernous restaurant and bar—replete with soaring ceilings, Chesterfield sofas, and open shelves filled with wine bottles—is popular for aperitivo and *apericena* (light evening meal with small plates). The menu eschews pasta and focuses instead on *pinsa* (Roman-style oval pizzas) as well as *fritti* (fried foods), burgers and steaks, and some salads and other light fare. **Known for:** industrial design; pinsa; cool local crowd. [$] *Average main: €15* ✉ *Piazza Dante 8, Esquilino* ☎ *06/85384091* [M] *Vittorio Emanuele.*

☕ Coffee and Quick Bites

Forno Conti & Co.

$ | **BAKERY** | **FAMILY** | At this spot on a quiet street near Piazza Vittorio, Scandinavian-inspired minimalist design is the backdrop for bread and pastries by fourth-generation baker Sergio Conti. You'll find staples like excellent croissants and pain au chocolat as well as special items like apple strudel, cheesecake, or brioche with salted caramel and peanuts. **Known for:** sleek minimalist design; bread naturally leavened with sourdough starter; pastries and cakes. [$] *Average main: €5* ✉ *Via Giusti 18, Esquilino* ☎ *339/2109591* 🌐 *www.fornoconti.co* 🕒 *Closed Sun.* [M] *Vittorio Emanuele.*

Mercato Centrale Roma

$ | **INTERNATIONAL** | **FAMILY** | This gourmet food hall is in the last place you'd expect—Termini Station—and it's great for a quick bite even if you're not catching a train. There are stalls from some of Rome's best food purveyors, including Stefano Callegari (of *trapizzino* fame), pizzaiolo Marco Quintili, and fritti by Arcangelo Dandini. **Known for:** gourmet food hall; trapizzino (stuffed triangle-shaped pizza dough) outpost; Sicilian specialties. [$] *Average main: €5* ✉ *Termini Station, Via Giovanni Giolitti 36, Esquilino* ☎ *06/46202900* 🌐 *www.mercatocentrale.it* [M] *Termini.*

Panella

$ | **BAKERY** | **FAMILY** | Opened in 1929, this bakery sells both sweet and savory items, including more than 70 types of bread. Line up for the pizza *al taglio* (by the slice) at lunchtime, or sit down at one of the outdoor tables for a cappuccino and cornetto or an aperitivo replete with mini sandwiches made on homemade buns. **Known for:** one of Rome's best bakeries; crostata, tartlets, and other sweet treats; espresso with zabaione. [$] *Average main: €10* ✉ *Via Merulana 54, Esquilino* ☎ *06/4872435* 🌐 *www.panellaroma.com* [M] *Vittorio Emanuele.*

Regoli Pasticceria

$ | **BAKERY** | **FAMILY** | Established in 1916, this family-run pasticceria is famous for its maritozzi, which often sell out by lunchtime. Other pastries include cream puffs, cannoli, and tarts made with tiny wild strawberries from Nemi. **Known for:** wild strawberry tarts; cream-filled pastries; maritozzi. [$] *Average main: €3* ✉ *Via dello Statuto 60, Esquilino* ☎ *06/4872812* 🌐 *www.pasticceriaregoli.com* 🕒 *Closed Tues.* [M] *Vittorio Emanuele.*

🛏 Hotels

Budget-conscious travelers who want to be near Rome's major transport hub, Termini Station, often stay here. There are a number of cheap, clean, no-frills hotels and pensioni, as well as a few more-stylish options.

The Beehive

$$ | **HOTEL** | Run by an American couple, this welcoming, community-oriented hostel near Termini Station offers private rooms as well as regular hostel beds in dorms. **Pros:** owners make the best bagels in Rome; convenient to Termini Station; very good prices, even in high season. **Cons:** some rooms do not have private baths; standard rooms lack

TV; no 24-hour reception. $ *Rooms from: €125* ✉ *Via Marghera 8, Esquilino* ☎ *06/44704553* ⊕ *www.the-beehive.com* ⬂ *8 rooms, 2 female-only dormitories, 2 co-ed dormitories* ‖⊙‖ *No Meals* ☞ *Check-in hours are 9 am–9 pm* Ⓜ *Termini.*

Britannia Hotel

$$$ | **HOTEL** | Situated in an elegant Art Nouveau palazzo, built in 1876 as a residence for Prince Philip Don Orsini, this charming hotel is furnished with original artwork and British textiles and feels like a luxurious private home. **Pros:** nice, friendly staff; great breakfast options; spacious marble bathrooms, many with Jacuzzi baths. **Cons:** rooms can be noisy for light sleepers; removed from the main attractions; some furnishings are out of date. $ *Rooms from: €242* ✉ *Via Napoli 64, Esquilino* ☎ *06/4883153* ⊕ *www.hotelbritanniaroma.com* ⬂ *34 rooms* ‖⊙‖ *No Meals* Ⓜ *Repubblica.*

Hotel Morgana

$$ | **HOTEL** | A nice, cozy hotel just a stone's throw from Termini Station sounds like some sort of a miracle, and yet, the Morgana welcomes guests with elegant, classically designed accommodations and top amenities. **Pros:** practical base for public transportation; great breakfast; pet-friendly. **Cons:** run-down neighborhood; removed from most sightseeing; some bathrooms are on the small side. $ *Rooms from: €197* ✉ *Via Filippo Turati 33/37, Esquilino* ☎ *06/4467230* ⊕ *www.hotelmorgana.com* ⬂ *123 rooms* ‖⊙‖ *Free Breakfast* Ⓜ *Termini.*

Nightlife

The area around Termini can be a bit sketchy, especially at night, but there are a few pubs around Santa Maria Maggiore and a happening scene around Piazza Vittorio.

BARS

Fiddler's Elbow

PUB | This traditional Irish pub, the oldest in Rome, probably hasn't changed much since it first installed its rustic wooden features in 1976. Expect raucous nights of beer and singing. ✉ *Via dell'Olmata 43, Esquilino* ☎ *06/4872110* ⊕ *www.thefiddlerselbow.com* Ⓜ *Piazza Vittorio, Cavour.*

Machiavelli 64

WINE BAR | This unpretentious enoteca is a popular spot to gather over excellent wines and creative small plates. Guests can take one of the bottles right off the well-stocked shelves or choose from a selection of wines by the glass, including some prized wines for very reasonable prices. ✉ *Via Machiavelli, 64, Esquilino* ☎ *06/77206673* ⊕ *www.instagram.com/machiavelli_64* Ⓜ *Vittorio Emanuele.*

Shopping

Home to a variety of ethnic communities, the shops in Esquilino feel very authentic. The market here is a fabulous place to explore.

MALLS AND SHOPPING CENTERS

Roma Termini

MALL | **FAMILY** | Rome's handiest central shopping mall is this cluster of shops that stays open until 10 pm (even on Sunday), conveniently located right inside Rome's biggest train station, Stazione Termini. In a city not exactly known for its convenient shopping hours, this "shop before you hop" hub is a good spot for last-minute goodies. Stores include ever-popular chains like Mango, Moleskine, and Sephora; bookshops with good selections of English-language best sellers; a grocery store; and a well-stocked food court. ✉ *Piazza dei Cinquecento 1, Esquilino* ⊕ *www.instazione.shop/roma-termini* Ⓜ *Termini.*

MARKETS

Nuovo Mercato Esquilino

MARKET | FAMILY | This massive covered market is an excellent place to wander thanks to its Italian, Asian, and African specialties. Many of Rome's top restaurants get their main ingredients here. ✉ *Via Principe Amedeo 184, Esquilino* [M] *Vittorio Emanuele.*

Pigneto

Connected to the rest of Rome by the Metro Line C, Pigneto is a hip neighborhood full of young people and famed for its street art and cool eateries and cafés. It comes alive at night, with most bars and restaurants clustered around the section of Via del Pigneto, between Via l'Aquila and Circonvallazione Casilina, and around the junction of Via Braccio da Montone and Via Fanfulla da Lodi.

🍴 Restaurants

Pigneto is Rome's up-and-coming *zona*, or area: gritty cafés, artsy bars, and youth-driven, modern Italian restaurants are what you'll find.

★ Necci dal 1924

$$ | ITALIAN | Pigneto is full of hip restaurants and bars now, but Necci is the neighborhood's original hangout, the haunt of famed director Pier Paolo Pasolini, who grew up in Pigneto when it was still a rough-and-tumble working-class area. There's a full menu of pastas and other Italian fare, but the servers won't bat an eye if you just want drinks or a small bite; it also hosts wine tastings in its recently discovered, 1st-century BC hypogeum. **Known for:** laid-back hipster hangout; large patio with lots of outdoor seating; all-day dining and drinking. [$] *Average main: €16* ✉ *Via Fanfulla da Lodi 68, Pigneto* ☎ *06/97601552* 🌐 *www.necci1924.com* [M] *Pigneto.*

Pigneto Quarantuno

$$ | MODERN ITALIAN | Reservations are a good idea (especially if you'd like to sit outside) at this popular spot, where the changing menu of Roman dishes reflects the use of seasonal produce. Start with one of the many foccacie, such as thyme, goat cheese, and grilled zucchini, and then move on to a primo—perhaps a hearty ragù in cooler months or a more-delicate vegetarian pasta dish in the summer. **Known for:** impressive local and Italian wine list; homemade pasta; legendary meatballs. [$] *Average main: €15* ✉ *Via del Pigneto 41, Pigneto* ☎ *06/70399483* 🌐 *www.facebook.com/PignetoQuarantuno* ⏲ *No lunch weekdays* [M] *Pigneto.*

Trattoria Pigneto

$ | ROMAN | This casual, relaxed trattoria follows the style of a *fraschetta*, a type of countryside restaurant where the menu focuses on porchetta—here, it's served on butcher's paper according to how many people are in your party. Accompany the main attraction with a cheese-and-charcuterie board followed by pasta all'amatriciana or cacio e pepe. **Known for:** affordable prices; old-school classics; rustic picnic table decor. [$] *Average main: €14* ✉ *Via del Pigneto 68, Pigneto* ☎ *06/45650417* 🌐 *www.trattoriapignetoroma.business.site* ⏲ *Closed Mon.* [M] *Pigneto.*

🍸 Nightlife

Co.So. Cocktails & Social

COCKTAIL BARS | This funky cocktail bar features street art murals and pendant lamps made from mixing glasses. The menu is inspired by Roman, Sicilian, and Japanese flavors, with a bento box aperitivo and a list of creative club sandwiches. Try something playful on the cocktail list like the Carbonara Sour, made with guanciale-infused vodka. ✉ *Via Braccio da Montone 80, Pigneto* ☎ *06/45435428* 🌐 *www.cosoroma.business.site* [M] *Pigneto.*

Did You Know?

Rome's cathedral is not
St. Peter's, but rather
the Arcibasilica di San
Giovanni in Laterano,
which was built by
Emperor Constantine 10
years before the church
dedicated to Peter and
restored in both the 16th
and 17th centuries.

San Giovanni

Rome's cathedral, the Basilica of San Giovanni in Laterano, is the crown jewel of San Giovanni, a neighborhood just west of Celio that has 19th- and 20th-century apartment buildings and modern shops. You can reach it by walking south along Via Merulana from the Colosseum.

Sights

★ **Arcibasilica di San Giovanni in Laterano**
(*Basilica of St. John Lateran*)
CHURCH | The cathedral of Rome is San Giovanni in Laterano, not St. Peter's. The church was built here by Emperor Constantine 10 years before he built the church dedicated to Peter, making it the ecclesiastical seat of the Bishop of Rome (the pope). But thanks to vandals, earthquakes, and fires, today's building owes most of its form to 16th- and 17th-century restorations, including an interior designed by Baroque genius Borromini. Colossal statues stand watch over the towering facade: the 12 apostles plus Christ, John the Baptist, and the Virgin Mary.

Some earlier fragments do remain: under the portico on the left stands an ancient statue of Constantine, while the central portal's ancient bronze doors were brought here from the Forum's Curia. The altar's rich Gothic tabernacle, holding what the faithful believe are the heads of saints Peter and Paul, dates from 1367. The last chapel on the left aisle houses the cloister, which is encrusted with 12th-century cosmatesque mosaics. Around the corner stands one of the oldest Christian structures in Rome: Emperor Constantine's octagonal baptistery. Despite several restorations, a 17th-century interior redecoration, and even a 1993 Mafia-related car bombing, the baptistery from AD 315 remains true to its ancient form. ⊠ *Piazza di San Giovanni in Laterano 4, San Giovanni* ☎ *06/69886433*

⊕ *www.vatican.va/various/basiliche/san_giovanni/index_it.htm* 🖾 *Basilica free; cloister €3* Ⓜ *San Giovanni.*

★ **Scala Santa** (*Holy Stairs*)
RELIGIOUS BUILDING | According to tradition, the Scala Santa was the staircase from Pilate's palace in Jerusalem—and, therefore, the one trod by Christ himself. St. Helena, Emperor Constantine's mother, brought the 28 marble steps to Rome in 326. As they have for centuries, pilgrims still come to climb the steps on their knees. At the top, they can glimpse the Sancta Sanctorum (Holy of Holies)—the pope's richly decorated private chapel (long before the Sistine Chapel), which contains an image of Christ "not made by human hands." You can sneak a peek, too, by taking one of the (non-sanctified) staircases on either side. ⊠ *Piazza di San Giovanni in Laterano 14, San Giovanni* ☎ *06/7726641* ⊕ *www.scala-santa.com* 🖾 *Scala Santa free, Sancta Sanctorum €3.50* ⊙ *Sancta Sanctorum closed Sun.* Ⓜ *San Giovanni.*

🍴 Restaurants

Pizzeria I Quintili
$ | **PIZZA** | **FAMILY** | Hailing from the province of Caserta, where some of Italy's best pizzerias are located, Marco Quintili is quietly taking Rome by storm. His dough is heavenly light, with a soft, puffy crust, and he uses high-quality toppings like San Marzano tomatoes, mozzarella di bufala, and sausage from Caserta to make traditional and creative pizzas that are among the city's best. **Known for:** light, Neapolitan-style pizza dough; top-notch toppings; excellent fried starters. 🟩 *Average main: €12* ⊠ *Via Eurialo 7c, San Giovanni* ☎ *06/80077157* ⊕ *www. iquintilifuriocamillo.superbexperience. com* Ⓜ *Furio Camillo.*

Santo Palato
$$ | **ROMAN** | Though she hails from Abruzzo, the young chef-owner Sarah Cicolini earned her place as one of the

rising stars in Rome's restaurant scene at this trendy trattoria, where she embraces *quinto quarto*—or the fifth quarter of an animal, like tripe, tail, and heart. Be sure to book ahead for the vintage vibes and superlative carbonara. **Known for:** retro vibes; oxtail meatballs with peanut sauce and cacao; one of the city's best carbonaras. $ *Average main: €19* ⊠ *Piazza Tarquinia, 4 A/B, San Giovanni* ⊕ *www. santopalatoroma.it* Ⓜ *Re di Roma.*

Sbanco

$$ | PIZZA | At this award-winning pizzeria in the Appio-Latino area between San Giovanni and the Appia Antica, the dough is thicker than traditional Roman-style pizza and sturdier than Neapolitan-style pizza. Creative offerings include a cacio e pepe pizza and the "Tropeana" topped with mozzarella di bufala, Tropea onions, taggiasca olives, 'nduja from Calabria, and lemon zest. **Known for:** creative pizzas; wide range of fried starters; Stefano Callegari's influence. $ *Average main: €15* ⊠ *Via Siria, 1, San Giovanni* ☎ *06/789318* ⊕ *www.sbanco.eatbu.com* Ⓜ *Ponte Lungo.*

🛍 Shopping

Marella

CLOTHING | Marella was born as a collection in 1976 and became its own brand in 1988. Part of the Max Mara group, it's sometimes described as Max Mara's little sister, as it sells slightly more youthful and affordable clothes than the original. Expect elegant, high-quality coats, jackets, and pants; dresses, skirts, and blouses that are often done in colorful prints; and accessories such as shoes, bags, scarves, and sunglasses. During semi-annual sales (in January and July), you can find especially good deals. There's also a location near the Spanish Steps on Via Frattina. ⊠ *Via Appia Nuova 7, San Giovanni* ☎ *06/70491664* ⊕ *www. marella.com* Ⓜ *San Giovanni.*

Pifebo

SECOND-HAND | Vintage aficionados, university students, musicians, and the occasional costume designer looking for something a little offbeat all love browsing through the racks of this hip vintage clothing emporium. The clothes fly off the racks quite quickly thanks to its eclectic selection of 1970s, '80s, and '90s apparel and shoes at hard-to-beat prices. The shop has another location on Via dei Serpenti in Monti. ⊠ *Via dei Valeri 10, San Giovanni* ☎ *06/98185845* ⊕ *www.pifebo. com* Ⓜ *San Giovanni.*

San Lorenzo

This traditionally working-class neighborhood north of Termini Station and close to the university is inundated with students and faculty, which makes it quite lively in the evening. It's also a bohemian, creative enclave thanks to its artist studios and galleries.

👁 Sights

Fondazione Pastificio Cerere

ART GALLERY | This small nonprofit art foundation is housed inside the turn-of-the-century Cerere factory, which produced pasta until 1960 and embodies San Lorenzo's transition from industrial to artsy. Although the foundation was established in 2004 to promote the work of young contemporary artists, artists have been renting studio space in the factory since the 1970s. Part of the exhibition space has remained raw, which makes for interesting site-specific installations. Check in advance to see what's happening as exhibitions typically change every couple of months. ⊠ *Via degli Ausoni 7, San Lorenzo* ☎ *06/45422960* ⊕ *www. pastificiocerere.it* 🎟 *Free* ⊗ *Closed Sun. and Mon. Oct.–May; closed weekends Jun.–Sept.*

Matèria

ART GALLERY | If you're keen to delve deeper into Rome's contemporary art scene, come to this stark-white gallery, which represents local and international artists whose work gets shown at international art fairs and prestigious museums like MAXXI and MACRO. The gallery has four exhibitions per year. ⊠ *Via dei Latini 27, San Lorenzo* ☎ *331/8336692* ⊕ *www. materiagallery.com* 🖃 *Free* ☉ *Closed Sat.–Mon.* Ⓜ *Vittorio Emanuele.*

🍴 Restaurants

San Lorenzo is a university quarter, where student budgets dictate low prices and good value. There are also a few hidden gems here.

I Fratelli

$$ | SOUTHERN ITALIAN | FAMILY | The four owners of this pizzeria and restaurant come from the deep south (Sicily, Calabria, Campania, and Puglia), and the influence can clearly be seen in the menu, especially in the pizza, which is of the thicker Neapolitan variety. There are classic pizzas and interesting combinations like pear and Gorgonzola or Brie and speck. **Known for:** casual atmosphere popular with locals; cacio e pepe dressed up with black truffle; Neapolitan-style pizza. $ *Average main: €15* ⊠ *Via degli Umbri 14, San Lorenzo* ☎ *06/4469856* ⊕ *www.ristoranteifratelli.it* ☉ *Closed 10 days in Aug.*

Pastificio San Lorenzo

$$ | MODERN ITALIAN | Not to be confused with the art foundation also located inside the former Cerere pasta factory, this industrial-chic restaurant wouldn't be out of place in New York or London. Some dishes combine Italian and international flavors with out-of-the-box results, while others feature subtle touches like adding salted ricotta to the *fusilloni* pasta with smoked tomato sauce. **Known for:** house-made pastas; industial-chic ambiance; nicely priced wine list as well as cocktails. $ *Average main: €22* ⊠ *Via*

Tiburtina 196, San Lorenzo ☎ *06/5042669* ⊕ *www.pastificiosanlorenzo.com.*

Tram Tram

$$ | ROMAN | The name refers to its proximity to the tram tracks, but it could also be used to describe the small interior of the restaurant, which is often packed with diners (in warmer weather there's a "side car" of tables along the sidewalk). Founded by Rosanna Di Vittorio and her two daughters, the restaurant gives Roman cuisine slight Puglian touches, emphasizing meat and vegetables—pappardelle with a white ragù of lamb and artichokes, for example—as well as a variety of homemade pastas. **Known for:** spaghetti with fresh anchovies; rigatoni con pajata (intestines of an unweaned calf); organic wine list. $ *Average main: €16* ⊠ *Via dei Reti 46, San Lorenzo* ☎ *06/490416* ⊕ *www.tramtram.it* ☉ *Closed Mon. No lunch Sun. in July and Aug.*

☕ Coffee and Quick Bites

Gelato San Lorenzo

$ | ICE CREAM | FAMILY | While San Lorenzo is filled with cheap fast food popular among students, this gelateria (open until midnight) places quality above all else and can easily rival some of Rome's most storied ice-cream shops. All flavors are properly labeled for special dietary restrictions. **Known for:** local favorite spot; raspberry basil sorbetto; vegan, sugar-free, and gluten-free options. $ *Average main: €3* ⊠ *Via Tiburtina 6, San Lorenzo* ☎ *06/4469440* ⊕ *www. gelatosanlorenzo.com.*

SAID dal 1923

$ | DESSERTS | FAMILY | Tucked away in a little alley, this historical shop and tearoom is heaven for chocolate lovers. Third-generation owner Fabrizio de Mauro carries on the tradition started by his grandfather, who lost his original shop during the bombings of WWII, though the factory has always been here. **Known for:** thick hot chocolate with cinnamon or hot pepper; cozy atmosphere with industrial relics; savory dishes made with chocolate. $ *Average main: €12* ⊠ *Via Tiburtina 135, San Lorenzo* ☎ *06/4469204* ⊕ *www.said.it* ☉ *Closed Mon.*

 Hotels

Soho House Rome
$$$$ | HOTEL | Drawing inspiration from the neighborhood's artsy ethos, the first international hotel brand to open in San Lorenzo functions as a members club, with both traditional rooms and apartments. **Pros:** sleek modern design with art from local galleries; rooftop pool and bar; cool events programming. **Cons:** some find the vibe a bit pretentious; far from the city's main sights, with no metro nearby; no-photo and no-video policy. $ *Rooms from: €330* ⊠ *Via Cesare de Lollis, 12, San Lorenzo* ☎ *06/94808000* ⊕ *www.sohohouse.com* ⇥ *49 rooms, 20 apartments* ◎ *No Meals.*

 Shopping

BOOKS
Giufà Libreria Caffè
BOOKS | This funky little bookshop has a large selection of comics and graphic novels, most of which are in Italian. It also sells posters and prints by local artists, which can make nice souvenirs. The café inside serves coffee, cocktails, and light bites and has seating outside. ⊠ *Via degli Aurunci, 38, San Lorenzo* ☎ *06/44361406* ⊕ *www.libreriagiufa.it.*

CLOTHING
L'Anatra all'Arancia
CLOTHING | Colorful Chie Mihara shoes, chunky handbags, luxurious perfumes, boutique jewelry, and funky dresses make this one of the best local shops in boho San Lorenzo. The focus is on innovative clothes from local and international designers like Alice Marrone, Apuntob, Hannoh, and Rundholz. ⊠ *Via Tiburtina, 105, San Lorenzo* ☎ *06/4456293* ⊕ *www.lanatraallarancia.com* Ⓜ *Castro Pretorio.*

Via Appia Antica

Far south of Esquilino lies catacomb country, where the fabled underground graves of Rome's earliest Christians are arrayed on either side of the Queen of Roads, the Via Appia Antica (Appian Way). Completed in 312 BC by Appius Claudius, the route was designed to connect Rome with settlements in the south, in the direction of Naples. Although time and vandals have taken their toll on the ancient sites along the road, it still evokes images of chariots and legionnaires returning from imperial conquests.

Pagans, Jews, and Christians all used underground burial sites, but the latter group developed them on a massive scale. Indeed, persecution of Christians under pagan emperors resulted in the creation of many martyrs, whose bones, once interred underground, became objects of veneration. Today, the dark, gloomy catacombs contrast strongly with the Appia Antica's fresh air, verdant meadows, and evocative classical ruins.

The initial stretch of the Via Appia Antica is not pedestrian-friendly—there is fast, heavy traffic and no sidewalk all the way from Porta San Sebastiano to the Catacombe di San Callisto. To reach the catacombs, take Bus No. 218 from San Giovanni in Laterano. Alternatively, take Metro A to Colli Albani and then Bus No. 660 to the Tomba di Cecilia Metella. Another attractive alternative is to rent a bike—for example, at the Appia Antica Caffè near the Cecilia Metella bus stop.

 Sights

Catacombe di San Callisto
(*Catacombs of St. Calixtus*)
CEMETERY | Burial place of several very early popes, this is Rome's oldest and best-preserved underground cemetery. One of the (English-speaking) friars who acts as custodian of the catacomb will guide you through its crypts and

Walk in the footsteps of St. Peter along the Via Appia Antica, stretches of which seem barely altered from the days of the Caesars.

galleries, some adorned with early Christian frescoes. Watch out for wrong turns: this catacomb is five stories deep! ■ TIP➔ **This site has a large parking area and is favored by big groups; it can get busy.** ✉ *Via Appia Antica 110* ☎ *06/5130151* ⊕ *www.catacombesancallisto.it* ✐ *€10* ✆ *Closed Wed. and mid-Jan.–Feb.*

★ **Catacombe di San Sebastiano** (*Catacombs of St. Sebastian*)
CEMETERY | The 4th-century church at this site was named after the saint who was buried in its catacomb, which burrows underground on four different levels. This was the only early Christian cemetery to remain accessible during the Middle Ages, and it was from here that the term "catacomb" is derived—it's in a spot where the road dips into a hollow, known to the Romans as a *catacumba* (Greek for "near the hollow"). ✉ *Via Appia Antica 136* ☎ *06/7850350* ⊕ *www.catacombe. org* ✐ *€10* ✆ *Closed Dec.*

Chiesa del Domine Quo Vadis (*Church of Quo Vadis*)
CHURCH | This church was built on the spot where tradition says Christ appeared to St. Peter as the apostle was fleeing Rome and persuaded him to return and face martyrdom. A paving stone in the church bears an imprint said to have been made by the feet of Christ. ✉ *Via Appia Antica 51* ☎ *06/5120441* ⊕ *www. dominequovadis.com.*

Cinecittà Studios
FILM/TV STUDIO | **FAMILY** | Film buffs may want to make the trip out to Cinecittà Studios—stomping ground of Fellini, Audrey Hepburn, and Elizabeth Taylor and birthplace of such classics as *Roman Holiday, Cleopatra,* and *La Dolce Vita.* You can take a guided tour of the sets and see the exhibition *Cinecittà Shows Off,* with memorabilia like original gowns, suits, and props from movies and TV series. Cinecittà is about 25 minutes southeast of the city center on Metro A. Sometimes tours in English are available; inquire via email (✐ *visit@*

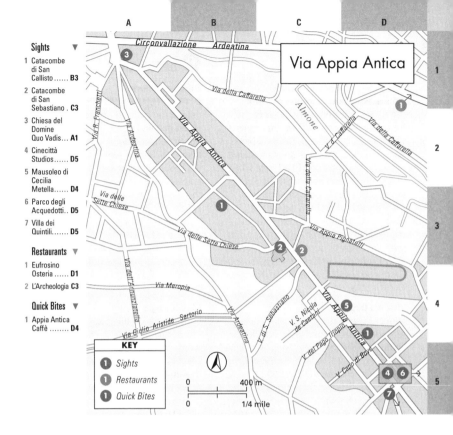

Sights ▼

1 Catacombe di San Callisto **B3**

2 Catacombe di San Sebastiano . **C3**

3 Chiesa del Domine Quo Vadis... **A1**

4 Cinecittà Studios **D5**

5 Mausoleo di Cecilia Metella **D4**

6 Parco degli Acquedotti.. **D5**

7 Villa dei Quintili **D5**

Restaurants ▼

1 Eufrosino Osteria **D1**

2 L'Archeologia **C3**

Quick Bites ▼

1 Appia Antica Caffè **D4**

KEY

- ❶ Sights
- ❶ Restaurants
- ❶ Quick Bites

Via Appia Antica

---

cinecitta.it). ✉ *Via Tuscolana 1055, Via Appia Antica* ☎ *06/72293269* ⊕ *www. cinecittasimostra.it* 🎟 *€10 exhibition (Mon. and Wed.–Fri.), €14 exhibition and tour (weekends), €15 combined ticket with MIAC (Italian Museum of Moving Images)* ⊙ *Closed Tues.* Ⓜ *Cinecittà.*

Mausoleo di Cecilia Metella

CEMETERY | For centuries, sightseers have flocked to this famous landmark, one of the most complete surviving tombs of ancient Rome. One of the many round mausoleums that once lined the Appian Way, this tomb is a smaller version of the Mausoleum of Augustus, but impressive nonetheless. It was the burial place of a Roman noblewoman: the wife of the son of Crassus, who was one of Julius Caesar's rivals and known as the richest man in the Roman Empire (infamously entering the English language as "crass").

The original decoration includes a frieze of bulls' skulls near the top. The travertine stone walls were made higher, and the medieval-style crenellations were added when the tomb was transformed into a fortress by the Caetani family in the 14th century. An adjacent chamber houses a small museum with exhibits on the area's geological phases. Entrance to this site also includes access to the splendid Villa dei Quintili. ✉ *Via Appia Antica 161* ☎ *06/7886254* ⊕ *www. parcoarcheologicoappiaantica.it* 🎟 *€8, includes all the sites in the Parco dell'Appia Antica (Villa dei Quintili, Antiquarium di Lucrezia Romana, Complesso di Capo di Bove, Tombe della Via Latina, and the Villa dei Setti Bassi)* ⊙ *Closed Mon.*

★ Parco degli Acquedotti

CITY PARK | FAMILY | This massive park, technically part of the Parco dell'Appia Antica, was named for the six remaining aqueducts that formed part of the famously elaborate system that carried water to ancient Rome. The park has some serious film cred: it was featured in the opening scene of *La Dolce Vita* and in a rather memorable scene depicting some avant-garde performance art in *La Grande Bellezza*. On weekends, it's a popular place for locals to picnic, exercise, and generally enjoy a day out with their kids or dogs. ⊠ *Via Lemonia 221, Via Appia Antica* ⊕ *www.parcodegliacquedotti.it* ⊠ *Free* Ⓜ *Giulio Agricola, Subaugusta.*

Villa dei Quintili

RUINS | Even in ruins, this villa conveys a real sense of ancient Rome's opulence, as do the archaeological finds in its small on-site museum. Indeed, Emperor Commodus—the villain in the 2000 film epic *Gladiator*—coveted this once-splendid villa so much that he accused its owners, the Quintili family, of plotting against him, had them executed, and then moved in. He may have used the exedra as a space in which to train for the ostrich fights that were held in the Colosseum. The villa is 5 km (3 miles) from the catacombs and is accessible from both the modern Appia Nuova and from the Appia Antica (by bicycle or on foot only). ⊠ *Via Appia Nuova 1092, Via Appia Antica* ☎ *06/7129121* ⊕ *www.parcoarcheologicoappiaantica.it* ⊠ *€8, includes all the sites in the Parco dell'Appia Antica (Mausoleo di Cecilia Metella, Antiquarium di Lucrezia Romana, Complesso di Capo di Bove, Tombe della Via Latina, and the Villa dei Setti Bassi)* ⊕ *Closed Mon.*

🍴 Restaurants

Eufrosino Osteria

$ | ITALIAN | FAMILY | At this welcoming osteria run by three young owners, wood-paneled walls, terrazzo floors, and green pendant lamps evoke 1970s nostalgia. The menu adheres to the Roman tradition, with homestyle dishes like chicken cacciatora, squid with peas, and the quartet of Roman pastas. **Known for:** old school Roman dishes; slow-food principles; neighboring pizzeria. Ⓢ *Average main: €14* ⊠ *Via di Tor Pignattara, 188, Via Appia Antica* ☎ *348/5883932* ⊕ *www.facebook.com/EufrosinoRoma* ⊙ *Closed Mon. and Tues. No lunch weekdays* Ⓜ *Malatesta, Porta Furba.*

L'Archeologia

$$$ | ITALIAN | In this circa-1804 farmhouse you can dine beside the fireplace in cool weather or in the garden under age-old vines in summer. Specialties include risotto with blue cheese and chestnuts, rack of lamb with Jerusalem artichoke, and fresh seafood. **Known for:** ancient wine cellar La Cantina; hand-painted frescoes; romantic setting. Ⓢ *Average main: €28* ⊠ *Via Appia Antica 139* ☎ *06/7880494* ⊕ *www.larcheologia.it* ⊙ *Closed Tues. No lunch weekdays.*

☕ Coffee and Quick Bites

Appia Antica Caffè

$ | ROMAN | FAMILY | In addition to serving the usual array of sandwiches, salads, pastries, and gelato, this café—conveniently situated at the No. 660 bus stop on the corner of Via di Cecilia Metella—has teamed up with Bicycle Roma to rent bikes to use on the Appian Way and arranges guided tours (book via ⊕ *www.bicycleroma.com*). **Known for:** classic Roman espresso; good people-watching; charming outdoor seating. Ⓢ *Average main: €8* ⊠ *Via Appia Antica, 175* ☎ *06/89879575* ⊕ *www.appiaanticacaffe.it* ⊙ *Closed Mon. and 2 wks in Jan.*

Chapter 12

SIDE TRIPS
FROM ROME

Updated by
Natalie Kennedy

◉ Sights   🍽 Restaurants   🛏 Hotels   🛍 Shopping   🎭 Nightlife
★★★★☆   ★★★☆☆   ★☆☆☆☆   ★☆☆☆☆   ★☆☆☆☆

WELCOME TO SIDE TRIPS FROM ROME

TOP REASONS TO GO

★ **Ostia Antica:** This excavated ancient Roman port city is brimming with ruins, mosaics, and structures, which convey a picture of everyday life in the empire.

★ **Tivoli's Villa d'Este:** Hundreds of fountains cascading and shooting skyward (one even plays music on organ pipes) will delight you at this spectacular garden.

★ **Castelli Romani:** Enjoy a raucous Roman lunch and an escape to the ancient hilltop wine towns on the city's doorstep.

★ **Viterbo:** This town may be modern, but it has a Gothic papal palace, a Romanesque cathedral, and the magical medieval quarter of San Pellegrino. It's also the gateway to the *terme* (hot springs) closest to Rome.

★ **Bizarre and beautiful gardens:** The 16th-century proto-Disneyland Parco dei Mostri (Monster Park) is famed for its fantastic sculptures; the stately Villa Lante, a few miles away, is a postcard-perfect Renaissance garden of swirling, manicured hedges.

1 Viterbo. The capital of Tuscia and a 13th-century time capsule with papal connections.

2 Bagnaia. The site of a 16th-century cardinal's summer home with an elaborate garden.

3 Caprarola. A hilltop village that is home to the huge Palazzo Farnese.

4 Bomarzo. The town with the eccentric Monster Park forest.

5 Ostia Antica. An ancient Roman port, now an archaeological site.

6 Tivoli. A fitting setting for the regal Villa Adriana and the unforgettable Villa d'Este, a park filled with gorgeous fountains.

7 Palestrina. Originally an ancient pagan sanctuary and home to the father of musical counterpoint.

8 Frascati. A historic getaway amid the Alban Hills and famed for its wine.

9 Castel Gandolfo. A lakeside town otherwise known as the pope's summer retreat.

10 Ariccia. Home to the grand Palazzo Chigi.

11 Nemi. A pretty hamlet, with an eagle's-nest perch above a volcanic lake.

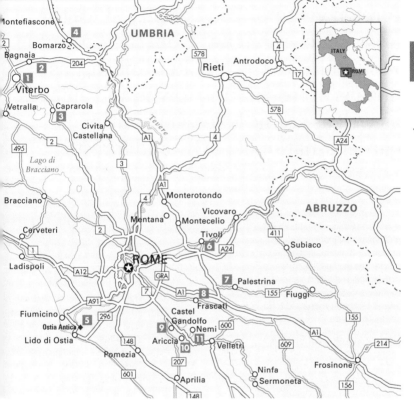

Less well known than neighboring Tuscany, Lazio, the region that encompasses Rome, is often bypassed by foreign visitors. This is a pity, since the area, which stretches from the Apennine Mountains to the Mediterranean, has dozens of fascinating towns and villages, as well as scenic lakes, enchanting gardens, national parks, and forests.

A trip outside Rome introduces you to a more intimate aspect of Italy, where local customs and feast days are still enthusiastically observed, and local gastronomic specialties take precedence on restaurant menus. Despite proximity to the capital and the increased commuter traffic congestion of today, each of the towns here has managed to preserve its unique character.

Ostia Antica, ancient Rome's seaport, is one of the region's top attractions—it rivals Pompeii in the quality of its preservation, and it easily outshines the Roman Forum thanks to its beautiful setting. Emperors, cardinals, and popes have long escaped to verdant retreats in Tivoli, Viterbo, and the Alban Hills, and their amazing villas, palaces, and gardens add to nature's allure.

So if the nonstop Vespa traffic and long lines at the Colosseum start to wear on you, do as the Romans do: spend a day out of town. There's plenty to explore and experience.

MAJOR REGIONS

Tuscia. Tuscia (the modern name for the Etruscan domain of Etruria) is a region of dramatic beauty punctuated by deep, rocky gorges and thickly forested hills, with dappled light falling on wooded paths. This has been a preferred locale for the retreats of wealthy Romans for ages, a place where they could build grand villas and indulge their sometimes-eccentric gardening tastes.

The provincial capital, Viterbo, which overshadowed Rome as a center of papal power for a time during the Middle Ages, lies in the heart of Tuscia. The farmland east of Viterbo conceals small quarries of the dark, volcanic *peperino* stone, which shows up in the walls of many buildings here. Lake Bolsena lies in an extinct volcano, and the sulfur springs still bubbling up in the modern spas were once used by the ancient Romans. Bagnaia and Caprarola are home to palaces and gardens; the garden statuary at Bomarzo is in a league of its own—somewhere between the beautiful and the bizarre.

Although the ideal way to explore this region is by car, from Rome you can reach Viterbo by train and then get to Bagnaia by local bus. If you opt to travel by train or bus, however, check schedules carefully; you may have to allow for an overnight if you want to do a round of the region's sights.

Tivoli and Palestrina. Tivoli is a five-star draw, its main attractions being its two villas. There's an ancient one in which Hadrian reproduced the most beautiful monuments in the then-known world, and a Renaissance one, in which Cardinal Ippolito d'Este created a water-filled wonderland. Unfortunately, the Via Tiburtina from Rome to Tivoli passes through miles of industrial areas with chaotic traffic, so whether you are driving or taking the bus, follow the A24 motorway to avoid it. Or take the train, which offers a slightly more scenic journey.

You'll know you're close to Tivoli when you see vast quarries of travertine marble and smell the sulfurous vapors of the little spa, Bagni di Tivoli. Both sites are outdoors and entail walking. With a car, you can continue your loop through the mountains east of Rome, taking in the ancient pagan sanctuary at Palestrina, with its ancient Roman treasures housed in a museum that is spectacularly set on the slopes of Mt. Ginestro.

The Castelli Romani. These *castelli* aren't really castles, as their name would seem to imply. Rather, they're little towns on the slopes of the Alban Hills just to the southeast of Rome. And the Alban Hills aren't really hills, but extinct volcanoes. There were castles here in the Middle Ages, however, when each of these towns, fiefs of rival Roman lords, had its own fortress to defend it.

Some centuries later, the area was given over to villas and retreats, notably the pope's summer residence at Castel Gandolfo and the 17th- and 18th-century villas that transformed Frascati into the Beverly Hills of Rome. Arrayed around the rim of an extinct volcano that encloses two crater lakes, the string of picturesque towns of the Castelli Romani are surrounded by vineyards, olive groves, and chestnut woods—no wonder overheated Romans have always loved to escape here.

In addition to their lovely natural settings, the Castelli have also been renowned for

their wine since the ancient Roman times. In the narrow, medieval alleyways of the oldest parts of the various villages, you can still find old-fashioned taverns where the locals sit on wooden benches, quaffing the golden nectar straight from the barrel.

Traveling around the countryside, you can also pop into some of the local vineyards for tastings. Exclusive local gastronomic specialties include the bread of Genzano, baked in traditional wood-fired ovens; the *porchetta* (roast suckling pig) of Ariccia; and the *pupazza* biscuits of Frascati, shaped like women or mermaids with three or more breasts (an allusion to ancient fertility goddesses).

Each town has its own feasts and saints' days, celebrated with costumed processions and colorful events. Some are quite spectacular, like the annual Marino Wine Festival in October, when the town's fountains flow with wine; or the Flower Festival of Genzano in June, when an entire street is carpeted with millions of flower petals, arranged in elaborate patterns.

Planning

Getting Here and Around

There's reliable public transit from Rome to Ostia Antica, Frascati, Tivoli, and Viterbo. Castel Gandolfo is also reachable by train—so long as you don't mind a short uphill walk from the station. COTRAL is the regional bus company outside of Rome, but timetables can be limited. For other destinations, having a car is a big advantage—going by bus or Trenitalia can add hours to your trip, and the routes and schedules are often puzzling.

CONTACTS COTRAL. ⊠ *Via Bernardino Alimena 105* ☎ *800/174471* ⊕ *www.cotralspa.it.* **Trenitalia.** (*Italian National Railway System*) ☎ *199/892021, 06/3000* ⊕ *www.trenitalia.com.*

12

Side Trips from Rome **PLANNING**

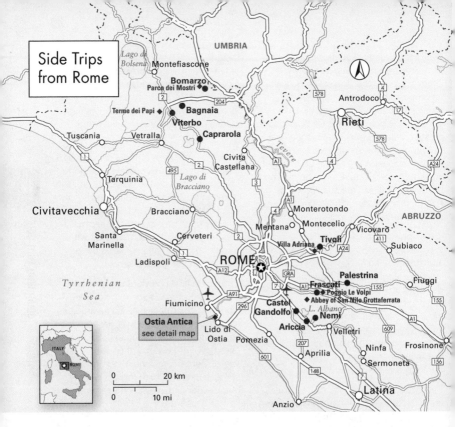

Making the Most of Your Time

Ostia Antica is in many ways an ideal day trip from Rome: it's fascinating, it's not far from the city, it's reachable by public transit, and it takes about half a day to do. Villa d'Este and Villa Adriana in Tivoli also make for a manageable, though fuller, day trip. There's so much to see at these two sights alone, but also be sure to visit Tivoli's picturesque gorge, which is strikingly crowned by an ancient Roman temple to Vesta (which is now a part of the incomparable outdoor terrace at the famed Sibilla restaurant). Other destinations can be visited in a day, but you'll get more out of them if you stay the night.

One classic five-day itinerary that takes in the area's grand villas, ancient ruins, and pretty villages begins with Ostia Antica, the excavated port town of ancient Rome. You can then head north to explore Viterbo's medieval streets on Day 2. On Day 3, take in the hot springs or the gardens of Bomarzo, Bagnaia, and Caprarola. For Day 4, head to Tivoli's delights. Then, on Day 5, take a relaxing trip to the Castelli Romani, where Frascati wine is produced. Admire the sparkling volcanic lakes, visit quiet museums, find a spot at a family-run local restaurant, and explore the narrow streets of these small hill towns.

Hotels

Former aristocratic villas with frescoed ceilings, *agriturismi* farmhouses, luxury spas at natural hotsprings, and cozy bed-and-breakfasts in the village center are just a few of the lodging options here. You won't find much in the way of major chain hotels, though.

Restaurants

You certainly won't go hungry while exploring the Roman countryside. Whether you choose a five-star establishment or a simple eatery, you can be sure of a fresh, clean tablecloth and friendly, attentive service. Odds are that the ingredients will come from the farmer down the road, and the owner will be in the kitchen, personally preparing the time-honored dishes that have made Italian cuisine so celebrated around the world.

⇨ *Hotel and restaurant reviews have been shortened. For full information, visit Fodors.com. Prices in the lodging reviews are the lowest cost of a standard double room in high season. Prices in the dining reviews are the average cost of a main course at dinner, or, if dinner is not served, at lunch.*

What It Costs in Euros			
$	$$	$$$	$$$$
HOTELS			
under €125	€125–€200	€201–€300	over €300
RESTAURANTS			
under €15	€15–€24	€25–€35	over €35

Visitor Information

City information kiosks, around Rome's main squares and at tourist sights, can give you information about the Castelli Romani, Ostia Antica, and Tivoli. The Tuscia area is served by the central tourist office in Viterbo.

CONTACT Visit Lazio. ⊕ *www.visitlazio. com.*

Viterbo

104 km (64 miles) northwest of Rome.

Viterbo is a regional commercial center, and much of the modern city is loud and industrial. But the city's charming medieval core still sits within 12th-century walls and reflects a time when it became the seat of the papal court.

Old buildings and their characteristic exterior staircases made of peperino, the deep-gray local stone, are contrasted here and there with the golden tufa rock of walls and towers. Window boxes are bright with geraniums. Artisan shops and bottegas still operate in settings that have remained practically unchanged over the centuries. The Papal Palace and the cathedral, which sit at the heart of the oldest part of the city, enhance the effect.

Viterbo is also a spa center. Just outside town are renowned natural hot springs that have been frequented by popes and mere mortals alike since the Middle Ages.

GETTING HERE AND AROUND

Direct train service from Rome's Stazione Trastevere takes one hour and 40 minutes. Note that many commuters live in towns along the line, so stops can be more frequent, and travel times longer, during peak transit times. Viturbo's *centro storico* (historic center) is a short walk from the train station.

By car, take either the old Roman consular road, the Via Cassia, which passes near Caprarola, or, the faster A1 toll highway to the Orte exit and then the 204 highway, with a detour to Bomarzo. On good days, the drive is just over an hour and 30 minutes but the trip can take a couple of hours or more, depending on traffic.

VISITOR INFORMATION
CONTACT Viterbo Tourism Office.
✉ *Piazza Martiri D'Ungheria, Viterbo*
☎ *0761/226427* ⊕ *www.promotuscia.it.*

Sights

Cattedrale di San Lorenzo
CHURCH | Viterbo's Romanesque cathedral was built over the ruins of the ancient Roman Temple of Hercules. During World War II, the roof and the vault of the central nave were destroyed, and you can still see the mark the shrapnel left on the columns closest to the pulpit. Subsequently, the church was rebuilt to reflect its medieval design, and it still has many original details, including a beautiful Cosmati floor that dates from the 13th century.

Three popes are buried here, including Pope Alexander IV (1254–61), whose body was hidden so well by the canons, out of fear that it would be desecrated, that it has never been found. The adjoining Museo del Colle del Duomo has a collection of 18th-century reliquaries, Etruscan sarcophagi, and a painting of the Crucifixion that has been attributed to Michelangelo. The ticket to the museum also grants you entrance to the Palazzo Papale, located on the same square. ✉ *Piazza San Lorenzo, Viterbo* ☎ *320/7911328* ⊕ *www.archeoares.it* 🎟 *€10, includes tour of Cattedrale di San Lorenzo, Palazzo dei Papi, and Museo del Colle del Duomo* ⊙ *Closed Tues. during Mar.–Nov.*

Palazzo dei Papi (*Papal Palace*)
CASTLE/PALACE | This Gothic palace was built in the 13th century as a residence for popes looking to get away from the city. At the time, Rome was notoriously ridden with malaria and the plague, not to mention rampaging factions of rival barons. In 1271 the palace was the scene of a novel type of rebellion. A conclave held that year to elect a new pope dragged on for months. The people of Viterbo were exasperated by the delay, especially as custom decreed that they had to provide for the cardinals' board and lodging for the duration of the conclave. To speed up the deliberations, the townspeople tore the roof off the great hall where the cardinals were meeting, and put them on bread and water. A new pope—Gregory X—was elected in short order.

Today, you can visit the great hall, step out on the pretty loggia, and admire the original frescoes in the small adjoining room. ■ TIP➔ **An audio guided tour is free with the purchase of a ticket and lasts 45 minutes, starting from Museo del Colle del Duomo.** ✉ *Piazza San Lorenzo, Viterbo* ☎ *393/0916060* ⊕ *www.archeoares.it* 🎟 *€10, includes tour of Cattedrale di San Lorenzo, Palazzo dei Papi, and Museo del Colle del Duomo* ⊙ *Closed Tues. during Mar.–Nov.*

San Pellegrino
HISTORIC DISTRICT | One of the best-preserved medieval districts in Italy, San Pellegrino has charming vistas of arches, vaults, towers, exterior staircases, worn wooden doors on great iron hinges, and tiny hanging gardens. You pass many antiques shops and craft workshops, as well as numerous restaurants, as you explore the little squares and byways. The Fontana Grande in the piazza of the same name is the largest and most extravagant of Viterbo's Gothic fountains. ✉ *Via San Pellegrino, near Palazzo dei Papi and Cattedrale di San Lorenzo, Viterbo.*

★ Terme dei Papi
HOT SPRING | Viterbo has been a spa town for centuries, and this excellent complex just a few miles outside the town walls continues the tradition, providing health and beauty treatments with an Etruscan

twist: try a facial with local volcanic mud or a steam bath in an ancient cave. The main draw, however, is the 21,000-square-foot outdoor limestone pool, into which Viterbo's famous 59°C (138°F) mineral water pours—and gives a jolt with its sulfurous odor.

You can rent floats and deck chairs, but you'll need your own bathrobe and towel unless you're staying the night at the spa hotel. Day passes tend to sell out but can be booked online up to five days ahead of your visit. ✉ *Strada Bagni 12, 5 km (3 miles) west of town center, Viterbo* ☎ *0761/3501* 🌐 *termedeipapi.it* 🎫 *Pool €18 weekdays, €25 weekends, €30 on holidays* 🕒 *Closed Tues.*

Restaurants

★ Osteria del Vecchio Orologio

$ | **ITALIAN** | Tucked on a side street off the medieval Piazza delle Erbe, the Osteria del Vecchio Orologio offers top-quality Tuscia specialties like wild boar ragu and local lake fish in a warm and informal atmosphere. Overflow seating for this popular eatery can be found at the cozy wine bar two doors down. **Known for:** cute, cupboard-lined walls; local ingredients; extensive wine list. [$] *Average main: €14* ✉ *Via Orologio Vecchio 25, Viterbo* ☎ *335/337754* 🌐 *www.alvecchioorologio.it* 🕒 *Closed Tues. No lunch Mon. or Wed.–Fri.*

Taverna Etrusca

$$ | **ITALIAN** | **FAMILY** | Located between the heart of San Pellegrino and Porta Romana, this friendly trattoria is known for its excellent home cooking and pizza. Be sure to admire the Etruscan-inspired decorations and check out the dessert—all the gelato is made on-site. **Known for:** homemade pasta alla viterbese (spicy red sauce with fennel); tagliolini (ribbon pasta) with lemon; great gelato. [$] *Average main: €15* ✉ *Via Annio 8, Viterbo* ☎ *347/8516619* 🌐 *www.tavernaetrusca.it* 🕒 *Closed Sun.*

Tre Re

$$ | **ITALIAN** | Viterbo's oldest restaurant—and one of the most ancient in Italy—has been operating in the centro storico since 1622. The small, wood-paneled dining room, chummily packed with tables, was a favorite haunt of movie director Federico Fellini and, before that, of British and American soldiers during World War II. **Known for:** traditional local dishes; roasted suckling pig; locals touch the historic Tre Re (Three Kings) sign for luck. [$] *Average main: €15* ✉ *Via Macel Gattesco 3, Viterbo* ☎ *0761/304619* 🌐 *www.ristorantetrere.com* 🕒 *Closed Thurs.*

Hotels

Palazzo Ubertini Urban Suites

$$ | **HOTEL** | Set in a historic building on the edge of Viterbo's medieval district, Palazzo Ubertini has converted the stately space into ten bright, modern rooms with small kitchenettes. **Pros:** welcome box with local food products for self-catering breakfast; elegant modern design; options for self check-in and check-out. **Cons:** no on-site restaurant; reception only open 8 am–8 pm; location in limited traffic zone complicates parking. [$] *Rooms from: €170* ✉ *Via Chigi, 7, Viterbo* ☎ *07/611871137* 🌐 *www.palazzoubertini.eu* 🛏 *10 rooms* 🍴 *No Meals.*

Bagnaia

5 km (3 miles) east of Viterbo.

The tranquil village of Bagnaia is the site of the 16th-century cardinal Alessandro Montalto's summer retreat, which is quite an extravaganza.

GETTING HERE AND AROUND

Local buses run here from nearby Viterbo. By train, the stop here is 10 minutes beyond that for Viterbo stop—few local trains actually do stop, though, so check beforehand. If you prefer to drive, take the A1 to the exit for Orte and follow signs for Bagnaia. There is free parking across the bridge from the main square, but competition for a spot can be high on the weekends.

Sights

Villa Lante
CASTLE/PALACE | FAMILY | The main draw of the sweet but underwhelming village of Bagnaia is the hillside garden and park that surround the two small, identical residences. They were both built in the 16th century but by different owners and more than 30 years apart. The first belonged to Cardinal Gianfrancesco Gambara. Cardinal Alessandro Montalto built the second and commissioned the virtuoso architect Giacomo Barozzi (circa 1507–73)—who was known as Vignola and who later worked with Michelangelo on St. Peter's—to design a stunning garden filled with grottoes, fountains, and immaculately manicured hedges.

An adjacent untamed park contrasts with the symmetry of the formal gardens, where the lowest terrace has a center-piece fountain fed by water channeled down the hillside. On another terrace, water runs through a groove carved in the long stone table where the cardinal entertained his friends, chilling wine in the running water. It's just one of the whimsical water features that were devised for the cardinal. ⊠ *Via Jacopo Barozzi 71, Bagnaia* ☎ *07/61288008* ⊕ *direzioneregionalemuseilazio.cultura.gov.it* 🎫 *€8* ⊗ *Closed Mon.*

Caprarola

21 km (13 miles) southeast of Bagnaia, 19 km (12 miles) southeast of Viterbo.

The wealthy and powerful Farnese family took over this sleepy village in the 1500s and had the architect Vignola design a huge palace and gardens to rival the great residences of Rome. Farnese also rearranged the little town of Caprarola to enhance the palazzo's setting, which sits on top of a hill overlooking the town.

GETTING HERE AND AROUND
Caprarola is served by COTRAL bus, leaving from Rome's Saxa Rubra Station on the Roma Nord suburban railway line. By car from the city, take the Via Cassia to Civita Castellana, and follow the fork towards Ronciglione then onto to Caprarola.

Sights

★ Palazzo Farnese
CASTLE/PALACE | When Cardinal Alessandro Farnese, Pope Paul III's grandson, retired to Caprarola, he intended to build a residence that would reflect the family's grandeur. In 1559, he entrusted the task to the leading architect Giacomo Barozzi da Vignola, who came up with some innovative ideas. A magnificent spiral staircase, lavishly decorated with allegorical figures, mythical landscapes, and grotesques by Antonio Tempesta, connected the main entrance with the cardinal's apartments on the main floor. The staircase was gently inclined, with very deep but low steps, so that the cardinal could ride his horse right up to his bedchamber.

A tour of the five-sided palatial villa includes the Hall of Farnese Triumphs, the Hercules Room, and the Antechamber of the Council of Trent, all painted by the Zuccari brothers. Of special interest is the Hall of the Maps, with the ceiling depicting the zodiac and the walls frescoed with maps of the world as known to 16th-century cartographers. The palace is surrounded by a formal, two-tiered Renaissance garden. ⊠ *Piazza Farnese 1, Caprarola* ☎ *0761/646052* ⊕ *direzioneregionalemuseilazio.cultura.gov.it* 🎫 *€10, includes garden; free the first Sun. of the month* ⊗ *Closed Mon.*

🍴 Restaurants

Antica Trattoria del Borgo

$$ | ROMAN | FAMILY | Visitors to Caprarola's landmark Palazzo Farnese often round out the experience with a hearty meal at this celebrated trattoria. There's a cozy, familial atmosphere inside, and when the weather permits, a pleasant seating area outside. **Known for:** local salumi (cured) and grilled meat; chestnut flour pasta; homemade desserts. $ *Average main: €20* ✉ *Via Borgo Vecchio 107, Caprarola* ☎ *0761/645252* ⊕ *www.anticatrattoriadelborgo.it* ⏱ *Closed Mon. No dinner Sun., Tues., or Wed.*

Bomarzo

15 km (9 miles) northeast of Viterbo.

Once a fief of the powerful Orsini family, Bomarzo is home to the Parco dei Mostri, the town's main attraction, which was created in the nearby woodlands to amuse and astound the Orsinis' guests. In the village center, the 16th-century Palazzo Orsini is now the seat of the town council. Inside, there is a princely hall, frescoed by Pietro da Cortona, the famous Italian Baroque fresco painter and architect.

GETTING HERE AND AROUND
Bomarzo is easily reached by car from the A1 autostrada. If you want to go there directly, carry on to the Attigliano exit. Parco dei Monstri is some 6 km (4 miles) from that point. Alternatively, come out at Orte and branch off at Casalone on the Viterbo road. A COTRAL bus also travels here four times a day from Viterbo and takes about half an hour.

👁 Sights

Parco dei Mostri (*Monster Park*)
GARDEN | FAMILY | This eerie fantasy, originally known as the Village of Marvels, or the Sacred Wood, was created in 1552 by Prince Vicino Orsini, with the aid of the famous artist Pirro Ligorio. The surreal park is populated with weird and fantastic sculptures of mythical creatures intended to astonish illustrious guests. The works, carved in outcroppings of mossy stone in shady groves and woodland, include giant tortoises and griffins and an ogre's head with an enormous gaping mouth and a table with chairs set inside. Children love it, and there are photo ops galore. The park has a self-service café (open Sunday only, in winter) and a gift shop. ✉ *Localita Giardino, 1½ km (1 mile) west of Bomarzo, Bomarzo* ☎ *0761/924029* ⊕ *www.sacrobosco.eu* 🎟 *€13; €8 children (4–13 years).*

🍴 Restaurants

Trattoria Quattro e Quattro 8

$ | ITALIAN | FAMILY | The name of this cozy trattoria between Bomarzo's Sacro Bosco and the historic center is a reference to its eight tables—four upstairs and four downstairs. The small family-run restaurant serves up lunches of traditional pastas and simple main courses with friendly and speedy efficiency. **Known for:** lombrichelli (local long pasta); coveted outdoor tables in good weather; beef with porcini mushrooms. $ *Average main: €12* ✉ *Via Madonna della Valle, 9, Bomarzo* ☎ *334/7871945* ⊕ *www.facebook.com/pasticceriadolcissima* ⏱ *Closed Mon. No dinner.*

Ostia Antica

30 km (19 miles) southwest of Rome.

Founded around the 4th century BC, Ostia served as Rome's port city for several centuries until the Tiber changed course, leaving the town high and dry. What has been excavated here is a remarkably intact Roman town. A visit to the excavations takes two to three hours, including 20 minutes for the museum. Good walking shoes are essential, and, on hot days, arrive when the gates open or late in the afternoon, so you can tour during the coolest times of the day.

Inside the site, there's a coffee bar with snacks and a bookshop, but the best idea is to plan to have lunch outside the archaeological area, in the town's compact medieval quarter.

GETTING HERE AND AROUND

The best way to get to Ostia Antica is by train. The Ostia Lido train leaves every 15 minutes from the Porta San Paolo station adjacent to Rome's Piramide station on Metro B, stopping off at Ostia Antica en route; the trip takes 35 minutes. By car, take the Via del Mare that leads off from Rome's EUR district. Be prepared for heavy traffic, especially at peak hours, on weekends, and in summer.

Sights

Castello di Giulio II

CASTLE/PALACE | FAMILY | The distinctive castle, easily spotted as you come off the footbridge from the train station and part of the medieval *borgo* (old town), was built in 1483 by the future Pope Julius II when he was the cardinal bishop of Ostia. The structure's triangular form is unusual for military architecture, but it was strategically placed for defense when the Tiber River still flowed below its walls. After crossing a drawbridge to gain access the castle's interior, you'll find a small exhibit of historical sketches on the second floor. ⊠ *Piazza della Rocca 13, Ostia Antica* ⊕ *www.ostiaantica. beniculturali.it* 🎟 *€6* ⊗ *Closed Mon.*

★Scavi di Ostia Antica (*Ostia Antica Excavations*)

RUINS | FAMILY | At its peak, the ancient port town at this site was home to a cosmopolitan population of rich businessmen, wily merchants, sailors, slaves, and their respective families. Great warehouses were built here in the 2nd century AD to handle goods that passed through, notably huge shipments of grain from Africa. Indeed, the port did so much

business that it necessitated the construction of *insulae* (apartment buildings) to provide housing for the city's growing population.

The increasing importance of nearby Portus and the inexorable decline of the Roman Empire eventually led to the port's abandonment. In addition, the coastline retreated over the millennia, and a 16th-century flood diverted the course of the Tiber. Tidal mud and windblown sand buried the ancient port town until the 19th century, when it was extensively excavated.

You can wander through the massive archaeological site and explore its curious corners, mosaic floors, fallen columns, and huge Roman amphitheater. There's also an on-site cafeteria. ■ TIP→ **The recently excavated ports of Tiberius and Claudius are nearby and included in the ticket.** ⊠ *Viale dei Romagnoli 717, Ostia Antica* ☎ *06/56358099* ⊕ *www.ostiaantica.beniculturali.it* 🎟 *€18, valid for 8 consecutive days; free 1st Sun. of month* ⊗ *Closed Mon.*

Restaurants

Arianna al Borghetto

$$ | ROMAN | FAMILY | A short walk from the excavations—tucked away in the charming walled medieval borgo of Ostia Antica next to the Castello di Giulio II—this cozy trattoria is an ideal spot to restore your energy with some seasonal dishes and Roman specialties. On warm days, request an outdoor table. **Known for:** traditional carbonara; seasonal artichokes; charming outdoor seating. 🟊 *Average main: €15* ⊠ *Via del Forno 11, Ostia Antica* ☎ *06/56352956* ⊕ *www. facebook.com/alborghetto.ostia* ⊗ *Closed Mon. No dinner Sun.*

Pizzeria Clementina

$$ | PIZZA | FAMILY | A 10-minute drive from Ostia Antica in Fiumicino, modern Rome's fishing port, Pizzeria Clementina is set on a seaside promenade

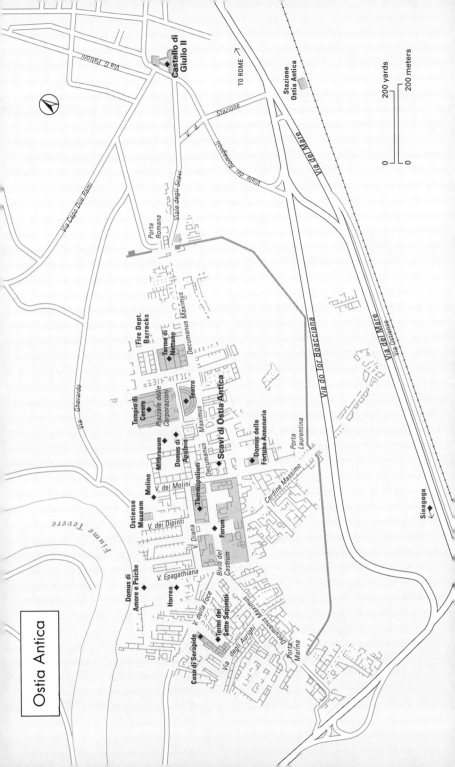

Ostia Antica

with views of bobbing boats. The fried appetizers and the pizzas are made using ingredients sourced from the hills around the city or from the daily catches brought in by local fishermen. **Known for:** supplì (fried risotto balls) with braised oxtail; savory cornetto with smoked provola and roasted mushrooms; porchetta-topped pizza. [$] *Average main: €18* ✉ *Via della Torre Clementina, 158, Fiumicino* ☎ *328/8181651* 🌐 *www.pizzeriaclementina.it* 🕒 *Closed Mon. No lunch Tues.–Sat.*

Tivoli

36 km (22 miles) northeast of Rome.

In ancient times, anyone who was anyone had a villa in Tivoli, including Crassus, Trajan, Hadrian, Horace, and Catullus. The town fell into obscurity, however in the medieval era until the Renaissance, when popes and cardinals returned and built villas showy enough to rival those of their extravagant predecessors.

Nowadays Tivoli is small but vibrant, with winding streets and views over the surrounding countryside. The deep Aniene River gorge, which runs through the center of town, is crossed by a romantically sited bridge over cascading waterfalls. Two jewels of ancient Roman architecture also crown its cliffs—the round Temple of Vesta (or the Sybil, the prophetess credited with predicting the birth of Christ) and the ruins of the rectangular temple of the hero-god Tibur, the mythical founder of the city. These can be viewed across the gorge from the Villa Gregoriana Park, named for Pope Gregory XVI, who saved Tivoli from chronic water damage by diverting the river through a tunnel, weakening its flow. An unexpected side effect was the creation of the Grande Cascata (Grand Cascade), a waterfall formed by the huge jet of water that shoots picturesquely into the valley below.

You may also want to set your sights on the Antico Ristorante Sibilla, set up against the Temple of Vesta. From its dining terrace you can take in one of the most remarkable and romantic landscape views in Italy.

GETTING HERE AND AROUND

Unless you have nerves of steel, it's best to skip the drive to Tivoli. Hundreds of businesses line the Via Tiburtina from Rome, and bottleneck traffic is nearly constant. You can avoid some of the congestion by taking the Roma–L'Aquila toll road. Luckily, there are abundant public transport options (although not having a car makes visiting Hadrian's Villa slightly less convenient).

Buses leave every 15 minutes from the Ponte Mammolo stop on Metro B; the ride takes an hour. Regional Trenitalia trains from both Termini and Tiburtina stations will have you in Tivoli in about an hour—or a swift 30 minutes if you plan ahead and catch one of the few express trains each day. Villa d'Este is in the town center, and there is a bus service from Tivoli's main square to Hadrian's Villa.

VISITOR INFORMATION

CONTACT PIT (Punto Informativo Turistico). (*Tivoli Tourist Office*) ✉ *Piazzale Nazioni Unite, Tivoli* ☎ *0774/313536* 🌐 *www.visittivoli.eu.*

Sights

★ **Villa Adriana** (*Hadrian's Villa*)
RUINS | Set below the ancient settlement of Tibur, this astonishingly grand 2nd-century villa was an exclusive retreat, where the marvels of the classical world were reproduced for a ruler's pleasure. Hadrian, who succeeded Trajan as emperor in AD 117, was a man of genius and intellectual curiosity, fascinated by the accomplishments of the Hellenistic world. From AD 125 to 134, architects, laborers, and artists worked on his dreamy villa, re-creating some of the monuments and sights that the emperor had seen on his travels in Egypt, Asia Minor, and Greece.

During the Middle Ages, the site was sacked by barbarians and Romans alike, and many of the statues and architectural features ended up in the Vatican Museums. Nonetheless, the colossal remains are impressive: the ruins rise in a garden setting of green lawns framed with oleanders, pines, and cypresses. Not surprisingly, Villa Adriana is a UNESCO World Heritage site, and it's one that has not yielded up all its secrets. Archaeologists recently discovered the site of the Temple of Isis, complete with several sculptures, including one of the falcon-headed god Horus. ■ **TIP→ A visit to the villa, which sits outside town, takes at least two hours (carry water on hot days); maps dispensed at the ticket office will help you get your bearings.** ✉ *Largo Margherite Yourcenar 1, 6 km (4 miles) southwest of Tivoli, Tivoli* ☎ *0774/39967200* 🌐 *www.coopculture.it/en/poi/hadrians-villa* 🎫 *€12; free 1st Sun. of month.*

★ Villa d'Este

GARDEN | FAMILY | One of Italy's UNESCO World Heritage sites, Villa d'Este was created by Cardinal Ippolito d'Este in the 16th century. This villa in the center of Tivoli was the most amazing pleasure garden of its day, and it still stuns modern visitors with its beauty. Cardinal d'Este (1509–72), a devotee of the Renaissance celebration of human ingenuity over nature, was inspired by the excavation of nearby Villa Adriana. He paid architect Pirro Ligorrio an astronomical sum to create an extraordinary garden filled with nymphs and grottoes. In addition, the Aniene River was diverted to water the garden and feed the several hundred fountains that cascade, shoot skyward, imitate birdsong, and simulate rain. Note especially the musical Fontana dell'Organo, whose water dances to an organ tune every two hours starting at 10:30 am. Romantics will love the night tour of the gardens and floodlit fountains that takes place on Friday and Saturday in summer. ■ **TIP→ Allow at least an hour for a visit, which involves steep inclines and many stairs. There are vending machines for refreshments by the bookshop.** ✉ *Piazza Trento 5, Tivoli* ☎ *0774/39967900* 🌐 *www.coopculture.it/en/poi/villa-deste* 🎫 *€15; free 1st Sun. of month Oct.–Mar.*

🍴 Restaurants

★ Antico Ristorante Sibilla

$$ | ITALIAN | Founded as a hotel and restaurant in 1720 and set beside the striking Roman Temple of Vesta and the Sanctuary of the Sybil, this establishment has an idyllic, wisteria-draped terrace overlooking the deep gorge of the Aniene River, with a thundering waterfall in the background. Standards are high, and the trip to Tivoli is worth it even if you do nothing more than order a lunch of upscale versions of local dishes and take in the spectacular view. **Known for:** beautiful terrace with a superb view; salt-baked fish; homemade pasta with seasonal ingredients. [$] *Average main: €20* ✉ *Via della Sibilla 50, Tivoli* ☎ *0774/335281* 🌐 *www.ristorantesibilla.com* 🕒 *Closed Mon.*

🛏 Hotels

Torre Sant'Antonio

$ | B&B/INN | Set inside a tower that dates from the 1300s, this small but cozy hotel offers two private rooms on the edge of the historic center. **Pros:** historic setting; modern interior design; easy walk to most major sites. **Cons:** limited parking nearby; old windowpanes let in some street noise; no 24-hour front desk. [$] *Rooms from: €90* ✉ *Vicolo Sant'Antonio 35, Tivoli* ☎ *347/8037983* 🌐 *www.torresantantonio-tivoli.it* 🛏 *2 rooms* 🍴 *No Meals.*

Palestrina

27 km (17 miles) southeast of Tivoli, 37 km (23 miles) east of Rome.

Except to students of ancient history and music lovers, Palestrina is little known outside Italy. Romans, however, flock to the small hillside town filled with sherbet-colored houses in summer, when its famed breezes offer a refreshing break from the hot city. In addition to the relatively cooler weather, the town is known for its most famous native son, Giovanni Pierluigi da Palestrina, born here in 1525, and considered the master of counterpoint and polyphony. He composed 105 Masses, as well as madrigals, Magnificats, and motets. There is a small museum dedicated to his life and work in the town center.

Ancient Praeneste (modern Palestrina) flourished much earlier than Rome. It was the site of the Temple of Fortuna Primigenia, which dates from the 2nd century BC and was one of the largest, richest, most frequented temple complexes in all antiquity—people came from far and wide to consult its famous oracle. In modern times no one had any idea of the extent of the complex until World War II bombings exposed ancient foundations built upon huge artificial terraces, which stretch from the upper part of the town as far downhill as its central duomo.

GETTING HERE AND AROUND

COTRAL buses leave from the Anagnina terminal on Rome's Metro A as well as from the Tiburtina railway station. Alternatively, you can take a train to Zagarolo, where a COTRAL bus takes you on to Palestrina. The total trip takes 45 minutes. By car, take the A1 (Autostrada del Sole) to the San Cesareo exit and follow the signs to Palestrina. The drive takes about an hour.

Sights

Palazzo Barberini

HISTORY MUSEUM | FAMILY | A bomb blast during World War II exposed the remains of the immense Temple of Fortune that covered the entire hillside under present-day Palestrina. Large arches and terraces are now visible, and you can walk or take a local bus up to the imposing Palazzo Barberini, which crowns the highest point and was built in the 17th century along the semicircular lines of the original Roman temple.

The palace now contains the Museo Nazionale Archeologico di Palestrina, with items found on the site that date from throughout the classical period, including Etruscan bronzes, pottery, and terra-cotta statuary as well as Roman artifacts. In addition, a model of the temple as it was in ancient times helps you appreciate its original immensity. The museum highlight, however, is a massive, incredibly preserved, 1st-century BC mosaic that colorfully details a Nile River scene, complete with ancient Egyptian boats, waving palm trees, and animals. ✉ *Piazza della Cortina 1, Palestrina* ☎ *06/9538100* 🌐 *direzioneregionalemuseilazio.cultura.gov.it* 🎫 *€7.*

Restaurants

Il Piscarello

$$ | ITALIAN | FAMILY | Tucked away in a garden at the bottom of a steep side road, this elegant restaurant comes as a bit of a surprise. The menu has both seafood and meat dishes (some topped with white and black truffles), and the pasta can be made gluten-free if you call at least one day ahead of time. **Known for:** truffle-topped dishes; excellent service; outdoor seating in summer. [$] *Average main: €20* ✉ *Via delle Pratarine 2, Palestrina* ☎ *06/9574326* 🌐 *www.ristoranteilpiscarello.it* 🕒 *Closed Mon. No lunch Tues.–Thurs. No dinner Sun.*

Frascati

20 km (12 miles) south of Rome.

Frascati is one of the easiest villages of the Castelli Romani to get to from central Rome, as well as one of the most enjoyable to navigate. After climbing the stairs from the train station or driving uphill to the entrance of the town, stroll through Frascati's lively old center. Via Battisti, leads away from the looming Villa Aldobrandini and into Piazza San Pietro with its imposing gray-and-white cathedral. Inside is the cenotaph of Prince Charles Edward, last of the Scottish Stuart dynasty, who tried unsuccessfully to regain the British Crown and died an exile in Rome in 1788.

A little arcade beside the monumental fountain at the back of the piazza leads into Market Square. Here, the smell of fresh baking will entice you into the Purificato family bakery to see the traditional honey-flavored pupazza biscuits, modeled on pagan fertility symbols.

Take your pick from the cafés and trattorias fronting the central Piazzale Marconi, or do as the locals do: buy fruit from the market gallery at Piazza del Mercato, then get a huge slice of porchetta from one of the stalls, a hunk of *casareccio* bread, and a few *ciambelline frascatane* (ring-shaped cookies made with wine), and take your picnic to any one of the nearby *cantine* (homey wine bars) to settle in for some sips of tasty, inexpensive vino. Or continue on to nearby Grottaferrata to take in its one-of-a-kind abbey.

GETTING HERE AND AROUND

An hourly train along a single-track line through vineyards and olive groves takes you to Frascati from Rome's central Stazione Termini. The trip takes 45 minutes. By car, take the Via Tuscolano, which branches off the Appia Nuova road just after the Archbasilica St. John Lateran in Rome, and drive straight up.

VISITOR INFORMATION

CONTACT Frascati Point (Tourism Office). ⊠ *Piazza G. Marconi 5, Frascati* ☎ *06/94184406* ⊕ *www.comune.frascati. rm.it.*

Sights

Abbey of San Nilo Grottaferrata

CHURCH | In Grottaferrata, a busy village a couple of miles from Frascati, the main attraction is a walled citadel founded by St. Nilo, who brought his group of Basilian monks here in 1004, when he was 90. The order is unique in that it's Roman Catholic but observes Greek Orthodox rites. It is the last surviving Byzantine-Greek monastery in Italy, and has a distinctive blend of art and architecture.

The fortified abbey with its soaring bell tower, considered a masterpiece of martial architecture, was restructured in the 15th century by Antonio da Sangallo for the future Pope Julius II. The abbey church, inside the second courtyard, has glittering Byzantine mosaics and a revered icon of Mary with child set into a marble tabernacle designed by Bernini. The Farnese chapel, leading from the right nave, contains a series of frescoes by Domenichino.

If you make arrangements in advance, you can visit the library, which is one of the oldest in Italy. The abbey also has a famous laboratory for the restoration of antique books and manuscripts, where Leonardo's *Codex Atlanticus* was restored in 1962 and more than a thousand precious volumes were saved after the disastrous Florence flood in 1966. ⊠ *Corso del Popolo 128, Grottaferrata* ☎ *06/9459309* ⊕ *www.abbaziasannilo. org* ⊠ *Free.*

★ Poggio Le Volpi

WINERY | Lazio's wines may not be as famous as those of Tuscany or Piedmont, but this award-winning family-run winery is leading the way for the region. The family's wine-making roots stretch back to 1920, but it was third-generation winemaker Felice Mergè who turned the winery into a destination with two restaurants: the casual Epos bistro and the fine-dining Barrique, where a tasting menu is served in the barrel aging room. Tours are available by appointment only, which means the best way to experience this place is to book a table at one of the restaurants and request a tour. ✉ *Via Fontana Candida 3/C, Monte Porzio Catone* ☎ *06/9426980* 🌐 *www.poggiolevolpi.com* 🎫 *Tours available by appointment* 🕒 *Closed Mon.*

Villa Falconieri

HISTORIC HOME | In the mid-1500s, Bishop Alessandro Rufini of Melfi constructed a stunning country retreat on the site of an earlier Roman villa in the hills outside the city. Pope Paul III soon played a hand in enlarging the villa, as a part of his broader plan to enhance the village of Frascati. The villa was eventually purchased by the Falconieri family in 1628, who gave their name to the estate, and commissioned an extension by Borromini—though the extent of the famed architect's contributions are debatable. What is certain is that the Falconieri family built a legacy-worthy library that hosted intellectuals and writers from around Europe, and established a tradition of offering 20 annual scholarships to promising young art students. The villa is now home to the Academy *Vivarium Novum,* a humanities institute based on the educational tradition of Renaissance schools, that opens the doors to its fresco-filled campus every Sunday with guided tours (in Italian) from 10 am–12 pm. Reserve a spot by emailing 📧 *visite@vivariumnovum.net.* ✉ *Viale Borromini, 5, Frascati* ☎ *06/6689034* 🌐 *www.vivariumnovum.net* 🕒 *Closed Mon.–Sat.*

🍴 Restaurants

Antica Fontana

$$ | **ROMAN** | Across the road from the Abbey of San Nilo is one of Grottaferrata's most esteemed restaurants, which has been run by the Consoli family since 1989. The decor is rustic but stylish, with plants hanging from the ceiling and rows of polished antique copper pans and molds decorating the walls. **Known for:** homemade pizza with excellent dough; fettuccine with porcini; pleasant outdoor terrace. [$] *Average main: €22* ✉ *Via Domenichino 24, Grottaferrata* ☎ *347/4044492* 🌐 *www.facebook.com/ristoranteanticafontana* 🕒 *Closed Mon.*

★ Cacciani

$$ | **ITALIAN** | The Cacciani family has been running this stylish restaurant in the heart of Frascati old town since 1922, when it was a popular hangout for the likes of Clark Gable and Gina Lollobrigida. Perched high on a rise overlooking the town and the Roman plain, there are spectacular views from the Cacciani terrace, but you can also keep an eye on the gorgeous food being prepared in the open kitchen. **Known for:** tonnarelli cacio e pepe prepared at the table; great views; elegant local wines. [$] *Average main: €22* ✉ *Via Armando Diaz 13, Frascati* ☎ *06/9420378* 🌐 *www.cacciani.it* 🕒 *Closed Mon. No dinner Sun.*

Il Grottino Frascati

$$ | **ITALIAN** | This former wine cellar just beyond Frascati's market square is now a cheerful trattoria serving hearty portions of traditional Roman dishes and pizza. In summer you can sit under an awning outside and enjoy the sweeping view over the plain toward Rome. **Known for:** pasta alla gricia (with pecorino cheese, black pepper, and guanciale); casual atmosphere; extensive wine list. [$] *Average main: €15* ✉ *Viale Regina Margherita 41–43, Frascati* ☎ *06/9416873* 🌐 *www.facebook.com/IlGrottinoDiAlfredo.*

★ **Osteria del Fico Vecchio**

$$ | ITALIAN | Only a couple of miles out-
side Frascati, this 16th-century coaching
inn has a tastefully renovated dining
room and an old fig tree (its namesake)
that shades a charming, table-filled garden. Long known for its excellent cooking, which was beloved by Italian director
Federico Fellini, the classic restaurant still
prepares typical Roman dishes, among
them *pollo al diavolo* (spicy braised
chicken) and *abbacchio allo scottadito*
(sizzling grilled lamb). **Known for:** pretty
garden for outdoor dining; classic cacio
e pepe; grilled meats. $ *Average main:
€20* ✉ *Via Anagnina 257, Grottaferrata*
☎ *06/9459261* ⊕ *www.alfico.it* ☾ *No
lunch Thurs.*

 Hotels

★ **Park Hotel Villa Grazioli**

$ | HOTEL | One of the region's most
famous residences, this patrician villa
halfway between Frascati and Grottaferrata is now a first-class hotel with
frescoed halls and salons—though the
guest rooms are admittedly less ornate
and standard-issue. **Pros:** incredible
frescoes in the main building; elegant
atmosphere; wonderful views of the
countryside. **Cons:** situated at the end of
a long, narrow lane; not all rooms are in
the main building; rather basic breakfast.
$ *Rooms from: €120* ✉ *Via Umberto
Pavoni 19, Grottaferrata* ✣ *Narrow
turnoff from the SP216 road going from
Grottaferrata roundabout to Frascati*
☎ *06/945400* ⊕ *www.villa-grazioli.it* ⇥ *62
rooms* ⧯ *Free Breakfast.*

Castel Gandolfo

*8 km (5 miles) southwest of Frascati, 25
km (15 miles) south of Rome.*

This scenic little town has been the
preferred summer retreat of popes for
centuries. It was the Barberini Pope
Urban VIII who first headed here, eager

to escape the malarial miasmas that
afflicted summertime Rome. before long,
the city's princely families also set up
country estates around here.

The 17th-century Villa Pontificia has a
superb position overlooking Lake Albano
and amid one of Italy's most gorgeous
gardens. Fortunately, these treasures are
now open to the public as papal audiences are no longer held in the Castel Gandolfo villa. There's a fountain on the little
square in front of the palace by Bernini,
who also designed the nearby Church
of San Tommaso da Villanova, which has
works by Pietro da Cortona.

The village has a number of whimsical
craft workshops and traditional food pur-
veyors, in addition to the souvenir shops
on the square. On the horizon, the silver
astronomical dome belonging to the
Specola Vaticana observatory—one of the
first in Europe and where the scientific
Pope Gregory XIII indulged his interest in
stargazing—is visible for miles around.

GETTING HERE AND AROUND
There's hourly train service for Castel
Gandolfo from Termini Station (Rome–
Albano line), and buses leave frequently
from the Anagnina terminal of Metro A.
The trip takes about 40 minutes, and the
village is reachable by a 10-minute uphill
walk from the station.

By car, take Via Appia from San Giovanni
in Rome and follow it straight to Albano,
where you branch off for Castel Gandolfo
(which takes about 45 minutes, depending on traffic).

VISITOR INFORMATION
**CONTACT PIT Tourist Office Castel Gan-
dolfo.** ✉ *Via Massimo D'Azeglio, Castel
Gandolfo* ✣ *A green kiosk on your right
as you walk up the road, just outside the
town walls* ⊕ *www.comune.castelgan-
dolfo.rm.it.*

Sights

Lakeside Lido

BEACH | FAMILY | This waterside promenade—down a steep incline from the pretty town—is lined with restaurants, ice-cream parlors, and cafés and is a favorite spot for Roman families to relax on summer days. No motorized craft are allowed on the lake, but you can rent paddleboats and kayaks. In summer, you can also take a short guided boat trip to learn about the geology and history of the lake, which lies at the bottom of an extinct volcanic crater. The deep sapphire waters are full of swans, herons, and other birds, and there is a nature trail along the wooded end of the shore for those who want to get away from the crowds.

Deck chairs are available for rent on the small beach, and you can stop for a plate of freshly prepared pasta or a gigantic Roman sandwich at one of the little snack bars under the oak and alder trees. There's also a small permanent fairground for children, and local vendors often set up temporary shops selling crafts, toys, and snacks on the warmer weekends. ⊠ *Lake Albano, Castel Gandolfo* 🎫 *Free.*

Palazzo Apostolico di Castel Gandolfo

CASTLE/PALACE | For centuries, the Apostolic Palace of Castel Gandolfo was the summer retreat of popes, who kept the papal villa and extensive grounds completely private. Luckily for tourists, Pope Francis decided that he was too busy to use it and had it opened to the public. Inside you can view the Gallery of Pontifical Portraits, ceremonial garments, and the imposing papal throne in the Sala degli Svizzeri. The private area of the palace with the pope's bedchamber, his library, study, and offices are also open to visitors. ⊠ *Piazza della Libertà, Castel Gandolfo* 🎫 *06/69863111* ⊕ *www.museivaticani.va* 🎫 *€12 including pontifical gardens* 🕙 *Closed Mon.–Thurs. and on Catholic holidays.*

Pontifical Gardens Villa Barberini

GARDEN | FAMILY | In 2016, Pope Francis opened the 136-acre pontifical estate and its glorious gardens to the public, which includes the archaeological remains of the palace of the Roman Emperor Domitian (dating from the 1st century AD) and the home farm, which supplies the Vatican with fresh dairy products and eggs. ⊠ *Via Massimo D'Azeglio (entrance gate), Castel Gandolfo* ⊕ *www.museivaticani.va* 🎫 *€12 with pontifical palace* 🕙 *Closed Mon.–Thurs.* ⚠ *Reservations required.*

Restaurants

Antico Ristorante Pagnanelli

$$$ | ITALIAN | One of the most refined restaurants in the Castelli Romani has been in the same family since 1882. Its dining room windows open onto a breathtaking view across Lake Albano to the conical peak of Monte Cavo. **Known for:** homemade gnocchetti with clams and black truffles; elegant and cozy interior with an open fire in winter; impeccable wine list and famed wine museum in basement. $ *Average main: €30* ⊠ *Via Gramsci 4, Castel Gandolfo* 🎫 *06/9360004* ⊕ *www.pagnanelli.it.*

Bucci

$$$ | ITALIAN | Situated in the heart of the village of Castel Gandolfo, Bucci occupies a splendid position overlooking Lake Albano far below with an outdoor terrace shaded by a grape pergola. Food has traditional roots but offers a modern twist, ranging from lasagna with crispy *guanciale* (Roman bacon) to spicy stewed calamari. **Known for:** contemporary Italian menu; vine-covered terrace; chilled local wine. $ *Average main: €28* ⊠ *Via De' Zecchini 31, Castel Gandolfo* 🎫 *06/9323334* ⊕ *ristorantebucci.it* 🕙 *Closed mid-Jan.–Feb.*

Hotels

Hotel Castelgandolfo

$$ | HOTEL | Overlooking the volcanic crater of Lake Albano and a minute's walk from the Apostolic Palace, this intimate hotel in the heart of Castel Gandolfo is a romantic retreat. **Pros:** convenient location; ideal for romantics; full breakfast buffet. **Cons:** some rooms only have street views; small, narrow balconies; no designated parking. *§ Rooms from: €140 ⊠ Via De' Zecchini 27, Castel Gandolfo ☎ 06/9360521 ⊕ www.hotelcastelgandolfo.com ⇗ 18 rooms ⦙◉⦙ Free Breakfast.*

Ariccia

8 km (5 miles) southwest of Castel Gandolfo, 26 km (17 miles) south of Rome.

Ariccia is a gem of Baroque town planning. When Fabio Chigi, scion of the superwealthy banking family, became Pope Alexander VII, he commissioned Gian Lorenzo Bernini to redesign his country estate and make it worthy of his new station. Bernini restructured not only the existing 16th-century palace, but also the town gates, the main square—with its graceful loggias and twin fountains—and the round church of Santa Maria dell'Assunzione (with a dome said to be modeled on the Pantheon). The rest of the village was coiled around the apse of the church down into the valley below.

Ariccia's splendid heritage was largely forgotten in the 20th century, and yet it was once one of the highlights of every artist's and writer's Grand Tour. Corot, Ibsen, Turner, Longfellow, and Hans Christian Andersen all stayed here. Today's village visitors are drawn by both the artistic landmarks and celebrated local culinary traditions.

GETTING HERE AND AROUND

For Ariccia, take the COTRAL bus from the Anagnina terminal of Metro A. Buses on the Albano–Genzano–Velletri line stop under the monumental bridge that spans the Ariccia Valley, where an elevator whisks you up to the main town square. If you take a train or COTRAL bus to Albano Laziale, you can proceed by local bus to Ariccia or continue on foot through the first town and over the bridge (it's just under 1½ km [1 mile]). If you're driving, follow the Via Appia Nuova to Albano and carry on to Ariccia.

Sights

★ Palazzo Chigi

CASTLE/PALACE | This is a true rarity: a Baroque residence whose original furniture, paintings, drapes, and decorations are largely intact. The Italian film director Luchino Visconti used the villa, which sits just at the end of Ariccia's famous bridge, for most of the interior scenes in his 1963 film *The Leopard*. The rooms of the *piano nobile* (main floor)—which, unlike Rome's Palazzo Chigi, are open to the public, but only on guided tours—contain intricately carved pieces of 17th-century furniture, as well as textiles and costumes from the 16th to the 20th century.

The Room of Beauties is lined with paintings of the loveliest ladies of the day, and the Nuns' Room showcases portraits of 10 Chigi sisters, all of whom took the veil. You can get a close look (with a guide) at Le Stanze del Cardinale (Cardinal's Rooms), the suites occupied by the pleasure-loving Cardinal Flavio Chigi. *⊠ Piazza di Corte 14, Ariccia ☎ 06/9330053 ⊕ www.palazzochigiariccia.it ⛬ €15 guided visit to piano nobile, Cardinal's Rooms, and Baroque Museum; €12 for self-visit ⊗ Palazzo closed Mon. Park closed Oct.–Mar.*

The monumental bridge connects Ariccia to Albano and offers beautiful views of Palazzo Chigi and Santa Maria Assunta.

Santa Maria Assunta in Cielo
(*Church of the Assumption*)

CHURCH | Directly across from Palazzo Chigi is the Church of the Assumption, with its distinctive blue dome and round shape designed by none other than Gian Lorenzo Bernini. The artistic architect had his best students execute most of the work of building and decorating the Pantheon-inspired church, creating porticoes outside and an elaborately plastered cupola inside, which steals the show in the otherwise simple interior. ⊠ *Piazza di Corte, Ariccia* ☎ *06/9330637* ⊘ *Closed noon–4 daily.*

🍴 Restaurants

A visit to Ariccia isn't complete without tasting the local gastronomic specialty: porchetta, a delicious whole-roasted pig stuffed with herbs, that goes well with the local Romanella wine. The shops on the central Piazza di Corte will make up a sandwich for you, or you can do what the Romans do: head for one of the *fraschetta* (a casual, boisterous countryside restaurant) wine cellars, which also serve cheese, cold cuts, pickled vegetables, olives, and the occasional plate of pasta.

Pass Palazzo Chigi and turn left under the arch to find several establishments in a long row on the other side of the street. Take your pick and ask for a seat on a wooden bench at a trestle table covered with simple white paper; be ready to make friends and maybe join in a sing-along.

L'Ariciarola
$ | **ITALIAN** | **FAMILY** | This fraschetta around the corner from Palazzo Chigi is great for people-watching, which you can do while enjoying a platter of cold cuts and assorted cheeses, washed down with a carafe of local Castelli wine. Order your own appetizers and slices of porchetta at the counter near the door, snag a table on the patio, flag down a waiter if you want to order a hot dish like pasta, and then settle into the rustic setting surrounded by Roman families who've abandoned the city for the day to enjoy the local food. **Known for:** classic porchetta; local

cold cuts; very casual and friendly atmosphere. $ *Average main: €12* ✉ *Via Borgo S. Rocco 9, Ariccia* ☎ *06/9334103* ⊕ *www.facebook.com/osterialariccciarola* ⊗ *Closed Mon. and 2 wks in Jan.*

Nemi

8 km (5 miles) east of Ariccia, 34 km (21 miles) south of Rome.

A bronze statue of Diana the Huntress greets you at the entrance to Nemi, the smallest and prettiest village of the Castelli Romani. Perched on a spur of rock 600 feet above the little oval-shaped lake of the same name, which is formed from a volcanic crater, the town has an eagle's-nest view over the rolling Roman countryside as far as the coast, some 18 km (11 miles) away.

The main street, Corso Vittorio Emanuele, takes you to the quaint Piazza Umberto I, lined with flower-box homes and outdoor cafés serving desserts made with the town's famous tiny wild strawberries which are harvested from the woodlands that line the crater bowl around the lake.

GETTING HERE AND AROUND
Nemi is hard to reach without a car. COTRAL buses from the Anagnina station on Metro A go to the town of Genzano, where a local bus travels to Nemi every two hours. If the times aren't convenient, you can sometimes find a taxi or simply walk the 5 km (3 miles) around Lake Nemi.

By car, take the panoramic route known as the Via dei Laghi (Road of the Lakes). Follow the Appia Nuova from St. John Lateran and branch off on the well-signposted route after Ciampino airport. Follow the Via dei Laghi toward Velletri until you see signs for Nemi. ■TIP→ **Only residents can drive through the village, so be sure to park at the entrance to the town.**

 ## Sights

Museo delle Navi Romane
(*Roman Ship Museum*)
HISTORY MUSEUM | FAMILY | In the 1930s, the Italian government drained Nemi's lake to recover two magnificent ceremonial ships, loaded with sculptures, bronzes, and art treasures, that were submerged for 2,000 years. The Museo delle Navi Romane, on the lakeshore below the town of Nemi, was built to house the ships, but they were destroyed in a fire during World War II. Inside are scale models, finds from the Bronze Age Diana sanctuary and the area nearby, and an excellent video exhibit explaining the history of the ships. There's also a colossal statue of the infamous and extravagant Roman emperor Caligula, who had the massive barges built; the Italian police once snatched the marble sculpture back from tomb robbers just as they were about to smuggle it out of the country. ✉ *Via del Tempio di Diana 13, Nemi* ☎ *06/9398040* ⊕ *direzioneregionalemuseilazio.cultura. gov.it* 🎟 *€5* ⊗ *Closed Mon.*

 ## Restaurants

★ La Fiocina
$$ | **ITALIAN** | Set on the tranquil shores of Lake Nemi, next to the Roman Ship Museum, La Fiocina has been serving local specialties, including lake fish and homemade gnocchi with porcini mushrooms, for more than 50 years. The interior is elegant and welcoming, with a roaring fireplace on cooler days; in warmer months, you can dine on the terrace overlooking the lake. **Known for:** coregone lake fish; garden terrace with lake views; wild Nemi strawberries. $ *Average main: €18* ✉ *Via delle Navi di Tiberio 9, Nemi* ☎ *06/9391120* ⊕ *ristorantelafiocin.wixsite.com/lafiocina* ⊗ *Closed Mon. and Tues.*

La Specchio di Diana

$$ | ITALIAN | Halfway down the main street on the left is the town's most historic inn (where Byron stayed when visiting the area) with a wine bar and café at street level and a full restaurant on the second floor. **■ TIP→ It also has several small apartments and rooms available to rent by the night in the village center.** **Known for:** polenta al sugo di lepre (hare sauce); spectacular lake views; desserts topped with local Nemi strawberries. [$] *Average main: €16* ✉ *Corso Vittorio Emanuele 13, Nemi* ☎ *06/9368714* 🌐 *www.specchiodidiana.it.*

Index

Photo Credits

Front Cover: Giorgio Filippin/Sime /eStock Photo[Descr.:Italy, Latium, Roma district, Rome, Vittorio Emanuele Monument, Seven Hills of Rome, The Altare della Patria, Trajan Forum in the foreground at sunset.]**Back cover, from left to right:** F11photo/Shutterstock. Catarina Belova/Shutterstock. Lucky-photographer/Shutterstock. **Spine:** Ecstk22/Shutterstock. **Interior, from left to right:** Evgeni Fabisuk/Shutterstock (1). Anton Aleksenko/iStockphoto (2-3). RPBaiao/Shutterstock (5). **Chapter 1: Experience Rome:** SJ Travel Photo and Video/Shutterstock (6-7). F11photo/Shutterstock (8-9). Fabrizio Troiani/Alamy Stock Photo (9). Graycat/Shutterstock (9). Fernando Guerra/La Galleria Nazionale (10). Pablo Debat/Shutterstock (10). Frank Bach/Alamy Stock Photo (10). Stefano Valeri/Dreamstime (10). Nikreates/Alamy Stock Photo (11). S.Borisov/Shutterstock (11). Muharremz/Shutterstock (12). Sant Eustachio Il Caffè (12). Alfredo Cerra/Shutterstock (12). Matteo Gabrieli/Shutterstock (12). ValerioMei/Shutterstock (13). Phant/Shutterstock (13). Catarina Belova/Shutterstock (14). Nido Huebl/Shutterstock (14). Gnoparus/Shutterstock (15). Marcomerry/Shutterstock (16). V_E/Shutterstock (16). David Rice/Alamy Stock Photo (16). Alexander Prokopenko/Shutterstock (16). Catarina Belova/Shutterstock (17). Sonse/Wikimedia (17). Beats1/Shutterstock (20). Mavo/Shutterstock (21). Lucian Milasan/Shutterstock (22). Andriy Blokhin/Shutterstock (22). Uly Prokopiv/Shutterstock (22). Cavan-Images/Shutterstock (23). Elena Pominova/Shutterstock (23). Christian Creixell/Alamy Stock Photo (24). Wjarek/Shutterstock (24). Valery Rokhin/Shutterstock (24). Isogood_patrick/Shutterstock (24). SimoneN/Shutterstock (25). Phant/Shutterstock (26). Boris Stroujko/Shutterstock (26). R.nagy/Shutterstock (26). Nattee Chalermtiragool/Shutterstock (27). Vasilii L/Shutterstock (27). Renata Sedmakova/Shutterstock (28). F11photo/Shutterstock (29). ValerioMei/Shutterstock (30). Scooteroma Tours (31). Paolo Costa/Shutterstock (32). Sandra Moraes/Shutterstock (33). **Chapter 2: Travel Smart:** Antonio gama/Shutterstock (64). **Chapter 3: Ancient Rome:** Leoks/Shutterstock (65). Paul D'Innocenzo (78). Preto_perola/iStock-photo (80-81). Javarman/Shutterstock (81). Angelo Campus (84). Nito/Shutterstock (85). Jolanta Wojcicka/Shutterstock (86). Amy Nichole Harris/Shutterstock (86). Pyty/Shutterstock (86). LifeCollectionPhotography/Shutterstock (86). David Ionut/Shutterstock (87). Viacheslav Lopatin/Shutterstock (87). Patryk Kosmider/Shutterstock (87). Mjols84/Shutterstock (88). Iakov Kalinin/Shutterstock (89). DaLiu/Shutterstock (89). David Ionut/Shutterstock (89). Kpapaioanno/Dreamstime (89). Anton_Ivanov/Shutterstock (90). Howard Hudson/Wikimedia Commons (91). Red-feniks/Shutterstock (91). Ilolab/Shutterstock (95). Sandro Pavlov/Shutterstock (98). **Chapter 4: The Vatican:** Banauke/Shutterstock (107). Vladimir Sazonov/Shutterstock (113). Gush Photography/Shutterstock (116-117). TTaylor/Wikimedia Commons (116). Rpbaiao/Shutterstock (118). Imaengine/Dreamstime (120-121). Imaengine/Dreamstime (122-123). Blue Planet Studio/Shutterstock (128). **Chapter 5: Piazza Navona, Campo de' Fiori, and the Jewish Ghetto:** Nikada/iStockphoto (135). Realy Easy Star/Alamy Stock Photo (141). Adam eastland/Alamy Stock Photo (146). Ale Argentieri/Shutterstock (165). **Chapter 6: Trevi and Piazza di Spagna:** Kondoros Eva Katalin/GettyImages (169). Suchart Boonyavech/Shutterstock (174-175). Sara Corso/Shutterstock (177). Slavson/Dreamstime (186). Rarrarorro/Dreamstime.com (194). Angelocordeschi/Dreamstime (196). **Chapter 7: Repubblica and the Quirinale:** Public Domain (201). Adam eastland/Alamy Stock Photo (208). V_E/Shutterstock (215). Stefano Valeri/Shutterstock (217). **Chapter 8: Villa Borghese and Environs:** Catarina Belova/Shutterstock (219). Public Domain (223). Agnese Sanvito/Alamy Stock Photo (233). ValerioMei/Shutterstock (235). **Chapter 9: Trastevere and Monteverde:** Catarina Belova/Shutterstock (237). Essevu/Shutterstock (240). **Chapter 10: Aventino and Testaccio:** Angelo Campus (253). Vlas Telino studio/Shutterstock (259). Marco Rubino/Shutterstock (263). Ella Ca/Shutterstock (265). **Chapter 11: Esquilino and Environs:** Stefano Tammaro/Shutterstock (269). Kiev.Victor/Shutterstock (277). Martina Birnbaum/Shutterstock (282). **Chapter 12: Side Trips from Rome:** Marco Rubino/Shutterstock (285). Ragemax/Shutterstock (306). **About Our Writers:** All photos are courtesy of the writers.

*Every effort has been made to trace the copyright holders, and we apologize in advance for any accidental errors. We would be happy to apply the corrections in the following edition of this publication.

Notes

Fodor's ROME 2025

Publisher: Stephen Horowitz, *General Manager*

Editorial: Douglas Stallings, *Editorial Director;* Jill Fergus, Amanda Sadlowski, *Senior Editors;* Brian Eschrich, Alexis Kelly, *Editors;* Angelique Kennedy-Chavannes, Yoojin Shin, *Associate Editors*

Design: Tina Malaney, *Director of Design and Production;* Jessica Gonzalez, *Senior Designer;* Jaimee Shaye, *Graphic Design Associate*

Production: Jennifer DePrima, *Editorial Production Manager;* Elyse Rozelle, *Senior Production Editor;* Monica White, *Production Editor*

Maps: Rebecca Baer, *Map Director;* David Lindroth, Mark Stroud (Moon Street Cartography), *Cartographers*

Photography: Viviane Teles, *Director of Photography;* Namrata Aggarwal, Neha Gupta, Payal Gupta, Ashok Kumar, *Photo Editors;* Jade Rodgers, Shanelle Jacobs, *Photo Production Interns*

Business and Operations: Chuck Hoover, *Chief Marketing Officer;* Robert Ames, *Group General Manager*

Public Relations and Marketing: Joe Ewaskiw, *Senior Director of Communications and Public Relations*

Fodors.com: Jeremy Tarr, *Editorial Director;* Rachael Levitt, *Managing Editor*

Technology: Jon Atkinson, *Executive Director of Technology;* Rudresh Teotia, *Associate Director of Technology;* Alison Lieu, *Project Manager*

Writers: Erica Firpo, Laura Itzkowitz, Natalie Kennedy

Editor: Yoojin Shin

Production Editor: Monica White

15th Edition

ISBN 978-1-64097-710-5

ISSN 0276-2560

All details in this book are based on information supplied to us at press time. Always confirm information when it matters, especially if you're making a detour to visit a specific place. Fodor's expressly disclaims any liability, loss, or risk, personal or otherwise, that is incurred as a consequence of the use of any of the contents of this book.

SPECIAL SALES
This book is available at special discounts for bulk purchases for sales promotions or premiums. For more information, e-mail SpecialMarkets@fodors.com.

PRINTED IN CANADA

10 9 8 7 6 5 4 3 2 1

MIX
Paper | Supporting responsible forestry
FSC® C016245
www.fsc.org

About Our Writers

 Erica Firpo is a travel and lifestyle journalist and podcaster based in Rome. She gets to the heart of Italian culture on her blog *Ciao Bella*, and keeps sharing la dolce vita as contributor to *AFAR, Washington Post, Insider, Condé Nast Traveler, Travel + Leisure, BBC Travel,* the *Guardian, Fathom,* and more. She has contributed to over a dozen travel books, including those by Fodor's, Insight Guides, and Lonely Planet. For this edition, she updated Trevi and Piazza di Spagna.

 Laura Itzkowitz is a freelance writer and editor based in Rome with an MFA in creative writing and a passion for covering travel, arts and culture, lifestyle, design, and food and wine. Her writing has appeared in *Travel + Leisure, Architectural Digest, Vogue, Food & Wine, Condé Nast Traveler, AFAR,* and others. Follow her on Instagram and Twitter @lauraitzkowitz, and subscribe to her weekly newsletter at ⊕ *newroman-times.substack.com*. For this edition, Laura updated Experience, Travel Smart, Ancient Rome, The Vatican, Repubblica and Quirinale, Villa Borghese and Environs, and Esquilino and Environs.

 Natalie Kennedy moved to Rome planning to stay for only a year but has now called the Eternal City home for over a decade. In between copious amounts of caffè and gelato while raising two little American-Irish Romans, she writes about Italy for international travel publications and runs a popular blog about life in Rome (⊕ *anamericaninrome.com*). For this edition, she updated Piazza Navona, Campo de' Fiori and the Jewish Ghetto, Trastevere and Monteverde, Aventino and Testaccio, and Side Trips from Rome.

Rome Metro and Suburban Railway

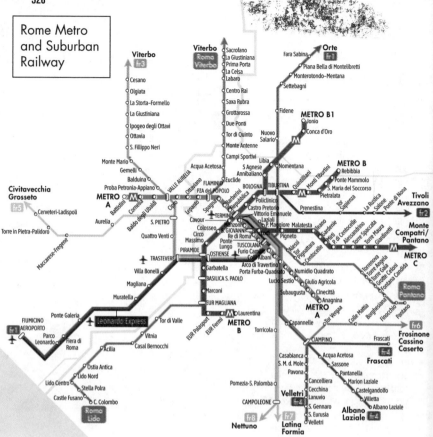

Tickets

A ticket (BIT) valid for 100 minutes on any combination of buses and trams and one entrance to the metro costs €1.50. Tickets are sold at newsstands, some coffee bars, ticket machines in metro stations, and ATAC and COTRAL ticket booths. Time-stamp your ticket when boarding the first vehicle, and stamp it again when boarding for the last time within 75 minutes. You stamp the ticket at Metro sliding electronic doors, and in the little yellow machines on buses and trams.

Fare fees	Price
Single fare	€1.50
Biglietto integrato giornaliero (Integrated Daily Ticket) BIG	€7
Biglietto turistico integrato (Three-Day Pass) BTI	€18
Weekly pass	€24
Monthly unlimited pass	€35